Pharmacy
Calculations
for Technicians

Succeeding in Pharmacy Math

Fourth Edition

Don A. Ballington, MS
Tova Wiegand Green, BS

Paradigm
PUBLISHING

St. Paul • Los Angeles • Indianapolis

Acquisitions Editor	Alison Brown Cerier
Senior Developmental Editor	Christine Hurney
Production Editor	Bob Dreas
Cover and Text Designer	Jaana Bykonich
Production Specialist	Jack Ross
Production Services	Publication Services, Inc.

Care has been taken to verify the accuracy of information presented in this book. However, the authors, editors, and publisher cannot accept responsibility for Web, e-mail, newsgroup, or chat room subject matter or content, or for consequences from application of the information in this book, and make no warranty, expressed or implied, with respect to its content.

Trademarks: Some of the product names and company names included in this book have been used for identification purposes only and may be trademarks or registered trade names of their respective manufacturers and sellers. The authors, editors, and publisher disclaim any affiliation, association, or connection with, or sponsorship or endorsement by, such owners.

Art and Photo Credits: © 2005 Abbott Laboratories, Used by permission. 86 top right; 94 top left; 128; 142 bottom left. Images courtesy of American Regent, Inc., Used with permission. 38 right; 65 top. Courtesy of Apothecary Products, Inc. 52; 53; 65 middle, bottom left; 135; 262. Reprinted with permission of APP BioScience, Inc. 40; 50 top left, bottom left; 86 bottom right; 92 top left and right; 146; 147 middle; 148 bottom; 149; 151 all; 152 all; 153 all; 155; 156 all; 157 all; 159 all; 164 all; 165 all; 171 all; 172 all; 173 all; 174, top left and right; 179 right; 182; 183 top and left; 198 left; 202 all; 205; 207 all; 208 all; 227 all. Images Courtesy of Baxter Healthcare Corporation. 93 bottom right; 147 top left; 148 top; 179 top, left, bottom. Copyright Boehringer Ingelheim Roxane, Inc. and/or affiliated companies 2008. All rights reserved. 93 bottom left; 122 top right; 142 top left. Images courtesy of Bristol Myers Squibb. Used with permission. 122 bottom left. © Eli Lilly Company. Used with permission. 67 bottom; 130 bottom; 142 right; 160 all; 161; 162; 163; 166 bottom left and right. Copyright GlaxoSmithKline. Used with permission. 51 right; 66; 67 top; 68 bottom right; 73 top; 75; 93 top and middle left. Copyright © Novartis Pharmaceuticals Corp. Used with permission. 8 top and bottom; 38 top left, middle left; 68 top and bottom left, top right; 73 bottom; 93 top right; 98; 99; 115; 141 top right; 283-287. Reproduced with permission of Pfizer Inc. All rights reserved. 63; 64; 91 top right. Images courtesy of Sanofi-Aventis. Used with permission. 166 top left; 167 left and right; 174 middle and bottom left. Images courtesy of Teva Pharmaceuticals. Used with permission. 183 middle left. Courtesy of Wallcur, Inc. 36. Courtesy of Tova Weigand Green. 65 bottom right.

We have made every effort to trace the ownership of all copyrighted material and to secure permission from copyright holders. In the event of any question arising as to the use of any material, we will be pleased to make the necessary corrections in future printings. Thanks are due to the aforementioned authors, publishers, and agents for permission to use the materials indicated.

ISBN 978-0-76383-465-4 (text and Study Partner CD)
ISBN 978-0-76383-463-0 (text)

© 2010 by Paradigm Publishing Inc., a division of EMC Publishing, LLC
875 Montreal Way
St. Paul, MN 55102
E-mail: educate@emcp.com
Web site: www.emcp.com

Brief Contents

Contents

Preface

Pharmacy Calculations for Technicians, Fourth Edition teaches the essential mathematics concepts and skills pharmacy technicians use on the job. Guided by clear, complete examples and practice problems, students will succeed in learning the skills required for calculating and preparing drug doses in both community pharmacy and institutional pharmacy settings. This comprehensive new edition offers basic skill reviews on fractions and percents as well as practice in pharmacy math calculations, conversions, measurements, and applications of equations, including calculations required for dose and solution preparations. The text also teaches business terms and business math skills essential to pharmacy practice, including calculations to determine inventory and purchasing needs, profit margins, and inventory control. Engaging activities on the Study Partner multimedia CD reinforce concepts taught in the text.

Chapter Features: A Visual Walk-Through

Chapter features are designed to help the aspiring pharmacy technician develop the calculation skills needed to work safely and effectively in the pharmacy.

1

LEARNING OBJECTIVES establish clear goals and help focus chapter study.

2

IMPORTANT TERMS are bolded and defined in context; margin boxes with the term plus definition reinforce learning. Students are encouraged to preview chapter terms on the Study Partner CD at the start of each chapter.

3

SAFETY NOTES highlight rules and guidelines for preventing medication errors.

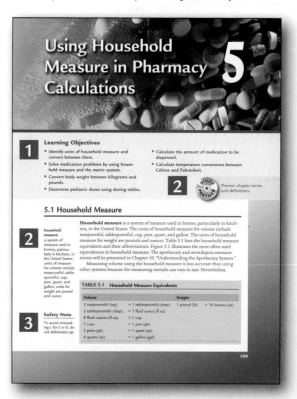

4

REMEMBER SIDE BARS emphasize previously learned information.

5

EXAMPLES provide realistic problem statements and show clear, step-by-step solutions. Where appropriate, solutions use both ratio-proportion and dimensional analysis methods.

6

PROBLEM SETS with answers showing work in Appendix A reinforce chapter content.

7

DRUG LITERACY is developed with examples and problems requiring students to read actual drug labels.

8

PRACTICE TESTS at the end of each chapter provide an opportunity to apply new skills. Students do not have access to the answers to the Practice Tests, and the Practice Tests parallel Chapter Tests provided for the instructor to use as possible assessment tools.

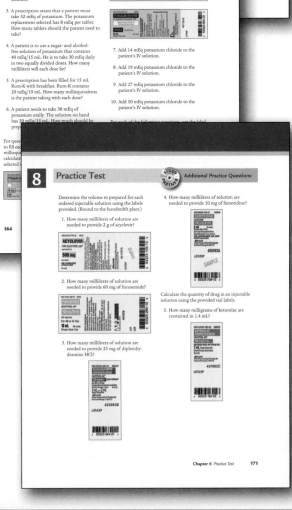

Resources for the Student

In addition to the textbook, students have access to valuable resources to help them perform pharmacy calculations safely and accurately.

Study Partner CD

A new, interactive, multimedia CD presents practice tests, matching exercises, and a comprehensive terms glossary.

The Study Partner CD, provided with each textbook, includes a rich bank of multiple-choice quizzes available in both Practice and Reported modes. In the Practice mode, students receive immediate feedback on each quiz item and report of his or her total score. In the Reported mode, the results are e-mailed to both the student and instructor. Book-level and chapter-specific quizzes are available.

The Study Partner CD also provides interactive matching activities and a glossary of terms and definitions.

Chapter Terms and Flash Cards help students learn key terminology. Chapter terms include audio.

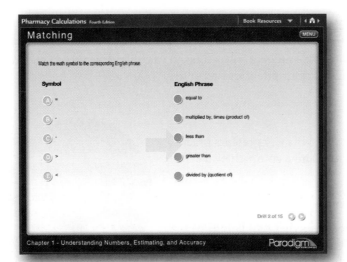

Matching Activities The Study Partner CD also includes interactive matching activities that require the student to demonstrate an understanding of chapter content.

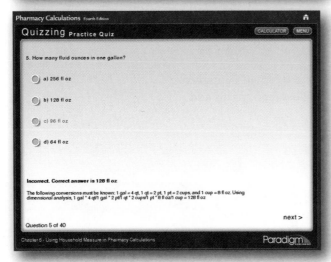

Quizzes The Study Partner CD includes a rich bank of multiple-choice quizzes available in both Practice and Reported modes. In the Practice mode, the student receives immediate feedback on each quiz item and a report of his or her total score. In the Reported mode, the results are e-mailed to both the student and the instructor. Both book-level and chapter-specific quizzes are available.

Internet Resource Center

The Internet Resource Center for this title at www.emcp.net/pharmcalc4e provides additional resources, chapter study notes, and interactive flash cards for learning the generic and brand names of the top prescribed drugs.

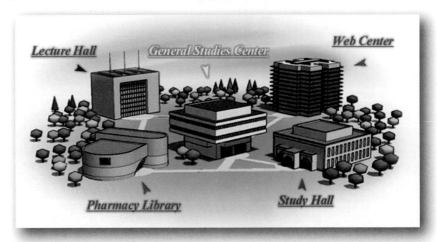

Resources for the Instructor

Pharmacy Calculations for Technicians, Fourth Edition is supported by several tools to help instructors plan their course and assess student learning.

Instructor's Guide with Instructor Resources CD

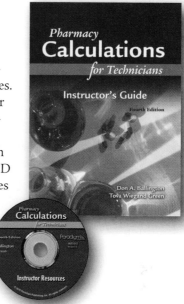

In addition to course planning tools and suggested syllabi, the *Instructor's Guide* provides answers, showing work, for all Practice Tests and appendix exercises. The *Instructor's Guide* also provides teaching hints for each chapter, Chapter Tests that parallel the end-of-chapter Practice Tests, and a 75-question, multiple-choice final exam. Available separately and with each print Instructor's Guide, the Instructor Resources CD includes Microsoft® Word documents of all resources in the print *Instructor's Guide* as well as Power-Point® presentations to enhance lectures.

All of the resources from the print *Instructor's Guide* and Instructor Resources CD are available on the password-protected Instructor section of the Internet Resource Center for this title at www.emcp.net/pharmcalc4e.

ExamView Computerized Test Generator

A full-featured computerized test generator on CD offers instructors a wide variety of options for generating both print and online tests. The test bank provides 50 questions for each chapter. Instructors can create custom tests using questions from the test bank, edit existing questions, or add questions of their own design.

Class Connection

Class Connection is a set of content files for Blackboard and other course management systems. Content includes chapter outlines, PowerPoint presentations, and quizzes.

Additional Textbooks in the Pharmacy Technician Series

In addition to *Pharmacy Calculations for Technicians, Fourth Edition,* Paradigm Publishing Inc. offers other titles designed specifically for the pharmacy technician curriculum.

- *Pharmacology for Technicians, Fourth Edition*
- *Pharmacology for Technicians, Fourth Edition Workbook*
- *Pharmacy Practice for Technicians, Fourth Edition*
- *Pharmacy Labs for Technicians*

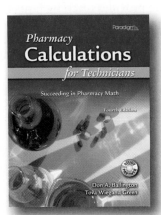
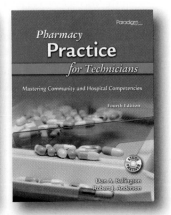
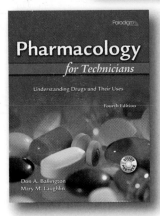
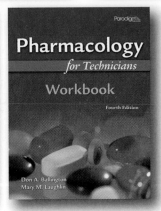
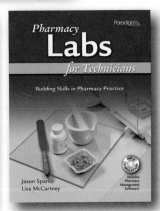

About the Authors

Don A. Ballington, MS, served as the program coordinator of the pharmacy technician training program at Midlands Technical College in Columbia, South Carolina for 27 years. He has also served as president of the Pharmacy Technician Educators Council and in 2005 received the council's Educator of the Year award. Mr. Ballington has conducted site visits for pharmacy technician accreditation and helped develop the American Society of Health-System Pharmacists model curriculum. He has also been a consulting editor for the *Journal of Pharmacy Technology*. Over the course of his career at Midlands Technical College, he developed a set of high-quality training materials for pharmacy technicians. These materials have been made available in three textbooks: *Pharmacology for Technicians, Pharmacy Practice for Technicians*, and this title, *Pharmacy Calculations for Technicians*. All are now available in fourth editions.

Tova Wiegand Green, BS, is a department chair in the School of Health Sciences, which includes Medical Assisting, Therapeutic Massage, and several allied health programs, including the Pharmacy Technician program at Ivy Tech Community College of Indiana Northeast in Fort Wayne, Indiana. She has coordinated and taught the statewide pharmacy technician program that is delivered on a two-way video hybrid system in Indiana. She has been a guest speaker at the Indiana Pharmacy Alliance Annual Meeting for the Pharmacy Technician Track, speaking on pharmacy calculations and compounding math. In addition, she has served as a consultant for the Indiana Higher Education Technology Services on issues related to teaching on a hybrid, two-way video system, including teaching math skills through distance education. In addition, she has worked as a pharmacy intern for Kroger pharmacies in Indiana.

Acknowledgments

The quality of this body of work is a testament to the feedback we have received from the many contributors and reviewers who participated in *Pharmacy Calculations for Technicians, Fourth Edition*.

Robert W. Aanonsen, CPhT
Platt College
Tulsa, Oklahoma

Cheryl Aiken, BS Pharm, PharmD, RPh
Hotel Pharmacy, Inc.
Brattleboro, Vermont

Ken Barker, PharmD
The Dupont Hospital
Fort Wayne, Indiana

Donald Becker, CPhT
San Jacinto College-North Campus
Houston, Texas

Danika Braaten, RPhT, CPhT
Northland Community and
    Technical College
East Grand Forks, Minnesota

Verender Gail Brown, CPhT
High-Tech Institute
Orlando, Florida

Linda M. Calvert, CPhT
Front Range Community College
Westminster, Colorado

Debborah G. Cummings, CPhT
Southeast Technical Institute
Sioux Falls, South Dakota

Andrea N. Curry, BS, CPhT
Concorde Career College
Memphis, Tennessee

Sharon Dalrymple
North Harris Community College
Houston, Texas

Jennifer Danielson, PharmD, RPh,
    MBA, CDE
University of Washington School of
    Pharmacy
Mill Creek, Washington

Cathy Dunne
North Orange County Community
    College District
Anaheim, California

Donna E. Guisado, RDA, BSOM
North-West College
West Covina, California

Carla May, RPh
Vance Granville Community College
Henderson, North Carolina

Michelle C. McCranie, CPhT
Ogeechee Technical College
Statesboro, Georgia

Ann Oberg, BS, CPhT
National American University
Sioux Falls, South Dakota

Andrea R. Redman, PharmD, RPh
Emory University Hospital
Atlanta, Georgia

Rebecca Schonscheck, CPhT
High-Tech Institute
Phoenix, Arizona

Mary Ann Stuhan, RPh
Cuyahoga Community College
Cleveland, Ohio

The authors and editorial staff invite your feedback on the text and its supplements. Please reach us by clicking the "Contact us" button at www.emcp.com.

Understanding Subdivisions of Numbers, Number Systems, Estimating, and Accuracy

1

Learning Objectives

- Understand fractions and be able to compare them, express them as decimals, and find common denominators.

- Manipulate fractions by adding, subtracting, multiplying, and dividing them.

- Interpret Roman and Arabic numbers and convert values between the two systems.

- Read scientific notation and convert large and small numbers to scientific notation.

- Determine the value of a decimal and accurately round off decimal values.

- Estimate drug doses in order to check the accuracy of final calculations.

- Perform calculations while retaining accuracy and the correct number of significant figures.

Preview chapter terms and definitions.

1.1 Fractions

fraction
a portion of a whole that is represented as a ratio

When something is divided into parts, each part is considered a **fraction** of the whole. For example, a pie might be divided into eight slices, each one of which is a fraction, or $\frac{1}{8}$, of the whole pie. The pie is still whole but has been divided into eight slices. Each slice is a selection—an eighth—of the whole pie, or 1 (the number of slices in the selection) over 8 (the number of slices in the whole pie). In the fraction $\frac{3}{8}$, the selection is for 3 of the 8 slices (see Figure 1.1).

Just as we talked about dividing a pie into parts, we can speak of dividing a tablet into parts, a common procedure for both pharmacist and patient. Figure 1.2 shows how cutting a tablet into smaller parts relates to fractions.

FIGURE 1.1
Fractions of the Whole Pie

8 slices = 1 whole pie = $\frac{8}{8}$ of the whole pie   3 slices = $\frac{3}{8}$ of the whole pie   1 slice = $\frac{1}{8}$ of the whole pie

1

FIGURE 1.2
**Fractions of
a Tablet**

1 tablet = 1000 mg

$\dfrac{1}{2}$ tablet = 500 mg

$\dfrac{1}{4}$ tablet = 250 mg

numerator
the number in the
upper part of a
fraction

denominator
the number in the
bottom part of a
fraction

Fractions are either common (³⁄₂, ²⁄₃, etc.) or decimal (0.5, 0.66, etc.—decimals are discussed in detail in a later section). A common fraction is composed of a **numerator** (top number) and a **denominator** (bottom number). The numerator represents the portion (1 piece in the case of the pie), and the denominator represents the whole (8 pieces of pie).

$$\text{numerator} \longrightarrow \dfrac{1}{8} \longleftarrow \text{denominator}$$

A fraction with the same numerator and denominator has a value equivalent to 1.

$$\frac{8}{8} = \frac{5}{5} = \frac{3}{3} = \frac{10}{10} = \frac{15}{15} = 1$$

proper fraction
a fraction with a
value of less than
1 (the value of
the numerator
is smaller than
the value of the
denominator)

A fraction with a value of less than 1 (numerator smaller than denominator) is called a **proper fraction.**

$$\frac{1}{4}, \quad \frac{2}{3}, \quad \frac{7}{8}, \quad \frac{9}{10}$$

improper fraction
a fraction with a
value greater than
1 (the value of the
numerator is larger
than the value of
the denominator)

A fraction with a value greater than 1 (numerator greater than denominator) is called an **improper fraction.**

$$\frac{6}{5}, \quad \frac{7}{5}, \quad \frac{9}{6}, \quad \frac{15}{8}$$

mixed number
a whole number
and a fraction

A **mixed number** consists of a whole number and a fraction and can be converted to an improper fraction by multiplying the whole number by the denominator and adding the numerator.

$$5\frac{1}{2} = \frac{(5 \times 2) + 1}{2} = \frac{11}{2}$$

complex fraction
a fraction in
which both the
numerator and the
denominator are
fractions

A fraction in which both the numerator and the denominator are fractions is called a **complex fraction.**

$$\frac{\frac{1}{4}}{\frac{1}{8}}$$

Comparing Fraction Size

Remember

The symbol
> means "is
greater than,"
and < means
"is less than."

When fractions that have the same numerator are compared, the fraction with the smaller denominator will have the larger value.

$$\frac{1}{10} > \frac{1}{25}$$

If two fractions have the same denominator, the fraction with the larger numerator will have the larger value.

$$\frac{3}{6} > \frac{2}{6}$$

When medications are dosed using fractions, it is important to recognize which strengths are largest and smallest.

Example 1.1.1

Which of the following nitroglycerin tablets is the smallest dose?

$$\frac{3}{10} \text{ mg tablet} \qquad \frac{4}{10} \text{ mg tablet} \qquad \frac{6}{10} \text{ mg tablet}$$

The $^1/_{10}$ mg tablet is the smallest dose because when fractions have the same denominator, the fraction with the smallest numerator will have the smallest value.

Example 1.1.2

Which of the following nitroglycerin tablets is the largest dose?

$$\frac{1}{200} \text{ grain tablet} \qquad \frac{1}{150} \text{ grain tablet} \qquad \frac{1}{100} \text{ grain tablet}$$

The $^1/_{100}$ grain tablet is the largest dose because when fractions have the same numerator, the fraction with the smaller denominator will have the largest value.

Expressing Fractions as Decimals

As the section on decimals later in the chapter will explain, in decimal fractions the denominator is not written but is represented by the location of the number in relation to the decimal point. For now, it is sufficient to know that any fraction may be expressed in decimal form by dividing the numerator by the denominator.

$$\frac{1}{2} = 1 \div 2 = 0.5$$

$$\frac{7}{10} = 7 \div 10 = 0.7$$

Adding and Subtracting Fractions

common denominator
a number into which each of the unlike denominators of two or more fractions can be divided evenly

When adding or subtracting fractions with unlike denominators, it is necessary to create a **common denominator,** a number into which each of the unlike denominators can be divided evenly. Think of it as making both fractions into the same kind of "pie." Creating a common denominator requires transforming each fraction by multiplying it by a form of 1 that represents one entire "pie."

Multiplying a number by 1 does not change the value of the number ($5 \times 1 = 5$). Therefore, if you multiply a fraction by a fraction that equals 1 (such as $^5/_5$), you do not change the value of the fraction. It is this mathematical rule that allows for the conversions in the following examples.

Example 1.1.3   Find the sum of $\dfrac{1}{2} + \dfrac{3}{5}$.

The lowest number that can be divided evenly by both 2 and 5 is 10. A quick way to determine a possible common denominator is to multiply the two denominators together ($5 \times 2 = 10$). Thus, tenths will be the common denominator for the two fractions, and each fraction must be converted to tenths.

To convert ½ to tenths, multiply ½ by ⅗ (one "pie" of fifths), which equals ⁵⁄₁₀.

$$\frac{1}{2} = \frac{1}{2} \times \frac{5}{5} = \frac{5}{10}$$

To convert ⅗ to tenths, multiply ⅗ by ²⁄₂ (one "pie" of halves), which equals ⁶⁄₁₀.

$$\frac{3}{5} = \frac{3}{5} \times \frac{2}{2} = \frac{6}{10}$$

Then add ⁵⁄₁₀ + ⁶⁄₁₀, which equals ¹¹⁄₁₀ or 1 and ¹⁄₁₀ (¹¹⁄₁₀).

$$\frac{5}{10} + \frac{6}{10} = \frac{11}{10} = 1\frac{1}{10}$$

Example 1.1.4   Find the sum of $\dfrac{1}{4} + \dfrac{3}{7}$.

The common denominator is 28, since $4 \times 7 = 28$.

$$\frac{1}{4} = \frac{1}{4} \times \frac{7}{7} = \frac{7}{28} \qquad \frac{3}{7} = \frac{3}{7} \times \frac{4}{4} = \frac{12}{28}$$

$$\frac{7}{28} + \frac{12}{28} = \frac{19}{28}$$

$$\frac{1}{4} + \frac{3}{7} = \frac{19}{28}$$

Sometimes, especially when there are three or more fractions, multiplying the denominators is not the best method to use to find a common denominator. In that case, follow the basic steps given in Table 1.1.

After two fractions have been converted to a common denominator and added together, it may be necessary to reduce the fraction. This requires canceling. To understand why this works, remember that multiplying a fraction by 1 will not change its value.

$$\frac{a}{b} \times 1 = \frac{a}{b}$$

Rewrite 1 as $\dfrac{c}{c}$.

$$\frac{a}{b} = \frac{a}{b} \times 1 = \frac{a}{b} \times \frac{c}{c} = \frac{ac}{bc}$$

Reversing the above steps illustrates the process of canceling.

$$ac = a \times c = a$$

Once the largest number possible has been canceled out of the numerator and denominator, the fraction is said to be in its lowest terms.

Example 1.1.5   **Simplify the fraction $\dfrac{3}{27}$.**

$$\frac{3 \div 3}{27 \div 3} = \frac{1}{3}$$

When subtracting fractions that have the same denominator, subtract the numerators and place the number over the common denominator. It may be necessary to reduce the answer fraction to its lowest terms.

Example 1.1.6   **Perform the following subtraction.**

$$\frac{5}{6} - \frac{3}{6}$$

Since these fractions already have the common denominator 6, subtract the numerators.

$$\frac{5}{6} - \frac{3}{6} = \frac{2}{6}$$

$$\text{Reduce: } \frac{2}{6} = \frac{1}{3}$$

TABLE 1.1   Steps for Finding a Common Denominator

Step 1. Examine each denominator in the given fractions for its divisors, or factors.

$$\frac{1}{15} = \frac{1}{3 \times 5} \qquad \frac{5}{6} = \frac{5}{2 \times 3} \qquad \frac{11}{36} = \frac{11}{2 \times 2 \times 3 \times 3}$$

Step 2. See what factors any of the denominators have in common.

$$\frac{1}{15} = \frac{1}{3 \times 5} \text{ has a 3 in its denominator}$$

$$\frac{5}{6} = \frac{5}{2 \times 3} \text{ and } \frac{11}{36} = \frac{11}{2 \times 2 \times 3 \times 3} \text{ both have 2 and 3 in their denominators.}$$

Step 3. Form a common denominator by multiplying all the factors that occur in all of the denominators. If a factor occurs more than once, use it the largest number of times it occurs in any denominator.

$$\text{Common denominator} = 5 \times 2 \times 2 \times 3 \times 3$$
$$= 5 \times 4 \times 9$$
$$= 180$$

Note: The product of all of the original denominators is $15 \times 6 \times 36 = 3240$.

Example 1.1.7   Simplify the following subtraction.

$$3\frac{3}{4} - \frac{2}{4}$$

Change the mixed fraction to an improper fraction.

$$3\frac{3}{4} = \frac{15}{4}$$

Replace the mixed fraction with the improper fraction in the subtraction, and confirm that the denominators are the same.

$$3\frac{3}{4} - \frac{2}{4} = \frac{15}{4} - \frac{2}{4} \qquad \text{(Both denominators are 4.)}$$

Solve the problem by subtracting the numerators.

$$\frac{15}{4} - \frac{2}{4} = \frac{13}{4}$$

Change the improper fraction to a mixed fraction.

$$\frac{13}{4} = 3\frac{1}{4}$$

When subtracting fractions that have different denominators, find the lowest common denominator, convert to equivalent fractions, subtract the numerators, and place the number over the denominator. It may be necessary to reduce the answer fraction to its lowest terms.

Example 1.1.8   Perform the following calculation.

$$\frac{3}{4} - \frac{2}{3}$$

The lowest common denominator is 12, so to convert to equivalent fractions, $\frac{3}{4}$ must be multiplied by $\frac{3}{3}$ and $\frac{2}{3}$ by $\frac{4}{4}$, giving

$$\frac{3}{4} = \frac{9}{12} \qquad \frac{2}{3} = \frac{8}{12}$$

Replace the original fractions and subtract the numerators.

$$\frac{9}{12} - \frac{8}{12} = \frac{1}{12}$$

Example 1.1.9   Subtract the two given fractions.

$$2\frac{1}{2} - \frac{6}{3}$$

Change the mixed number to a fraction.

$$2\frac{1}{2} = \frac{(2 \times 2) + 1}{2} = \frac{5}{2}$$

Replace the mixed fraction with the improper fraction.

$$2\frac{1}{2} - \frac{6}{3} = \frac{5}{2} - \frac{6}{3}$$

The lowest common denominator is 6; convert to equivalent fractions.

$$\frac{5}{2} \times \frac{3}{3} = \frac{15}{6} \qquad \frac{6}{3} \times \frac{2}{2} = \frac{12}{6}$$

Rewrite the original problem and subtract the numerators.

$$\frac{15}{6} - \frac{12}{6} = \frac{3}{6}$$

Simplify the answer.

$$\frac{3}{6} = \frac{1}{2}$$

So $2\frac{1}{2} - \frac{6}{3} = \frac{1}{2}$.

Multiplying and Dividing Fractions

The basic step in multiplying fractions is to multiply numerators by numerators and denominators by denominators. Another way to state this rule is the following: multiply all numbers above the line; then multiply all numbers below the line. Finally, cancel if possible and reduce to lowest terms.

$$\frac{1}{8} \times \frac{1}{2} = \frac{1 \times 1}{8 \times 2} = \frac{1}{16}$$

$$\frac{1}{8} \times \frac{1}{2} \times \frac{2}{3} = \frac{1 \times 1 \times 2}{8 \times 2 \times 3} = \frac{2}{48} = \frac{1}{24}$$

$$5 \times \frac{3}{4} = \frac{5}{1} \times \frac{3}{4} = \frac{15}{4} = 3\frac{3}{4}$$

When partial doses such as ½ tablet or ¾ teaspoonful are prescribed, it may become necessary to multiply fractions as part of the calculations needed to determine the amount of medication to dispense. The following examples will demonstrate these calculations.

Example 1.1.10

A patient needs to take a half of a Diovan 40 mg tablet each day for 30 days. How many tablets will the patient need to last 30 days?

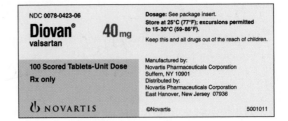

This problem may be solved by multiplying the number of days by the amount of medication taken per day.

$$\frac{30 \text{ days}}{1} \times \frac{1 \text{ tablet}}{2} = \frac{30 \times 1}{1 \times 2} = \frac{30}{2} = 15 \text{ tablets will last 30 days}$$

Example 1.1.11

How many milligrams are in half of a Diovan tablet shown in the following label?

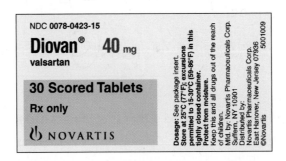

$$\frac{40 \text{ mg}}{1 \text{ tablet}} \times \frac{1 \text{ tablet}}{2} = \frac{40 \times 1}{1 \times 2} = \frac{40}{2} = 20 \text{ mg}$$

Alternatively, you can divide the strength of the tablet by 2, because ²⁄₁ is the reciprocal of ½.

$$40 \text{ mg} \div 2 = 20 \text{ mg}$$

Table 1.2 lists guidelines for multiplying and dividing fractions. To divide by a fraction, turn it upside down, multiply by the result (called the reciprocal of the original fraction), and then reduce if necessary.

$$\frac{10}{\frac{1}{4}} = \frac{10 \times 4}{1} = \frac{40}{1} = 40$$

$$\frac{1}{\frac{1}{3}} = \frac{1 \times 3}{1} = \frac{3}{1} = 3$$

$$\frac{6}{8} \div \frac{2}{3} = \frac{6}{8} \times \frac{3}{2} = \frac{18}{16} = \frac{9}{8} = 1\frac{1}{8}$$

TABLE 1.2 Guidelines for Multiplying and Dividing Fractions

1. Multiplying the numerator by a number increases the value of a fraction.

$$\frac{1}{4} \times \frac{2}{1} = \frac{1 \times 2}{4 \times 1} = \frac{2}{4} = \frac{1}{2}$$

2. Multiplying the denominator by a number decreases the value of a fraction.

$$\frac{1}{4} \times \frac{1}{2} = \frac{1 \times 1}{4 \times 2} = \frac{1}{8}$$

3. The value of a fraction is not altered by multiplying or dividing both the numerator and the denominator by the same number.

$$\frac{1}{4} \times \frac{4}{4} = \frac{1 \times 4}{4 \times 4} = \frac{4}{16} = \frac{1}{4}$$

4. Dividing the denominator by a number is the same as multiplying the numerator by that number.

$$\frac{3}{\frac{20}{5}} = \frac{3}{4} \qquad \frac{3 \times 5}{20} = \frac{15}{20} = \frac{3}{4}$$

5. Dividing the numerator by a number is the same as multiplying the denominator by that number.

$$\frac{\frac{6}{3}}{4} = \frac{2}{4} = \frac{1}{2} \qquad \frac{6}{4 \times 3} = \frac{6}{12} = \frac{1}{2}$$

1.1 Problem Set

Circle the fraction with the highest value.

1. $\left(\frac{1}{2}\right)$ $\frac{1}{3}$ $\frac{1}{4}$

2. $\frac{3}{10}$ $\frac{3}{12}$ $\left(\frac{3}{8}\right)$

Circle the fraction with the lowest value.

3. $\frac{3}{1}$ $\frac{4}{1}$ $\left(\frac{2}{1}\right)$

4. $\left(\frac{2}{6}\right)$ $\frac{3}{6}$ $\frac{4}{6}$

5. $\left(\frac{1}{10}\right)$ $\frac{1}{8}$ $\frac{1}{6}$

Complete the following operations.

6. $\frac{5}{6} + \frac{7}{10} + \frac{2}{5} =$ 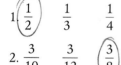 $\frac{50}{60} + \frac{42}{60} + \frac{24}{60} = \frac{116}{60} = \frac{29}{15} = 1\frac{14}{15}$

7. $\frac{21}{32} + \frac{1}{12} + \frac{31}{48} =$ 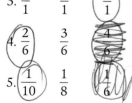 $\frac{63}{96} + \frac{8}{96} + \frac{62}{96} = \frac{133}{96} = 1\frac{37}{96}$

Reduce the following fractions to their lowest form.

8. $\frac{25}{100}$ $\frac{1}{4}$

9. $\frac{67}{10}$ $6\frac{7}{10}$

10. $\frac{11}{5}$

11. $\frac{27}{30}$ $\frac{9}{10}$

12. $\frac{12}{30}$

13. $\frac{\frac{1}{2}}{6}$ $\frac{1}{12}$

Express the following fractions in decimal form.

14. $\frac{1}{5}$

15. $\frac{1}{20}$ .05

16. $4\frac{2}{4}$

17. $\frac{30}{100}$ $\frac{3}{10} = .3$

18. $\frac{1}{200}$

19. $\frac{1}{500}$ $.002$

20. $1\frac{8}{10}$

21. $\frac{1}{25}$ $.04$

22. $\frac{1}{125}$

Applications

$\frac{1}{2} + \frac{4}{5} + \frac{1}{4} + \frac{5}{2} = \frac{10 + 16 + 5 + 50}{20\ 20\ 20\ 20}$

$= \frac{81}{20}$

$4\ \frac{1}{20}$ lbs

23. A patient has taken ¼ tablet, ½ tablet, 1½ tablet, and ¾ tablet. In total, how many tablets has the patient taken?

$\frac{1}{4} + \frac{1}{2} + \frac{3}{2} + \frac{3}{4} = \frac{1}{4} + \frac{2}{4} + \frac{6}{4} + \frac{3}{4} = \frac{12}{4} = \boxed{3}\ \text{tablets}$

24. Which dose contains the largest amount of medication: a tablet containing ¹/₁₅₀ g or 2 tablets containing ¹/₁₀₀ g in each tablet?

25. You are to measure ¼ grain of medication each into unit dose oral containers. Your bulk container holds 375 grains. How many containers will be prepared?

$\frac{375}{\frac{1}{4}} = 375 \times 4 = 1,500$

Table sugar is needed for making simple syrup. One formula calls for ½ lb to make enough syrup, a second formula requires ⁴/₅ lb, a third formula needs ¼ lb, and the last formula requires 2½ lb. You need to make one batch of all four formulas.

26. How many bags should you buy if the sugar is packaged in 2 lb bags?

27. How many bags must be purchased if the sugar is packaged in 5 lb bags?

1 bag

Self-check your work in Appendix A.

1.2 Number Systems

Two types of numbers are used in pharmaceutical calculations: Roman and Arabic. The Arabic system is more commonly used in healthcare, although the Roman system is used on a limited basis.

Safety Note

Roman numerals are often used on prescriptions because they are harder to alter than Arabic numbers.

Roman Numerals

The Roman numbering system (numerals) can be traced back to ancient Rome. This system uses letters to represent quantities or amounts, whereas the Arabic system uses numbers, fractions (such as ³/₈), and decimals. **Roman numerals** are expressed in either lowercase letters (particularly in calculations) or as capital letters. The most frequently used numerals are the uppercase I, V, and X, which represent 1, 5, and 10, respectively. In writing prescriptions, however, the lowercase letter i is often used to represent the number one, ii to represent two, and so on; and to prevent errors in interpretation, a line is drawn above the symbol, with the dot above the line (for example: ī, īī, īīī). The symbol for ½, if placed after a Roman numeral, is ss (for example: 5½ is vss). Roman numerals are used to record amount or quantity but have little use in calculations.

Roman numerals a numbering system that uses alphabetic symbols to indicate a quantity; uses the letters I, V, and X to represent 1, 5, and 10, respectively

TABLE 1.3	Comparison of Roman and Arabic Numerals				
Roman		**Arabic**	**Roman**		**Arabic**
ss	=	½	L or l	=	50
I or i or ī	=	1	C or c	=	100
V or v	=	5	D or d	=	500
X or x	=	10	M or m	=	1000

Table 1.3 lists the common units and their values in the Roman system. The following example shows a prescription that uses Roman numerals to indicate both the amount to take at each dose and the quantity to dispense.

Example 1.2.1

The following prescription is received in the pharmacy. According to this prescription, how many tablets are in a daily dose and how many tablets are to be dispensed?

> **metformin 850 mg**
>
> Sig: ï tab daily with food
>
> Disp: C tablets

Determine the dose.

$$\text{ï tablet per day} = 1 \text{ tablet}$$

Determine the quantity to dispense.

$$\text{C tablets} = 100 \text{ tablets}$$

Roman numerals may be grouped together to express different quantities. To interpret these numbers, addition and subtraction must be used, as specified in the guidelines shown in Table 1.4. Example 1.2.2 will demonstrate reading grouped Roman numerals.

TABLE 1.4 Guidelines for Interpreting Roman Numerals

1. When a numeral is repeated or a smaller numeral follows a larger one, the values are added together.

   ii or II = 1 + 1 = 2   VII = 5 + 2 = 7
   LVII = 50 + 5 + 1 + 1 = 57   XXI = 10 + 10 + 1 = 21
   CXIII = 100 + 10 + 1 + 1 + 1 = 113   LXV = 50 + 10 + 5 = 65

2. When a smaller numeral comes before a larger numeral, subtract the smaller value.

   IV = 5 − 1 = 4   IX = 10 − 1 = 9
   CD = 500 − 100 = 400

3. Numerals are never repeated more than three times in sequence.

   III = 3   IV = 4   XXX = 30   XL = 40

4. When a smaller numeral comes between two larger numerals, subtract the smaller numeral from the numeral following.

   XIX = 10 + (10 − 1) = 19   XIV = 10 + (5 − 1) = 14

Example 1.2.2 **The following prescription is received in the pharmacy. How many milligrams are in a dose and how many tablets are to be dispensed?**

> ℞ **diphenhydramine XXV mg**
>
> Sig: take ïi tab each night
>
> Disp: XXXII tablets

To calculate the number of milligrams in a dose, start by calculating the amount of milligrams in a tablet. Add the Roman numerals on the prescription.

$$\frac{\text{XXV mg}}{1 \text{ tablet}} = 10 + 10 + 5 = \frac{25 \text{ mg}}{1 \text{ tablet}}$$

Then, determine the number of tablets taken each night.

$$\text{ïi tab} = 1 + 1 = 2 \text{ tablets}$$

Determine the daily dose by multiplying the amount of milligrams in each tablet by the number of tablets taken each night.

$$\frac{25 \text{ mg}}{1 \text{ tablet}} \times 2 \text{ tablets} = 50 \text{ mg}$$

Calculate the number to dispense by adding the Roman numerals on the prescription.

$$\text{XXXII tablets} = 10 + 10 + 10 + 1 + 1 = 32 \text{ tablets}$$

The Arabic Number System

place value
the location of a numeral in a string of numbers that describes the numeral's relationship to the decimal point

Arabic numbers
a numbering system that uses numeric symbols to indicate a quantity, fractions, and decimals; uses the numerals 0, 1, 2, 3, 4, 5, 6, 7, 8, 9

The Arabic system is also called the decimal system. Ten figures are used: 0, 1, 2, 3, 4, 5, 6, 7, 8, 9. The decimal point serves as the anchor. Each place to the left of the decimal point signals a tenfold increase, and each place to the right signals a tenfold decrease. Figure 1.3 illustrates the relative value of each unit. Memorize the **place values,** which describe each numeral's relationship to the decimal point, for future reference.

In expressions using **Arabic numbers,** the whole numbers are to the left of the decimal point while the fractions are on the right. The positions for the numbers to the right of the decimal point are called decimal places. Table 1.5 provides guidelines for interpreting Arabic numbers.

FIGURE 1.3
**Decimal Units
and Values**

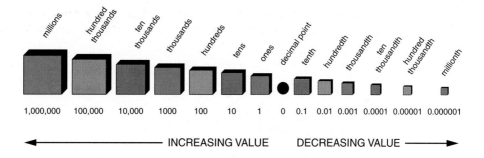

INCREASING VALUE   DECREASING VALUE

TABLE 1.5   Guidelines for Interpreting Arabic Numbers

1. The value of a decimal equal to 1 or more depends on the size of the whole numbers. The higher the value of the whole numbers, the higher the overall value.

   8.2 > 6.2
   20.1 > 14.6
   3.08 > 2.39

2. If the decimal fraction does not have a whole number preceding the decimal point, a zero is used in front of the decimal point. This is called a leading zero. The fraction with the highest tenth will have the highest value.

   0.4 > 0.3
   2.41 > 2.39

3. When the tenths are identical, a number with a decimal fraction that is higher in hundredths will have a higher value.

   0.17 > 0.15
   0.35 > 0.30
   10.66 > 10.64

4. Look at the tenths first. If these are identical, the hundredths will determine the value unless they are also identical. Then the value will be determined by the thousandths.

   0.125 > 0.124

5. The total value of a number is therefore the sum of the different parts, depending on their position.

467.43 represents	400.00	=	four hundreds
	+60.00	=	six tens
	+ 7.00	=	seven ones
	+ 0.40	=	four tenths
	+ 0.03	=	three hundredths

Scientific Notation

scientific notation a method used to write numbers that have a very large or very small numerical value; uses "× 10" with an exponent

Scientific notation is a method used to write numbers that have a very large or very small numerical value. Because of space issues as well as readability, it is not practical to write out numbers that have a large number of zeros, such as 5,200,000,000,000 or very small numbers such as 0.00000025. Numbers such as these are written as a group of significant figures multiplied by 10 with an exponent. The number in the exponent

TABLE 1.6 Scientific Notation Equivalences

Arabic Number	Scientific Notation	Decimal Place Movement
6500	6.5×10^3	3 places to the left
120,000	1.2×10^5	5 places to the left
921,000,000	9.21×10^8	8 places to the left
4,800,000,000,000	4.8×10^{12}	12 places to the left
0.109	1.09×10^{-1}	1 place to the right
0.000587	5.87×10^{-4}	4 places to the right
0.00000026	2.6×10^{-7}	7 places to the right
0.000000000049	4.9×10^{-11}	11 places to the right

indicates how many places the decimal has been moved, and the value of the exponent (positive or negative) indicates the direction the decimal was moved. A positive exponent indicates a number greater than 1, and a negative exponent indicates a number smaller than 1. Table 1.6 shows examples of values written in Arabic numbers and in scientific notation.

1.2 Problem Set

Give the equivalent Arabic numeral for each of the following Roman numerals.

1. X   10

2. V

3. DCXXIV   624

4. MML

5. XLVIII   48

Give the equivalent Roman numeral for each of the following Arabic numerals.

6. 17

7. 67   LX VII

8. 1995

In each group of numbers, circle the highest value.

9. 3.1   1.7   (4.1)

10. 0.5   0.56   0.6

In each group of numbers, circle the lowest value.

11. (2.02)   2.12   2.1

12. 0.16   0.167   0.017

Using the following number, list the quantity of each numeral in the named places.

92,375.046

13. tenth place   0

14. thousandth place

15. hundreds place   3

State the place value of the underlined digit.

16. 18,2̲40.6

17. 7.23̲91   hundredths

18. 621.508̲

19. 0̲.98   ones

20. 40.0̲23

Write the following numbers without using scientific notation.

21. 6.8×10^4 *68,000*

22. 1.87×10^6

23. 1.03×10^7 *10,300,000*

24. 8.4×10^{-4}

25. 7.68×10^{-3} *.00768*

26. 6.239×10^{-5}

Write the following numbers using scientific notation.

27. 0.00000000329   *32.9×10^{10}*

28. 390,000,000,000

29. 0.0038   *3.8×10^3*

30. 52,000,000,000,000,000

31. 3,779,000   *3.779×10^6*

32. 0.000000000202

Applications

33. A patient is to take "VII ss tablets three times daily." How many tablets must be dispensed to last 7 days?   *$7\frac{1}{2} \times 7 \times 3 =$* *$52\frac{1}{2} \times 3 = 157\frac{1}{2}$*

34. Using the prescription below, answer the following questions.

> ℞   **ASA gr X**
>
> Sig: i po daily
>
> Disp: C

  a. What is the strength of the tablet?

  b. What is the daily dose?

  c. What is the quantity to be dispensed?

35. Using the prescription below, answer the following questions.

> ℞   **Drug XYZ gr ss**
>
> Sig: gr ii QAM
>
> Disp: C

Note: QAM (or qam or q am) means "every morning."

  a. What is the dosage strength of the drug XYZ?   *1/2 grains*

  b. How many grains are ordered each day?   *2 grains or 4 tab*

  c. How many tablets will be needed for 7 days?   *14*

  d. How long will C tablets last the patient?   *25 days*

36. Using the prescription below, answer the following questions.

> ℞   **Erythromycin 250 mg**
>
> i qid with food
>
> XXVIII

Note: qid (or QID) means "four times a day."

  a. How many tablets will be dispensed?

  b. How many days will the prescription last?

37. Using the prescription below, answer the following questions.

> ℞   **Glucotrol Tablet 5 mg**
>
> ii q am
>
> i with lunch
>
> ii 8 pm
>
> 30 days' supply

  a. How many tablets are taken each day?   *5*

  b. How many tablets will be dispensed?   *150*

  c. How long would C tablets last?   *20 days*

Self-check your work in Appendix A.

1.3 Decimals

A fraction in which the denominator is 10 or some multiple of 10 is a decimal fraction or, more simply, a **decimal.** In decimal fractions, the denominator is not written but is represented by the location of the number in relation to the decimal point. (Refer to the section on the Arabic number system.) The decimal point represents the center. Numbers written to the right of the decimal point are decimal fractions with a denominator of 10 or a multiple of 10 and so have a value of less than 1. Numbers written to the left of the decimal point have a value of 1 or greater (whole numbers).

An understanding of decimals is *crucial* to pharmacy calculations because most medication orders are written in metric, which uses decimals. Remember, numbers to the left of the decimal point are whole numbers; numbers to the right of the decimal point are decimal fractions (parts of a whole).

Reading and Writing Decimals

A decimal is read by first reading the whole number, if there is one, to the left of the decimal point, then the decimal point (say "and" or "point"), and then the decimal fraction, to the right of the decimal point.

A decimal is written as a whole number or a zero, then the decimal point (indicating the value of the number to the right of the decimal), and then the fractional portion. The values to the right of the decimal point are multiples of one-tenth: tenths, hundredths, thousandths, ten thousandths, and so on. Figure 1.4 illustrates this relationship in terms of medication.

To further emphasize the value of the calculation when there is no whole number, a zero should be placed to the left of the decimal point. This zero is called a **leading zero.** Using a leading zero will help prevent errors by ensuring a correct reading of the value.

Adding and Subtracting Decimals

When adding or subtracting decimals, place the numbers in columns so that the decimal points are aligned directly under each other. Add or subtract from the far-right column to the left column.

$$
\begin{array}{r} 20.4 \\ +21.8 \\ \hline 42.2 \end{array}
\qquad
\begin{array}{r} 11.2 \\ 13.6 \\ +16.0 \\ \hline 40.8 \end{array}
\qquad
\begin{array}{r} 15.36 \\ -3.80 \\ \hline 11.56 \end{array}
$$

Multiplying and Dividing Decimals

Multiply the two decimals as whole numbers. Add the total number of decimal places that are in the two numbers being multiplied (count from right to left), count that number of places from right to left in the answer, and insert a decimal point.

FIGURE 1.4
Decimal Places

1000 mg	500 mg	50 mg	5 mg	0.5 mg
whole	0.5 tenths (1 place to the right)	0.05 hundredths (2 places to the right)	0.005 thousandths (3 places to the right)	0.0005 ten thousandths (4 places to the right)

$$
\begin{array}{r}
1.23 \\
\times 2.3 \\
\hline
369 \\
+2460 \\
\hline
2.829
\end{array}
$$

(A zero is added to align the columns. Note that no value is added to the number.)

To divide decimal numbers, change both the divisor (the number doing the dividing; the denominator) and the dividend (the number being divided; the numerator) to whole numbers by moving their decimal points the same number of places to the right. If the divisor and the dividend have a different number of digits after the decimal point, choose the one that has more digits and move its decimal point a sufficient number of places to make it a whole number. Then move the decimal point in the other number the same number of places, adding a zero at the end if necessary. In the first example, the divisor has more digits after the decimal point, so move its decimal point three places to the right to make it a whole number. Then move the decimal point in the dividend the same number of places, adding a zero at the end. In the second example, the dividend has more digits after the decimal point, so move its decimal point three places to the right to make it a whole number. Then move the decimal point in the divisor three places to the right also.

$$1.45 \div 3.625 = 0.4 \qquad 1.617 \div 2.31 = 0.7$$

$$\frac{1.45}{3.625} = \frac{1450}{3625} = 0.4 \qquad \frac{1.617}{2.31} = \frac{1617}{2310} = 0.7$$

Rounding Decimals

Rounding numbers is essential for daily use of mathematical operations. The purpose of rounding is to keep the number we are working with to a manageable size. It is important to recognize, however, that rounding will affect the **accuracy** to which a medication can be determined. In some cases, it may be appropriate to calculate a dose to the nearest whole milliliter and, in other cases, to round to the nearest tenth or hundredth of a milliliter. Depending on the drug and strength prescribed, it may not be possible to accurately measure a very small quantity such as a hundredth of a milliliter.

When numbers with decimals are used to calculate a volumetric dose, a number with multiple digits beyond the decimal often results. It is not practical to retain all of these numbers, as a dose cannot be accurately measured beyond the hundredth or thousandth place for most medications. Most commonly, the dose is rounded to the nearest tenth. It is common practice to round the weight of a dose at the hundredth or thousandth place, or as accurate as the particular measuring device (or medication) will permit.

To round off an answer to the nearest tenth, carry the division out two places, to the hundredth place. If the number in the hundredth place is 5 or greater, add 1 to the tenth place number. If the number in the hundredth place is less than 5, round the number down by omitting the digit in the hundredth place.

5.65 becomes 5.7   4.24 becomes 4.2

accuracy
the correctness of a number in its representation of a given value

The same procedure may be used when rounding to the nearest hundredth place or thousandth place.

$$3.8421 = 3.84 \quad \text{(hundredth)}$$
$$41.2674 = 41.27 \quad \text{(hundredth)}$$
$$0.3928 = 0.393 \quad \text{(thousandth)}$$
$$4.1111 = 4.111 \quad \text{(thousandth)}$$

As mentioned earlier, when rounding numbers used in pharmacy calculations, it is common to round off to the nearest tenth. However, there are times when a dose is very small and rounding to the nearest hundredth or thousandth may be more appropriate.

The exact dose calculated is 0.08752 g
Rounded to nearest tenth: 0.1 g
Rounded to nearest hundredth: 0.09 g
Rounded to nearest thousandth: 0.088 g

When a number that has been rounded to the tenth place is multiplied or divided by a number that was rounded to the hundredth or thousandth place, the answer must be rounded back to the tenth place. The reason is that the answer can only be accurate to the place to which the highest rounding was made in the original numbers.

Example 1.3.1

Round off the answer of the following equation to the appropriate decimal. Note that 7.1 is a rounded figure.

$$3.46 \times 7.1 = 24.566$$

The answer must be rounded back to the tenth place.

Answer = 24.6

Example 1.3.2

Round off the answer of the following equation to the appropriate decimal. Note that 1.349 is a rounded figure.

$$0.3563 \times 1.349 = 0.4806487$$

The answer must be rounded to the thousandth place.

Answer = 0.481

Safety Note

Do not use a trailing zero unless it indicates accuracy of a number (is significant).

trailing zero
a zero that appears at the end of a decimal string and is not needed except when considered significant

In most cases, a zero occurring at the end of a string of digits is not written. This zero is called a **trailing zero.** The exception to this occurs when rounding results in a zero as the last place value. When the last digit resulting from rounding is a zero, this zero should be written because it is considered significant to that particular problem or dosage. In such cases, the amount can be measured out to an exact zero as the place value.

Example 1.3.3   **Round 9.98 to the nearest tenth.**

Answer = 10.0

Example 1.3.4   **Round 0.599 to the nearest hundredth.**

Answer = 0.60

1.3 Problem Set

Write the following decimals.

1. seven hundred eighty-four and thirty-six hundredths *784.036*

2. nine tenths

Add the following decimals.

3. 0.34 + 1.54 = *1.88*

4. 1.39 + 1.339 =

Subtract the following decimals.

5. 15.36 − 0.987 = *15.36*
   − 0.987
   14.373

6. 3.09875 − 0.00045 =

7. 12.901 − 0.903 = *12.901*
   − 0.903
   11.998

Multiply the following decimals and round to the hundredth place.

8. 21.62 × 21.62 =

9. 0.9 × 500 =

Divide the following decimals and round to the thousandth place.

10. 12 ÷ 6.5 =

11. 0.8 ÷ 0.6 =

Round the following to the nearest hundredth.

12. 3.872

13. 0.138

14. 0.076

Round the following to the nearest thousandth.

15. 0.1961

16. 0.0488

Multiply the following and round to the appropriate place.

17. 6.7 × 5.21 =

18. 0.45 × 3.1 =

Applications

19. Using the prescription below, answer the following questions.
    Note: QID means "four times a day."

Alprazolam 0.25 mg
Sig: 3 tabs po QID
Disp: 100 tablets

    a. How many milligrams is the patient taking with each dose?

    b. How many milligrams is the patient taking each day?

    c. How many tablets will the patient need for 14 days?

    d. Is the prescription written for enough tablets to last the patient until the next office visit in two weeks?

    e. The pharmacy plans to charge $7.59 plus the cost of the medication. The available products include:

alprazolam 0.25 mg #100/$14.95
alprazolam 0.5 mg #100/$17.46
alprazolam 1 mg #100/$23.87

Select the appropriate product and calculate the price for the patient. Based on the prescription provided, the pharmacy can only dispense 100 tablets.

20. The physician changes the prescription at the patient's next visit. The prescription is shown below.

 Alprazolam 0.25 mg

    Sig: 4 tabs po QID

    Disp: 175 tablets

The available products include:

alprazolam 0.25 mg #100/$14.95
alprazolam 0.5 mg #100/$17.46
alprazolam 1 mg #100/$23.87

a. How many milligrams at each dose is this?

b. How much would #125 alprazolam 0.5 mg tablets cost the pharmacy?

c. How much would #50 alprazolam 1 mg tablets cost the pharmacy?

d. How many days would #50 alprazolam 1 mg tablets taken QID last?

21. Sterile water comes in bottles of 1 L. You will need to pour out 120 mL bottles for each patient.

a. How many 120 mL bottles will you get from a 1 L bottle? (1 L = 1000 mL)

b. How much will be left over?

22. How many milliliters total will need to be dispensed for the following prescription? *Note:* bid means "twice a day."

 Augmentin 125 mg/5 mL susp

    8.5 mL bid days 1–2

    5.75 mL bid days 3–7

23. Round the following to the nearest whole dollar.

a. $46.92

b. 12 @ $1.26

c. $7.37 divided by 2

24. Calculate the following dollar amounts and round to the nearest cent.

a. $5.84 \times 12 =$

b. $0.415 \times 269 =$

25. Calculate the following test scores to the nearest tenth of a percent.

a. 34 of 38 questions correct

b. 51 of 60 questions correct

c. 83 of 90 questions correct

Self-check your work in Appendix A.

1.4 Estimates

Estimating an answer prior to calculating the solution is a simple way of checking to see whether the answer we arrive at is reasonable. Estimating can be used in both simple mathematical equations and more complicated algebraic equations.

There are no set mathematical rules for estimating. Most commonly, estimating is performed by rounding to the nearest whole unit that makes sense for the numbers involved. This may be the ones place, tens place, hundreds place, or even larger. A very common estimate that is used daily is rounding to the nearest whole dollar while shopping.

Estimating Sums

A **sum** is the result of adding two or more numbers together. When estimating sums, it is common to round the numbers to be added to the nearest ten or hundred or thousand first and then add these rounded numbers. When this is done, the values in the ones place and lower are often ignored. The following calculations compare an actual mathematical computation with a corresponding estimate.

Actual $73.8 + 42.03 + 18.3 + 87.32 = 221.45$
Estimate $70 \ + 40 \ \ + 20 \ + 90 \ \ \ \ = 220$

Actual $623 + 1493 + 1631 + 794 + 86 \ = 4627$
Estimate $600 + 1500 + 1600 + 800 + 100 = 4600$

Actual $6425 + 2652 + 2328 + 4490 = 15{,}895$
Estimate $6000 + 3000 + 2000 + 4000 = 15{,}000$

Another common method of estimating sums is to stack the numbers by aligning them on their decimal points; add the numbers in the far left column using their place value (6428 would be 6000 because the 6 is in the thousands place, for example); and then add one half of the place value of the far-left column for each number with a value in the second-from-left column. If the second-to-left column is the hundreds column, each number that had a numeral in the column would represent 500 (one-half of the next left column of 1000). This is loosely based on the assumption that on average each of the entries with a numeral in the column will contribute about half of the next place value.

Estimating is a process that becomes easier and more accurate with practice. A small list of numbers will often generate a fairly accurate estimate, while longer lists of numbers may require more practice and may be less accurate. For a long list of numbers, it is helpful to estimate the sums on paper using the method shown in Table 1.7. The following examples demonstrate this stepped method for estimating. The sum determined by estimating cannot be relied on as accurate when dispensing prescriptions.

Example 1.4.1

Estimate the sum of 73.80, 42.05, 18.30, and 87.32.

Step 1. Stack these four numbers so that their decimal points are aligned.

73.80
42.05
18.30
87.32

TABLE 1.7   Steps for Estimating Sums

Step 1. Stack the numbers whose sum is to be estimated so that their decimal points are aligned.

Step 2. Add the numbers in the far-left column using their column place value. For example, if the first number is 735, use 700 as that number's value.

Step 3. Multiply one-half of the place value of the far-left column by the total number of numbers that have place values in the second-from-the-left column.

Step 4. Add the totals determined in Steps 2 and 3 to estimate the sum.

Step 2. Add the numbers in the far-left column using their place value, in this case, the tens column.

$$70 + 40 + 10 + 80 = 200$$

Step 3. Multiply one-half of the place value of the far-left column by the total number of numbers that have place values in the second-from-the-left column in the original problem.

$$(10 \text{ far-left column value} \div 2) \times 4 \text{ numbers} = 20$$

Step 4. Add the totals determined in Steps 2 and 3 to determine the estimate.

$$200 + 20 = 220$$

Compare this number to the actual sum of the original numbers, which is 221.47.

Example 1.4.2

Estimate the sum of 623, 1493, 1631, 794, and 86.

Step 1. Stack these five numbers so that their decimal points are aligned.

$$623$$
$$1493$$
$$1631$$
$$794$$
$$86$$

Step 2. Add the numbers in the far-left column using their place value, in this case, the thousands column.

$$1000 + 1000 = 2000$$

Step 3. Multiply one-half of the place value of the far-left column by the total number of numbers that have place values in the second-from-the-left column in the original problem.

$$(1000 \text{ far-left column value} \div 2) \times 4 \text{ numbers} = 2000$$

Note that because 86 does not have a hundreds place value, the number 4, not 5, is used in this step.

Step 4. Add the totals determined in Steps 2 and 3 to determine the estimate.

$$2000 + 2000 = 4000$$

Compare the estimate with the actual sum of the original numbers, which is 4627.

Example 1.4.3	**Estimate the sum of 6425, 2652, 2328, and 4490.**

Step 1. 6425
2652
2328
4490

Step 2. 6000 + 2000 + 2000 + 4000 = 14,000

Step 3. (1000 far-left column value ÷ 2) × 4 numbers = 2000

Step 4. 14,000 + 2000 = 16,000

Compare the estimate with the actual sum of the numbers, which is 15,895.

Estimating Products and Quotients

product
the result of multiplying one number by another

quotient
the result of dividing one number by another

A **product** is the result of multiplying two numbers together. A **quotient** is the result of dividing one number by another number. When estimating products or quotients, it is common to round each of the original numbers, divided by the place value of its leftmost column, to the nearest whole number. The rounded numbers can be quickly multiplied or divided, and the appropriate number of zeros can be added to the answer.

Example 1.4.4

Estimate the product of 325 × 618.

Round the two numbers and multiply leftmost digits.

$$3 \times 6 = 18$$

Add four zeros to this answer to account for the four places of "25" and "18" in the original problem.

$$180,000$$

Compare the estimate to the actual product, which is 200,850.

Example 1.4.5

Estimate the product of 843 × 41.

Round the two numbers and multiply them.

$$8 \times 4 = 32$$

Add three zeros for the "43" and "1."

$$32,000$$

Compare the estimate to the actual product, which is 34,563.

Example 1.4.6   **Estimate the product of 843 × 56.**

Round the two numbers, and multiply them. Note that 56 is rounded up to 6, not down to 5.

$$8 \times 6 = 48$$

Add 3 zeros for the "43" and "6."

$$48,000$$

Compare the estimate to the actual product, which is 47,208.

Example 1.4.7   **Estimate the quotient of 5355 ÷ 4.79.**

Round the two numbers and divide them.

$$5 \div 5 = 1$$

Add three zeros for the "355." Do not add zeros for the numbers to the right of the decimal place in 4.79.

$$1000$$

Compare the estimate to the actual product, which is 1117.95.

Example 1.4.8   **Estimate the product of 14.3 × 0.19.**

Round the two numbers.

14.3 is rounded to 14
0.19 is rounded to 0.2

To avoid the decimal in the estimate operation, simplify 0.2 to 2. The decimal point will be inserted after we have multiplied the two rounded numbers.

$$14 \times 2 = 28$$

We ignored one decimal place in order to perform the estimating process quickly, so now we must account for the decimal. To do this, move the decimal point the same number of places that we ignored, in this case, one place. Thus, 28 becomes 2.8.

Compare the estimate to the actual product, which is 2.717.

In other cases, it may make sense to round to a near factor of 10 or 100 or even larger.

Actual $18.79 × 6 = $112.74
Estimate $20.00 × 6 = $120.00

Actual $424.00 × 2 = $848.00
Estimate $420.00 × 2 = $840.00

$$\begin{array}{ll} \text{Actual} & 4326 \div 3.78 = 1144.44 \\ \text{Estimate} & 4000 \div 4 = 1000 \end{array}$$

$$\begin{array}{ll} \text{Actual} & 820 \div 42 = 19.52 \\ \text{Estimate} & 800 \div 40 = 20 \end{array}$$

Example 1.4.9

A patient needs to take 3.75 mL daily for 30 days. Estimate the total number of milliliters needed. The pharmacy technician can select between a 120 mL bottle and 180 mL bottle for dispensing this liquid mediation. Which bottle should the technician use?

$$\begin{array}{ll} \text{Estimate} & 4 \text{ mL} \times 30 \text{ days} = 120 \text{ mL for 30 days} \\ \text{Actual} & 3.75 \text{ mL} \times 30 \text{ days} = 112.5 \text{ mL for 30 days} \end{array}$$

Because the 120 mL bottle has more than enough room, the 180 mL bottle is not necessary, and the 120 mL bottle will be used to dispense the medication.

Estimating a Drug Dose

Safety Note

As stated before, an estimated value can be used to double-check a dose but cannot be relied on for accuracy.

Estimating a drug dose before calculating the actual dose is helpful because the estimate can be used to double-check the accuracy of the calculated actual dose. If the amounts do not match, then the answer should be checked carefully. When estimating a drug dose, the first step is to determine whether the dose is going to be more or less than the unit dose or available drug strength. Continue estimating the dose by rounding the given dose to simplify the problem and dividing this rounded dose by the available drug strength.

Example 1.4.10

An order for 12.5 mg of a drug needs to be filled using a 5 mg tablet. Estimate the number of tablets needed for this dose.

The requested solution has 5 mg of drug for each tablet. Since the order is for 12.5 mg of drug, the dose to be measured out will be larger than 1 tablet.

Simplify the estimation by rounding 12.5 mg down to 10 mg. This will make it easier to use the available dose to determine the value of the requested dose.

$$10 \text{ mg (requested amount)} \times \frac{1 \text{ tablet}}{5 \text{ mg}} \text{ (available amount)} = 2 \text{ tablets}$$

Therefore, the estimate indicates that the dose will be at least 2 tablets.

The actual calculated dose of 2.5 tablets can then be checked by comparing it with the estimate. If an actual dose of 0.25 tablet or 25 tablets was calculated instead, then a quick comparison with the estimated dose of 2 tablets would immediately indicate that the actual dose was calculated incorrectly.

In addition to drug doses, the volume to be dispensed and the size of the container needed can be useful estimates when preparing a drug for dispensing.

Example 1.4.11   The pharmacy receives an order for a 10 day supply of liquid antibiotic to be taken in a dose of 8.5 mL of medication three times a day. The pharmacy has 100 mL, 200 mL, and 300 mL bottles of this antibiotic in stock. Which size bottle of antibiotic should be dispensed?

Begin by simplifying the problem by rounding the dose of 8.5 mL/dose to 10 mL/dose. It is important to round up to make sure the patient has enough drug.

Using this rounded value, calculate the amount of drug needed per day by multiplying the estimated dose by the number of doses each day.

$$\frac{10 \text{ mL}}{1 \text{ dose}} \times \frac{3 \text{ doses}}{1 \text{ day}} = \frac{30 \text{ mL}}{1 \text{ day}}$$

In other words, the patient will need about 30 mL of drug a day.

Since the patient needs to take this drug for 10 days, multiply the amount of drug per day by the number of days of therapy.

$$\frac{30 \text{ mL}}{\text{day}} \times 10 \text{ days} = 300 \text{ mL}$$

Therefore, the patient will need about 300 mL of the medication. The actual amount needed is 255 mL, but the 300 mL bottle is the correct choice to fill this prescription.

1.4 Problem Set

Using the stack-up process described in Table 1.7, estimate the sum to the nearest ten place and then calculate the actual value.

1. $231 + 718 + 357 + 609 =$

2. $176 + 34 + 49 + 16 =$

3. $12.38 + 6.26 + 18.95 + 16.52 =$

4. $93.7 + 16 + 48.7 + 12.02 =$

5. $0.95 + 6.96 + 0.49 + 12.42 =$

Use rounding to estimate the dollar amounts to the nearest whole dollar, and then calculate the actual value.

6. $\$12.53 - \$6.15 =$

7. $\$6.28 + \$1.99 + \$3.98 =$

8. $\$40 - \$34.81 =$

9. $\$100 - \$18.29 =$

10. $\$100 - \$17.52 - \$31.90 =$

Estimate the products by rounding the two numbers and then multiplying them. Also calculate the actual value.

11. $6.8 \times 7656 =$

12. $4.02 \times 350.07 =$

13. $598.4 \times 0.015 =$

14. $4569 \times 0.0972 =$

15. $6183 \times 18 =$

16. $1253 \times 9.1 =$

Estimate the quotients by rounding the two numbers and then dividing them. Also calculate the actual value.

17. $185 \div 18 =$

18. $18,015 \div 56 =$

19. $584.0 \div 8 =$

20. $844.23 \div 4.4 =$

21. $123 \div 14 =$

Applications

Round and estimate to find the following.

22. An employee of the pharmacy is being sent to the grocery store to buy the following items. Estimate how much petty cash he will need.

Food dye	$1.89
Sugar, 2@	$4.25
Baking soda	$0.79
Cherry flavoring	$2.39
1 gallon bleach	$1.97
Distilled water, 4@	$0.89

23. Estimate how much sterile water for injection (SWFI) you will need for the following reconstitutions: 3.2 mL, 7.6 mL, 1.6 mL, and 4.1 mL. Choose the appropriate vial from the available vials (15 mL SWFI, 30 mL SWFI, and 50 mL SWFI).

24. A patient is receiving the following fluids: IV fluids, 1723 mL; juice, 150 mL; coffee, 126 mL. Estimate the patient's intake to the nearest 10 mL.

25. The following is a patient's parenteral fluid intake for the first 24 hours of admittance: 780 mL NS, 3×50 mL piggybacks, 250 mL NS, 3×1000 mL NS. Estimate the total to the nearest 100 mL amount.

Self-check your work in Appendix A.

1.5 Significant Figures and Measurement Accuracy

significant figures
the figures in a numeral that are known values and have not been rounded or estimated in the process of mathematical calculation, plus the digit in the lowest place value, which is approximate

lowest known place value
the last digit on the right of a written numeral

Rounding and estimating have been discussed as a practical way of using numbers to calculate and measure a dose. In the process, one should not lose sight of the mathematical principle that each numerical value has a certain number of **significant figures.** These significant figures consist of those that are known to be accurate plus the digit in the lowest place value, which is approximate.

The **lowest known place value** is the last digit on the right of a written numeral. This lowest known value is approximate because of many sources of error including the limitation of the instrument used to measure, operator error, temperature variation, and the need to round at a certain point to make the number practical for calculations.

Significant figures are digits that have a practical meaning or value. A leading zero that marks the place of the decimal is not significant, because it only marks the place value of the numbers that follow the decimal. Counting of significant figures begins at the first nonzero digit. Table 1.8 provides a short list of "rules" to follow when counting significant figures. Table 1.9 shows several numbers and indicates how many significant figures they have.

In certain cases, when the accuracy of the measurement is known, the trailing zero to the right of the apparent last significant figure may also be considered significant. For example, if the device used to measure a substance is accurate to the nearest tenth,

---

TABLE 1.8 Rules for Counting Significant Figures

Rule 1. Begin counting at the first nonzero digit.

Rule 2. Continue counting to the right until you reach the place value that is last (or rounded).

Rule 3. Zeros that are located between digits are significant and should be counted.

Rule 4. Do not count zeros that are placed to the left of the first digit. They only mark the place of the decimal.

Rule 5. One or more final zeros may or may not be significant depending on the accuracy to which the number is held.

TABLE 1.9 Counting Significant Figures

Number	Number of Significant Figures	Rule Applied
1.8	2	1, 2
18.3	3	1, 2
183	3	1, 2
1.832	4	1, 2
1832	4	1, 2
0.183	3	1, 2
0.108	3	1, 2, 3, 4
0.0108	3	1, 2, 3, 4
0.01	1	1, 2, 4
0.8	1	1, 2, 4
8	1	1, 2

the tenth place may be considered significant even if the last digit is a zero. The zero may be retained to indicate the accuracy of the number. For example,

1.0 has 2 significant figures

Larger numbers have significant figures based on their accuracy to the nearest factor of 10. If a very large amount of a substance is measured, at some point the person doing the measuring must "estimate" the closest amount represented by the device being used. As a result, the last digit recorded cannot be considered to be accurate and is thus not significant. For example, if 2788 is considered accurate from 2780 to 2790, it has only 3 significant figures. Similarly, if 8,341,274 is considered accurate from 8,341,270 to 8,341,280, it has only 6 significant figures.

When the degree of accuracy is known to a certain place value, the significant figures are counted only to that place value. Knowing the level of accuracy is important when considering the weighing capacity and sensitivity of a scale or balance in the pharmacy.

Example 1.5.1

An item is weighed on a balance with a degree of accuracy to the nearest tenth when measuring milligrams. The balance indicates that an item weighs 1.459 mg. How many significant figures does this weight have? What would the rounded value be?

Because the accuracy of the scale can be relied on only to the tenth place, the number of significant figures is 2. The "59" is not considered significant due to the sensitivity of the scale being used.

The weight would be rounded to 1.5 mg.

Significant figures are also used to describe the relative accuracy of a given number or value. For practical purposes, a number may be considered accurate to within two figures and up to five figures. More significant digits indicate a greater accuracy of known values. A number that is accurate to within two figures has a practical 5% error from the actual measurement. Table 1.10 demonstrates these accuracy translations.

TABLE 1.10   Accuracy Ranges

Accuracy Level	Example
Two-figure accuracy is within 5%	100 mg is in the range of 95 mg to 105 mg
Three-figure accuracy is within 0.5%	100 mg is in the range of 99.5 mg to 100.5 mg
Four-figure accuracy is within 0.05%	100 mg is in the range of 99.95 mg to 100.05 mg
Five-figure accuracy is within 0.005%	100 mg is in the range of 99.995 mg to 100.005 mg

In studying mathematics, numbers may be considered accurate for an infinite number of figures. In the study of pharmacy, however, for practical purposes a range of two to five figures is common.

Numbers greater than 100 have significant figures based on the relative accuracy of the measurement. If a number over 100 is accurate to the nearest 10, the first two digits are considered significant, and the last zero is considered an estimate and thus not significant. This is also true for numbers that are accurate to the nearest 100 or 1000. For example, if the following numbers are accurate to the nearest 10, they will have the indicated number of significant figures.

200 has 2 significant figures
1800 has 3 significant figures
30,000 has 4 significant figures

Similarly, if the following numbers are accurate to the nearest 100, they will have the indicated number of significant figures.

200 has 1 significant figure
1800 has 2 significant figures
30,000 has 3 significant figures

Just as with rounding, when performing calculations with numbers that have a different number of significant figures or have been rounded to different place values, the answer must be rounded to the place value of the least number of decimals.

Example 1.5.2

Determine the product of 6.5 mg × 4.18 using the appropriate number of accurate and significant figures.

Note the number of significant figures and the level of accuracy for each number: 6.5 has two significant figures and is accurate to the tenth place, whereas 4.18 has three significant figures and is accurate to the hundredth place. Now, determine the product of the two numbers.

$$6.5 \times 4.18 = 27.17$$

Because 6.5 is accurate only to the tenth place, the answer is only accurate to the tenth place. Therefore, 27.17 needs to be rounded to the tenth place. The answer, 27.2, has three significant figures.

Example 1.5.3   **Determine the product of 12.59 × 1572 using the appropriate number of accurate and significant figures.**

Note the number of significant figures and the accuracy of the numbers. Both factors have 4 significant figures. The number 12.59 is accurate to the hundredth place, but 1572 is accurate only to the ones place.

Now, determine the product of the two numbers.

$$12.59 \times 1572 = 19{,}791.48$$

The accuracy of the product is considered only to the ones place. Therefore, the answer must be rounded to that place, and the acceptable answer is 19,791.

1.5 Problem Set

Identify the number of significant figures in the following amounts. Assume that all final zeros are not significant.

1. 15.4324 grains

2. 1500 mL

3. 0.21 mg

4. $1.07

5. 100,000 mcg

6. 507.2 mg

7. 1.0 kg

8. 0.001 mg

9. 21,204.075 mcg

10. 100 mL

Round the following numbers to three significant figures.

11. 42.75

12. 100.19

13. 0.04268

14. 18.426

15. 0.003918

Round the following to two decimal places and state how many significant figures each has.

16. 0.3479

17. 0.056921

18. 1.9947

19. 0.00986

20. 1.0277

Calculate the following and retain the correct number of decimal places in the calculation.

21. 0.67 × 95.2 =

22. 1.26 × 24 =

23. 325 × 0.5 =

Applications

24. You are to prepare capsules that contain 0.125 g of a drug. You have four partial containers of medication, which weigh 3.2 g, 1.784 g, 2.46 g, and 5.87 g. Assume you have weighed each of the four containers with the same scale, and the accuracy is known to the hundredth gram.

    a. Which amount will need to be rounded?

    b. Which amount is not as accurate as it should be?

    c. What is the amount of the medication that will be left over after making the 0.125 g capsules?

25. A unit dose of an oral medication requires 21.65 mg. You are to prepare 45 doses.

    a. How many milligrams will you need?

    b. How many significant figures does this amount have?

    Self-check your work in Appendix A.

Circle the fraction with the highest value.

1. $\dfrac{4}{8}$ $\dfrac{3}{8}$ $\dfrac{2}{8}$

2. $\dfrac{1}{100}$ $\dfrac{1}{400}$ $\dfrac{1}{500}$

Express the following fractions in decimal form. Round to the nearest thousandth or zero.

3. $\dfrac{1}{5}$

4. $\dfrac{7}{8}$

Give the equivalent Arabic numeral for each of the following Roman numerals.

5. XXXIX

6. CCXVI

Give the equivalent Roman numeral for each of the following Arabic numerals.

7. 1200

8. 473

Write the following numbers without using scientific notation.

9. 9.1×10^8

10. 7.2×10^2

11. 2.538×10^{-5}

12. 2.01×10^{-4}

Write the following numbers using scientific notation.

13. 375,940,000,000

14. 0.000000109

15. 1,800,000

16. 920

In each group of numbers, circle the highest value.

17. 0.31   0.61   0.91

18. 0.33   0.3   0.31

State the place value of the underlined digit.

19. 1.3̲6

20. 56.7̲8̲

21. 0.231̲

22. 1̲4.02

Write the following decimals.

23. one thousand ninety and six tenths

24. twelve and nine thousand six hundred forty-sevenths

Add the following decimals.

25. $12.2 + 19.7 + 16.57 =$

26. $3.89 + 0.257 + 9.023 =$

Multiply the following decimals.

27. $6.08 \times 3.24 =$

28. $10.728 \times 4.23 =$

Calculate the following, retaining the correct number of decimal places.

29. $15.432 \times 3 =$

30. $208 \times 62.1 =$

Round the following to the nearest tenth.

31. 6.52

32. 83.97

Round the following to the nearest thousandth.

33. 643.7308

34. 4.2619

Multiply the following and round to the appropriate place.

35. $8.23 \times 0.23 =$

36. $0.8015 \times 0.9921 =$

Calculate the following test scores to the nearest tenth of a percent.

37. 34 of 38 questions correct

38. 51 of 60 questions correct

Applications

39. A prescription is to be filled for a patient who needs to take 11 mL of medication two times daily. She needs a 7 days' supply. You have amber ovals (bottles) in three sizes: 120 mL, 240 mL, and 360 mL. Estimate the total volume needed and choose the appropriate container size.

40. The following list indicates the value of various drugs that were destroyed: $41.71, $11.50, $8.93, $10.50, $3.29, $14.34, $68.20. Estimate the total dollar amount to be documented for the loss.

Using Ratios, Percents, and Proportions

2

Learning Objectives

- Describe the use of ratios and proportions in the pharmacy.
- Solve pharmacy calculations by using ratios and proportions.
- Calculate percentage of error in measurements.

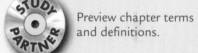

Preview chapter terms and definitions.

2.1 Numerical Ratios

ratio
a numerical representation of the relationship between two parts of the whole or between one part and the whole

A **ratio** is a numerical representation of the relationship between two parts of a whole or of the relationship of one part to the whole. Ratios are written with a colon (:) between the numbers, which may be read as "per," "of," "to," or "in." The ratio 1:2 could mean that the second part has twice the value (e.g., size, number, weight, volume) of the first part, or it could mean that one part is something within a total of two parts. Ratios may also be written as fractions, and it is the ratio in fraction form that is most useful to the pharmacy technician.

1:2	is read as	1 part to 2 parts	and may also be written as $\frac{1}{2}$
3:4	is read as	3 parts to 4 parts	and may also be written as $\frac{3}{4}$
1:20	is read as	1 part to 20 parts	and may also be written as $\frac{1}{20}$
1:10	is read as	1 part to 10 parts	and may also be written as $\frac{1}{10}$

In the above ratios, you may use the words *per, in,* or *of* in place of *to* when reading the ratio. Any unit of description may be substituted for the word *part* or *parts*. For example, we say there are 250 mg per tablet. Other common unit labels include capsule, bottle, gram, milligram, microgram, and liter.

A ratio can be any numerical relation we wish it to be. With medications, we commonly use a ratio to express the weight or strength of a drug per dose or

FIGURE 2.1
**Ratios on an
Ampule Label**

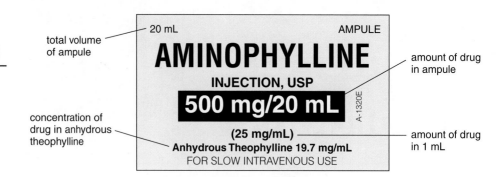

total volume
of ampule

20 mL

AMPULE

AMINOPHYLLINE

INJECTION, USP

500 mg/20 mL

A-1320E

(25 mg/mL)
Anhydrous Theophylline 19.7 mg/mL
FOR SLOW INTRAVENOUS USE

amount of drug
in ampule

amount of drug
in 1 mL

concentration of
drug in anhydrous
theophylline

volumetric measurement. Ratios are commonly used to express concentrations of a drug in solution. For example, a 1:100 concentration of a drug means that there is 1 part of the drug in 100 parts of the solution (1 g per 100 mL). It is also common to reverse the order of the values written in a ratio.

250 mg:1 tablet	or	1 tablet:250 mg
1 g:100 mL	or	100 mL:1 g
500 mg:20 mL	or	20 mL:500 mg

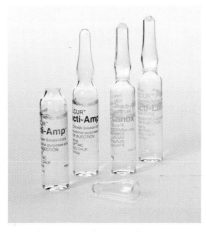

Ampules are small, single dose containers of medication that are opened at the time of use.

The ratio may be manipulated by multiplying or dividing both parts of the ratio by the same factor. We use this application when calculating the volume of a medication to be given or, in some cases, the amount of drug per volume of drug given. See the drug label below when reviewing the following examples.

Some drug labels, especially those of injectable drugs have more than one ratio listed. For example, the aminophylline label shown in Figure 2.1 includes three ratios, each descriptive of the drug's concentration. The first ratio, 500 mg/20 mL, represents the total amount of drug in the ampule. The second ratio, 25 mg/mL, represents the amount of drug in 1 mL. The third ratio, 19.7mg/mL, describes the concentration of drug in its anhydrous-theophylline state. The pharmacist may use this concentration to further analyze the dosage. The ratio indicating the total amount of drug in the ampule is of the most importance to the pharmacy technician. Typically, this ratio is the most prominent one on the label, as is the case for this label.

Example 2.1.1

How much aminophylline was ordered if two ampules were administered and each ampule contained 500 mg/20 mL?

For 2 ampules, we multiply both parts of the ratio by 2.

$$\frac{500 \text{ mg} \times 2}{20 \text{ mL} \times 2} = \frac{1000 \text{ mg}}{40 \text{ mL}}$$

So, 1000 mg were given.

Example 2.1.2

How much aminophylline was ordered if half an ampule was administered and each ampule contained 500 mg/20 mL?

For half of an ampule, we divide both parts of the ratio by 2.

$$\frac{500 \text{ mg} \div 2}{20 \text{ mL} \div 2} = \frac{250 \text{ mg}}{10 \text{ mL}}$$

So, 250 mg were given.

Some medications are ordered in concentrations that are expressed in a ratio. Typically, these medications are available in a very small percentage (less than 1%). The dose form (such as a cream, solution, or liquid mixture) will influence the ratio. The following examples use a 1:10,000 ratio.

1 g active ingredient:10,000 g product for a solid such as a cream
1 g active ingredient:10,000 mL solution for a solution
1 mL active ingredient:10,000 mL mixture for a liquid

Example 2.1.3

A 1:100 solution has 1 g active ingredient in 100 mL. How much active ingredient is present in 300 mL of this solution?

Set up a ratio and solve for x. In this problem, x equals the active ingredient.

$$\frac{x \text{ g}}{300 \text{ mL}} = \frac{1 \text{ g}}{100 \text{ mL}}$$

$$\frac{(300 \text{ mL}) \, x \text{ g}}{300 \text{ mL}} = \frac{(300 \text{ mL}) \, 1 \text{ g}}{100 \text{ mL}}$$

$$x \text{ g} = 3 \text{ g}$$

Therefore, there are 3 g of active ingredient in 300 mL of this solution.

2.1 Problem Set

Express the following ratios as fractions and reduce to the lowest terms.

1. 3:7 $\frac{3}{7} = \frac{3}{7}$
2. 8:6 $\frac{8}{6} = \frac{4}{3} = 1\frac{1}{3}$
3. 3:4 $\frac{3}{4}$
4. 4:6 $\frac{4}{6} = \frac{2}{3}$
5. 1:7 $\frac{1}{7}$

Reduce the following fractions to the lowest terms and express each as a ratio.

6. $\frac{2}{3}$ 2:3
7. $\frac{6}{8}$ 3:4
8. $\frac{5}{10}$ 1:2
9. $\frac{1}{9}$ 1:9
10. $\frac{1}{10,000}$ 1:10,000

Applications

State the ratio for the following doses.

11. 40 mg tablet Diovan   40mg : 1 tab

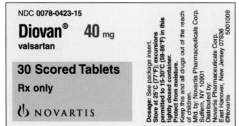

NDC 0078-0423-15
Diovan® **40** mg
valsartan
30 Scored Tablets
Rx only
Ⴆ **NOVARTIS**

12. 5 mL dose of Trileptal containing 300 mg

300mg : 5mL

Trileptal®
(oxcarbazepine)
Oral Suspension   Rx only
300 mg/5 mL   100 mL

13. 5 mL dose of oral suspension containing 250 mg amoxicillin

250mL : 5mL

00000-0000-00   reconstitute w/ 105 mL water
Amoxicillin for Oral Suspension, USP
250 mg per 5 mL
when reconstituted according to directions
Caution: Federal law prohibits dispensing without prescription.
150 mL bottle

Use the ratios calculated in the preceding problems to calculate how much drug is in the following doses. Write a sentence explaining how you calculated each answer.

14. ½ tablet Diovan

$$\frac{40mg}{1\,tab} = \frac{Xmg}{.5\,tab}$$

$$40 \times .5 = 1 \times X$$

$$40 \times .5 = 20\,mg$$

15. 10 mL Triletal suspension, 300 mg in 5 mL
    600 mg

16. 15 mL amoxicillin suspension, 250 mL in 5 mL
    750 mL

Fill in the blanks.

17. A 10:1000 solution contains __10__ g of active ingredient and __1000__ mL of product, and 100 mL of that solution contains __1__ g.

18. A 1:100 solution contains __1__ g of active ingredient and __100__ mL of product, and 500 mL of that solution contains __5__ g.

19. A 1:250 solution contains __1__ g of active ingredient and __250__ mL of product, and 1000 mL of that solution contains __4__ g.

20. A 1:1000 solution contains __1__ g of active ingredient and __1000__ mL of product, and 50 mL of that solution contains __1/20__ g. As indicated on the label below, this can be reduced to 1 mg/1 mL.

50mg

NDC 0517-1071-25
EPINEPHRINE
INJECTION, USP
1:1000 (1 mg/mL)
1 mL AMPULE
FOR SC AND IM USE. FOR IV AND IC USE AFTER DILUTION.
Rx Only
CONTAINS NO SULFITES.
PRESERVATIVE FREE.
Store below 23°C (73°F). Do not freeze.
AMERICAN REGENT, INC.
SHIRLEY, NY 11967   Rev. 5/05

Self-check your work in Appendix A.

2.2 Percents

percent
the number of parts per 100; can be written as a fraction, a decimal, or a ratio

Percent expresses the number of parts compared to a total of 100 parts. Percent means, literally, "per 100" (from the Latin) or hundredths and is the same as a fraction in which the denominator is 100. Percent is represented by the symbol %. Percents can be visualized by comparing a stack of 100 pennies (equivalent to 1 dollar) next to smaller stacks of pennies (see Figure 2.2). A stack of 5 pennies equals 5 cents and

FIGURE 2.2
Comparison
of Percents

100% of a dollar

40% of a dollar

5% of a dollar

100 pennies

40 pennies

5 pennies

represents 5% of a dollar. Similarly, a stack of 40 pennies equals 40 cents and represents 40% of a dollar.

A percent can be written as a fraction, a decimal, or a ratio. For example, 30% means there are 30 parts in a total of 100 parts.

$$30{:}100, \quad \frac{30}{100}, \text{ or } 0.30$$

If a test has 100 questions and you receive a score of 89%, you got 89 of the 100 questions correct.

$$89{:}100, \quad \frac{89}{100}, \text{ or } 0.89$$

Safety Note

The higher the percentage of a dissolved substance, the greater the strength.

Percent strengths are often used to describe intravenous solutions and topically applied drugs. The higher the percentage of dissolved substances (in a solute or a topical drug), the greater the strength. Both of the following examples may be expressed as 1:100, $\frac{1}{100}$, or 0.01.

A 1% solution contains 1 g of drug per 100 mL of fluid

A 1% hydrocortisone cream contains 1 g of hydrocortisone per 100 g of cream

By multiplying the first number in the ratio (the solute) while keeping the second number unchanged, we can increase the strength. Conversely, by dividing the first number in the ratio while keeping the second number unchanged, we can decrease the strength.

Example 2.2.1

A 5% solution contains 5 g of solute per 100 mL of solution. If the patient is to receive a 10% solution, how many grams of solute will the solution have to contain?

$$\frac{5 \text{ g} \times 2}{100 \text{ mL}} = \frac{10 \text{ g}}{100 \text{ mL}} = 10\% \text{ solution}$$

Thus, a 10% solution contains 10 g of solute per 100 mL of solution.

Example 2.2.2

A 2% solution contains 2 g of solute per 100 mL of solution. If the patient is to receive a 1% solution, how many grams of solute will the solution have to contain?

$$\frac{2 \text{ g} \div 2}{100 \text{ mL}} = \frac{1 \text{ g}}{100 \text{ mL}} = 1\% \text{ solution}$$

Thus, a 1% solution contains 1 g of solute per 100 mL of solution.

Example 2.2.3

Convert the percent lidocaine to a ratio and then convert the grams to milligrams.

A 1% solution of lidocaine contains 1 g of lidocaine in 100 mL solution. This could also be written as 1000 mg solute per 100 mL solution (1 g is equivalent to 1000 mg). Equivalent to this ratio is the strength indicated on the label above (10 mg/mL). The label uses both percentage and milligrams per milliliter expressions to describe the concentration of the drug.

$$1\% = \frac{1 \text{ g}}{100 \text{ mL}} = \frac{1000 \text{ mg}}{100 \text{ mL}} = \frac{10 \text{ mg}}{1 \text{ mL}}$$

When working in the pharmacy, the technician will need to know how to convert between ratios, percents, and decimals. The values in each row of Table 2.1 are equivalent to each other. They are simply expressed in different ways.

Converting a Ratio to a Percent

To express a ratio as a percent, designate the first number of the ratio as the numerator and the second number as the denominator. Multiply the fraction by 100 and add a percent sign after the number.

$$5{:}1 = \frac{5}{1} \times 100 = 5 \times 100 = 500\%$$

$$1{:}5 = \frac{1}{5} \times 100 = \frac{100}{5} = 20\%$$

$$1{:}2 = \frac{1}{2} \times 100 = \frac{100}{2} = 50\%$$

TABLE 2.1 Equivalent Values

Percent	Fraction	Decimal	Ratio
45%	$\frac{45}{100}$	0.45	45:100
0.5%	$\frac{0.5}{100}$	0.005	0.5:100

Example 2.2.4

A 1:1000 solution has been ordered. You have a 1% solution, a 0.5% solution, and a 0.1% solution in stock. Will one of these work to fill the order?

$$1:1000 = \frac{1}{1000} \times 100 = \frac{100}{1000} = 0.1\%$$

The 0.1% solution is the same concentration as the ordered 1:1000 solution.

Converting Percents and Decimals

To convert a percent to a ratio, first change it to a fraction by dividing it by 100 and then reduce the fraction to its lowest terms. Express this as a ratio by making the numerator the first number of the ratio and the denominator the second number.

$$2\% = 2 \div 100 = \frac{2}{100} = \frac{1}{50} = 1:50$$

$$10\% = 10 \div 100 = \frac{10}{100} = \frac{1}{10} = 1:10$$

$$75\% = 75 \div 100 = \frac{75}{100} = \frac{3}{4} = 3:4$$

$$\frac{1}{2}\% = \frac{1}{2} \div 100 = \frac{\frac{1}{2}}{100} = \frac{1}{2} \times \frac{1}{100} = \frac{1}{200} = 1:200$$

Example 2.2.5

A 0.02% solution has been ordered. You have a 1:1000 solution, a 1:5000 solution, and a 1:10,000 solution in stock. Will one of these work to fill the order?

$$0.02\% = \frac{0.02}{100} = 0.0002 = 0.02:100$$

Simplify the ratio by dividing both sides of the ratio by 0.02.

$$0.02 \div 0.02 = 1$$
$$100 \div 0.02 = 5000$$

The percent 0.02% is represented by the ratio 1:5000. The supply of 1:5000 solution may be used to fill this order.

FIGURE 2.3
10% Bleach
Solution

> **1:10 Bleach Solution**
>
> **Materials:** Storage container, measuring cup or graduated cylinder, bleach, water, label
>
> **Instructions:** Measure one quantity of bleach (such as 1 cup) and place it into the storage container. Measure the same quantity of water nine times (9 cups) and place it into the storage container. Mix well, label, and date the container.

A solution commonly used for cleaning in healthcare facilities is a 1:10 solution of bleach and water. This solution is available commercially or may be made fresh daily using regular bleach. Figure 2.3 shows the recipe for making a 1:10 bleach solution. In the recipe, one part bleach is mixed with nine parts of water. The amounts can be adjusted, but the ratio should not change. Because it chemically degrades, a bleach solution prepared according to this recipe is only good for one day.

Example 2.2.6

You have been asked to prepare a 480 mL (1 pint) of 1:10 bleach solution. How much bleach and water will you need to measure out?

Determine the size of a "part" by dividing 10 parts into the total volume.

$$\text{total volume} \div \text{number of parts} = \text{volume per one part}$$

$$480 \text{ mL} \div 10 \text{ parts} = \frac{48 \text{ mL}}{1 \text{ part}}$$

We know from the recipe for a 10% bleach solution that the bleach volume is equal to one part, or 48 mL. Determine the amount of water needed by subtracting the known amount of bleach from the total volume.

$$\text{total volume} - \text{bleach volume} = \text{water volume}$$
$$480 \text{ mL} - 48 \text{ mL} = 432 \text{ mL}$$

The following ratio and fractions show the relationship of the 1:10 solution.

$$1{:}10 = \frac{1 \text{ part bleach}}{10 \text{ parts water and bleach solution}} = \frac{48 \text{ mL bleach}}{480 \text{ mL water and bleach solution}}$$

Converting a Percent to a Decimal

To convert a percent to a decimal, drop the percent symbol and divide the number by 100. Dividing a number by 100 is equivalent to moving the decimal two places to the left and inserting zeros if necessary.

$$4\% = 4 \div 100 = 0.04$$
$$15\% = 15 \div 100 = 0.15$$
$$200\% = 200 \div 100 = 2.0$$

To change a decimal to a percent, multiply by 100 or move the decimal point two places to the right and add a percent symbol.

$$0.25 = 0.25 \times 100 = 25\%$$
$$1.35 = 1.35 \times 100 = 135\%$$
$$0.015 = 0.015 \times 100 = 1.5\%$$

2.2 Problem Set

Express the following fractions as percents.

1. $\frac{6}{7}$ 85.7%

2. $\frac{5}{12}$ 41.6̄6̄%

3. $\frac{1}{4}$ 25%

4. $\frac{2}{3}$ 66.0̄6̄%

5. $\frac{0.5}{10}$ 5%

Express the following ratios as percents.

6. 2:3   66.6̄6̄%

7. 1.5:4.65   32.3%

8. 1:250   0.4%

9. 1:10,000   .01%

10. 1:6   16.6̄6̄%

Convert the following percents to fractions.

11. 50% $\frac{5}{10} = \frac{1}{2}$ 12. 2% $\frac{1}{50}$

Convert the following percents to decimals.

13. 6% 0.06   15. 126% 1.26

14. 12.5% 0.125

Calculate the following, rounding off to the nearest hundredth when necessary.

16. 5% of 20   1

17. 20% of 60   12

18. 19% of 63   11.97

19. 110% of 70   77

20. 0.2% of 50   0.1

Fill in the missing values.

	Percent	Fraction	Ratio	Decimal
21.	33%	$\frac{1}{3}$	1:3	0.33
22.	2.5%	$\frac{1}{40}$	1:40	0.025
23.	50%	$\frac{1}{2}$	1:2	0.5
24.	1%	$\frac{1}{100}$	1:100	0.01
25.	90%	$\frac{9}{10}$	9:10	0.90
26.	67%	$\frac{2}{3}$	2:3	0.67
27.	0.2%	$\frac{1}{500}$	1:500	0.002
28.	0.45%	$\frac{.09}{20}$	.09:20	0.0045
29.	5%	$\frac{1}{20}$	1:20	0.05
30.	20%	$\frac{1}{5}$	1:5	.20

Applications

Choose the appropriate solution from the available stock.

31. A 1:10,000 solution has been ordered. You have a 0.05% solution, a 0.01% solution, and a 1% solution in stock. Which will you choose?

32. A 1:20 solution has been ordered. You have a 5% solution, a 10% solution, and a 20% solution in stock. Which will you choose?

33. A 1:25 solution has been ordered. You have a 0.4% solution, a 0.05% solution, and a 4% solution in stock. Which will you choose?

34. A 1:800 solution has been ordered. You have a 0.01% solution, a 0.125% solution, and a 1.25% solution in stock. Which will you choose?

35. A 1:10 solution has been ordered. You have a 0.09% solution, a 0.01% solution, and a 10% solution in stock. Which will you choose?

Self-check your work in Appendix A.

2.3 Proportions

proportion
an expression of equality between two ratios

A **proportion** is an expression of equality between two ratios. A proportion can be visualized by thinking of two triangles that resemble one another in shape but are of different sizes. The triangles in Figure 2.4 have equal proportions.

A proportion is notated by an equal sign or a double colon (::) between the ratios. It can also be noted by using fractions.

$$3{:}4 = 15{:}20 \quad \text{or} \quad 3{:}4 :: 15{:}20 \quad \text{or} \quad \frac{3}{4} = \frac{15}{20}$$

In a proportion, the first and fourth, or outside, numbers are called the extremes. The second and third, or inside, numbers are called the means.

$$3{:}4 \quad = \quad 15{:}20$$

means

extremes

The product of the means must always equal the product of the extremes in a proportion. You can check for the correctness of the proportion by using this formula.

Given a proportion

$$a{:}b = c{:}d$$

the product of means = the product of extremes

or

$$b \times c = a \times d$$

FIGURE 2.4
Triangles with Equal Proportions

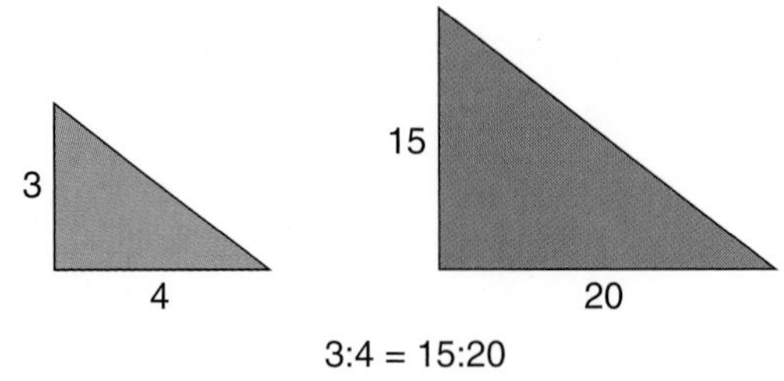

3

4

15

20

3:4 = 15:20

Example 2.3.1   **Confirm that the proportion 3:4 equals the proportion 15:20.**

$$3:4 = 15:20$$
$$4 \times 15 = 3 \times 20$$
$$60 = 60$$

---

ratio-proportion method
a conversion method based on comparing a complete ratio to a ratio with a missing component

The **ratio-proportion method** is one of the most frequently used methods for calculating drug doses in the pharmacy. We can use this method any time one ratio is complete and the other one has a missing component. In other words, if we know three of the four values in a proportion, we can solve for the missing value. When setting up ratios in the proportion, it is important that the numbers remain in the correct ratio and that the numbers have the correct units of measurement in both the numerator and the denominator. Table 2.2 lists the rules for using the ratio-proportion method. Table 2.3 lists the steps for solving for an unknown quantity, which we usually label x.

Example 2.3.2   **A drug is available as 250 mg/5 mL. How many milliliters represent a dose of 375 mg?**

In this case, set the ordered dose ratio equal to the pharmacy stocked drug ratio. In setting up a proportion, the ratios on the two sides of the equal sign may be flipped over as long as *both* ratios are reversed.

$$\text{prescription order ratio} = \text{pharmacy shelf ratio}$$

$$\frac{x \text{ mL}}{375 \text{ mg}} = \frac{5 \text{ mL}}{250 \text{ mg}}$$

Be sure to check that the unit of measurement in the numerators is the same (both are milliliters) and that the unit of measurement in the denominators is the same (both are milligrams). Multiply both sides by 375 mg to cancel the milligram unit and isolate the unknown.

$$\frac{(375 \text{ mg}) \, x \text{ mL}}{375 \text{ mg}} = \frac{(375 \text{ mg}) \, 5 \text{ mL}}{250 \text{ mg}}$$

$$x \text{ mL} = \frac{1875 \text{ mL}}{250}$$

Simplify the fraction by dividing 1875 by 250.

$$x \text{ mL} = 7.5 \text{ mL}$$

Check that the product of the means equals the product of the extremes.

$$7.5 \text{ mL}:375 \text{ mg} = 5 \text{ mL}:250 \text{ mg}$$
$$375 \times 5 = 7.5 \times 250$$
$$1875 = 1875$$

TABLE 2.2   Rules for Using the Ratio-Proportion Method

Rule 1. Three of the four amounts must be known.
Rule 2. The numerators must have the same unit of measurement.
Rule 3. The denominators must have the same unit of measurement.

Example 2.3.3

The label shown below is the stock your pharmacy has available of tobramycin sulfate. How many milliliters will need to be dispensed to the patient if the prescription is for 150 mg?

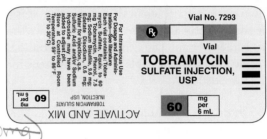

$$\frac{x\ \text{mL}}{150\ \text{mg}} = \frac{6\ \text{mL}}{60\ \text{mg}}$$

$$\frac{(150\ \text{mg})\ x\ \text{mL}}{150\ \text{mg}} = \frac{(150\ \text{mg})\ 6\ \text{mL}}{60\ \text{mg}}$$

$$x\ \text{mL} = \frac{900\ \text{mL}}{60}$$

$$x\ \text{mL} = 15\ \text{mL}$$

Check that the product of the means equals the product of the extremes.

$$15\ \text{mL}:150\ \text{mg} = 6\ \text{mL}:60\ \text{mg}$$
$$150 \times 6 = 15 \times 60$$
$$900 = 900$$

TABLE 2.3   Steps for Solving for *x* in the Ratio-Proportion Method

Step 1. Create the proportion by placing the ratios in fraction form so that the *x* is in the upper-left corner.

Step 2. Check that the unit of measurement in the numerators is the same and the unit of measurement in the denominators is the same.

Step 3. Solve for *x* by multiplying both sides of the proportion by the denominator of the ratio containing the unknown, and cancel.

Step 4. Check your answer by seeing if the product of the means equals the product of the extremes.

Example 2.3.4

The label shown below is the stock available at your pharmacy. How many milligrams of diazepam will need to be dispensed to the patient if the prescription is for 4 mL?

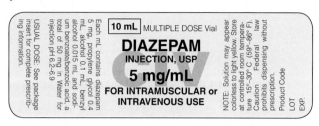

$$\frac{x \text{ mg}}{4 \text{ mL}} = \frac{5 \text{ mg}}{1 \text{ mL}}$$

$$\frac{(4 \text{ mL}) \, x \text{ mg}}{4 \text{ mL}} = \frac{(4 \text{ mL}) \, 5 \text{ mg}}{1 \text{ mL}}$$

$$x \text{ mg} = 20 \text{ mg}$$

Check that the product of the means equals the product of the extremes.

$$20 \text{ mg:4 mL} = 5 \text{ mg:1 mL}$$
$$4 \times 5 = 20 \times 1$$
$$20 = 20$$

Remember

When setting up a proportion to solve a conversion, the units in the numerators must match, and the units in the denominators must match.

conversion factor
an equivalency equal to 1 that can be used when converting units of measure using the ratio-proportion method

In addition to being useful for calculating drug doses in the pharmacy, the ratio-proportion method can be used for converting between units of measure. To solve a conversion problem, put the unknown and the specific value that is to be converted on the left side of the proportion. On the right side of the proportion, put the conversion factor. The **conversion factor** is an equivalency equal to 1. For example, since 1 g = 1000 mg, an example of a conversion factor is 1 g/1000 mg or 1000 mg/1 g. Additional conversion factors are presented in Appendix D.

Example 2.3.5

How many milligrams are equivalent to 3 g?

Begin the solution by setting up a ratio and solving for x, using the conversion factor 1000 mg = 1 g.

$$x \text{ mg:3 g} = 1000 \text{ mg:1 g}$$

$$\frac{x \text{ mg}}{3 \text{ g}} = \frac{1000 \text{ mg}}{1 \text{ g}}$$

The unit of measurement in the numerators is the same (both are milligrams), and the unit of measurement in the denominators is the same (both are grams). Multiply both sides by 3 g to cancel the grams and isolate the unknown.

$$\frac{(3 \text{ g}) \, x \text{ mg}}{3 \text{ g}} = \frac{(3 \text{ g}) \, 1000 \text{ mg}}{1 \text{ g}}$$

$$x \text{ mg} = \frac{3000 \text{ mg}}{1} = 3000 \text{ mg}$$

Check that the product of the means equals the product of the extremes.

$$3000 \text{ mg}:3 \text{ g} = 1000 \text{ mg}:1 \text{ g}$$
$$3 \times 1000 = 3000 \times 1$$
$$3000 = 3000$$

Example 2.3.6

Change 44 lb to kilograms. Your conversion chart in Appendix D states that 1 kg = 2.2 lb.

$$\frac{x \text{ kg}}{44 \text{ lb}} = \frac{1 \text{ kg}}{2.2 \text{ lb}}$$

$$\frac{(44 \text{ lb}) \, x \text{ kg}}{44 \text{ lb}} = \frac{(44 \text{ lb}) \, 1 \text{ kg}}{2.2 \text{ lb}}$$

$$x \text{ kg} = \frac{44 \text{ kg}}{2.2}$$

$$x \text{ kg} = 20 \text{ kg}$$

Make sure the product of the means equals the product of the extremes.

$$20 \text{ kg}:44 \text{ lb} = 1 \text{ kg}:2.2 \text{ lb}$$
$$44 = 44$$

The ratio-proportion method can also be used to solve many types of percentage problems. When setting up the ratios, remember that a percentage may be written in fraction form, with the percent value over 100. For example, 95% is equivalent to $^{95}/_{100}$.

Example 2.3.7

A patient needs to take 75% of a recommended dose before it may be discontinued. The recommended dose is 650 mg. How much must the patient take before it is discontinued?

Write the percentage (75%) as a fraction ($^{75}/_{100}$) and solve for x.

$$\frac{x \text{ mg}}{650 \text{ mg}} = \frac{75 \text{ mg}}{100 \text{ mg}}$$

$$\frac{(650 \text{ mg}) \, x \text{ mg}}{650 \text{ mg}} = \frac{(650 \text{ mg}) \, 75 \text{ mg}}{100 \text{ mg}}$$

$$x \text{ mg} = 487.5 \text{ mg}$$

Example 2.3.8

A patient has taken 85% of a recommended dose. If the amount taken is 320 mg, what was the recommended dose?

Another way of phrasing this question is "320 mg is 85% of what?"

$$\frac{x \text{ mg}}{320 \text{ mg}} = \frac{100 \text{ mg}}{85 \text{ mg}}$$

$$\frac{(320 \text{ mg}) \, x \text{ mg}}{320 \text{ mg}} = \frac{(320 \text{ mg}) \, 100 \text{ mg}}{85 \text{ mg}}$$

$$x \text{ mg} = 376.47 \text{ mg}$$

2.3 Problem Set

Solve for x for each of the following ratios. Round your answers to the nearest hundredth when necessary.

1. $\dfrac{x}{10} = \dfrac{20}{40}$

2. $\dfrac{x}{0.6} = \dfrac{0.8}{6.12}$

3. $\dfrac{x}{9} = \dfrac{5}{10}$

4. $\dfrac{x}{1} = \dfrac{0.5}{5}$

5. $\dfrac{x}{50} = \dfrac{0.4}{125}$

6. $\dfrac{13}{15} = \dfrac{5}{x}$

7. $\dfrac{x}{68} = \dfrac{72}{90}$

8. $\dfrac{14}{3} = \dfrac{x}{52}$

9. $\dfrac{x}{27} = \dfrac{49}{51}$

10. $\dfrac{13}{x} = \dfrac{52}{64}$

11. $\dfrac{14}{23} = \dfrac{27}{x}$

12. $\dfrac{31}{13} = \dfrac{51}{x}$

13. $\dfrac{47}{9} = \dfrac{x}{15}$

14. $\dfrac{9}{26} = \dfrac{x}{31}$

15. $\dfrac{37}{x} = \dfrac{11}{23}$

Set up proportions and solve for x to answer the following questions. Round your answers to the hundredth place.

16. 72 is what percent of 254?

17. 90% of what number is 44?

18. 44% of what number is 100?

19. 28% of what number is 34?

20. 24.5 is what percent of 45?

Change the following weights using the conversion factor 1 g = 1000 mg.

21. 100 mg = _____ g

22. 247 mg = _____ g

23. 1420 mg = _____ g

24. 495 mg = _____ g

25. 3781 mg = _____ g

26. 0.349 g = _____ mg

27. 1.5 g = _____ mg

28. 0.083 g = _____ mg

29. 0.01 g = _____ mg

30. 2.1 g = _____ mg

Change the following weights using the conversion factor 1 kg = 2.2 lb. Round your answer to the tenth place.

31. 6.3 lb = _____ kg

32. 15 lb = _____ kg

33. 97 lb = _____ kg

34. 115 lb = _____ kg

35. 186 lb = _____ kg

36. 7.5 kg = _____ lb

37. 3.6 kg = _____ lb

38. 79.2 kg = _____ lb

39. 90 kg = _____ lb

40. 0.5 kg = _____ lb

Applications

Set up a proportion using x as the unknown and solve the following. Explain in your own words how you set up your proportion.

41. A drug is available as 50 mg/mL. The order calls for 100 mg. How many milliliters will you prepare?

42. Maxicillin is available as a 125 mg tablet. How many tablets are needed to give a dose of 375 mg?

43. Soakamycin is available as a concentration of 20 mg/mL. How many milliliters are needed to prepare a foot soak that contains 300 mg?

44. You are going to buy some folders to file your orders. After checking around, you find that the most cost-effective price is $7.40 per box of 100 folders. You have $15 to spend. How many folders can you buy? (The boxes may not be broken.)

45. The patient is to get an intramuscular injection of 10,000 units of Musclesporin. You have a bottle containing 250,000 units per 15 mL. How many milliliters must be prepared to administer this dose?

48. A dose of 300 mg is ordered. The drug is available as a 500 mg/10 mL solution. How many milliliters are needed to provide the ordered dose?

46. A dose of 60 mg gentamicin is ordered. The drug is available as a 40 mg/mL solution. How many milliliters are needed to provide the ordered dose?

49. A dose of 30 mg Epivir oral solution is ordered. The drug is available in a 5 mg/mL oral solution. How many millilitres are needed to provide the ordered dose?

47. A dose of 60 mg famotidine is ordered. The drug is available as a 40 mg/4 mL solution. How many milliliters are needed to provide the ordered dose?

50. A dose of 30 mg is ordered. The drug is available as a 20 mg/mL solution. How many milliliters are needed to provide the ordered dose?

Use the following drug label to determine the dose needed for questions 51–55.

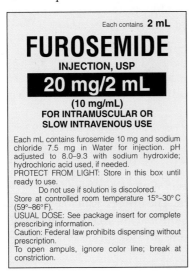

Each contains **2 mL**

FUROSEMIDE
INJECTION, USP

20 mg/2 mL
(10 mg/mL)
FOR INTRAMUSCULAR OR
SLOW INTRAVENOUS USE

Each mL contains furosemide 10 mg and sodium chloride 7.5 mg in Water for injection. pH adjusted to 8.0–9.3 with sodium hydroxide; hydrochloric acid used, if needed.
PROTECT FROM LIGHT: Store in this box until ready to use.
Do not use if solution is discolored.
Store at controlled room temperature 15°–30° C (59°–86° F).
USUAL DOSE: See package insert for complete prescribing information.
Caution: Federal law prohibits dispensing without prescription.
To open ampuls, ignore color line; break at constriction.

51. The order calls for 5 mL. How many milligrams is this?

52. The order calls for 80 mg. How many milliliters is this?

53. The order calls for 50 mg. How many milliliters is this?

54. The order calls for 12.5 mg. How many milliliters is this?

55. The order calls for 3.5 mL. How many milligrams is this?

Self-check your work in Appendix A.

2.4 Percentage of Error

Graduated cylinders are used to accurately measure liquids in the pharmacy.

Percentages are used in a variety of ways when preparing medication doses. In the compounding pharmacy, percentages are used in determining the possible percentage of error and the least weighable quantity of a substance for safe preparation. Percentages are also used when doing the business of the pharmacy, such as calculating the percentage of sales, percentage of discount, and percentage of markup. These applications will be covered in Chapter 9, *Using Business Math in the Pharmacy.*

When measuring a liquid or weighing a solid ingredient in the pharmacy, a certain amount of error is expected. Not all graduated cylinders used in the pharmacy are equally accurate, although they are usually much more accurate than the measuring devices found in patients' homes. Graduated cylinders used in pharmacies may be conical or cylindrical, with the cylindrical shape being more accurate. Similarly, pharmacy balances, though generally very accurate when compared to other small scales, may exhibit slight variations. A Class III balance is a type of balance commonly used to weigh very small

A Class III prescription balance can accurately weigh small quantities.

quantities in the pharmacy. Regardless of the measuring tool being used, it is important to know the margin of error that a particular balance or graduated cylinder has.

When weighing any substance, the balance will appear to have weighed correctly. A very small sample, however, may have an unacceptable margin of error. Pharmacy balances are generally marked with their degree of accuracy. This degree of accurateness has been determined by comparing quantities weighed on the balance with the weights obtained from another balance whose accuracy is known. This determination of accuracy is performed in the factory and normally is not done in the pharmacy.

If a substance was weighed or measured incorrectly, and we have something that will allow us to more accurately measure the amount in question, then we can determine the **percentage of error** by using the following formula:

percentage of error
the percentage by which a measurement is inaccurate

$$\frac{\text{amount of error}}{\text{quantity desired}} \times 100 = \text{percentage of error}$$

In this equation, the amount of error is the difference between the actual amount and the quantity desired, or

$$\text{actual amount} - \text{quantity desired} = \text{amount of error}$$

The percentage of error is considered to be a range both above and below the target measurement. It is inconsequential whether the result is over or under the target (i.e., whether it is positive or negative).

Example 2.4.1

You are to dispense 120 mL of a liquid. The original measurement is 120 mL. When you double-check the amount, using a more accurate graduated cylinder, the actual amount is 126 mL. What is the percentage of error of the first measurement?

Determine the difference in the two measurements in order to determine the amount of error.

$$\text{actual amount} - \text{quantity desired} = \text{amount of error}$$
$$126 \text{ mL} - 120 \text{ mL} = 6 \text{ mL}$$

Use the percentage of error equation to determine the percentage of error of the measurement.

$$\frac{\text{amount of error}}{\text{quantity desired}} \times 100 = \frac{6 \text{ mL}}{120 \text{ mL}} \times 100 = 5\%$$

The percentage of error is 5%.

Example 2.4.2

You are to dispense 30 g of a powder. The original measurement is 30 g. When you double-check the amount, using a more accurate balance, the actual amount is 31.8 g. What is the percentage of error of the first measurement?

Determine the difference in the two amounts in order to determine the amount of error.

$$31.8 \text{ g} - 30 \text{ g} = 1.8 \text{ g}$$

Use the percentage of error equation to determine the percentage of error of the measurement.

$$\frac{\text{amount of error}}{\text{quantity desired}} \times 100 = \frac{1.8 \text{ g}}{30 \text{ g}} \times 100 = 6\%$$

The percentage of error is 6%.

Example 2.4.3

You are to dispense 453 mg of a powder. The original measurement is 453 mg. When you double-check the amount, using a more accurate balance, the actual amount is 438 mg. What is the percentage of error of the first measurement?

Determine the difference in the two measurements in order to determine the amount of error.

$$453 \text{ mg} - 438 \text{ mg} = 15 \text{ mg}$$

Use the percentage of error equation to determine the percentage of error of the measurement.

$$\frac{\text{amount of error}}{\text{quantity desired}} \times 100 = \frac{15 \text{ mg}}{453 \text{ mg}} \times 100 = 3.3\%$$

Example 2.4.4

You are to weigh 60 g of a cream base for a topical compound. Your error range is 3%. What will be the least amount and the largest amount acceptable?

Multiply the percentage (in decimal form) by the target weight.

$$60 \text{ g} \times 0.03 = 1.8 \text{ g}$$

Determine the range.

$$60 \text{ g} - 1.8 \text{ g} = 58.2 \text{ g} \qquad 60 \text{ g} + 1.8 \text{ g} = 61.8 \text{ g}$$

Therefore, the acceptable range is 58.2 g to 61.8 g.

Example 2.4.5

You are preparing an order by measuring 800 mL from a 1 L normal saline IV bag. When you check the volume of the fluid in a graduated cylinder, the amount measured is actually 820 mL. You have an acceptable range of 2%. What is the percentage of error in this measurement? Did you meet your target?

Determine the difference in the two measurements in order to determine the amount of error.

$$820 \text{ mL} - 800 \text{ mL} = 20 \text{ mL}$$

Use the percentage of error equation to determine the percentage of error of the measurement.

$$\frac{\text{amount of error}}{\text{quantity desired}} \times 100 = \frac{20 \text{ mL}}{800 \text{ mL}} \times 100 = 2.5\%$$

Because 2.5% is larger than the acceptable percentage of error, the target range was not met.

2.4 Problem Set

Calculate the percentage of error for the following measurements. Assume that the measured amount is equal to the quantity desired.

1. The measured weight was 185 mg, but the actual weight is 189 mg.

2. The measured weight was 500 mg, but the actual weight is 476 mg.

3. The measured weight was 1200 mg, but the actual weight is 1507 mg.

4. The measured weight was 15 mg, but the actual weight is 12.5 mg.

5. The measured weight was 400 mcg, but the actual weight is 415 mcg.

6. The measured volume was 5 mL, but the actual volume is 6.3 mL.

7. The measured volume was 15 mL, but the actual volume is 13 mL.

8. The measured volume was 15 mL, but the actual volume is 20 mL.

9. The measured volume was 1.5 L, but the actual volume is 1.45 L.

10. The measured volume was 700 mL, but the actual volume is 726 mL.

Determine the percentage of error for the following measurements, and identify those within a percentage of error of 3%.

11. The measured volume was 3 mL, but the actual volume is 2.6 mL.

12. The measured volume was 12.5 mL, but the actual volume is 12.1 mL.

13. The measured volume was 1.8 mL, but the actual volume is 1.5 mL.

14. The measured volume was 3.2 mL, but the actual volume is 3.29 mL.

Determine the percentage of error for the following measurements, and identify those within a percentage of error of 6%.

15. The measured weight was 150 mg, but the actual weight is 149 mg.

16. The measured weight was 200 mg, but the actual weight is 192 mg.

17. The measured weight was 30 mg, but the actual weight is 31.5 mg.

18. The measured weight was 454 mg, but the actual weight is 450 mg.

State the acceptable range of error for each of the following.

19. The desired volume is 200 mL, and the percentage of error is 0.5%.

20. The desired volume is 10.3 mL, and the percentage of error is 0.75%.

21. The desired volume is 830 mL, and the percentage of error is 2%.

22. The desired weight is 18 g, and the percentage of error is 0.15%.

23. The desired weight is 750 mg, and the percentage of error is 0.4%.

Applications

24. If a generic drug manufacturer meets a bioavailability comparison to within 20% and a drug normally has a bioavailability of 100 mg, what is the range of accuracy?

25. A new brand of vitamins claims to have bioavailability within 12% of a national brand of vitamin C. The national brand has 500 mg of vitamin C per tablet. What is the range of vitamin C contained in the tablet?

Self-check your work in Appendix A.

Practice Test

State the ratio for the following doses.

1. 10 mg tablet of glipizide

2. 5 mL dose of azithromycin containing 250 mg

3. 5 mL dose of diphenhydramine containing 12.5 mg

4. 2 mL ampule containing 500 mg

5. A 1:10 solution contains _____ g of active ingredient and _____ mL of product, and 1000 mL of that solution contains _____ g.

6. A 1:100 solution contains _____ g of active ingredient and _____ mL of product, and 250 mL of that solution contains _____ g.

Convert the following percent to fractions.

7. 12.5%

8. 66.67%

Convert the following percents to decimals.

9. 0.5%

10. 93%

Choose the appropriate solution from the available stock.

11. A 1:5 solution has been ordered. You have a 5% solution, a 10% solution, and a 20% solution in stock. Which solution will you choose?

12. A 1:250 solution has been ordered. You have a 0.4% solution, a 0.05% solution, and a 4% solution in stock. Which solution will you choose?

Convert the following using the ratio 1 g:1000 mg.

13. 120 mg = _____ g

14. 1800 mg = _____ g

Use the ratio-proportion method to determine the unknown quantity.

15. A dose of 50 mg is ordered. The drug is available as a 1 mg tablet. How many whole tablets are needed to provide the ordered dose?

16. A dose of 30 mg is ordered. The drug is available as a 20 mg/mL solution. How many milliliters are needed to provide the ordered dose?

Determine the percentage of error for the following measurements. Round to the hundredth place when needed. Assume the measured amount is equal to the quantity desired.

17. The measured weight was 325 mg, but the actual weight was 343 mg.

18. The measured weight was 850 mg, but the actual weight was 790 mg.

19. The measured volume was 480 mL, but the actual volume was 473 mL.

20. The measured volume was 30 mL, but the actual volume was 32 mL.

21. The measured volume was 125 mL, but the actual volume was 119 mL.

   a. What is the actual percentage of error?

   b. Is the percentage of error within the 3% range?

22. The measured volume was 50 mL, but the actual volume was 57 mL.

   a. What is the actual percentage of error?

   b. Is the percentage of error within the 3% range?

State the acceptable range of error for the following situations.

23. The desired volume is 467 mL and the percentage of error is 1%.

24. The desired weight is 30 g and the percentage of error is 0.25%.

Developing Literacy Skills

3

Learning Objectives

- Identify the elements of a complete prescription order.
- Apply calculation operations in handling prescription orders.
- Recognize the elements of a medication label.
- Apply calculation operations to information on medication labels.

Preview chapter terms and definitions.

3.1 Elements of the Prescription Order

prescription
an order for medication for a patient that is written by a physician or a qualified licensed practitioner to be filled by a pharmacist

A **prescription** is an order for a medication or mixture of medications written (or otherwise recorded and/or transmitted) by a practitioner to be filled by a pharmacist. The pharmacy technician will need to interpret the prescription to determine which calculations will be necessary to fill this order correctly and appropriately. Although the legal requirements for information necessary on a prescription are regulated by state law and vary from one state to another, the following elements will appear on every prescription: patient information, prescriber information, and drug designation. Figure 3.1 illustrates the parts of a prescription written for a community pharmacy, and Figure 3.2 illustrates the parts of a prescription written for a hospital pharmacy.

Patient Information

Every prescription order must have enough information to uniquely identify the patient for whom the order was written. This will always include the patient's full name (first and last). Most states also require outpatient prescriptions to include the patient's address (street, city, state). In addition, it is good practice to include the patient's age or date of birth on every prescription, and some states and most insurers require this information.

Prescriptions for inpatients, often referred to as "orders," usually substitute the patient's hospital identification number and room number for the address and are often written on a form prestamped with the patient's admission date, the admitting physician's name, and the patient's date of birth in addition to the patient's

FIGURE 3.1
**Elements of a
Prescription
for a
Community
Pharmacy**

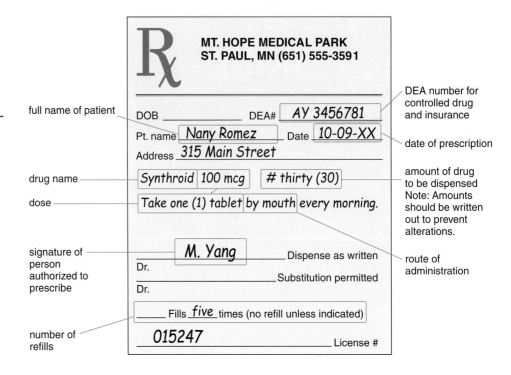

Ｒ MT. HOPE MEDICAL PARK
ST. PAUL, MN (651) 555-3591

full name of patient

DEA number for
controlled drug
and insurance

DOB _____ DEA# | AY 3456781 |

Pt. name | Nany Romez | Date | 10-09-XX |

date of prescription

Address | 315 Main Street |

drug name — | Synthroid | 100 mcg | | # thirty (30) |

dose — | Take one (1) tablet | by mouth | every morning. |

amount of drug
to be dispensed
Note: Amounts
should be written
out to prevent
alterations.

signature of
person
authorized to
prescribe

| M. Yang | _____ Dispense as written

Dr.

_____ Substitution permitted

Dr.

route of
administration

number of
refills

____ Fills _five_ times (no refill unless indicated)

015247 _____ License #

name and hospital number. Hospital medication order forms frequently require a notation of the patient's allergy information as well.

Many pharmacies require that the patient's height and weight be available, either on the prescription itself or in the patient's file. (Hospital order forms, as well as outpatient prescription forms, frequently have blanks where the height and weight are to be written.) If height and weight are included, it is important to know the units in which they were determined. Patient weights may be measured in either kilograms (kg) or pounds (# or lb); heights are generally measured in centimeters (cm) or inches (sometimes abbreviated as ″ or in.). These are quite different from one another: a 100 kg patient is more than twice the size of a 100 lb patient; a 76 cm patient is most likely a child under three years of age, whereas a 76″ patient is a very tall adult! (Conversions of height and weight units are covered in Chapters 4 and 5.)

Prescriber Information

In most states, outpatient prescription orders must include the name, authority (medical doctor, doctor of osteopathy, etc.), and address of the prescribing practitioner. Frequently, the prescriber's telephone number is noted. Prescriptions for controlled substances must also bear a registration code known as the **DEA number.** DEA numbers are issued by the Drug Enforcement Administration (DEA), an agency of the federal government, and signify the authority of the holder to prescribe or handle controlled substances. They are *always* formatted to begin with two letters, which are followed by seven digits. The last of the seven digits is a "checksum" digit, calculated by following the steps in Table 3.1.

The first two letters of the DEA number provide information about the prescriber. The first letter usually (but not always) designates the type or authority of the holder. For example, A or B is used for primary-level practitioners such as physicians and dentists, and M is used to indicate mid-level practitioners such as nurse midwives and advanced practice nurses. The second letter in the DEA number is the first letter of the prescriber's

FIGURE 3.2
**Elements of a
Hospital
Medication
Order**

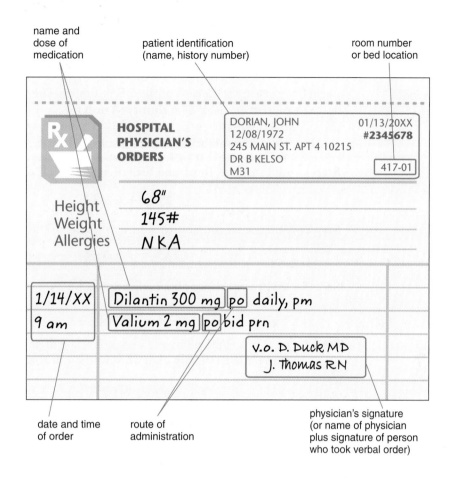

name and
dose of
medication

patient identification
(name, history number)

room number
or bed location

	HOSPITAL PHYSICIAN'S ORDERS	DORIAN, JOHN	01/13/20XX
		12/08/1972	**#2345678**
		245 MAIN ST. APT 4 10215	
		DR B KELSO	
		M31	417-01

Height 68"
Weight 145#
Allergies NKA

1/14/XX Dilantin 300 mg po daily, pm
9 am   Valium 2 mg po bid prn

v.o. D. Duck MD
J. Thomas RN

date and time
of order

route of
administration

physician's signature
(or name of physician
plus signature of person
who took verbal order)

last name. So, the first two letters of the DEA number for Dr. Mary Smith might be AS or BS, whereas the first two letters for nurse practitioner David Jones might be MJ.

DEA numbers are carefully regulated, and a DEA number that does not have a correct checksum digit (as determined by the steps in Table 3.1) is considered to be invalid. The checksum digit gives pharmacists and pharmacy technicians one way to check whether a DEA number was falsified. Note that passing the checksum test does not necessarily mean that a DEA number is valid. Many unethical or criminally minded people know the formula and are able to compose DEA numbers that *look* valid but were not issued by the government authority. If a pharmacy technician discovers an invalid DEA number or suspects a problem with the authenticity of a prescription, he or she should notify a pharmacist immediately.

The following examples demonstrate how the steps in Table 3.1 can be used to check for false DEA numbers.

Safety Note

The checksum digit calculation is a necessary but not sufficient condition for the validity of a DEA number.

TABLE 3.1   DEA Checksum Formula

Step 1. Add the first, third, and fifth digits of the DEA number.

Step 2. Add the second, fourth, and sixth digits of the DEA number.

Step 3. Double the sum obtained in Step 2 (i.e., multiply it by 2).

Step 4. Add the results of Steps 1 and 3. The last digit of this sum should match the checksum digit, the last digit of the DEA number.

Example 3.1.1

A patient brings a prescription for methylphenidate tablets to the pharmacy, signed by Dr. Johnson and bearing a DEA number of BJ 2345678. Is this DEA number valid?

Begin by reviewing the letters of the DEA number. The first letter is consistent with the prescriber's level of authority (A or B for a primary practitioner), and the second letter matches the last name of the physician (J).

Now, check the validity of the checksum digit.

Step 1. Add the first, third, and fifth digits of the DEA number.

$$2 + 4 + 6 = 12$$

Step 2. Add the second, fourth, and sixth digits of the DEA number.

$$3 + 5 + 7 = 15$$

Step 3. Multiply the sum obtained in Step 2 by 2.

$$15 \times 2 = 30$$

Step 4. Add the results of Steps 1 and 3. The last digit of this sum should match the checksum digit, the last digit of the DEA number.

$$12 + 30 = 42$$

Because the checksum digit is 8, not 2, this DEA number is invalid.

Example 3.1.2

A patient brings a prescription for oxycodone to the pharmacy, signed by nurse-midwife Ann Johnson and bearing a DEA number of MJ 3456781. (In the state where the prescription is received, advanced practice nurses are authorized to prescribe narcotic analgesics.) Is this DEA number valid?

Begin by reviewing the letters of the DEA number. The first letter is consistent with the prescriber's level of authority (M for a nurse practitioner), and the second letter matches the last name of the prescriber (J).

Now, check the validity of the checksum digit.

Step 1. Add the first, third, and fifth digits of the DEA number.

$$3 + 5 + 7 = 15$$

Step 2. Add the second, fourth, and sixth digits of the DEA number.

$$4 + 6 + 8 = 18$$

Step 3. Multiply the sum obtained in Step 2 by 2.

$$18 \times 2 = 36$$

Step 4. Add the results of Steps 1 and 3. The last digit of this sum should match the checksum digit, the last digit of the DEA number.

$$15 + 36 = 51$$

Because the checksum digit is 1, this DEA number meets the criteria for a valid registration.

Inpatient prescriptions are most often written or transcribed on the premises where the patient is located and where the medication will be administered; such prescriptions may be ordered only by practitioners with privileges within that institution. Physician addresses and DEA numbers are generally not required on the actual medication orders because the institutional pharmacy that will fill the orders usually has this information on file for each authorized practitioner.

Drug Designation

A prescription order must always designate the medication that is intended for the patient. Sometimes, the drug will be identified by its **generic name,** the name by which it was approved by the Food and Drug Administration (FDA) as a unique chemical product safe and effective for use in its approved indication. The generic name of a drug is the same, regardless of the company that manufactures it or the dosage form or packaging in which it is supplied. At other times, a physician will specify a brand name drug. The **brand name** is a registered trademark of the manufacturer and may indicate the dose form or packaging of the drug as well. State law and (in the case of inpatients) institutional policy govern the extent to which generic products can be substituted for brand name drugs. In some cases, the pharmacy can automatically substitute an equivalent product with the same generic name (but a different brand name) for cost savings or convenience. In other situations, the pharmacy must supply the exact brand prescribed, unless the pharmacist has discussed a substitution with the prescriber.

Figure 3.3 identifies the standard parts of a drug label for Cleocin Phosphate. As shown in this example, the label of a brand name drug will indicate both the trade and generic names. Medications with a given name (brand or generic) are frequently avail-

generic name
the name under which a drug is approved by the Food and Drug Administration; sometimes denotes a drug that is not protected by a trademark; also referred to as a USAN (United States Adopted Name)

brand name
the name under which the manufacturer markets a drug; a registered trademark of the manufacturer; also known as the trade name

FIGURE 3.3
Parts of a Drug Label

Reproduced with permission of Pfizer Inc. All rights reserved.

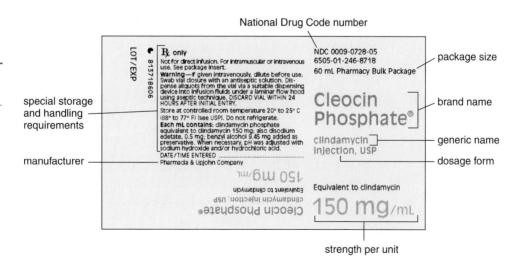

FIGURE 3.4
Comparison of Dosage Forms

(a) 25 mg/5 mL liquid, (b) 25 mg capsules, (c) 50 mg capsules

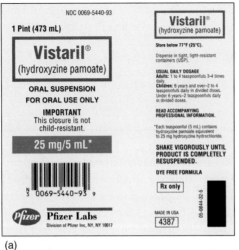

(a)

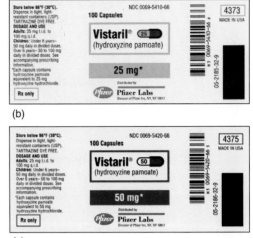

(b)

(c)

able in a variety of strengths, doses, or dosage forms, and information about the particular strength, dose and dosage form is also clearly stated on the drug label. Digoxin, for instance, is available as a generic product and as several branded preparations. It is available as a tablet in two different strengths (0.125 mg and 0.25 mg), a capsule in three strengths (0.05 mg, 0.1 mg, and 0.2 mg), an elixir of 0.05 mg/mL, and injections of 0.1 mg/mL and 0.25 mg/mL. Many other drugs present a similar array of choices (brand names, dosage forms, strengths or concentrations), and the proper product to select must be made clear in the prescription order. Figure 3.4 shows labels for the same drug in different dosage forms. Note how the labels use color to help distinguish the unique information.

It is important to correctly match a prescription order with the appropriate medication available in the pharmacy. The following example demonstrates this procedure.

Example 3.1.3

The pharmacy receives an order for Epinephrine 1 mg/mL. Epinephrine 1:10,000, 1:2000, and 1:1000 injections are available in stock. Which one matches the order?

As discussed in Chapter 2, the available drug concentrations are 1:10,000, or 1 g/10,000 mL; 1:2000, or 1 g/2000 mL; and 1:1000, or 1 g/1000 mL.

Convert the strength of 1 mg/mL into a concentration ratio. Begin by setting up a ratio and solving for x, using the conversion factor 1000 mg = 1 g.

$$\frac{x \text{ mL}}{1000 \text{ mg}} = \frac{1 \text{ mL}}{1 \text{ mg}}$$

$$\frac{(\cancel{1000 \text{ mg}}) \, x \text{ mL}}{1000 \text{ mg}} = \frac{(\cancel{1000 \text{ mg}}) \, 1 \text{ mL}}{1 \cancel{\text{ mg}}}$$

$$x \text{ mL} = 1000 \text{ mL}$$

Therefore x mL/1000 mg = 1000 mL/1000 mg, and 1000 mL/1000 mg = 1000 mL/1 g = 1 g/1000 mL, or a ratio of 1:1000. Thus, the 1:1000 injection should be chosen to fill this order. The label appears on the next page.

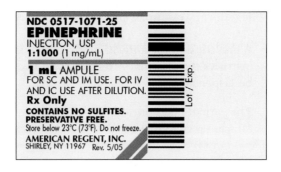

NDC 0517-1071-25
EPINEPHRINE
INJECTION, USP
1:1000 (1 mg/mL)

1 mL AMPULE
FOR SC AND IM USE. FOR IV
AND IC USE AFTER DILUTION.
Rx Only
CONTAINS NO SULFITES.
PRESERVATIVE FREE.
Store below 23°C (73°F). Do not freeze.
AMERICAN REGENT, INC.
SHIRLEY, NY 11967 Rev. 5/05

Lot / Exp.

Quantity to Dispense

Every outpatient prescription order must indicate to the pharmacist what quantity to dispense. Sometimes, the indication is straightforward, as in Figure 3.1, where the physician has written the number of tablets to dispense next to "#" (used as a number sign). This number is often written as a Roman numeral or spelled out ("thirty" for #30) to hinder alteration. At other times, the physician will indicate the number of doses the patient is to take, or the number of days the therapy is to last, and the pharmacy staff will calculate the quantity to dispense from the information on the prescription.

When the quantity to dispense has been determined, the pharmacy technician selects the proper dispensing container. Commonly, amber ovals (bottles) are used for liquids and amber vials for tablets or capsules. Amber ovals are often marked with both fluid ounce and milliliter lines. Common practice utilizes the metric system, so the quantity indicated on the prescription drug label will be indicated in milliliters. When preparing tablets or capsules to fill a prescription, the tablets or capsules are generally counted out, using a specially designed tray and plastic or metal spatula, and placed in amber vials. Tablets and capsules are typically counted out by "fives."

Amber medication bottles come in several sizes. The pharmacy technician will need to select the appropriate size to match the dispensed volume.

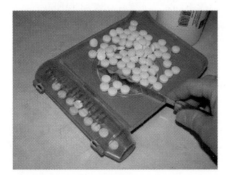

Tablets are frequently counted out by fives on a tray with a spatula and then placed in the dispensing container.

One fluid ounce is the size of most plastic dispensing cups.

The following examples show how the quantity to dispense is calculated.

Example 3.1.4

A prescription for antacid reads "Take one ounce three times a day" and instructs the pharmacy to dispense a five-day supply. What volume is to be dispensed?

The patient takes one ounce three times a day, so first determine the number of ounces taken in one day. Note that the units cancel out, as shown below.

$$\frac{x \text{ oz}}{1 \text{ day}} = \frac{1 \text{ oz}}{1 \text{ dose}} \times \frac{3 \text{ doses}}{1 \text{ day}} = \frac{3 \text{ oz}}{1 \text{ day}}$$

You can determine the amount to dispense by multiplying the daily dose by the number of days.

$$x \text{ oz} = \frac{3 \text{ oz}}{1 \text{ day}} \times 5 \text{ days} = 15 \text{ oz}$$

Example 3.1.5

A prescription for Zovirax reads "Take 400 mg every 12 hours" and instructs the pharmacy to dispense a one-week supply. The pharmacy has the following product in stock. How many tablets are dispensed?

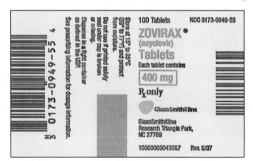

Because one table contains 400 mg, the patient will take one tablet every 12 hours, and there are 24 hours in a day. You can determine the number of tablets the patient will need in a single 24 hour period (a day) by setting up a ratio.

$$\frac{x \text{ tablets}}{24 \text{ hours}} = \frac{1 \text{ tablet}}{12 \text{ hours}}$$

$$\frac{(24 \text{ hours}) \, x \text{ tablets}}{24 \text{ hours}} = \frac{(24 \text{ hours}) \, 1 \text{ tablet}}{12 \text{ hours}}$$

$$x \text{ tablets} = 2 \text{ tablets}$$

A week is 7 days, so the pharmacist will dispense the following number of tablets.

$$\frac{x \text{ tablets}}{1 \text{ week}} = \frac{2 \text{ tablets}}{1 \text{ day}} \times \frac{7 \text{ days}}{1 \text{ week}} = \frac{14 \text{ tablets}}{1 \text{ week}}$$

3.1 Problem Set

Which of the following DEA numbers meet the standard validity test?

1. DEA number JC 2169870 for Dr. James Collins   *16+(7×2)=50* ✗

2. DEA number MG 3081659 for nurse-midwife Laura Green

3. DEA number BH 9998070 for Dr. Margaret Hall   *18+(24×2)=66* ✗

4. DEA number AL 6230618 for Dr. George Lewis

5. DEA number AD 7638224 for Dr. Daniel Lopez   *12+(16×2)=44* ✗

6. DEA number BP 4412209 for Dr. Sarah Parker

7. DEA number AP 3051492 for Dr. Donna Perez   *12+(10×2)=32* ✓

8. DEA number MW 2864228 for clinical nurse specialist Thomas Wright

Choose a drug product to fill the following orders.

9. acetic acid 1:400 irrigation   *1/400 =*
   a. glacial acetic acid
   b. *(0.25% acetic acid)*
   c. 25% acetic acid
   d. 4% acetic acid

10. isoproterenol 5 mg/mL solution
    a. isoproterenol 5% solution
    b. isoproterenol 0.05% solution
    c. isoproterenol 1:200 solution
    d. isoproterenol 1:2 solution

Identify the information indicated for each provided drug label.

11. Brand/trade name: _Epivir_

    Generic name: _Lamivudine_

    Dosage form: _Oral solution_

    Strength: _10 mg/mL_

    Total quantity: _240 mL_

    Storage requirement(s): _store in tight bottles 25°C_

    Manufacturer: _GlaxoSmithKline_

    NDC number: _0173-0471-00_

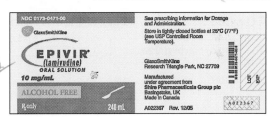

12. Brand/trade name: _____

    Generic name: _____

    Dosage form: _____

    Strength: _____

    Total quantity: _____

    Storage requirement(s): _____

    Manufacturer: _____

    NDC number: _____

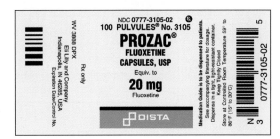

13. Brand/trade name: _____

Generic name: _____

Dosage form: _____

Strength: _____

Total quantity: _____

Storage requirement(s): _____

Manufacturer: _____

NDC number: _____

NDC 0078-0358-34   85081901

Diovan®   80 mg
valsartan
90 Tablets

Rx only

NOVARTIS

FPO

EXP
LOT

14. Brand/trade name: _____

Generic name: _____

Dosage form: _____

Strength: _____

Total quantity: _____

Storage requirement(s): _____

Manufacturer: _____

NDC number: _____

NDC 0078-0315-34   85082901

Diovan HCT®
valsartan and hydrochlorothiazide, USP

160 mg/12.5 mg

90 tablets

Rx only

NOVARTIS

FPO

EXP
LOT

15. Brand/trade name: _____

Generic name: _____

Dosage form: _____

Strength: _____

Total quantity: _____

Storage requirement(s): _____

Manufacturer: _____

NDC number: _____

NDC 0078-0357-52   85042802

Trileptal® 300 mg/5 mL
(oxcarbazepine)
Oral Suspension
250 mL   **Rx only**

IMPORTANT: Shake well before using.
Each 5 mL contains 300 mg oxcarbazepine.
Use within 7 weeks of first opening the
bottle.

NOVARTIS   ©Novartis

US 04 A/H - 32563

Lot Number

Expiration date

16. Brand/trade name: _____

Generic name: _____

Dosage form: _____

Strength: _____

Total quantity: _____

Storage requirement(s): _____

Manufacturer: _____

NDC number: _____

USUAL DOSAGE: See package insert.

STORAGE: Store at 20° to 25°C (68° to 77°F) [see USP Controlled Room Temperature].

Dispense in a well-closed, light-resistant container with a child-resistant closure.

Do not accept if seal over bottle opening is broken or missing.

Mallinckrodt Inc.
St. Louis, MO 63134

tyco / Healthcare

NDC 0406-9915-01
100 Capsules

Restoril® IV
temazepam
capsules USP

7.5 mg

Each capsule contains
Temazepam USP ... 7.5 mg

Rx only.

Mallinckrodt   Rev 081406

How much medication should be dispensed for the following prescriptions?

17.

℞ **Ibuprofen 400 mg tablet #XX**

take one four times daily with food

18.

℞ **Amoxicillin capsule 500 mg**

take one capsule three times daily for 10 days

19.

R̥   **Prednisone 5 mg tablet**

take four tablets twice daily
for two days,

then three tablets twice daily for two
days,

then four tablets once daily
for two days,

then three tablets once daily for two
days,

then two tablets once daily
for two days,

then one tablet daily for two days

20.

R̥   **Milk of Magnesia**

take one ounce every night at bedtime
for one week

21.

R̥   **Phenytoin 100 mg capsule #CL**

take three capsules every morning

Self-check your work in Appendix A.

3.2 Prescription Directions

***signa* (sig)**
from the Latin
for "write"; the
instructions for
proper use of
the medication
included on each
prescription,
including the dose,
route of admin-
istration, and
dosing schedule

dose
on a prescription,
the indication of
how much medi-
cation the patient
will take at each
administration

**route of
administration**
on a prescription,
the indication of
how the medica-
tion is to be given

dosing schedule
on a prescription,
the indication of
how often the
drug is to be taken

A very important part of each prescription is the ***signa* (sig),** a term that comes from the Latin for "write." It consists of the prescriber's instructions for proper use of the medication and usually includes the following information.

Dose: how much medication the patient will take at each administration. It is generally expressed as a number of units (e.g., tablets, capsules), an amount of drug (e.g., weight in milligrams or grains), or a volume of medication (e.g., ounces, teaspoonfuls).

Route of administration: how the drug is to be administered. Routes of administration include oral (by mouth), injection (into veins, into muscles, under the skin), rectal, or topical (to the eye, ear, skin, or mucous membranes), among others.

Dosing schedule: how often the drug is to be taken and, in some cases, how long therapy is to be continued.

Abbreviations

Healthcare professionals have developed their own shorthand for many aspects of patient care, and it is reflected in the abbreviations used in prescription directions. Many of the abbreviations used in prescriptions are derived from the initials of Latin or Greek phrases. Others come from medical terminology in English, and some even combine terms from multiple languages. Table 3.2 lists some of the most common abbreviations used on prescriptions.

When abbreviations are standardized (to have only one meaning) and are clearly written or printed, they are useful because they save space and time. Abbreviations can cause problems, however, if they are misinterpreted. Sometimes, this occurs when the same set of letters can have two different meanings. For example, the abbreviation "IVP" means "IV Push" or "administer by injection into the vein from a syringe" when used on a hospital prescription order for an intravenous medication. In another context, however, "IVP" designates "intravenous pyelogram," an X-ray examination of the kidneys, bladder, and urinary tract.

Abbreviations are also problematic when they are not typed or written clearly. The abbreviation "q6 pm," for example, means "every evening at 6 P.M.," but if written

TABLE 3.2　Common Prescription Abbreviations

Abbreviation	Translation	Abbreviation	Translation
ac	before meals	NKA	no known allergy
am	morning	NKDA	no known drug allergy
bid	twice a day	npo	nothing by mouth
c̄	with	pc	after meals
cap	capsule	po	by mouth
DAW	dispense as written	prn	as needed
D/C	discontinue	q	every
g	gram	qh	every hour
gr	grain	q2 h	every 2 hours
gtt	drop	qid	four times a day
h or hr	hour	qs	a sufficient quantity
IM	intramuscular	stat	immediately
IV	intravenous	tab	tablet
L	liter	tid	three times daily
mcg	microgram	ud	as directed
mEq	milliequivalent	wk	week
mL	milliliter		

Note: Some prescribers may write abbreviations using capital letters or periods. However, periods should not be used with metric units or medical abbreviations as they can be a source of medication errors.

hastily or printed on a fax machine low in toner, it may appear to say "q6 h," meaning every six hours. The abbreviation "qhs" means "nightly at bedtime" but could be misread as "qhr," meaning "every hour." Some abbreviations are so error-prone that the Joint Commission on Accreditation of Healthcare Organizations (JCAHO) has declared that they are absolutely unacceptable for use in accredited institutions. These are listed in Table 3.3.

TABLE 3.3　Unacceptable Abbreviations Formerly in Common Use

Unapproved Abbreviation	Intended Meaning	Misinterpretation	Correct Form to Use
μg	microgram	milligram	microgram or mcg
hs	half-strength or hours of sleep, bedtime	hours of sleep, bedtime or half-strength	half-strength or hours of sleep, bedtime
qd	every day	four times a day	every day or daily
qhs	every night at bedtime	every hour (qhs)	nightly at bedtime
qod	every other day	daily or four times a day	every other day
U	unit	number 0 or 4	units
$MgSO_4$	magnesium sulfate	morphine sulfate	magnesium sulfate
MSO_4	morphine sulfate	magnesium sulfate	morphine sulfate

Note: Additional error-prone abbreviations are listed at www.ismp.org.

qs = a sufficient quantity
ud = as directed

6, 16, 500

Directions for Patients

Safety Note

Instructions to patients on dispensed medications must be clear and should not include abbreviations.

Because most patients are not familiar with the abbreviations and shorthand used on prescriptions, directions must be "translated" from the sig and "written" on the label placed on the dispensing packaging. Sometimes, descriptive terms are added if appropriate. For example, a prescription for a fentanyl transdermal patch may have the sig "ī q 3d." The pharmacy label on the patient's package, however, will read "Apply one patch every 72 hours." Similarly, a prescription for hydrochlorothiazide 25 mg tablets may bear a sig of "12.5 mg po qam," but the patient's label must read "Take one-half tablet by mouth every morning." It is important that directions for patients be set forth in clear and unambiguous terms on the label, even if the doctor and the pharmacist explain verbally in great detail how the medication is to be used. It is easy for patients to misunderstand or forget what they were told days or weeks earlier, and having the label available for instructions at every dose is necessary for safe medication use.

3.2 Problem Set

Write out the meaning (in complete words) of these common abbreviations used on prescriptions.

1. bid twice per day
2. DAW dispense as written
3. IM intramuscular
4. IV intravenous
5. mL milliliter
6. NKA no known allergies
7. npo nothing by mouth
8. q3 h every 3 hours
9. qid 4 times/day
10. tid 3 times/day

Answer the following questions.

11. What is a route of administration?
    how med is taken
12. Name four routes of administration.
    by mouth, injected, applied to skin, through ears
13. Give one abbreviation for a route of administration and write out its meaning.
    p.o: By mouth
14. Give one abbreviation for a dosing schedule and write out its meaning.
    qid: 4 X/day
15. List one error-prone abbreviation and give its intended meaning. Explain why it is prone to error. μg = microgram could be interpretated as mg, miligram.

Translate the following directions from a prescription order into wording that would be proper on a label for the patient's use.

16. (for diphenhydramine capsules) īī cap po qid prn itching Take 2 capsules by mouth ~~every 6 hours~~ (or 4x/day) as needed for itching
17. (for nitroglycerin transdermal systems) ī on qhs off qam Put 1 patch on at every bedtime, take off every morning

18. (for nitroglycerin ointment) ½ in q6 h

Apply ½ inch of ointment every 6 hours

19. (for nateglinide 60 mg tablets) 120 mg po tid ac

Take 2 tablets by mouth 3 times/day ~~(everytime)~~ before meals.

20. (for potassium chloride 20 mEq tablets) 10 mEq bid

Take ½ tablet twice a day

21. (for tobramycin eyedrops) ii gtt q4 h right eye

apply 2 drops to the right eye every 4 hours

22. (for alendronate tablets) i q wk 30 minutes ac breakfast c̄ H₂O

Take one every 7 days 30 minutes before breakfast, with water

Check the validity of the DEA numbers used by the following prescribers.

1. DEA number BA 4412209 for Albert King, MD ✗

2. DEA number BA 4412209 for Norma Aborra, DO ✓

3. DEA number MB 9231971 for Joanne Burgess, CRNP ✓

4. DEA number AK 1521964 for Harold Kwong, DDS ✗

Calculate the quantity to dispense for the following prescriptions.

5. #XC   90 tab

   Sig: one tablet daily

6. 30 day supply   30 tab

   Sig: one tablet daily

7. Sig: one cap TID × 10 days   30 cap

8. Sig: one ounce TID × 10 days   30 oz

9. Dispense 30 day supply   90 tab

   Sig: 1½ tablet BID

10. Dispense 60 day supply   180 cap

    Sig: 3 cap daily

11. Brand/trade name: Epivir-HBV

    Generic name: lamivudine

    Dosage form: Oral solution

    Strength: 5 mg/mL

    Total quantity: 240 mL

Storage requirement(s): _____

Manufacturer: _____

NDC number: _____

12. Brand/trade name: _____

    Generic name: _____

    Dosage form: _____

    Strength: _____

    Total quantity: _____

    Storage requirement(s): _____

    Manufacturer: _____

    NDC number: _____

Write out (in words) what the following abbreviations mean.

13. cap

14. DAW

15. gr

16. IM

17. IV

18. mL

19. NKA

20. po

21. q6 h

22. stat

Write the abbreviations that correspond to these phrases.

23. a sufficient quantity

24. as directed

25. discontinue

26. four times a day

27. gram

28. liter

29. milliequivalent

30. nothing by mouth

31. tablet

32. with

Translate the following directions from a prescription order into wording that would be proper on a label for the patient's use.

33. ī tab po q2 h prn

34. īī gtt right eye bid

35. ī patch q wk

36. ī cap po tid ac ud

37. to rash prn itch

38. ī tablet qam c̄ food

What is missing from these prescriptions?

39.

R̟x

MT. HOPE MEDICAL PARK
ST. PAUL, MN (651) 555-3591

DOB _____ DEA# _AY 3456781_

Pt. name _Kimberly Evans_ Date _1/6/20XX_

Address _2888 Main St. Townville, OH_

   ibuprofen   600 mg tab

   Sig: i q6 h prn pain

_____ Dispense as written
Dr.
_____M. Yang_____ Substitution permitted
Dr.

_____ Fills _____ times (no refill unless indicated)

_____ License #

40.

R̟x

MT. HOPE MEDICAL PARK
ST. PAUL, MN (651) 555-3591

DOB _____ DEA# _AY 3456781_

Pt. name _Kevin Hall_ Date _1/7/20XX_

Address _3333 Broadway Blvd. Metro, NY_

   amoxicillin   250 mg

          # thirty (30)

_____ Dispense as written
Dr.
_____M. Yang_____ Substitution permitted
Dr.

_____ Fills _1_ times (no refill unless indicated)

_____ License #

Calculate the quantity and write out directions for the patient for each of the following prescriptions.

41.

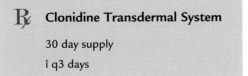

℞ Clonidine Transdermal System

30 day supply

i̅ q3 days

42.

℞ Ampicillin 250 mg cap

500 mg po tid × 10 days

43

℞ Tobradex 5 mL

i̅ gtt left eye bid × 7 days

44. Using the label below, how many bottles will be needed to provide the quantity ordered?

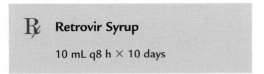

℞ Retrovir Syrup

10 mL q8 h × 10 days

Answer the following questions.

41. What is a dosing schedule?

42. What are four routes of administration?

43. What are two examples of error-prone abbreviations?

44. What are the intended meanings of the abbreviations you gave in question 43?

45. Why are the abbreviations you gave in question 43 prone to error, and how might they be mistakenly interpreted?

Applying Metric Measurements and Calculating Doses

4

Learning Objectives

- Identify the basic units and prefixes of the metric system.

- Convert units within the metric system by moving the decimal place, using the ratio-proportion method, and using the dimensional analysis method.

- Calculate drug doses using the ratio-proportion and dimensional analysis methods.

- Calculate doses based on weight and body surface area (BSA).

- Calculate a pediatric dose using the patient's weight or age and the appropriate adult dose.

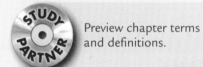

Preview chapter terms and definitions.

4.1 Basic Metric Units

metric system
a measurement system based on subdivisions and multiples of 10; made up of three basic units: meter, gram, and liter

meter
the basic unit for measuring length in the metric system

gram
the basic unit for measuring weight in the metric system

liter
the basic unit for measuring volume in the metric system

Chapter 1 presented a brief overview of the decimal number system. Because of its accuracy, the decimal system is used in pharmacy measurements: based on subdivisions and multiples of 10, the **metric system** uses decimals to indicate tenths, hundredths, and thousandths.

Identifying Metric Units of Measure

The metric system's three basic units of measure are the meter, the gram, and the liter (see Table 4.1). The **meter,** the unit for measuring length, has limited use in the pharmacy; consequently, we discuss its properties only in comparison to common measures used in daily life. The **gram,** the unit for measuring weight, is used in the pharmacy for measuring the amount of medication in solid form and for indicating the amount of solid medication in a solution. The gram is the weight of one cubic centimeter of water at 4 °C. The **liter** is the unit used for measuring the volume of liquid medications and liquids for solutions. One liter is equal to 1000 milliliters, and one milliliter is equal to the volume in one cubic centimeter.

Using Metric Prefixes and Abbreviations

The set of prefixes shown in Table 4.2 are used to designate multiples of the basic metric units. The three prefixes most widely used in pharmaceutical calculations

TABLE 4.1 Metric Units of Measure

Metric Unit	Measurement
meter (m)	length
gram (g)	weight
liter (L)	volume

TABLE 4.2 Metric System Prefixes

Prefix	Value
nano (n)	1/1,000,000,000 (one-billionth of the basic unit, or 0.000000001)
micro (mc)	1/1,000,000 (one-millionth of the basic unit, or 0.000001)
milli (m)	1/1000 (one-thousandth of the basic unit, or 0.001)
centi (c)	1/100 (one-hundredth of the basic unit, or 0.01)
deci (d)	1/10 (one-tenth of the basic unit, or 0.1)
kilo (k)	1000 (one thousand times the basic unit)

TABLE 4.3 Metric Abbreviations

Measurement	Metric Unit	Abbreviation
Weight	kilogram	kg
	gram	g
	milligram	mg
	microgram	mcg
Volume	kiloliter	kL
	liter	L
	milliliter	mL*
	microliter	mcL
Length	kilometer	km
	meter	m
	millimeter	mm
	micrometer	mcm†

* equivalent to cc, which stands for cubic centimeters, but cc is considered a dangerous abbreviation

† sometimes abbreviated as μm, but μm is considered a dangerous abbreviation

are kilo-, milli-, and micro-. The abbreviations shown in Table 4.3 are commonly used for metric measurements.

It is important to memorize the basic metric units along with their prefixes. All units in the metric system use the same prefixes. An example is the gram: the larger unit is the kilogram while two of the smaller units are the milligram and microgram.

Most people can visualize an object that weighs a kilogram or a gram, and many can create a mental picture of a container that can hold a liter or milliliter of a liquid. However, it is impossible even to see something that weighs only a microgram.

A kilogram is equivalent to a little more than two 1 lb boxes of pasta.

A single large paper clip, or two small paper clips, weighs about 1 g.

Remembering the amount of liquid that is contained in a standard, 2 L soda bottle will help you visual the amount of liquid in a single liter.

Medications that contain micrograms, or even milligrams, of an active ingredient will almost always contain an inactive filler so that the dosage form becomes measurable. For example, a tablet with a weight of 300 micrograms would be hard to see and far too small to handle safely. The tablets shown in Figure 4.1 all contain different amounts of levothyroxine, but they are all the same size. Even though levothyroxine is available in a variety of doses, the tablet sizes remain the same. The colors of the tablets and the package labeling differentiate the amount of active ingredient in each.

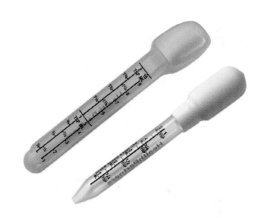

Dosing spoons and droppers are frequently marked with metric and household measures.

Safety Note

For a decimal value less than 1, use a leading zero to prevent errors.

Safety Note

Pharmacy technicians should use the medication labels, not the color or shape of the pills, to confirm the amount of drug contained in a tablet or capsule.

Parts of a unit are written as a decimal fraction. For example, two and a half milligrams is written as 2.5 mg. A zero is used if there is no whole number preceding the decimal point. For example, one-half liter is written as 0.5 L, and one-quarter gram is 0.25 g. These place-saving zeros help prevent medication errors.

When writing dosage strengths, unnecessary zeros after the decimal point are generally left off to reduce the chance of misreading the value. For example, 0.25 mL, 5 L, and 15.6 mL should not be written as 0.250 mL, 5.0 L, and 15.60 mL.

FIGURE 4.1
Levothyroxine

25 mcg orange	50 mcg white	75 mcg violet	88 mcg olive	100 mcg yellow	112 mcg rose	125 mcg brown	137 mcg turquoise	150 mcg blue	175 mcg lilac	200 mcg pink	300 mcg green

4.1 Problem Set

State the abbreviation for each of the following metric units.

1. microgram *mcg*

2. milligram *mg*

3. liter *L*

4. gram *g*

5. kilogram *kg*

6. meter *M*

7. centimeter *cm*

8. milliliter *mL*

9. cubic centimeter *cc*

10. deciliter *dL*

Write the following numbers using an Arabic number with a decimal value and the appropriate abbreviation.

11. six-tenths of a gram *0.6 g*

12. fifty kilograms *50 kg*

13. four-tenths of a milligram *0.4 mg*

14. four-hundredths of a liter *0.04 L*

15. four and two-tenths of a gram *4.2 g*

16. five-thousandths of a gram *0.005 g*

17. six-hundredths of a gram *0.06 g*

18. two and six-tenths liters *2.6 L*

19. three-hundredths of a liter *0.03 L*

20. two-hundredths of a milliliter *0.02 mL*

Applications

21. The Taro Pharmaceutical Company has donated a container labeled 5 kg of bulk Maxicillin granules. The standard dose is 375 mg. How many single dose units can be obtained from the container? *13,333*

22. The pharmacy receives the following prescription.

   > **℞ Levothyroxine Tablets 0.05 mg**
   >
   > ii q am
   >
   > i with lunch
   >
   > ii 8 pm
   >
   > 30 days' supply

   a. How many days will the dispensed medication last? *30 days*

   b. How many milligrams will the patient take over the course of one month (30 days)? *0.25 mg x 30 = 7.5 mg*

23. If the total daily dose of a drug is 0.9 g and it is given tid, what is the amount of each dose in grams? *0.3 g*

24. A patient is to receive 1.2 g of cimetidine per day in four divided doses.

a. How many grams will be in each dose?

    0.3g = 300 mg

b. If the available dosage forms are shown in the following labels, which will be chosen?

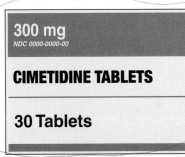

300 mg
NDC 0000-0000-00

CIMETIDINE TABLETS

30 Tablets

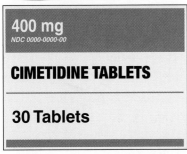

400 mg
NDC 0000-0000-00

CIMETIDINE TABLETS

30 Tablets

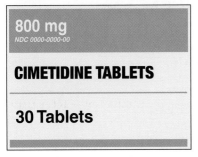

800 mg
NDC 0000-0000-00

CIMETIDINE TABLETS

30 Tablets

25. The following prescription for potassium permanganate has been brought into the compounding pharmacy.

℞ **potassium permanganate**

1. Weigh out 1 g of potassium permanganate.

2. Add to a 1 L bottle of sterile water for irrigation. (Be sure to wear gloves, as this chemical stains.)

3. Replace cap on bottle and swirl to dissolve potassium permanganate.

The solution expires 30 days after mixing.

a. What is the percentage of potassium permanganate in this solution?

    0.1%

b. If today is August 1, 2011, what expiration date will you place on the bottle?

    Aug 31, 2011

Self-check your work in Appendix A.

4.2 Conversions within the Metric System

This section will present three ways to convert units within the metric system: moving the decimal point, using the ratio-proportion method, and using the dimensional analysis method. Once you learn the three methods of conversion, you should select the method you are most comfortable with and stick to that method when making conversions. Before calculating a needed dose, you should be confident that the number you are working with is accurate and that the correct conversion has been made.

Moving the Decimal Point

To change the metric units of a number to smaller or larger units, you can multiply or divide by an appropriate multiple of 1000, as determined from Table 4.4. For instance,

TABLE 4.4 Metric Unit Equivalents

Kilo	Base	Milli	Micro
0.001 kg	1 g	1000 mg	1,000,000 mcg
0.001 kL	1 L	1000 mL	1,000,000 mcL
0.001 km	1 m	1000 mm	1,000,000 mcm

to convert 5 grams to milligrams, multiply by 1000 to get 5000 milligrams. (Move the decimal point three places to the right.) Multiplying 17 liters by 1,000,000 yields 17,000,000 microliters. (Move the decimal point six places to the right.) Conversely, changing to a larger unit requires division. So, to convert 25 meters to kilometers, divide by 1000 to get 0.025 kilometers. (Move the decimal point three places to the left.) Similarly, 3 microliters divided by 1000 yields 0.003 milliliters, and 22 milliliters divided by 1000 yields 0.022 liters. In each case, move the decimal point three places to the left.

The key to understanding the relationships in the metric system is to remember that the decimal point must be moved three places when converting from one unit to the next. Moving the decimal point three places is essentially equivalent to multiplying or dividing the number by 1000. The three "places" are representative of the three zeros in 1000.

$$1 \text{ kg} = 1000 \text{ g}$$
$$1 \text{ g} = 1000 \text{ mg}$$
$$1 \text{ mg} = 1000 \text{ mcg}$$
$$1 \text{ L} = 1000 \text{ mL}$$

Remember

Moving the decimal point three spaces to the right is the same as multiplying by 1000. Moving the decimal three places to the left is the same as dividing by 1000.

When converting from a smaller to a larger unit of measure, move the decimal point three places to the left.

$$4500 \text{ mL} = 4.5 \text{ L}$$
$$1287 \text{ mg} = 1.287 \text{ g}$$
$$480 \text{ mL} = 0.48 \text{ L}$$

When converting from a larger to a smaller unit of measure, move the decimal point three places to the right.

$$0.954 \text{ g} = 954 \text{ mg}$$
$$1.5 \text{ g} = 1500 \text{ mg}$$
$$0.238 \text{ g} = 238 \text{ mg}$$
$$0.621 \text{ mg} = 621 \text{ mcg}$$

Remember

When setting up proportions, units in the numerators must match, and units in the denominators must match.

Using the Ratio-Proportion Method

If you have difficulty remembering which way to move the decimal point when converting between units of measure in the metric system, the ratio-proportion method introduced in Chapter 2 is an effective alternative. This method is a "foolproof" way to convert metric units. Set up the conversion by placing the unknown and the value to be converted on one side of the equation and the conversion factor (the ratio of the desired unit to the given unit) on the other side.

When setting up proportions to solve for a variable, remember that the units in the numerators must match and so must the units in the denominators. Checking to make sure the units match prior to completing the calculation will ensure accuracy in the conversion. The next examples will each demonstrate a conversion by moving the decimal point, followed by the same conversion using the ratio-proportion method.

Example 4.2.1   **Change 2300 mg to grams.**

One method is to divide by 1000 by moving the decimal point three places to the left.

$$2300 \text{ mg} = 2.300 \text{ g} = 2.3 \text{ g}$$

Another method is to use a proportion to solve for the unknown.

$$\frac{x \text{ g}}{2300 \text{ mg}} = \frac{1 \text{ g}}{1000 \text{ mg}}$$

$$\frac{(2300 \text{ mg}) \, x \text{ g}}{2300 \text{ mg}} = \frac{(2300 \text{ mg}) \, 1 \text{ g}}{1000 \text{ mg}}$$

$$x \text{ g} = \frac{2300 \text{ g}}{1000}$$

$$x \text{ g} = 2.3 \text{ g}$$

Example 4.2.2   **Change 3.2 mg to micrograms.**

We can multiply by 1000 by moving the decimal point three places to the right.

$$3.2 \text{ mg} = 3200. \text{ mcg} = 3200 \text{ mcg}$$

Alternatively, we can use a proportion.

$$\frac{x \text{ mcg}}{3.2 \text{ mg}} = \frac{1000 \text{ mcg}}{1 \text{ mg}}$$

$$\frac{(3.2 \text{ mg}) \, x \text{ mcg}}{3.2 \text{ mg}} = \frac{(3.2 \text{ mg}) \, 1000 \text{ mcg}}{1 \text{ mg}}$$

$$x \text{ mcg} = (3.2) \, 1000 \text{ mcg}$$

$$x \text{ mcg} = 3200 \text{ mcg}$$

Example 4.2.3   **Change 3.785 L to milliliters.**

Multiply by 1000 by moving the decimal point three places to the right.

$$3.785 \text{ L} = 3785. \text{ mL} = 3785 \text{ mL}$$

Or, alternatively,

$$\frac{x \text{ mL}}{3.785 \text{ L}} = \frac{1000 \text{ mL}}{1 \text{ L}}$$

$$\frac{(\cancel{3.785 \text{ L}}) \, x \text{ mL}}{\cancel{3.785 \text{ L}}} = \frac{(\cancel{3.785 \text{ L}}) \, 1000 \text{ mL}}{1 \cancel{\text{L}}}$$

$$x \text{ mL} = (3.785) \, 1000 \text{ mL}$$

$$x \text{ mL} = 3785 \text{ mL}$$

Example 4.2.4

Change 454 g to kilograms.

Divide by 1000 by moving the decimal point three places to the left.

$$454 \text{ g} = 0.454 \text{ kg} = 0.454 \text{ kg}$$

Or set up a proportion.

$$\frac{x \text{ kg}}{454 \text{ g}} = \frac{1 \text{ kg}}{1000 \text{ g}}$$

$$\frac{(\cancel{454 \text{ g}}) \, x \text{ kg}}{\cancel{454 \text{ g}}} = \frac{(\cancel{454 \text{ g}}) \, 1 \text{ kg}}{1000 \cancel{\text{g}}}$$

$$x \text{ kg} = \frac{454 \text{ kg}}{1000}$$

$$x \text{ kg} = 0.454 \text{ kg}$$

---

dimensional analysis method
a conversion method in which the given number and unit are multiplied by the ratio of the desired unit to the given unit, which is equivalent to 1

Using the Dimensional Analysis Method

The **dimensional analysis method** is based on the principle that multiplying a number by 1 does not change its value. In this method, the given number and unit are multiplied by the ratio of the desired unit to the given unit, which is equivalent to 1. The unit in the denominator will match the given unit, so the units will cancel each other out and the unit remaining in the numerator will be the unit to which we are converting.

Example 4.2.5

Convert 486 mg to grams.

$$486 \text{ \cancel{mg}} \times \frac{1 \text{ g}}{1000 \text{ \cancel{mg}}} = 0.486 \text{ g}$$

Example 4.2.6   Convert 4.5 L to milliliters.

$$4.5 \, \cancel{L} \times \frac{1000 \text{ mL}}{1 \, \cancel{L}} = 4500 \text{ mL}$$

Example 4.2.7   Convert 240 mL to liters.

$$240 \, \cancel{\text{mL}} \times \frac{1 \text{ L}}{1000 \, \cancel{\text{mL}}} = 0.24 \text{ L}$$

Example 4.2.8   Convert 0.725 mg to micrograms.

$$0.725 \, \cancel{\text{mg}} \times \frac{1000 \text{ mcg}}{1 \, \cancel{\text{mg}}} = 725 \text{ mcg}$$

4.2 Problem Set

Convert the following units within the metric system by using the ratio-proportion method. Retain all significant figures and do not round the answers.

1. 1964 mcg = __1.964__ mg

2. 418 mg = __0.418__ g

3. 651 mg = __651,000__ mcg

4. 0.84 mg = __840__ mcg

5. 0.012 g = __12__ mcg

6. 9,213,406 mcg = __9,213.406__ g

7. 284 mg = __0.284__ g

8. 9382.5 mcg = __9.3825 0.0093825__ mg

9. 12,321 mcg = __0.012321__ g

10. 184 g = __0.184__ kg

Convert the following units within the metric system by using the dimensional analysis method. Retain all significant figures and do not round the answers.

11. 52 mL = __0.01152__ L

12. 2.06 g = __2,060__ mg

13. 16 mg = __16,000__ mcg

14. 256 mg = __0.256__ g

15. 2,703,000 mcg = __2.703__ g

16. 6.9 L = __6,900__ mL

17. 62.5 mg = __0.0625__ g

18. 15 kg = __15,000__ g

19. 2,785,000 mcg = __2.785__ g

20. 8.234 mg = __8,234__ mcg

Convert the following using the method you prefer. Show all work. Retain all significant figures and do not round the answers.

21. 2 kg = _____ mg

22. 21 L = _____ mL

23. 576 mL = _____ L

24. 823 kg = _____ mg

25. 27 mcg = _____ mg

26. 5000 mcg = _____ mg

27. 20 mcg = _____ mg

28. 4.624 mg = _____ mcg

29. 3.19 g = _____ mg

30. 8736 mcg = _____ mg

31. 830 mL = _____ L

32. 0.94 L = _____ mL

33. 1.84 g = _____ mg

34. 560 mg = _____ g

35. 1200 mcg = _____ mg

36. 125 mcg = _____ mg

37. 0.275 mg = _____ mcg

38. 480 mL = _____ L

39. 239 mg = _____ g

40. 1500 mg = _____ g

Applications

41. The following prescription has come into the pharmacy.

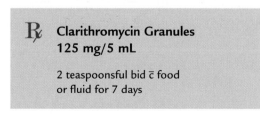

R℞ **Clarithromycin Granules**
125 mg/5 mL

2 teaspoonsful bid c̄ food
or fluid for 7 days

a. How many milliliters will the patient take daily?

b. How many milliliters should be dispensed for the patient?

c. How many grams will the patient take daily?

d. Using the following drug label, how many bottles of Biaxin will be needed to fill this prescription?

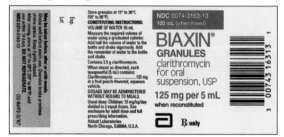

42. A patient is to take 1.5 g of amoxicillin prior to a dental procedure. The capsules available are shown in the following label. How many capsules will be dispensed to this patient?

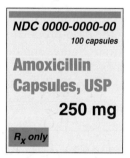

43. A patient is to receive 1000 mg vancomycin two times daily, diluted in IV solution. The following label shows the stock available.

a. How many doses are available in one vial?

b. How many days will one vial last?

Self-check your work in Appendix A.

TABLE 4.5 Steps for Using Ratio-Proportion Method for Solving Story Problems

Step 1. Read through the entire problem and identify what the question is asking for. This becomes the variable *x*, labeled with the unit you are looking for such as *x* mg or *x* mL.

Step 2. Identify the prescriber's order. Circle the dose ordered by the physician.

Step 3. Identify the appropriate stock available in the pharmacy. The ratio of pharmacy stock, such as 1 mg/tablet or 125 mg/5 mL, should be found on the labels of the drugs used in the pharmacy. Underline this information.

Step 4. Identify extraneous information. It is often helpful to draw a single pencil line through any information you identify as not needed. This prevents you from using that information in your setup.

Step 5. Estimate what your answer should be. Compare the ordered dose to what is on hand. Will the dose be larger or smaller than the dosage unit given?

Step 6. Use the ratio-proportion method to solve for *x*. When using the ratio-proportion method to solve your problem, place the physician-ordered dosage on the left side of the proportion and the pharmacy on-hand ratio on the right side.

Step 7. Round your answer to the appropriate number of significant figures. Weights are typically rounded to the nearest whole milligram, and volumes are typically rounded to the nearest tenth of a milliliter.

4.3 Problem Solving in the Pharmacy

Many pharmacy calculations require problem solving. When faced with a "story problem" or other problem where the calculation needed is not absolutely clear, it is important to begin by asking the question, "What am I looking for?" In dose calculations, this is usually a weight, expressed in milligrams, or a volume, expressed in milliliters.

Using the Ratio-Proportion Method to Solve Story Problems

vehicle
an inert medium, such as a syrup, in which a drug is administered

In Chapter 2, you learned some basic calculations using the ratio-proportion method and applied that same method to converting between units of measure in the metric system. Now you will use ratios and proportions mathematically to compare a readily available product, consisting of an active ingredient and a **vehicle,** to a desired (prescribed) dosage. Like the available product, the desired dosage will consist of an active ingredient and a vehicle. A vehicle is an inert medium, such as syrup, in which a drug is administered.

$$\frac{\text{active ingredient (desired)}}{\text{vehicle (desired)}} = \frac{\text{active ingredient (on hand)}}{\text{vehicle (on hand)}}$$

Remember
When setting up proportions, units in the numerators must match, and units in the denominators must match.

Keep in mind that the ratios on the two sides of the equation may be reversed, but the same units must appear in both numerators and the same units must appear in both denominators.

The steps outlined in Table 4.5 can be used as a basis for solving story problems or dose calculations using the ratio-proportion method. Usually, the following equation will be used to solve a story problem.

$$\frac{\text{desired amount of drug}}{\text{prescriber's order}} = \text{ratio of pharmacy stock}$$

Example 4.3.1

A physician has ordered 370 mg of a drug, and you have a 10 mL vial of solution containing 250 mg/3 mL on hand. How many milliliters will you measure out?

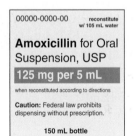

Step 1. Identify the question being asked. We need to find out how many milliliters, so *x* mL is the unknown.

Step 2. Identify the prescribed amount and circle it. In this problem, the physician has ordered 370 mg.

Step 3. Identify the product available in the pharmacy and underline it. In this problem, the pharmacy has 250 mg/3 mL of the drug.

Step 4. Identify extraneous information and draw a line through it. In this problem, it is not important to know that the drug comes in a 10 mL vial.

Step 5. Estimate the answer. The ordered dose of 370 mg is larger than the dosage strength of 250 mg, so the dose volume should be more than 3 mL.

Step 6. Use the ratio-proportion method to solve for *x* mL.

$$\frac{\text{desired amount of drug}}{\text{prescriber's order}} = \text{ratio of pharmacy stock}$$

$$\frac{x \text{ mL}}{370 \text{ mg}} = \frac{3 \text{ mL}}{250 \text{ mg}}$$

$$x \text{ mL} = 4.44 \text{ mL}$$

Step 7. Since this is a liquid and volumes are typically rounded to the nearest tenth of a milliliter, round to 4.4 mL.

Example 4.3.2

A physician has ordered 100 mg of amoxicillin to be given to a child three times a day for 10 days. Amoxicillin is available in a 150 mL bottle with a dose strength of 125 mg/5 mL. How many milliliters will the child need at each dose?

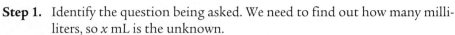

Step 1. Identify the question being asked. We need to find out how many milliliters, so *x* mL is the unknown.

Step 2. Identify the prescribed amount and circle it. In this problem, the physician has ordered 100 mg at each dose.

Step 3. Identify the product available in the pharmacy and underline it. In this problem, the pharmacy has 125 mg/5 mL of amoxicillin.

Step 4. Identify extraneous information and draw a line through it. In this problem, it is not important to know "three times a day for 10 days" and that the size of the amoxicillin bottle is 150 mL.

Step 5. Estimate the answer. The ordered dose of 100 mg is less than the dose strength of 125 mg, so the dose volume should be less than 5 mL.

Step 6. Use the ratio-proportion method to solve for *x* mL.

$$\frac{\text{desired amount of drug}}{\text{prescriber's order}} = \text{ratio of pharmacy stock}$$

$$\frac{x \text{ mL}}{100 \text{ mg}} = \frac{5 \text{ mL}}{125 \text{ mg}}$$

$$x \text{ mL} = 4 \text{ mL}$$

Step 7. No rounding is needed because the answer for this liquid measure does not extend beyond a tenth of a milliliter.

Some medications are ordered by a certain volume rather than by milligrams or weight. For example, a cough syrup may be ordered as 10 mL every four hours, and it may be necessary to calculate how much of the active ingredient is in this dose. The steps presented in Table 4.5 can also be used to solve this type of problem. In this case, however, the unknown will be the amount of the active ingredient instead of the overall volume.

Example 4.3.3

A physician has ordered 10 mL of amoxicillin to be given to a child three times daily for 7 days. Amoxicillin is available in a 150 mL bottle with a dosage strength of 250 mg/5 mL. How many milligrams will the child get at each dose?

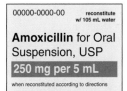

Step 1. The unknown is x mg.
Step 2. The prescribed amount is 10 mL amoxicillin.
Step 3. The pharmacy has 250 mg/5 mL of amoxicillin.
Step 4. The extraneous information includes "three times daily for 7 days" and that the size of the amoxicillin bottle is 150 mL.
Step 5. The answer will be more than 250 mg because 10 mL is larger than 5 mL.
Step 6. Use the ratio-proportion method to solve for x mg.

$$\frac{x \text{ mg}}{10 \text{ mL}} = \frac{250 \text{ mg}}{5 \text{ mL}}$$

$$x \text{ mg} = 500 \text{ mg}$$

Step 7. No rounding is needed because the answer for this weight does not have a decimal point and the significant figures are correct.

Example 4.3.4

A physician has ordered cefaclor 375 mg/5 mL oral suspension. A 100 mL bottle is prepared and is labeled to administer 7.5 mL twice daily for 5 days. How many milligrams is the patient receiving at each dose?

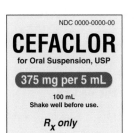

Step 1. The unknown is x mg.
Step 2. The prescribed amount is 7.5 mL suspension.
Step 3. Once the suspension is prepared, it contains 375 mg cefaclor/5 mL of suspension.
Step 4. The extraneous information includes "twice daily for 5 days" and that the size of the cefaclor bottle is 100 mL.
Step 5. The answer will be more than 375 mg because 7.5 mL is larger than 5 mL.

Step 6. Use the ratio-proportion method to solve for x mg.

$$\frac{x \text{ mg}}{7.5 \text{ mL}} = \frac{375 \text{ mg}}{5 \text{ mL}}$$

$$x \text{ mg} = 562.5 \text{ mg}$$

Step 7. The answer of 562.5 mg is rounded to the nearest whole milligram, or 563 mg.

Using Dimensional Analysis to Calculate a Drug Dose

Just as the dimensional analysis method was used in converting metric units earlier in this chapter, it can now be used to solve drug dosage problems by "converting" a dose from milligram to tablets, or milligrams to milliliters. This is accomplished by multiplying the dose ordered by the ratio for the on-hand product. As in the metric conversions practiced earlier in the chapter, the ratio is set up so that the units of the given dose and the units in the denominator will cancel out. When the dimensional analysis method is used to solve drug dosage problems, the steps shown in Table 4.5 can still be used to analyze the information. The only difference is in the setup in Step 6.

The dimensional analysis method tends to be used most frequently for simple dosage calculations such as the number of tablets. For example, if a doctor has prescribed 100 mg of a drug and you have that drug on hand in 50 mg tablets, you can quickly determine that the patient will need two 50 mg tablets for the prescribed 100 mg dose. Although you may be able to do the calculations in the following exercises in your head, it is important to work through the steps to be sure you understand them.

Example 4.3.5

A physician has ordered a 25 mg dose of hydrochlorothiazide. You have a 100 count bottle of 50 mg tablets. What will you prepare to fill the order?

NDC 0000-0000-00

50 mg

Hydrochlorothiazide

100 Scored Tablets

R_x only

Step 1. The unknown is x tablets.
Step 2. The prescribed amount is 25 mg.
Step 3. The pharmacy has 50 mg tablets.
Step 4. The extraneous information includes "100 count bottle."
Step 5. The answer will be less than 1 tablet, as the requested dose is less than the amount of milligrams in 1 tablet.
Step 6. Convert the units using the dimensional analysis method.

$$25 \text{ mg} \times \frac{1 \text{ tablet}}{50 \text{ mg}} = 0.5 \text{ tablet}$$

Step 7. No rounding is required.

Example 4.3.6

A physician has ordered a 750 mg dose of amoxicillin. You have 150 mL of a 250 mg/5 mL suspension. What will you prepare to fill the order?

$750 \text{mg} \times \dfrac{5 \text{mL}}{250 \text{mg}} = 15 \text{mL}$

Step 1. The unknown is x mL.
Step 2. The prescribed amount is 750 mg amoxicillin.
Step 3. The pharmacy has 250 mg/5 mL.

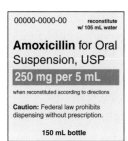

Step 4. The extraneous information includes "150 mL suspension."

Step 5. The answer will be approximately three times as large as the unit given.

Step 6. Convert the units using the dimensional analysis method.

$$750 \cancel{mg} \times \frac{5 \text{ mL}}{250 \cancel{mg}} = 15 \text{ mL}$$

Step 7. No rounding is required.

4.3 Problem Set

Calculate the following doses using the ratio-proportion method.

1. A patient has a prescription order for 30 mg of a drug. The pharmacy has a partial container of 7.5 mg tablets. How many tablets will the patient need?

2. A prescription order is written for 20 mg of medication. The pharmacy has on hand a 10 mL vial of 25 mg/2 mL solution. How many milliliters will be prepared for this patient?

3. A patient is to get 125 mg of carbamazepine suspension. The label at right shows the drug that the pharmacy has in stock. How many milliliters will be prepared for this patient?

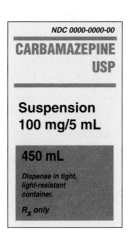

4. A patient is to receive 4 mg of haloperidol. The pharmacy has on hand a 1 mL vial of 5 mg/1 mL solution. How many milliliters are needed to fill this prescription?

5. A loading dose of 1750 mg is needed. The pharmacy has on hand a 500 count bottle of 250 mg capsules. How many capsules will be needed to fill this prescription?

6. A patient is to receive an 18 mg dose of hydroxyzine pamoate. The pharmacy has the following medication available. How many milliliters will be prepared for this patient?

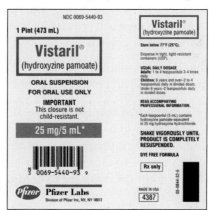

7. A patient is to receive 400 mg of erythromycin ethylsuccinate three times daily. The available drug is shown in the label. How many milliliters will be prepared for the morning dose?

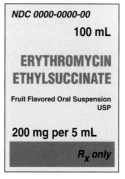

8. The following order is received by the pharmacy.

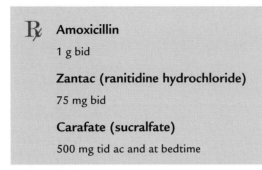

R̥ **Amoxicillin**

1 g bid

Zantac (ranitidine hydrochloride)

75 mg bid

Carafate (sucralfate)

500 mg tid ac and at bedtime

a. Amoxicillin is available as 250 mg/mL suspension. How many milliliters of medication would you draw up in each oral syringe for the patient?

b. Zantac is available as 15 mg/mL. How many milliliters will you draw up in each oral syringe for the patient?

c. Carafate is available as 1 g tablets. How many tablets will be needed for one day?

9. A total regimen of therapy calls for 10 mg of a medication to be given to a patient over several days. In the pharmacy, a solution is available with 40 mcg/mL. How many milliliters must be dispensed to complete the regimen?

10. A patient was given 2 mL of gentamicin, shown in the label below. How many milligrams were given to the patient?

11. A patient receives 1 mg of atropine, shown in the label. How many milliliters is this?

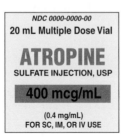

12. A patient receives 1.2 mL of the atropine solution shown in the preceding problem. How many micrograms is this?

13. A 0.63 mL dose of medication is to be given. The pharmacy stock solution contains 80 mg/15 mL. How many micrograms are in the dose?

14. A capsule contains 35 mg of an active ingredient. How many capsules would you need to accumulate 1.05 kg of ingredient?

15. A total regimen of a drug calls for 880 mg to be given. If two doses provide 80 mg, how many doses will have to be given?

16. You have 560 mL of a solution that contains 1600 mg. How many micrograms are in 4 mL of solution? (Round your answer to the nearest tenth.)

17. A total regimen of therapy calls for 10 mg of a medication to be given to a patient over several days. In the pharmacy, a solution is available with 40 mcg/mL. How many milliliters must be dispensed to complete the regimen?

18. A patient is to receive 2000 units of heparin. Use the following label to determine how many milliliters of heparin you will prepare.

Use the following label to answer questions 19 and 20.

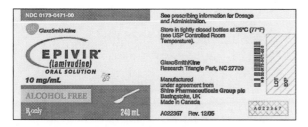

19. A patient is to take 20 mg of Epivir oral solution as shown. How many milliliters will this be?

20. A patient is to take 3.5 mL of Epivir oral solution as shown. How many milligrams will this be?

Use the following label to answer questions 21 and 22.

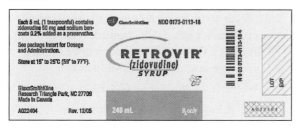

21. A patient is to take 12.5 mL of Retrovir syrup as shown. How many milligrams is this?

22. A patient is prescribed 100 mg Retrovir syrup as shown. How many milliliters is this?

Use this label to answer questions 23 and 24.

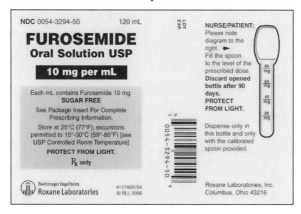

23. A pediatric patient is to take 0.5 mL of furosemide oral solution, and the medication shown in the label above is to be used to fill the order. How many milligrams will the child take with each dose?

24. A pediatric patient is to take 0.8 mL of furosemide oral solution, and the medication shown in the label above is to be used to fill the order. How many milligrams will the child take with each dose?

Use this label to answer questions 25 and 26.

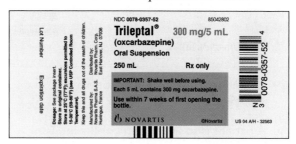

25. A patient is to take 150 mg Trileptal every 12 hours, and the medication is available as presented in the label shown above. How many milliliters will the patient take at each dose?

26. A patient is to take 0.5 g Trileptal. How many milliliters will be prepared?

Use this label to answer questions 27 and 28.

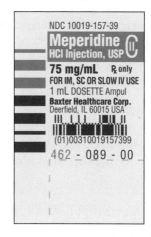

27. A patient is to receive 50 mg of meperidine intramuscularly every 4 to 6 hours as needed, and the medication shown in the label is to be used to fill the order. How many milliliters will the patient need for one dose?

28. A patient is to receive 0.8 mL meperidine solution IM stat. How many milligrams is this?

Use the following label to answer questions 29 and 30.

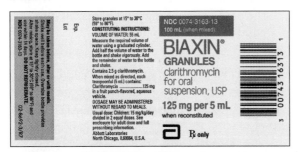

29. A patient is to take 100 mg of Biaxin. How many milliliters will this be?

30. A patient is to take 7.5 mL of Biaxin. How many milligrams is this?

Use the following label to answer questions 31 and 32.

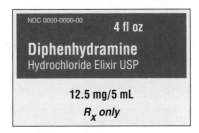

31. A pediatric patient is to receive 20 mg of diphenhydramine hydrochloride. How many milliliters of elixir will be administered?

32. An adult patient who has been stung by a wasp is to receive 50 mg diphenhydramine hydrochloride immediately. How many milliliters of elixir will be administered?

33. A patient is to take 150 mg of nortriptyline per day. The pharmacy has on hand 25 mg, 50 mg, and 75 mg capsules.

   a. Select the product that will result in the patient taking the fewest number of capsules daily.

   b. How many capsules will need to be dispensed for a week's supply?

34. The following order has been received by the pharmacy.

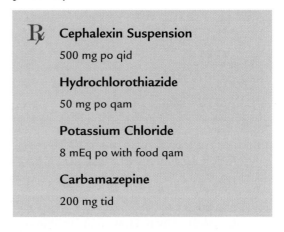

   a. Cephalexin is available in a 200 mL bottle of 250 mg/5 mL suspension. How many milliliters will the patient need for the first day?

   b. Hydrochlorothiazide is available from the pharmacy in a 1000 count bottle of 25 mg tablets. How many tablets will be needed for the first day of hospitalization?

   c. Potassium chloride is available as a 20 mEq/15 mL sugar-free solution. It contains 5% alcohol. How many milliliters will be measured out for the patient's morning dose?

   d. The pharmacy has a 450 mL bottle of 100 mg/5 mL carbamazepine solution. How many milliliters will be prepared for this patient for the first day?

4.4 Customized Doses

Most manufacturers offer dose ranges as prescribing guidelines. In some cases, the suggested dose may be based on the patient's weight or the patient's weight and height. Calculations to customize patient-specific doses are important in the pharmacy.

Calculating Doses Based on Weight

The patient's weight may be especially important when calculating a customized parenteral, pediatric, or geriatric dose of a medication. Medications that have a low margin of safety should have a customized dose. More commonly, children and elderly patients often need customized doses because they weigh significantly less than the "normal" adult patients the drugs are designed for. Also, their body systems may not metabolize or eliminate the drug as an adult's body might. In these cases, manufacturers will offer prescribing guidelines for a medication based upon a therapeutic amount or range per unit of body weight. The most common is unit used is milligram of a medication per kilogram of body weight. The following examples will demonstrate calculations used to customize a dose.

Example 4.4.1

A patient weighs 60 kg, and she is to receive a medication of 15 mg/kg. What will her dose be? If the medication is available in a 300 mg capsule, how many will be dispensed for 1 dose?

This problem has two parts. The first part asks for the dose, and the second part asks for the number of capsules to be dispensed for 1 dose. We can solve both parts of this problem using either the ratio-proportion method or the dimensional analysis method.

Part I. Determine the dose.
Solution 1: Using the ratio-proportion method,

$$\frac{x \text{ mg}}{60 \text{ kg}} = \frac{15 \text{ mg}}{1 \text{ kg}}$$

$$\frac{(60 \text{ kg}) \, x \text{ mg}}{60 \text{ kg}} = \frac{(60 \text{ kg}) \, 15 \text{ mg}}{1 \text{ kg}}$$

$$x \text{ mg} = (60) \, 15 \text{ mg}$$

$$x \text{ mg} = 900 \text{ mg}$$

Solution 2: Using the dimensional analysis method,

$$60 \text{ kg} \times \frac{15 \text{ mg}}{1 \text{ kg}} = 900 \text{ mg}$$

Part II. Determine the number of capsules to be dispensed for 1 dose.
Solution 1: Using the ratio-proportion method,

$$\frac{x \text{ capsules}}{900 \text{ mg}} = \frac{1 \text{ capsule}}{300 \text{ mg}}$$

$$\frac{(900 \text{ mg}) \, x \text{ capsules}}{900 \text{ mg}} = \frac{(900 \text{ mg}) \, 1 \text{ capsule}}{300 \text{ mg}}$$

$$x \text{ capsules} = \frac{900 \text{ capsules}}{300}$$

$$x \text{ capsules} = 3 \text{ capsules}$$

Solution 2: Using the dimensional analysis method,

$$900 \text{ mg} \times \frac{1 \text{ capsule}}{300 \text{ mg}} = 3 \text{ capsules}$$

Example 4.4.2

A patient weighs 74 kg, and he is to receive a medication of 0.4 mg/kg. What will his dose be? If the medication is available in a 15 mg/10 mL solution, how many milliliters of medication will the patient receive in a dose?

This problem has two parts. The first part asks for the dose, and the second part asks for the amount of milliliters to be dispensed. We can solve both parts of this problem using either the ratio-proportion method or the dimensional analysis method.

Part I. Determine the dose.
Solution 1: Using the ratio-proportion method,

$$\frac{x \text{ mg}}{74 \text{ kg}} = \frac{0.4 \text{ mg}}{1 \text{ kg}}$$

$$\frac{(74 \text{ kg}) \, x \text{ mg}}{74 \text{ kg}} = \frac{(74 \text{ kg}) \, 0.4 \text{ mg}}{1 \text{ kg}}$$

$$x \text{ mg} = (74) \, 0.4 \text{ mg}$$

$$x \text{ mg} = 29.6 \text{ mg}$$

Solution 2: Using the dimensional analysis method,

$$74 \text{ kg} \times \frac{0.4 \text{ mg}}{1 \text{ kg}} = 29.6 \text{ mg}$$

Part II. Determine the number of milliliters to be dispensed for 1 dose.
Solution 1: Using the ratio-proportion method,

$$\frac{x \text{ mL}}{29.6 \text{ mg}} = \frac{10 \text{ mL}}{15 \text{ mg}}$$

$$\frac{(\cancel{29.6 \text{ mg}}) \, x \text{ mL}}{\cancel{29.6 \text{ mg}}} = \frac{(\cancel{29.6 \text{ mg}}) \, 10 \text{ mL}}{15 \, \cancel{\text{mg}}}$$

$$x \text{ mL} = \frac{296 \text{ mL}}{15}$$

$$x \text{ mL} = 19.733 \text{ mL, rounded to } 19.7 \text{ mL}$$

Solution 2: Using the dimensional analysis method,

$$29.6 \, \cancel{\text{mg}} \times \frac{10 \text{ mL}}{15 \, \cancel{\text{mg}}} = 19.733 \text{ mL, rounded to } 19.7 \text{ mL}$$

body surface area (BSA)
a measurement related to a patient's weight and height, expressed in meters squared (m^2), and used to calculate patient-specific doses of medications

Calculating Doses Based on Body Surface Area (BSA)

Body surface area (BSA) is a measurement that is based on weight and height variables and expressed as meters squared (m^2). BSA is usually estimated using a nomogram. Table 4.6 outlines the steps for using a nomogram, and Figures 4.2 and 4.3 are nomograms used for estimating BSA for children and adults. Some medications, such as chemotherapy drugs, require BSA to calculate a patient-specific dose.

Example 4.4.3

A patient is to receive a medication with the dose based on 50 mg/m^2. If the patient has a BSA of 0.90 m^2, what will the dose be? If the medication is available only in 15 mg tablets, how many will be dispensed for 1 dose?

Part I. Since the dose is to be based on 50 mg/m^2, multiply by the number of square meters of the BSA, in this case 0.90.

$$0.90 \, \cancel{m^2} \times \frac{50 \text{ mg}}{\cancel{m^2}} = 45 \text{ mg}$$

Part II. Use the dose to determine the number of tablets to dispense.

$$45 \, \cancel{\text{mg}} \times \frac{1 \text{ tablet}}{15 \, \cancel{\text{mg}}} = 3 \text{ tablets}$$

TABLE 4.6 Steps for Reading a Nomogram for Estimating BSA
Step 1. Mark the patient's height on the left column.
Step 2. Mark the patient's weight on the right column.
Step 3. Draw a line or place a straight-edge ruler on the two marks.
Step 4. Read the BSA by noting where the straight edge crosses the center column. When the straight edge crosses between two numbers, the BSA should be estimated to the nearest one-half unit.

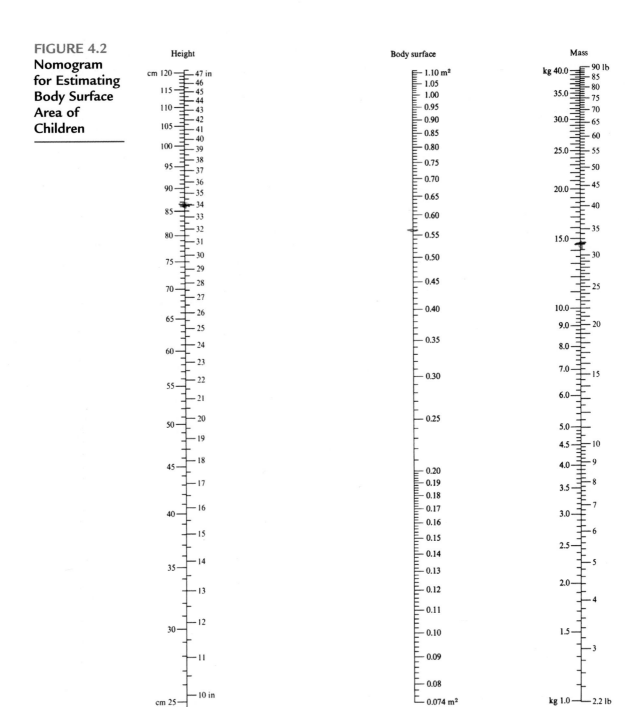

FIGURE 4.2
Nomogram for Estimating Body Surface Area of Children

Height

cm 120	47 in
115	46
	45
	44
110	43
105	42
	41
	40
100	39
95	38
	37
90	36
	35
85	34
	33
80	32
	31
75	30
	29
70	28
	27
65	26
	25
60	24
	23
55	22
	21
50	20
	19
45	18
	17
40	16
	15
35	14
	13
30	12
	11
cm 25	10 in

Body surface

1.10 m²
1.05
1.00
0.95
0.90
0.85
0.80
0.75
0.70
0.65
0.60
0.55
0.50
0.45
0.40
0.35
0.30
0.25
0.20
0.19
0.18
0.17
0.16
0.15
0.14
0.13
0.12
0.11
0.10
0.09
0.08
0.074 m²

Mass

kg 40.0	90 lb
	85
35.0	80
	75
	70
30.0	65
	60
25.0	55
	50
20.0	45
	40
	35
15.0	30
	25
10.0	
9.0	20
8.0	
7.0	15
6.0	
5.0	
4.5	10
4.0	9
3.5	8
3.0	7
	6
2.5	
	5
2.0	
	4
1.5	
	3
kg 1.0	2.2 lb

FIGURE 4.3
**Nomogram
for Estimating
Body Surface
Area of Adults**

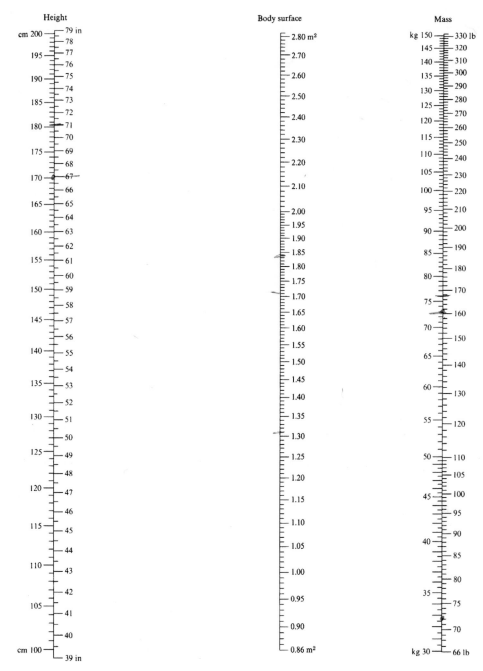

Height

cm 200 — 79 in
        78
195 — 77
        76
190 — 75
        74
185 — 73
        72
180 — 71
        70
175 — 69
        68
170 — 67
        66
165 — 65
        64
160 — 63
        62
155 — 61
        60
150 — 59
        58
145 — 57
        56
140 — 55
        54
135 — 53
        52
130 — 51
        50
125 — 49
        48
120 — 47
        46
115 — 45
        44
110 — 43
        42
105 — 41
        40
cm 100 —
        39 in

Body surface

2.80 m²
2.70
2.60
2.50
2.40
2.30
2.20
2.10
2.00
1.95
1.90
1.85
1.80
1.75
1.70
1.65
1.60
1.55
1.50
1.45
1.40
1.35
1.30
1.25
1.20
1.15
1.10
1.05
1.00
0.95
0.90
0.86 m²

Mass

kg 150 — 330 lb
145 — 320
140 — 310
135 — 300
        290
130 — 280
125 — 270
120 — 260
115 — 250
110 — 240
105 — 230
100 — 220
95 — 210
90 — 200
85 — 190
80 — 180
        170
75 — 160
70 — 150
65 — 140
60 — 130
55 — 120
50 — 110
        105
45 — 100
        95
        90
40 — 85
        80
35 — 75
        70
kg 30 — 66 lb

Example 4.4.4

A patient with a BSA of 1.30 m² is to receive a medication with the dose based on 0.80 mg/m². The prescription is to be divided into three equal doses. How much will each dose be? If the medication is available only as 50 mcg tablets, how many will be dispensed?

Part I. Multiply the number of mg/m² by the number of m², which is the BSA.

$$1.30 \, \cancel{m^2} \times \frac{0.80 \text{ mg}}{\cancel{m^2}} = 1.04 \text{ mg}$$

$$1.04 \text{ mg} \div 3 \text{ doses} = 0.35 \text{ mg/dose}$$

Part II. Convert the dose in milligrams to micrograms, the units of the tablets, by using the equivalency 1 mg = 1000 mcg.

$$0.35 \, \cancel{\text{mg}} \times \frac{1000 \text{ mcg}}{1 \, \cancel{\text{mg}}} = 350 \text{ mcg}$$

Therefore, a dose is 350 mcg. Since the tablets are 50 mcg each,

$$350 \, \cancel{\text{mcg}} \times \frac{1 \text{ tablet}}{50 \, \cancel{\text{mcg}}} = 7 \text{ tablets}$$

Calculating Pediatric Doses

Young's Rule
a formula used to determine an appropriate pediatric dose by using the child's age in years and the normal adult dose; [age in years/(age in years + 12 years)] × adult dose = pediatric dose

Clark's Rule
a formula used to determine an appropriate pediatric dose by using the child's weight in pounds and the normal adult dose; weight in lb/150 lb × adult dose = pediatric dose

If a manufacturer does not suggest an exact pediatric dose for a medication, such as a dose based on body weight or BSA, an appropriate dose may be calculated using the normal adult dose and one of several formulas. **Young's Rule** bases the suggested dose on a child's age in years, and **Clark's Rule** bases the suggested dose on a child's weight. Both formulas include the usual adult dose, but because the manufacturer often provides this as a range (such as 20–30 mg), the physician or pharmacist must determine the "usual dose" for purposes of the formula. Many medications have a wide dose range, and the patient's response and adverse reactions can vary widely, even in adults. For this reason, many physicians prefer to prescribe to children only those medications that have a known suggested pediatric dose. Consequently, Young's and Clark's formulas are used infrequently. A more common method for determining pediatric doses, using dosing tables, will be presented in Chapter 5.

Young's Rule

$$\frac{\text{age (in years)}}{\text{age} + 12 \text{ years}} \times \text{adult dose} = \text{pediatric dose}$$

Clark's Rule

$$\frac{\text{weight (in lb)}}{150 \text{ lb}} \times \text{adult dose} = \text{pediatric dose}$$

Example 4.4.5

A 6-year-old child needs a dose of a medication that has a suggested adult dose of 500 mg. Using Young's Rule, what is the appropriate pediatric dose?

$$\frac{6 \text{ years}}{6 \text{ years} + 12 \text{ years}} \times 500 \text{ mg} = 166.67 \text{ mg}$$

Example 4.4.6

An 80 lb child needs a dose of a medication that has a suggested adult dose of 250 mg. Using Clark's Rule, what is the appropriate pediatric dose?

$$\frac{80 \text{ lb}}{150 \text{ lb}} \times 250 \text{ mg} = 133.33 \text{ mg}$$

Example 4.4.7

Calculate the dose of acetaminophen for a 5-year-old child who weighs 44 lb (20 kg). The normal adult dose is 650 mg every 4 to 6 hours as needed. Determine the child's dose based on Young's Rule and Clark's Rule.

Young's Rule: $\dfrac{5 \text{ years}}{5 \text{ years} + 12 \text{ years}} \times 650 \text{ mg} = 191.18 \text{ mg}$

Clark's Rule: $\dfrac{44 \text{ lb}}{150 \text{ lb}} \times 650 \text{ mg} = 190.67 \text{ mg}$

Example 4.4.8

The manufacturer in Example 4.4.7 recommends a dosage range of 10–15 mg/kg for a child age 4–5 years. What is the dosage range for the five-year-old child who weighs 20 kg?

$$20 \text{ kg} \times \frac{10 \text{ mg}}{\text{kg}} = 200 \text{ mg}$$

$$20 \text{ kg} \times \frac{15 \text{ mg}}{\text{kg}} = 300 \text{ mg}$$

Thus, the manufacturer's suggested dosage range for this child is 200–300 mg. This is a little more than the dose determined by the formulas in Example 4.4.7. For this medication, in fact, the manufacturer specifically recommends a dose of 240 mg per dose for a child between the ages of 4 and 5 years.

4.4 Problem Set

Use the nomogram to determine the following BSA values. (Round to the hundredth place.)

1. Child of normal height and weight: 28 inches, 20 lb

2. Child of normal height and weight: 34 inches, 32 lb

3. Child of normal height and weight: 48 inches, 51 lb (approximate your answer)

4. Child of normal height and weight: 95 cm, 21 kg

5. Young adult of normal height and weight: 141 cm, 42.5 kg

6. Adult: 60 inches, 78 kg

7. Adult: 66 inches, 64 kg

8. Adult: 71 inches, 76 kg

9. Adult: 58 inches, 57 kg

10. Adult: 200 cm, 80 kg

Applications

Calculate the following weight-based doses based on the provided recommended dose. (Round to the hundredth place.)

11. Cortisone is dosed at 0.5 mg/kg per day. If the patient weighs 56 kg, what is the dose?

12. A postsurgical patient is to receive 125 mg/kg per day of cephalosporin divided into six doses daily. What will each dose be for a patient weighing 87 kg?

13. A premature infant is to receive 4 mL/kg of a medication. If the infant weighs 1.4 kg, how much medication will be administered?

14. A drug is to be given at a dose of 0.625 mg/kg.

   a. If a patient weighs 80 kg, what is the proper dose?

   b. The dose determined above is to be divided and given three times over the course of 24 hours. What is the size of each dose, to the nearest hundredth of a milligram?

15. A newborn weighs 6 kg and is to be given medication at 5 mg/kg per day in two divided doses. How much will each dose be?

16. A patient weighs 68.64 kg and is to be dosed at 125 mg/kg per day. How many milligrams is this?

17. A child weighs 10 kg and is to be dosed at 10 mg/kg per day. The medication should be administered in equal doses every 12 hours. How many milligrams are in each dose?

Calculate the following BSA-based doses based on the provided recommended dose.

18. A patient is to receive medication with the dose based on 25 mg/m² per day, divided into two equal doses. This patient has a BSA of 1.1 m². How much will each dose be?

19. A patient is to receive medication with the dose based on 0.75 mg/m². This patient has a BSA of 0.67 m². How much of the medication will you prepare? (Round to the nearest hundredth.)

20. The medication order for a patient says that the dose is to be based on 100 mg/m². If this patient has a BSA of 0.85 m², how much will be prepared?

21. A child is to receive acyclovir at 250 mg/m². The child's BSA is 0.71 m². What will the dose be?

22. Methotrexate is to be given at 3.3 mg/m². The patient has a BSA of 0.83 m². What will the dose be?

Determine if the following doses are safe according to the manufacturer's recommended doses.

23. A pediatric patient weighs 40 lb and is 43 inches in height. The manufacturer of vincristine has a recommended dose of 2 mg/m^2. The physician has ordered 1.9 mg of vincristine. Is the physician's order safe according to the recommended dose?

24. A pediatric patient weighs 27 lb and is 30 inches in height. The manufacturer of methotrexate has a recommended dose of 3.3 mg/m^2. The physician has ordered 2.5 mg of methotrexate. Is the physician's order safe according to the recommended dose?

25. A pediatric patient weighs 23 lb and is 32 inches in height. The manufacturer of acyclovir has a recommended dose of 250 mg/m^2 every 8 hours. The physician has ordered 200 mg acyclovir tid. Is the physician's order safe according to the recommended dose?

26. A patient weighs 40.9 kg and is 58 inches in height. The manufacturer of erythromycin has a recommended dose of 50 mg/kg per day. The physician has ordered 300 mg erythromycin tid. Is the physician's order safe according to the recommended dose?

Calculate dosage ranges for the following and determine whether the prescribed dose is in the recommended safe range.

27. A pediatric patient weighs 36.4 kg and is 48 inches in height. The manufacturer of cefazolin has a recommended dose of 50 to 100 mg/kg per day. The physician has prescribed 250 mg tid.

   a. What is the recommended minimum dose per day?

   b. What is the recommended maximum dose per day?

c. Is this physician's dose within the recommended safe range?

d. If the product is available as a 500 mg/50 mL solution, how many milliliters will be prepared for one prescribed dose?

28. A pediatric patient weighs 5.45 kg and has a length of 21 inches. The manufacturer of amoxicillin has a recommended dose of 20 to 40 mg/kg per day. The physician has ordered 125 mg tid.

   a. What is the recommended minimum dose per day?

   b. What is the recommended maximum dose per day?

   c. Is the physician's dose within the recommended range?

   d. How many milliliters will be prepared for one prescribed dose if the product is available as a 125 mg/5 mL suspension?

29. A pediatric patient weighs 11.8 kg and is 31 inches in height. The physician has ordered acetaminophen with codeine, and safe dosing of acetaminophen with codeine is based on the amount of codeine. The manufacturer of codeine has a recommended dose of 0.5 to 1 mg/kg per dose. The physician has ordered 10 mL of 12 mg codeine/5 mL oral elixir.

   a. What is the recommended minimum dose per day?

   b. What is the recommended maximum dose per day?

c. How many milligrams of codeine are in the 10 mL of oral elixir?

d. Is this dose within the recommended safe range?

30. A pediatric patient weighs 9.32 kg and is 28 inches in length. The manufacturer of ibuprofen has a recommended dose of 5 to 10 mg/kg every 6 to 8 hours. The physician has ordered 125 mg q8 h.

a. What is the recommended minimum dose per day?

b. What is the recommended maximum dose per day?

c. Is the physician's dose within the recommended range?

d. How many milliliters will be prepared for one prescribed dose if the product is available as a 100 mg/5 mL suspension?

31. A patient weighs 50 kg and is 65 inches in height. The manufacturer of cephalexin has a recommended dose of 25 to 50 mg/kg per day in 2 or 4 equal doses. The physician has ordered 500 mg bid.

a. What is the recommended minimum dose per day?

b. What is the recommended maximum dose per day?

c. Is the physician's dose within the recommended range?

d. How many milliliters will be prepared for one prescribed dose if the product is available as a 250 mg/5 mL suspension?

32. A pediatric patient weighs 28.6 kg and is 50 inches in height. The manufacturer of acetaminophen has a recommended dose of 10 to 15 mg/kg per day. The physician has ordered 325 mg/day.

a. What is the recommended minimum dose per day?

b. What is the recommended maximum dose per day?

c. Is the physician's dose within the recommended range?

d. How many milliliters will be prepared for one dose if the product is available as a 160 mg/5 mL suspension?

33. An 8-year-old child weighs 68 lb (30.9 kg) and is to take acyclovir, which has a normal adult dose of 600 mg.

a. Using Young's Rule, what is the appropriate pediatric dose?

b. Using Clark's Rule, what is the appropriate pediatric dose?

Self-check your work in Appendix A.

Convert the following units within the metric system.

1. 1821 mcg = _____ mg

2. 6864 mg = _____ g

3. 34.5 mg = _____ mcg

4. 186 g = _____ kg

Calculate the following.

5. A patient is to take 2.25 g of amoxicillin prior to a dental procedure. The capsules available are 250 mg per capsule. How many capsules will be dispensed to this patient?

6. A dose of an antacid is 30 mL. How many doses can be prepared from a 360 mL bottle?

7. A patient has a prescription order for 15 mg of a drug. The pharmacy has a partial container of 2.5 mg tablets. How many tablets will the patient need?

8. A patient is to receive 4 mg of haloperidol. The pharmacy has on hand a 1 mL vial of 5 mg/mL solution. How many milliliters are needed to fill this prescription?

9. A total regimen of therapy calls for 70 mg of a medication to be given to a patient over several days. In the pharmacy, a solution is available with 100 mcg/mL. How many milliliters must be dispensed to complete the regimen?

10. A patient receives 1.2 mg of atropine, shown in the label. How many milliliters is this?

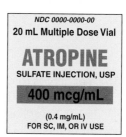

11. A patient receives 2.8 mL of the atropine solution shown in the label above. How many micrograms is this?

12. A total regimen of a drug calls for 720 mg to be given. If two doses equal 80 mg, how many doses will have to be given?

13. You have 480 mL of a solution that contains 8 g. How many micrograms are in 4 mL of solution? (Round your answer to the nearest tens place.)

14. A patient is to receive 7000 units of heparin. Heparin is available as 5000 units/mL. How many milliliters do you prepare?

15. A pediatric patient is to take 45 mcg of digoxin each morning. The pediatric elixir is available in a 60 mL dropper bottle with the concentration 0.05 mg/mL. How many milliliters will the patient take with each dose?

16. A patient is to take 200 mcg of a drug each morning. The medication is available in a 0.4 mg/5 mL solution. How many milliliters will the patient take each morning?

Calculate the following weight-based BSA doses based on the provided recommended dose. (Use the nomograms in Figures 4.2 and 4.3 to determine the BSA values when necessary.)

17. Medication is dosed at 8 mg/kg divided into three equal doses daily. The adult patient is 67 inches in height and weighs 63 kg. How many milligrams will be given at each dose?

18. The medication order is dosed at 0.5 mg/m² per day. The pediatric patient is 34 inches in height and weighs 32 lb. What is the recommended dose for this patient?

19. A newborn weighs 3.86 kg and is to be given medication at 5 mg/kg per day divided into two doses. How much will each dose be?

20. A patient weighs 73 kg and is 67 inches in height. He is to be dosed at 125 mg/m² per day. How many milligrams is this?

21. A pediatric patient weighs 15 kg and is 41 inches in height. The manufacturer of thioridazine recommends a dose between 0.5 mg/kg to a maximum of 3 mg/kg per day for children, to be given in divided doses. The physician has prescribed 15 mg every 12 hours.

   a. What is the minimum recommended dose?

   b. What is the maximum recommended dose?

   c. Is the prescribed dose within the recommended dose range?

   d. How many milliliters of 5 mg/mL strength thioridizine suspension will be given at each prescribed dose?

22. A pediatric patient weighs 21.8 kg and is 52 inches in height. The manufacturer of acetaminophen has a recommended dose of 10 to 15 mg/kg per day. The physician has ordered 325 mg.

a. What is the minimum dose per day?

b. What is the maximum dose per day?

c. Is the physician's dose within the recommended safe range?

d. If the product is available as a 160 mg/ 5 mL suspension, how many milliliters will be prepared for one prescribed dose?

23. A 12-year-old child weighs 80 lb (36.36 kg) and is to take zidovudine with a normal adult dose of 600 mg.

a. Using Young's Rule, what is the appropriate pediatric dose?

b. Using Clark's Rule, what is the appropriate pediatric dose?

24. A 9-year-old child weighs 62 lb (28.2 kg) and is to take Flumadine, which has a normal adult dose of 100 mg twice daily for 7 days.

a. Using Young's Rule, what is the appropriate pediatric dose?

b. Using Clark's Rule, what is the appropriate pediatric dose?

Using Household Measure in Pharmacy Calculations

5

Learning Objectives

- Identify units of household measure and convert between them.

- Solve medication problems by using household measure and the metric system.

- Convert body weight between kilograms and pounds.

- Determine pediatric doses using dosing tables.

- Calculate the amount of medication to be dispensed.

- Calculate temperature conversions between Celsius and Fahrenheit.

Preview chapter terms and definitions.

5.1 Household Measure

household measure
a system of measure used in homes, particularly in kitchens, in the United States; units of measure for volume include teaspoonful, tablespoonful, cup, pint, quart, and gallon; units for weight are pound and ounce

Household measure is a system of measure used in homes, particularly in kitchens, in the United States. The units of household measure for volume include teaspoonful, tablespoonful, cup, pint, quart, and gallon. The units of household measure for weight are pounds and ounces. Table 5.1 lists the household measure equivalents and their abbreviations. Figure 5.1 illustrates the more often used equivalences in household measure. The apothecary and avoirdupois measurements will be presented in Chapter 10, "Understanding the Apothecary System."

Measuring volume using the household measure is less accurate than using other systems because the measuring utensils can vary in size. Nevertheless,

Safety Note

To avoid misreading c for c̄ or 0, do not abbreviate *cup*.

TABLE 5.1 Household Measure Equivalents

Volume		Weight	
3 teaspoonsful (tsp)	= 1 tablespoonful (tbsp)	1 pound (lb)	= 16 ounces (oz)
2 tablespoonsful (tbsp)	= 1 fluid ounce (fl oz)		
8 fluid ounces (fl oz)	= 1 cup		
2 cups	= 1 pint (pt)		
2 pints (pt)	= 1 quart (qt)		
4 quarts (qt)	= 1 gallon (gal)		

FIGURE 5.1
Household Measure Equivalents

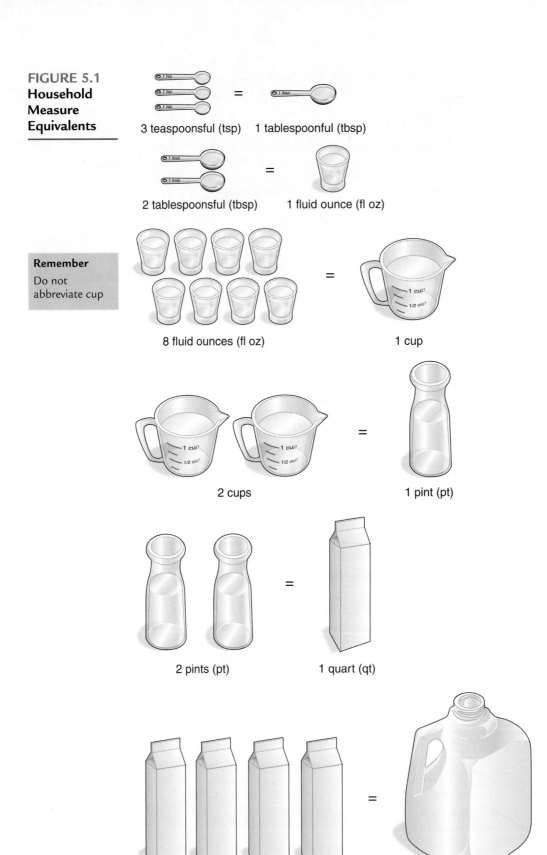

3 teaspoonsful (tsp) = 1 tablespoonful (tbsp)

2 tablespoonsful (tbsp) = 1 fluid ounce (fl oz)

Remember
Do not abbreviate cup

8 fluid ounces (fl oz) = 1 cup

2 cups = 1 pint (pt)

2 pints (pt) = 1 quart (qt)

4 quarts (qt) = 1 gallon (gal)

household volume measure may be used in community pharmacy practice when dispensing drugs that will be administered in the patient's home because patients may not have other measuring devices at home. Labels instructing patients on how to take a medication often use household measure units for this reason.

It is important to note that the fluid ounce is the same in household and in apothecary (pharmacy) volume measure. However, the ounces used to signify weight are different. There are 12 ounces in an apothecary pound, whereas there are 16 ounces in a household pound. The household pound is the more commonly used equivalence.

Converting Household Volume Measures

Like all systems, units of household volume measure can be converted to larger or smaller units. The following examples will demonstrate this type of conversion.

Example 5.1.1

How many tablespoonsful are in 2 cups of medication?

Begin the solution by noting the appropriate equivalences indicated in Table 5.1 and Figure 5.1.

$$2 \text{ tbsp} = 1 \text{ fl oz}$$
$$1 \text{ cup} = 8 \text{ fl oz}$$

Using these equivalences, the solution can be determined in two ways.

Solution 1: Using the ratio-proportion method, first determine the number of fluid ounces in 2 cups.

8 fl oz = 1 cup

$$\frac{x \text{ fl oz}}{2 \text{ cups}} = \frac{8 \text{ fl oz}}{1 \text{ cup}}$$

$$\frac{(2 \text{ cups}) \, x \text{ fl oz}}{2 \text{ cups}} = \frac{(2 \text{ cups}) \, 8 \text{ fl oz}}{1 \text{ cup}}$$

$$x \text{ fl oz} = 16 \text{ fl oz}$$

Second, determine the number of tablespoonsful in 16 fl oz.

2 tbsp = 1 fl oz

$$\frac{x \text{ tbsp}}{16 \text{ fl oz}} = \frac{2 \text{ tbsp}}{1 \text{ fl oz}}$$

$$\frac{(16 \text{ fl oz}) \, x \text{ tbsp}}{16 \text{ fl oz}} = \frac{(16 \text{ fl oz}) \, 2 \text{ tbsp}}{1 \text{ fl oz}}$$

$$x \text{ tbsp} = 32 \text{ tbsp}$$

Solution 2: Using the dimensional analysis method,

$$x \text{ tbsp} = 2 \text{ cups} \times \frac{8 \text{ fl oz}}{1 \text{ cup}} \times \frac{2 \text{ tbsp}}{1 \text{ fl oz}} = 32 \text{ tbsp}$$

Note that the cup units cancel, the fluid ounce units cancel, and the tablespoonful unit remains.

Safety Note

When converting several equivalence using dimensional analysis, it is helpful to make a notation of the units you want in the final answer. Here, we are starting the solution with x tbsp because we want the answer to be the number of tablespoonsful.

Example 5.1.2   **How many 1 tsp doses are in 3 cups of liquid medication?**

Begin the solution by noting the appropriate equivalences indicated in Table 5.1.

$$3 \text{ tsp} = 1 \text{ tbsp}$$
$$2 \text{ tbsp} = 1 \text{ fl oz}$$
$$8 \text{ fl oz} = 1 \text{ cup}$$

Using these equivalences, the solution can be determined in two ways.

Solution 1: Using the ratio-proportion method, first determine the number of fluid ounces in 3 cups.

8 fl oz   =   1 cup

$$\frac{x \text{ fl oz}}{3 \text{ cups}} = \frac{8 \text{ fl oz}}{1 \text{ cup}}$$

$$\frac{(3 \text{ cups}) \, x \text{ fl oz}}{3 \text{ cups}} = \frac{(3 \text{ cups}) \, 8 \text{ fl oz}}{1 \text{ cup}}$$

$$x \text{ fl oz} = 24 \text{ fl oz}$$

Second, determine the number of tablespoonful in 24 fl oz.

2 tbsp   =   1 fl oz

$$\frac{x \text{ tbsp}}{24 \text{ fl oz}} = \frac{2 \text{ tbsp}}{1 \text{ fl oz}}$$

$$\frac{(24 \text{ fl oz}) \, x \text{ tbsp}}{24 \text{ fl oz}} = \frac{(24 \text{ fl oz}) \, 2 \text{ tbsp}}{1 \text{ fl oz}}$$

$$x \text{ tbsp} = 48 \text{ tbsp}$$

Third, determine the number of teaspoonful in 48 tbsp.

3 tsp   =   1 tbsp

$$\frac{x \text{ tsp}}{48 \text{ tbsp}} = \frac{3 \text{ tsp}}{1 \text{ tbsp}}$$

$$\frac{(48 \text{ tbsp}) \, x \text{ tsp}}{48 \text{ tbsp}} = \frac{(48 \text{ tbsp}) \, 3 \text{ tsp}}{1 \text{ tbsp}}$$

$$x \text{ tsp} = 144 \text{ tsp}$$

Solution 2: Using the dimensional analysis method,

$$x \text{ tsp} = 3 \text{ cups} \times \frac{8 \text{ fl oz}}{1 \text{ cup}} \times \frac{2 \text{ tbsp}}{1 \text{ fl oz}} \times \frac{3 \text{ tsp}}{1 \text{ tbsp}} = 144 \text{ tsp}$$

Note that the cup units cancel, the fluid ounce units cancel, the tablespoonful units cancel, and the teaspoonful unit remains.

Example 5.1.3

How many 1 fl oz doses are in 3 pt of liquid medication?

Begin the solution by noting the appropriate equivalences indicated in Table 5.1.

$$8 \text{ fl oz} = 1 \text{ cup}$$
$$2 \text{ cups} = 1 \text{ pt}$$
$$2 \text{ pt} = 1 \text{ qt}$$

Using these equivalences, the solution can be determined in two ways.

Solution 1: Using the ratio-proportion method, first determine the number of cups in 3 pt.

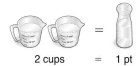

2 cups = 1 pt

$$\frac{x \text{ cups}}{3 \text{ pt}} = \frac{2 \text{ cups}}{1 \text{ pt}}$$

$$x \text{ cups} = 6 \text{ cups}$$

Second, determine the number of fluid ounces in 6 cups.

8 fl oz = 1 cup

$$\frac{x \text{ fl oz}}{6 \text{ cups}} = \frac{8 \text{ fl oz}}{1 \text{ cup}}$$

$$x \text{ fl oz} = 48 \text{ fl oz}$$

Solution 2: Using the dimensional analysis method,

$$x \text{ fl oz} = 3 \text{ pt} \times \frac{2 \text{ cups}}{1 \text{ pt}} \times \frac{8 \text{ fl oz}}{1 \text{ cup}} = 48 \text{ fl oz}$$

Example 5.1.4

How many 1 fl oz doses are in 2 qt of liquid medication?

Begin the solution by noting the appropriate equivalences indicated in Table 5.1.

$$8 \text{ fl oz} = 1 \text{ cup}$$
$$2 \text{ cups} = 1 \text{ pt}$$
$$2 \text{ pt} = 1 \text{ qt}$$

Using these equivalences, the solution can be determined in two ways.

Solution 1: Using the ratio-proportion method, first determine the number of pints in 2 qt.

2 pt = 1 qt

$$\frac{x \text{ pt}}{2 \text{ qt}} = \frac{2 \text{ pt}}{1 \text{ qt}}$$

$$x \text{ pt} = 4 \text{ pt}$$

Second, determine the number of cups in 4 pt.

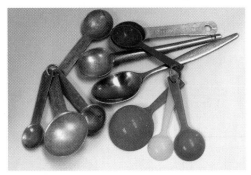

2 cups = 1 pt

$$\frac{x \, \text{cup}}{4 \, \text{pt}} = \frac{2 \, \text{cups}}{1 \, \text{pt}}$$

$$x \, \text{cup} = 8 \, \text{cups}$$

Third, determine the number of fluid ounces in 8 cups.

8 fl oz = 1 cup

$$\frac{x \, \text{fl oz}}{8 \, \text{cups}} = \frac{8 \, \text{fl oz}}{1 \, \text{cup}}$$

$$x \, \text{fl oz} = 64 \, \text{fl oz}$$

Solution 2: Using the dimensional analysis method,

$$x \, \text{fl oz} = 2 \, \text{qt} \times \frac{2 \, \text{pt}}{1 \, \text{qt}} \times \frac{2 \, \text{cups}}{1 \, \text{pt}} \times \frac{8 \, \text{fl oz}}{1 \, \text{cup}} = 64 \, \text{fl oz}$$

Converting between Household Measure and the Metric System

The volume held by a household teaspoon may vary, but a true teaspoon equals 5 mL.

Because of the inaccuracy of the measuring tools used in the household measure, it is often preferable to convert all quantities into the metric system. This may seem like additional work for some problems, but using the metric system will serve you better than relying on the household system, which is declining in use.

Prescriptions that are interpreted and entered into a computer as part of the patient's record will need to be converted to the metric system. Typically, such computer programs are set up to accept quantity measurements using milliliters for liquid prescriptions and grams for solid prescriptions such as for creams or ointments. When a prescription is written for a liquid, the volume to be

---

TABLE 5.2   Household Measure and Metric System Conversion Values

Volume		Weight	
1 tsp	= 5 mL	1 oz	= 30 g†
1 tbsp	= 15 mL	1 lb	= 454 g†
1 fl oz	= 30 mL*	2.2 lb	= 1 kg
1 cup	= 240 mL		
1 pt	= 480 mL*		
1 qt	= 960 mL		
1 gal	= 3840 mL		

* There are actually 29.57 mL in 1 fl oz, but 30 mL is usually used. When packaging a pint, companies will typically include 473 mL, rather than the full 480 mL.

† There are actually 28.34952 g in an avoirdupois ounce; however, we often round up to 30 g. It is common practice to use 454 g as the equivalent for a pound (28.35 g × 16 oz/lb = 453.6 g/lb, rounded to 454 g/lb).

FIGURE 5.2
Household Measure and Metric System Conversion Volume Values

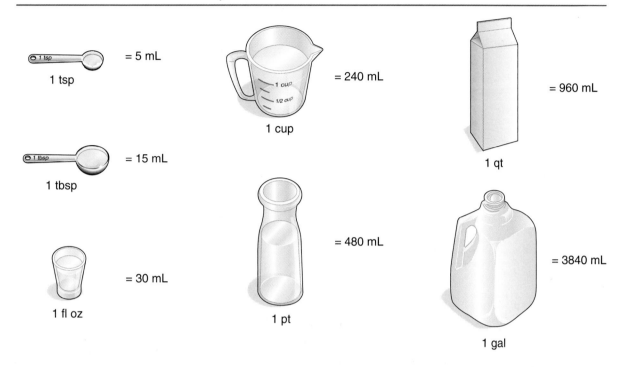

1 tsp = 5 mL

1 tbsp = 15 mL

1 fl oz = 30 mL

1 cup = 240 mL

1 pt = 480 mL

1 qt = 960 mL

1 gal = 3840 mL

dispensed and the quantity to be given at each dose will be used to calculate the amount of medication needed for 24 hours or one day.

Although some references list exact values for conversions between the household measure and the metric system, the equivalents shown in Table 5.2 and Figure 5.2 are generally accepted for use for these conversions in daily pharmacy practice. All of these conversion values should be committed to memory.

The following examples show some typical conversion problems the pharmacy technician must be able to solve.

Example 5.1.5

You are to dispense 300 mL of Trileptal Oral Suspension. The prescription states the child is to take 2 tsp BID. How many doses will the dispensed volume contain?

NDC 0078-0357-52

Trileptal®
(oxcarbazepine)

Oral Suspension

300 mg/5 mL

Shake well before using.

Each 5 mL contains 300 mg oxcarbazepine.

250 mL

Rx only

Ⓑ NOVARTIS

IMPORTANT: Shake well before using.
For oral use only.
Dosage: See package insert.
See enclosed Trileptal® (oxcarbazepine) Oral Suspension Instruction Sheet.
Store in original container.
Store at 25°C (77°F); excursions permitted to 15-30°C (59-86°F) [see USP Controlled Room Temperature].
Keep this and all drugs out of the reach of children.

Use within 7 weeks of first opening the bottle.

Ⓑ NOVARTIS

2 tsp = 10 mL

Begin solving this problem by converting to a common unit of measure using the conversion values in Table 5.2 and Figure 5.2.

$$1 \text{ dose} = 2 \text{ tsp} = 2 \times 5 \text{ mL} = 10 \text{ mL}$$

Using these converted measurements, the solution can be determined in two ways.

Solution 1: Using the ratio-proportion method and the metric system,

$$\frac{x \text{ doses}}{300 \text{ mL}} = \frac{1 \text{ dose}}{10 \text{ mL}}$$

$$\frac{(300 \text{ mL}) \, x \text{ doses}}{300 \text{ mL}} = \frac{(300 \text{ mL}) \, 1 \text{ dose}}{10 \text{ mL}}$$

$$x \text{ doses} = 30 \text{ doses}$$

Solution 2: Using the dimensional analysis method,

$$300 \text{ mL} \times \frac{1 \text{ dose}}{10 \text{ mL}} = 30 \text{ doses}$$

Example 5.1.6

Using the medication and dosing instructions in Example 5.1.5, how many days will the 300 mL last?

The patient is to take 1 dose twice daily (BID), and, as calculated in Example 5.1.5, there are 30 doses in the dispensed volume.

$$30 \text{ doses} \times \frac{1 \text{ day}}{2 \text{ doses}} = 15 \text{ days}$$

Example 5.1.7

A patient is to purchase a 12 fl oz bottle of antacid. The patient is to take 15 mL before each meal and at bedtime. How many doses does the bottle contain?

1 fl oz = 30 mL

Begin solving this problem by converting to a common unit of measure using the conversion values in Table 5.2 and Figure 5.2.

$$1 \text{ fl oz} = 30 \text{ mL, so } 0.5 \text{ fl oz} = 15 \text{ mL, and } 12 \text{ fl oz} = 360 \text{ mL}$$

Using these converted measurements, the solution can be determined in three ways.

Solution 1: Using the ratio-proportion method and the metric system,

$$\frac{x \text{ doses}}{360 \text{ mL}} = \frac{1 \text{ dose}}{15 \text{ mL}}$$

$$x \text{ dose} = 24 \text{ doses}$$

Solution 2: Using the dimensional analysis method and the metric system,

$$360 \text{ mL} \times \frac{1 \text{ dose}}{15 \text{ mL}} = 24 \text{ doses}$$

Solution 3: Using the dimensional analysis method and the household system,

$$12 \text{ fl oz} \times \frac{1 \text{ dose}}{0.5 \text{ fl oz}} = 24 \text{ doses}$$

Example 5.1.8

Using the medication and dosing instructions in Example 5.1.7, if the patient eats 3 times a day, how many days will the 12 fl oz bottle last?

The patient is to take 1 dose with every meal and at bedtime, so a daily dose is

$$\frac{1 \text{ dose}}{\text{meal}} \times \frac{3 \text{ meals}}{\text{day}} + 1 \text{ dose at bedtime} = \frac{4 \text{ doses}}{\text{day}}$$

If 24 doses are dispensed, as calculated in Example 5.1.7,

$$24 \text{ doses} \times \frac{1 \text{ day}}{4 \text{ doses}} = 6 \text{ days}$$

Example 5.1.9

How many 2 tbsp doses are in 480 mL?

Using the conversion values in Table 5.2 and Figure 5.2, 1 tbsp = 15 mL. Because 1 dose equals 2 tbsp,

$$1 \text{ dose} = 2 \text{ tbsp} = 2 \times 15 \text{ mL} = 30 \text{ mL}$$

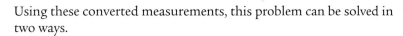

1 tbsp = 15 mL

Using these converted measurements, this problem can be solved in two ways.

Solution 1: Using the ratio-proportion method,

$$\frac{x \text{ doses}}{480 \text{ mL}} = \frac{1 \text{ dose}}{30 \text{ mL}}$$

$$x \text{ dose} = 16 \text{ doses}$$

Solution 2: Using the dimensional analysis method,

$$480 \text{ mL} \times \frac{1 \text{ dose}}{30 \text{ mL}} = 16 \text{ doses}$$

Example 5.1.10

Theophylline elixir contains 80 mg/15 mL. A dose is 2 tbsp. How many milligrams are in 1 dose of the theophylline elixir?

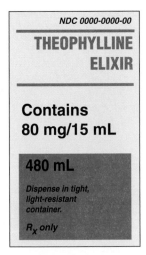

Using the conversion values in Table 5.2 and Figure 5.2,

$$1 \text{ dose} = 2 \text{ tbsp} = 2 \times 15 \text{ mL} = 30 \text{ mL}$$

This problem can be solved in two ways.

Solution 1: Using the ratio-proportion method,

$$\frac{x \text{ mg}}{30 \text{ mL}} = \frac{80 \text{ mg}}{15 \text{ mL}}$$

$$x \text{ mg} = 160 \text{ mg}$$

Solution 2: Using the dimensional analysis method,

$$30 \text{ mL} \times \frac{80 \text{ mg}}{15 \text{ mL}} = 160 \text{ mg}$$

1 tbsp = 15 mL

Like volumes, weights can be converted between household measure and metric measure. The most common conversions are between the household measurements of pounds and ounces and the metric kilograms and grams. These conversions were presented in Table 5.2.

Example 5.1.11

A physician has written a prescription for a 1.5 oz tube of ointment. How many grams is this?

Since 1 oz equals 30 g, this problem can be solved in two ways.

Solution 1: Using the ratio-proportion method,

$$\frac{x \text{ g}}{1.5 \text{ oz}} = \frac{30 \text{ g}}{1 \text{ oz}}$$

$$x \text{ g} = 45 \text{ g}$$

> **Remember**
> 30 g = 1 oz
> 454 g = 1 lb

Solution 2: Using the dimensional analysis method,

$$1.5 \text{ oz} \times \frac{30 \text{ g}}{1 \text{ oz}} = 45 \text{ g}$$

Example 5.1.12

You have a 1 lb jar of ointment available. You are instructed to use this stock to fill smaller jars with 20 g of ointment each. How many jars can you fill?

Because 1 lb equals 454 g, this problem can be solved in two ways.

Solution 1: Using the ratio-proportion method,

$$\frac{x \text{ jars}}{454 \text{ g}} = \frac{1 \text{ jar}}{20 \text{ g}}$$

$$x \text{ jar} = 22.7 \text{ jars, or 22 full jars}$$

Solution 2: Using the dimensional analysis method,

$$454 \text{ g} \times \frac{1 \text{ jar}}{20 \text{ g}} = 22.7 \text{ jars, or 22 full jars}$$

In both solutions, there is 0.7 jar of ointment remaining. You can figure out how many grams of ointment are left over with the following calculation:

$$\frac{20 \text{ g}}{\text{jar}} \times 0.7 \text{ jar leftover ointment} = 14 \text{ g leftover ointment}$$

Converting Body Weight

As discussed in the previous chapter, drugs are sometimes dosed based on the weight of the patient. Increasingly, drug manufacturers are providing a recommended dose based on a specific dose in milligrams per kilogram of the patient's weight. Because most drugs are dosed on the basis of kilograms, if a patient's weight is documented in pounds, the weight will have to be converted to kilograms before calculating the appropriate dose.

Example 5.1.13

A patient weighs 134 lb. What is this patient's weight in kilograms?

Since 1 kg equals 2.2 lb, this problem can be solved in two ways.

Remember
2.2 lb = 1 kg

Solution 1: Using the ratio-proportion method,

$$\frac{x \text{ kg}}{134 \text{ lb}} = \frac{1 \text{ kg}}{2.2 \text{ lb}}$$

$$x \text{ kg} = 60.909 \text{ kg, rounded to } 60.9 \text{ kg}$$

Solution 2: Using the dimensional analysis method,

$$134 \text{ lb} \times \frac{1 \text{ kg}}{2.2 \text{ lb}} = 60.909 \text{ kg, rounded to } 60.9 \text{ kg}$$

Example 5.1.14

A patient weighs 76 lb. What is this patient's weight in kilograms?

Because 1 kg equals 2.2 lb, this problem can be solved in two ways.

Solution 1: Using the ratio-proportion method,

$$\frac{x\,\text{kg}}{76\,\text{lb}} = \frac{1\,\text{kg}}{2.2\,\text{lb}}$$

$$x\,\text{kg} = 34.545\,\text{kg, rounded to }34.5\,\text{kg}$$

Solution 2: Using the dimensional analysis method,

$$76\,\text{lb} \times \frac{1\,\text{kg}}{2.2\,\text{lb}} = 34.545\,\text{kg, rounded to }34.5\,\text{kg}$$

A kilogram is equal to 2.2 lb, shown here.

Although it is important to understand the conversion using both the ratio-proportion and the dimensional analysis methods, a shorthand method for converting a patient's weight from pounds to kilograms is to divide the amount by 2.2 lb/kg. Similarly, you can convert a patient's weight from kilograms to pounds by multiplying it by 2.2 lb/kg.

Example 5.1.15

A patient weighs 58 kg. What is this patient's weight in pounds?

$$58\,\text{kg} \times 2.2\,\text{lb/kg} = 127.6\,\text{lb}$$

Check this answer by converting the answer from pounds back to kilograms.

$$127.6\,\text{lb} \times 1\,\text{kg}/2.2\,\text{lb} = 58\,\text{kg}$$

Example 5.1.16

A patient in the neonatal ICU weighs 1250 g. How many pounds is this?

First, convert the grams to kilograms.

$$1250\,\text{g} = 1.25\,\text{kg}$$

Second, convert kilograms to pounds.

$$1.25\,\text{kg} \times 2.2\,\text{lb/kg} = 2.75\,\text{lb}$$

Check the answer by converting the answer from pounds back to kilograms.

$$2.75\,\text{lb} \times 1\,\text{kg}/2.2\,\text{lb} = 1.25\,\text{kg}$$

5.1 Problem Set

Convert the given volumes within the household measure system.

1. 8 cups = _____ 4 _____ pt

2. 3 pt = _____ fl oz

3. 1 pt = _____ 32 _____ tbsp

4. 3 qt = _____ fl oz

5. 28 tsp = ~~140~~ 4.6666 fl oz

6. 1 pt = _____ qt

7. 6 cups = _____ 288 _____ tsp

Convert the given volumes between the household measure and metric systems.

8. 80 mL = _____ 5.333 _____ tbsp

9. 6 fl oz = _____ 180 _____ mL

10. 90 mL = _____ fl oz

11. 800 mL = _____ pt

12. 53 mL = _____ tsp

13. 35 mL = _____ tsp

14. 10 L = _____ gal

15. 4 tbsp = _____ mL

16. 15 mL = _____ tsp

17. 720 mL = _____ pt

18. 30 tsp = _____ mL

19. 120 mL = _____ fl oz

20. ½ gal = _____ mL

21. 2 L = _____ pt

Convert the following commonly used volumes to milliliters.

22. 3 tbsp = _____ mL

23. 1 fl oz = _____ mL

24. 2 fl oz = _____ mL

25. 3 fl oz = _____ mL

26. 4 fl oz = _____ mL

27. 5 fl oz = _____ mL

28. 6 fl oz = _____ mL

29. 7 fl oz = _____ mL

30. 8 fl oz = _____ mL

31. 12 fl oz = _____ mL

32. 16 fl oz = _____ mL

Convert the following weights between household measure and the metric system.

33. 2 oz = _____ g

34. 1.5 oz = _____ g

35. 8 oz = _____ g

36. 906 g = _____ lb

$6\,cups \times \dfrac{240\,ml}{1\,cup} \times \dfrac{1\,tsp}{5\,ml} = 288$

$80\,ml \times \dfrac{1\,tbsp}{15\,ml} = 5.333$

$6\,fl\,oz \times \dfrac{30ml}{1oz} = 180\,ml$

37. 30 g = _____ lb

38. 0.8 oz = _____ g

Convert the following patient weights from pounds to kilograms.

39. 3.5 lb

40. 14 lb

41. 42 lb

42. 97 lb

43. 112 lb

44. 165 lb

45. 178 lb

46. 247 lb

Applications

In solving these problems, convert all quantities into the metric system even when the problem could be solved using only the household measure.

47. How many 1 tsp doses are in 2 pt, 6 fl oz?

48. How many 2 tsp doses are in 3 cups?

49. How many 1 tbsp doses are in 12 bottles containing 16 fl oz each?

50. How many 5 mL doses are in a 5 fl oz bottle?

51. How many 3 tsp doses are in 1 pt?

52. A dose of 1.5 fl oz is to be given three times daily. How many milliliters will be given in one day?

53. How many 1½ tsp doses are in an 8 fl oz bottle of cough syrup?

Use the following label to answer questions 54 and 55.

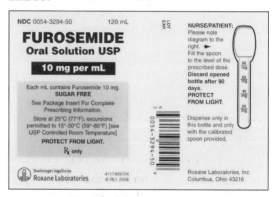

54. A prescription states that a patient is to take one-half tsp of furosemide oral solution daily. Using the furosemide label shown above, how many milligrams are in a dose?

55. Using the furosemide label shown above, how many days will a 4 fl oz bottle last a patient taking 20 mg daily?

Use the following label to answer questions 56 and 57.

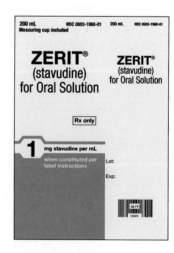

56. A prescription states that a patient is to take 10 mg of Zerit daily. Using the provided label, calculate the equivalent dose measured in teaspoonsful.

57. How many days will the bottle of Zerit last a patient if the patient is taking 1 tsp daily?

58. A medication is prescribed as 2 tsp/68 kg/day for an adult patient. How many doses would you get in a 300 mL bottle for a patient who weighs 180 lb?

59. A medication is prescribed as 1 tsp/20 kg/day for a pediatric patient. How many doses will a 4 fl oz bottle provide for a 52 lb patient?

60. A laxative medication is prescribed as 2 tbsp/50 kg. How long will a 12 fl oz bottle last for a patient who weighs 172 lb?

Self-check your work in Appendix A.

5.2 Oral Doses

It is important that pharmacy technicians be able to perform calculations involving oral dosing of medications. Oral medications are prescribed over other dosage forms whenever possible and appropriate because oral medications typically are safe and cost-effective. Most prescriptions taken orally come in tablet or capsule form, but liquid forms are also common. Liquid medications are used most commonly by children and by adults with a disease that impairs the swallowing reflex. For all dosing calculations, accuracy of conversions from the metric to the household system, dosing amounts, and dispensing amounts need to be checked for safety as well as billing purposes.

Determining Pediatric Doses Using Dosing Tables

Not all drugs that are safe and effective for adult use are appropriate for the pediatric population. In the past, formulas using the child's weight or age were used to reduce the normal adult dose to a smaller amount appropriate for the child patient. Today, prescribers are reluctant to use a medication for a child unless the pharmaceutical manufacturer indicates the proper dose. A manufacturer will provide specific age- and/or weight-related prescribing guidelines for pediatric-appropriate doses of a medication as soon as its safety and effectiveness for the pediatric population have been established. These guidelines are provided in dosing tables as a dose range that is a function of the patient's weight and/or age. When a recommended dose is not provided, often the reason is that the Food and Drug Administration has not approved the particular drug for use in children. The dosing tables are satisfactory for many purposes, but when a more accurate calculation is needed, either the weight-based dosing method or the body surface area (BSA) dosing method, which were discussed in Chapter 4, must be used.

dosing table
a table providing dose recommendations based on the age and/ or the weight of the patient; often used for determining the safe dose for a pediatric patient

A typical **dosing table** includes an age range and/or a weight range with corresponding doses. Dosing tables are used for both oral liquids and solid dosage forms, but oral liquids are easier for young patients to take and thus are more common.

Dosing tables often appear on over-the-counter (OTC) packaging for products used for children older than two years of age. For medications used for children under age two, the instruction "Consult your physician" appears. The table for children under age two is available to healthcare providers in pharmacies and physicians' offices. Physicians often instruct parents to purchase OTC medications for small children, so appropriate dosing instructions must be provided for these patients. Dosing may need to be translated from metric units to household measure units. The dosing information listed in Table 5.3 and Table 5.4 will be used to complete the following examples.

TABLE 5.3   Acetaminophen Dosing

Age	Dose
0–3 mo	40 mg
4–11 mo	80 mg
1–2 yr	120 mg
2–3 yr	160 mg
4–5 yr	240 mg
6–8 yr	320 mg
9–10 yr	400 mg
11 yr to adult	480 mg
adult	325–650 mg q4–6 h or 1000 mg 3–4 times daily
adult maximum	4000 mg daily

TABLE 5.4   Ibuprofen Dosing

Age	Weight	Dose
6–11 mo	12–17 lb	50 mg
12–23 mo	18–23 lb	75 mg
2–3 yr	24–35 lb	100 mg
4–5 yr	36–47 lb	150 mg
6–8 yr	48–59 lb	200 mg
9–10 yr	60–71 lb	250 mg
11 yr	72–95 lb	300 mg

Example 5.2.1

A 12-month-old child weighing 22 lb is to receive one dose of acetaminophen. According to the dosing information in Table 5.3, what is an appropriate dose?

Because the acetaminophen dosing is by age, not weight, use dosing for one to two years. The appropriate dose would be 120 mg.

Example 5.2.2

A parent wants to give her 15-month-old child who weighs 21 lb an appropriate dose of OTC ibuprofen. The package provides the dosing information in Table 5.4. What is the appropriate dose?

The dose can be determined by either age or weight, and for this child, the dosing would be the same. The appropriate dose would be 75 mg.

Dispensing Liquid Medications

Many oral liquid medications are actually solids, suspended in a liquid. These suspensions are often indicated by the number of milligrams per milliliter. For example,

FIGURE 5.3
Oral Syringe

This oral syringe is
marked with both
household and
metric units of
measure.

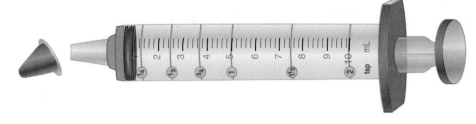

amoxicillin is available as a 125 mg/5 mL oral liquid. In other words, 5 mL of the liquid contains 125 mg of amoxicillin.

Oral liquid medications are most often dosed by teaspoonsful; tablespoonsful; fluid ounces; or now, in the metric system, milliliters. Being able to convert accurately between household measure and the metric measure system is a necessary skill for the pharmacy technician. When calculating volumes of oral medication, it is best to convert everything into the same units. The preferred method is to use the metric system. Patient instructions will usually indicate teaspoonsful if the amount is an even half or full teaspoon. However, the instructions should indicate milliliters if the dose is not easily measured using the household system. An oral syringe, as shown in Figure 5.3 is helpful to patients dosing oral liquids using the metric or household systems.

Usually, an oral liquid medication's written prescription includes a specific volume to be given at each dose, as well as the total volume to be dispensed. It is important to have a working knowledge of the volumes of oral liquid medications that are commonly prescribed. Most frequently, the dosage amount is between 2 mL and 60 mL, or roughly ½ tsp to 2 fl oz. Oral doses are often verified in the pharmacy by means of reference and established protocols.

Example 5.2.3

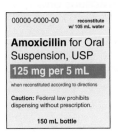

The pharmacy receives a prescription for 100 mg of amoxicillin to be taken three times daily for 10 days. The pharmacy has a 150 mL bottle of 125 mg/5 mL amoxicillin. How many milliliters of the suspension will be dispensed, and what will the patient's dosing instructions on the label say?

Determine what quantity of suspension contains 100 mg amoxicillin. This can be solved in two ways.

Solution 1: Using the ratio-proportion method,

$$\frac{x \text{ mL}}{100 \text{ mg}} = \frac{5 \text{ mL}}{125 \text{ mg}}$$

$$x \text{ mL} = 4 \text{ mL}$$

Solution 2: Using the dimensional analysis method,

$$100 \text{ mg} \times \frac{5 \text{ mL}}{125 \text{ mg}} = 4 \text{ mL}$$

Using the amount determined for a single dose, determine the total amount of suspension to be dispensed for 10 days.

$$4 \text{ mL} \times 3 \text{ doses/day} \times 10 \text{ days} = 120 \text{ mL}$$

The patient's instructions will say, "Take 4 mL three times daily for 10 days." The patient will need a dosing syringe to dispense the required amount of medication.

Example 5.2.4

If a 12 fl oz bottle of mouthwash contains 0.75 g of the active ingredient, how many milligrams will be in a 1 tbsp dose?

Begin the problem by converting all of the household measure units to metric units.

$$12 \text{ fl oz} = 360 \text{ mL}$$
$$1 \text{ tbsp} = 15 \text{ mL}$$

Also, convert 0.75 g to 750 mg. Using these converted values, this problem can be solved in two ways.

Solution 1: Using the ratio-proportion method,

$$\frac{x \text{ mg}}{15 \text{ mL}} = \frac{750 \text{ mg}}{360 \text{ mL}}$$

$$x \text{ mg} = 31.25 \text{ mg}$$

Solution 2: Using the dimensional analysis method,

$$15 \text{ mL} \times \frac{750 \text{ mg}}{360 \text{ mL}} = 31.25 \text{ mg}$$

Example 5.2.5

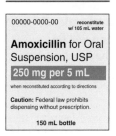

The pharmacy receives a prescription for amoxicillin suspension 1 g bid. The pharmacy has a supply of amoxicillin 250 mg/5 mL. How many milliliters are in one dose? What will the patient's dosing instructions on the bottle label say?

First determine how many milligrams are needed for one dose.

$$1 \text{ g} = 1000 \text{ mg}$$

Then determine what quantity of suspension contains 1000 mg.

Solution 1: Using the ratio-proportion method,

$$\frac{x \text{ mL}}{1000 \text{ mg}} = \frac{5 \text{ mL}}{250 \text{ mg}}$$

$$x \text{ mL} = 20 \text{ mL}$$

Solution 2: Using the dimensional analysis method,

$$1000 \text{ mg} \times \frac{5 \text{ mL}}{250 \text{ mg}} = 20 \text{ mL}$$

Translate the amount in milliliters to teaspoonful: 5 mL = 1 tsp, so 20 mL = 4 tsp. The patient's instructions will say, "Take 20 mL (or 4 teaspoonsful) two times daily."

Example 5.2.6

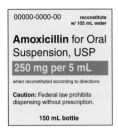

A patient is to take 7 mL of amoxicillin 250 mg/5 mL. How many milligrams are present in one dose?

Solution 1: Using the ratio-proportion method,

$$\frac{x \text{ mg}}{7 \text{ mL}} = \frac{250 \text{ mg}}{5 \text{ mL}}$$

$$x \text{ mg} = 350 \text{ mg}$$

Solution 2: Using the dimensional analysis method,

$$7 \text{ mL} \times \frac{250 \text{ mg}}{5 \text{ mL}} = 350 \text{ mg}$$

Example 5.2.7

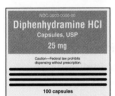

A patient is taking 4 tsp of diphenhydramine elixir at bedtime. He wishes to take oral capsules instead of the elixir. The 12.5 mg/5 mL elixir comes in a 4 fl oz bottle and is 14% alcohol. The 25 mg capsules come in a 100 count bottle. How many capsules will he need to take to equal the dose in the 4 tsp of elixir?

Begin by determining the milligrams per dose of the oral liquid using one of the following methods.

Solution 1: Using the ratio-proportion method,

$$\frac{x \text{ mg}}{20 \text{ mL}} = \frac{12.5 \text{ mg}}{5 \text{ mL}}$$

$$x \text{ mg} = 50 \text{ mg}$$

Solution 2: Using the dimensional analysis method,

$$20 \text{ mL} \times \frac{12.5 \text{ mg}}{5 \text{ mL}} = 50 \text{ mg}$$

Now, compare the milligrams to the alternative capsule product.

Solution 1: Using the ratio-proportion method,

$$\frac{x \text{ capsules}}{50 \text{ mg}} = \frac{1 \text{ capsule}}{25 \text{ mg}}$$

$$x \text{ capsule} = 2 \text{ capsules}$$

Solution 2: Using the dimensional analysis method,

$$50 \text{ mg} \times \frac{1 \text{ capsule}}{25 \text{ mg}} = 2 \text{ capsules}$$

Because the patient's dose is 50 mg, and the capsules come in 25 mg, he will need to take two capsules to provide the proper amount of the drug.

Example 5.2.8

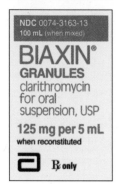

1 tbsp = 15 mL

1 tbsp = 15 mL

1 tsp = 5 mL

How many milligrams of medication are in 1 tbsp of medication that contains 125 mg/tsp?

Convert both volumes to the metric system using the following values from Table 5.2.

$$1 \text{ tbsp} = 15 \text{ mL}$$
$$1 \text{ tsp} = 5 \text{ mL}$$

Using these equivalences, this problem can be solved in two ways.

Solution 1: Using the ratio-proportion method,

$$\frac{x \text{ mg}}{15 \text{ mL}} = \frac{125 \text{ mg}}{5 \text{ mL}}$$

$$x \text{ mg} = 375 \text{ mg}$$

Solution 2: Using the dimensional analysis method,

$$15 \text{ mL} \times \frac{125 \text{ mg}}{5 \text{ mL}} = 375 \text{ mg}$$

Calculating the Amount to Dispense

How long the amount of medication dispensed will last the patient must be determined when the prescription is entered into the patient's computerized record. Pharmacies typically bill liquid medications by the milliliter and solid medications by the unit, such as a tablet. Insurance companies require claims for reimbursement for prescription drugs to include the amount of drug dispensed as well as the number of days that the dispensed amount should last. The amount dispensed is usually indicated by the prescriber; however, if it is not indicated, the amount to be dispensed is calculated by multiplying the amount of drug needed for a single day by the number of days of treatment. Not only is the dispensed amount needed for insurance purposes, but the pharmacy also needs to ensure that the patient is receiving enough medication to last for the duration of treatment, whether the medication is in liquid or solid form.

Example 5.2.9

1 tsp = 5 mL

1 fl oz = 30 mL

A patient is taking 2 tsp of medication every 8 hours. He has a 6 fl oz bottle of medication. How much medication will the patient take in one day, and how many days will the medication last?

Begin by converting all of the stated volumes to the metric system using the conversion values in Table 5.2.

$$1 \text{ tsp} = 5 \text{ mL}; \text{ therefore, } 2 \text{ tsp/dose} = 10 \text{ mL/dose}$$
$$1 \text{ fl oz} = 30 \text{ mL}; \text{ therefore, } 6 \text{ fl oz/bottle} = 180 \text{ mL/bottle}$$

Next, determine how much medication is needed for one day of treatment. The dose is every 8 hours, and there are 24 hours in a day, so

$$\text{24 hours/day} \times \text{1 dose/8 hour} = \text{3 doses/day}$$
$$\text{3 doses/day} \times \text{10 mL/dose} = \text{30 mL/day}$$

Finally, determine the number of days the medication will last.

$$\text{180 mL/bottle} \times \text{1 day/30 mL} = \text{6 days/bottle}$$

Example 5.2.10

A patient is to take 1 tsp of a medication twice daily, and she has a 4 fl oz bottle of medication. How much medication will the patient take in a day, and how many days will the medication last?

Begin by converting all of the stated volumes to the metric system using the conversion values in Table 5.2.

1 tsp = 5 mL

1 fl oz = 30 mL

$$\text{1 tsp} = \text{5 mL; therefore, 1 tsp/dose} = \text{5 mL/dose}$$
$$\text{1 fl oz} = \text{30 mL; therefore, 4 fl oz/bottle} = \text{120 mL/bottle}$$

Next, determine how much medication is needed for one day.

The dose is taken twice daily, so there are 2 doses/day.

$$\text{2 doses/day} \times \text{5 mL/dose} = \text{10 mL/day}$$

Finally, determine the number of days the medication will last.

$$\text{120 mL/bottle} \times \text{1 day/10 mL} = \text{12 days/bottle}$$

Example 5.2.11

A patient has a prescription that says the following: "Take Magic Cough syrup 1–2 tsp every 4–6 hours prn cough. Disp: 8 fl oz." How many days will the cough syrup last?

Begin by converting all of the stated volumes to the metric system using the conversion values in Table 5.2.

1 tsp = 5 mL

1 fl oz = 30 mL

$$\text{1 tsp} = \text{5 mL; therefore, 1–2 tsp/dose} = \text{5–10 mL/dose}$$
$$\text{1 fl oz} = \text{30 mL; therefore, 8 fl oz/bottle} = \text{240 mL/bottle}$$

Next, determine how much medication is needed for one day. Assume that the patient will take as much medication as possible as frequently as allowed. This will give the minimum number of days the medication will last.

There are 24 hours in a day, so if the patient takes a dose every 4 hours,

$$\text{24 hr/day} \times \text{1 dose/4 hour} = \text{6 doses/day}$$
$$\text{6 doses/day} \times \text{10 mL/dose} = \text{60 mL/day}$$

Finally, determine the number of days the medication will last.

$$\text{240 mL/bottle} \times \text{1 day/60 mL} = \text{4 days/bottle}$$

Note that the bottle will last longer if the patient takes 1 tsp every 6 hours.

Some prescriptions do not come with explicit instructions as to how much medication is to be dispensed. The prescription may say, "Take 2 tsp every morning for 10 days." The quantity indicated on the prescription may also say "QS," which means to dispense a "quantity sufficient" to meet the needs of the patient with the instructions given. When the duration of treatment is indicated, the amount of medication needed for a single day and the total amount to be dispensed can be calculated as demonstrated in the following examples.

Example 5.2.12

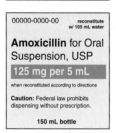

A patient comes to the pharmacy with a prescription that does not indicate a quantity. It says, "Amoxicillin 125 mg/5 mL, 1 tsp tid for 10 days." What is the total amount of medication to be dispensed?

Begin by converting all of the dosage volumes to the metric system using the conversion values in Table 5.2.

$$1 \text{ tsp} = 5 \text{ mL; therefore, } 1 \text{ tsp/dose} = 5 \text{ mL/dose}$$

Next, determine how much medication is needed for one day. Because "tid" means three times daily,

$$5 \text{ mL/dose} \times 3 \text{ doses/day} = 15 \text{ mL/day}$$

Finally, determine the amount of medication to dispense.

$$15 \text{ mL/day} \times 10 \text{ days} = 150 \text{ mL}$$

Example 5.2.13

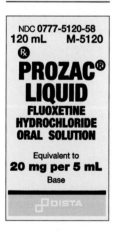

A patient is to take 2 tsp of Prozac each morning for 30 days. How many milliliters will be needed? How many bottles with the label shown below will be required to fill this prescription?

Begin by converting all of the dosage volumes to the metric system using the conversion values in Table 5.2 and Figure 5.2. Since 1 tsp = 5 mL, 2 tsp/dose = 10 mL/dose.

Next determine how many milliliters are needed for 30 days.

$$10 \text{ mL/day} \times 30 \text{ days} = 300 \text{ mL}$$

Finally, determine the number of bottles of medication are needed. The label indicates that each bottle contains 120 mL. Therefore,

$$2 \text{ bottles} \times 120 \text{ mL/bottle} = 240 \text{ mL}$$
$$3 \text{ bottles} \times 120 \text{ mL/bottle} = 360 \text{ mL}$$

So, two full bottles and part of a third bottle will be needed to fill this prescription. (There will be 60 mL left over.)

The same procedure is used when calculating the number of tablets needed to fill a prescription or the number of days a given prescription will last.

Example 5.2.14   **A patient has brought in a prescription for an antidiabetic drug. The prescription says, "Take 2 tablets before breakfast, 1 before lunch and supper, and 1 at bedtime." Determine the quantity needed for a 30 days.**

Begin by determining the number of tablets required for one day.

2 before breakfast + 1 before lunch + 1 before supper + 1 at bedtime = 5

The patient will take 5 tablets/day, so a 30 day supply wil be

5 tablets/day × 30 days = 150 tablets

Example 5.2.15   **A patient is to take a prescription for prednisone that uses a tapered dosing schedule. Determine the number of 5 mg tablets needed.**

In this problem, the number of tablets taken each day changes, so the most straightforward way to determine the number of tablets needed is to make a list of how many tablets the patient will take each day of treatment.

Day 1: 40 mg/day ÷ 5 mg/tablet = 8 tablets

 Prednisone 5 mg Oral Tablets

Take 40 mg for 2 days

Take 35 mg for 1 day

Take 30 mg for 2 days

Then decrease by 5 mg each day until gone.

Day 2: 40 mg/day ÷ 5 mg/tablet = 8 tablets
Day 3: 35 mg/day ÷ 5 mg/tablet = 7 tablets
Day 4: 30 mg/day ÷ 5 mg/tablet = 6 tablets
Day 5: 30 mg/day ÷ 5 mg/tablet = 6 tablets
Day 6: 25 mg/day ÷ 5 mg/tablet = 5 tablets
Day 7: 20 mg/day ÷ 5 mg/tablet = 4 tablets
Day 8: 15 mg/day ÷ 5 mg/tablet = 3 tablets
Day 9: 10 mg/day ÷ 5 mg/tablet = 2 tablets
Day 10: 5 mg/day ÷ 5 mg/tablet = 1 tablet

The sum of the daily totals is 50 tablets for a 10 day regimen.

5.2 Problem Set

Aspirin is typically contraindicated in children. If a child is unable to take acetaminophen or ibuprofen, however, aspirin may be used. Additionally, aspirin is indicated for some conditions in children such as antiplatelet therapy and antirheumatic therapy. Determine the milligram dose of aspirin every 4 hours for each child in the following questions using the dosing table provided.

Aspirin			
Age (years)	Weight		Dose (mg every 4 hr)
	lb	kg	
2–3	24–35	10.6–15.9	162
4–5	36–47	16–21.4	243
6–8	48–59	21.5–26.8	324
9–10	60–71	26.9–32.3	405
11	72–95	32.4–43.2	486
12–14	≥96	≥43.3	648

1. 4 years

2. 7 years

3. 10 years

4. 14 years

Levothyroxine is indicated for children with hypothyroidism. Many states require infants to be tested for hypothyroidism shortly after birth so that therapy can begin immediately if needed. In adult patients, the dose is adjusted up or down based on blood titers and clinical signs and symptoms. Newborn patients are more difficult to assess, so a standard dosing table based on kilograms has been developed. Determine the daily dose of levothyroxine for each child in the following questions using the dosing table provided.

Levothyroxine		
Age	Normal range per day (mg)	Daily dose per kg (mg)
0–<6 mo	7.5–30	2.4–6
6–<12 mo	30–45	3.6–4.8
1–5 yr	45–80	3–3.6
6–12 yr	60–90	2.4–3
>12 yr	.90	1.2–1.8

5. 6 lb, newborn

6. 7 lb, 12 oz, newborn

7. 23 lb, 11 months

8. 18 lb, 15 months

Applications

Calculate the following using either the dimensional analysis method or the ratio-proportion method.

9. A patient takes 1 tsp daily of a medication with the concentration 80 mg/15 mL. How many milligrams are in one dose?

10. A patient needs to have 60 mg of medication, and the drug has the concentration 120 mg/5 mL. How many teaspoonsful will the patient take?

11. If there are 24 mg in a teaspoonful of liquid medication, how many grams are in 8 fl oz?

12. How many milligrams are in 4 fl oz of liquid medication with the concentration of 65 mg/tbsp?

13. How many milligrams are in a 2 tsp dose of liquid medication if there are 2.5 g in 2 fl oz?

14. How many milligrams are in a 1 tbsp dose of liquid medication if there are 260 mg in 600 mL?

15. A prescription is received for Drug YXZ to be taken 2 tsp bid. The required strength of the drug is 25 mg/tsp. How many grams are needed to prepare 20 fl oz?

16. A prescription is received for Drug YXZ to be taken 1 tbsp qam. The required strength of the drug is 30 mg/15 mL. How many milligrams are in a 1 tsp dose?

17. A prescription is received for Drug YXZ to be taken 1 tbsp bid. The required strength of the drug is 40 mg/mL. How many grams of medication are needed to prepare 1 pint?

18. A patient is taking ¾ tsp of an antibiotic suspension three times a day.

    a. How long will a 150 mL bottle of antibiotic suspension last this patient?

    b. How many milliliters will be left after 10 days?

19. An antibiotic suspension is available in 80 mL, 150 mL, and 200 mL bottles.

    a. What size bottle of antibiotic suspension will a patient need in order to take 1 tsp twice daily for 14 days?

    b. How much will remain after 14 days?

20. How many days will a 12 fl oz bottle last if a patient takes 1 tbsp tid?

21. A patient is on an alternate-day therapy consisting of 2 tsp of a medication one day and 1 tbsp the next. How long will a 300 mL bottle last?

22. If there are 25 mg in a tablespoonful of liquid medication, how many grams are in 20 fl oz?

23. A patient uses an antacid 1 fl oz tid and hs. How many 12 fl oz bottles will this patient need to last 14 days?

24. How many prednisone 5 mg tablets are needed to fill the following prescription?

 Prednisone 5 mg

Take 4 tab × 2 days

Take 3 tab × 2 days

Take 1 tab × 1 day

25. How many milliliters of nystatin must be dispensed for the following prescription?

 Nystatin Suspension

use 1 mL in each cheek pouch q3 h, dispense qs 10 days

26. There are 25 mg in a teaspoonful of medication. You are dispensing 12 fl oz.

    a. How many milligrams will be in the bottle?

    b. If the patient is to get a total of 9 g for a full therapy program, how many refills will be needed?

27. For the prescription below, how many fluid ounces of nystatin must be dispensed?

 Nystatin Oral Suspension

Take ii teaspoonsful 3 times daily for 15 days.

28. A prescription received reads, "Take 2 tbsp of an oral suspension three times daily for 20 days." How many milliliters should be dispensed?

Use the label below to answer questions 29 and 30.

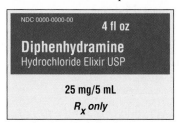

29. A mother has two children with poison ivy. One child takes 1 tsp tid and the other child takes 2 tsp tid. How many bottles of diphenhydramine elixir will be needed to supply both for 4 days?

30. How many milligrams are contained in each of the children's doses?

Use the label below to answer questions 31–34.

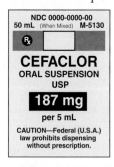

31. How many milligrams are in ¾ tsp?

32. How many milligrams are in 1½ tsp?

33. How many milliliters are needed to provide 125 mg?

34. How many milliliters are needed to provide 500 mg?

35. The following prescription for buttocks cream has been brought into the compounding pharmacy for compounding on January 3, 20XX.

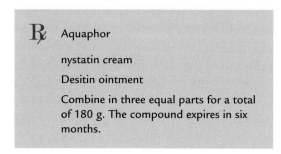

R̥   Aquaphor

nystatin cream

Desitin ointment

Combine in three equal parts for a total of 180 g. The compound expires in six months.

a. How much of each ingredient will you use?

b. What size of ointment jar (ounces) will you use to store the compound?

c. What expiration date will you put on the compound?

36. The following order for absolute (dehydrated) alcohol has been brought into the compounding pharmacy. How many syringes will be sent to the floor?

1. Obtain a 12 fl oz bottle of absolute alcohol from the narcotics cabinet.

2. Filter through a 0.2 micron filter.

3. Send to the floor in 60 mL syringes.

Self-check your work in Appendix A.

5.3 Temperature Measurement

Celsius
a thermometric scale in which 100 degrees is the boiling point of water and 0 degrees is the freezing point of water

Fahrenheit
a thermometric scale in which 212 degrees is the boiling point of water and 32 degrees is the freezing point of water

Temperature is a factor in dealing with chemical compounds. Two temperature scales are used to measure temperatures: the **Celsius** system and the **Fahrenheit** system. Both were developed almost 300 years ago.

Understanding Temperature Measurement Systems

Daniel Fahrenheit, a German physicist, invented an alcohol thermometer in 1709, a mercury thermometer in 1714, and a temperature scale in 1724. This temperature scale was based on ice water and salt as a low point (0 °F) and the human body temperature as the high point (100 °F). Fahrenheit used his own body temperature as the standard, but in the years that followed, scientists learned that body temperature varied. Therefore, the Fahrenheit scale was keyed to water for both the low point and the high point. The freezing point of water at sea level was set at 32 °F, and the boiling point of water at sea level was set at 212 °F.

About 1742 Anders Celsius, a Swedish astronomer, developed what became the Celsius or centigrade thermometer. In Celsius measurement, water freezes at 0 °C and boils at 100 °C.

Converting Celsius and Fahrenheit Temperatures

Both measurement systems are in common use today. Pharmacy personnel must know the two systems and be able to convert back and forth between them. The formulas for converting from one temperature measuring system to another are based on the fact that each Celsius degree equals 1.8 or $\frac{9}{5}$ of each Fahrenheit degree. The conversion formulas are as follows.

degrees Celsius to degrees Fahrenheit:

$$°F = \left(\frac{9 \times °C}{5} \right) + 32°$$

or

$$°F = (1.8 \times °C) + 32$$

degrees Fahrenheit to degrees Celsius:

$$°C = (°F - 32) \times \frac{5}{9}$$

or

$$°C = \frac{°F - 32°}{1.8}$$

Pharmacy technicians may be asked to help patients convert between temperature readings in degrees Celsius and Fahrenheit. As with all conversions, this calculation must be done accurately.

Example 5.3.1   Convert 40 °C to its equivalent in the Fahrenheit scale.

Solution 1:

$$°F = \left(\frac{9 \times °C}{5}\right) + 32°$$

$$= \left(\frac{9 \times 40°}{5}\right) + 32°$$

$$= \frac{360°}{5} + 32°$$

$$= 72° + 32°$$

$$= 104°$$

Solution 2:

$$°F = (1.8 \times °C) + 32°$$

$$= (1.8 \times 40°) + 32°$$

$$= 72° + 32°$$

$$= 104°$$

Example 5.3.2   Convert 82 °F to its equivalent in the Celsius scale.

Solution 1:

$$°C = (°F - 32°) \times \frac{5}{9}$$

$$= (82° - 32°) \times \frac{5}{9}$$

$$= 50° \times \frac{5}{9}$$

$$= 27.777°, \text{ rounded to } 27.8°$$

Solution 2:

$$°C = \frac{(°F - 32°)}{1.8}$$

$$= \frac{(82° - 32°)}{1.8}$$

$$= \frac{50°}{1.8}$$

$$= 27.777°, \text{ rounded to } 27.8°$$

Completing a Temperature Chart

Often medication comes with specific instructions regarding refrigeration. To store medication under "refrigerated" conditions means to store it between 2 °C and 5 °C (35.6 °F and 41 °F). It is very important that temperatures of refrigerators for storing medications be monitored daily.

Most pharmacies have specific charts for recording temperatures of refrigerators and freezers used for storage. See Figure 5.4 and Figure 5.5 for examples of these charts.

FIGURE 5.4
Refrigerator Temperature Chart (Celsius)

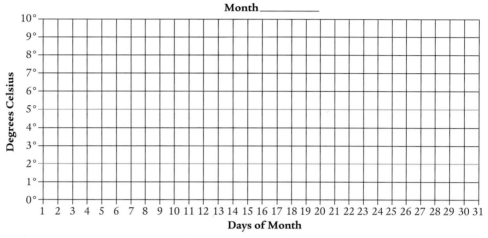

Graph refrigerator temperature on chart once daily. If temperature is less than **2 degrees** or greater than **5 degrees,** check the thermostat setting and correct as necessary. Recheck temperature in one hour, and if temperature is out of stated range, contact maintenance for evaluation and repair. Contact the appropriate area for storage of supplies.

Documentation of Repairs: _____

Documentation of Cleaning: _____

FIGURE 5.5
Refrigerator Temperature Chart (Fahrenheit)

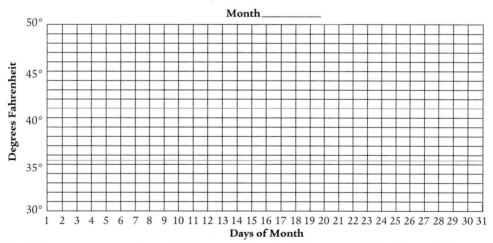

Graph refrigerator temperature on chart once daily. If temperature is less than **35.6 degrees** or greater than **41 degrees,** check the thermostat setting and correct as necessary. Recheck temperature in one hour, and if temperature is out of stated range, contact maintenance for evaluation and repair. Contact the appropriate area for storage of supplies.

Documentation of Repairs: _____

Documentation of Cleaning: _____

5.3 Problem Set

Convert the following Fahrenheit temperatures to Celsius.

1. 0 °F

2. 23 °F

3. 36 °F

4. 40 °F

5. 64 °F

6. 72 °F

7. 98.6 °F

8. 100.5 °F

9. 102.8 °F

10. 105 °F

Convert the following Celsius temperatures to Fahrenheit.

11. −15 °C

12. 18 °C

13. 27 °C

14. 31 °C

15. 38 °C

16. 40 °C

17. 49 °C

18. 63 °C

19. 99.8 °C

20. 101.4 °C

Applications

21. When making a mixture, you are instructed to heat the mixture to 130 °C. You have only a Fahrenheit thermometer. What is the equivalent temperature on the Fahrenheit scale?

22. The following prescription is sent to the hospital pharmacy.

> ℞ **Alteplase in a Syringe**
>
> | alteplase, 2 mg/mL | 50 mg |
> |---|---|
> | sterile water for injection | 25 mL |
>
> 1. Reconstitute the alteplase with SWFI.
> 2. Draw up 5 mL in 10 mL syringes.
> 3. Label syringes with contents, concentration, and date of preparation.
> 4. Place syringes in freezer. They should be frozen with the premix piggybacks.
>
> The syringes are stable for six months, or 180 days, −20° C.

a. What is the Fahrenheit temperature at which you should store this product?

b. What expiration date should you put on this compound if today is February 1, 2007?

23. A prescription is sent to the hospital pharmacy requesting a substance to be heated in a 300 °F oven for 12–18 hours. At what Celsius temperature does the oven need to be set?

24. Convert the following refrigerator temperatures and log them on the Celsius chart. Note any temperatures out of the safe range.

Date	Degrees F	Degrees C
5/5	36.1°	a. _____
5/6	37.7°	b. _____
5/7	39.0°	c. _____
5/8	35.7°	d. _____
5/9	36.9°	e. _____
5/10	34.9°	f. _____
5/11	36.4°	g. _____
5/12	36.8°	h. _____
5/13	35.5°	i. _____
5/14	38.8°	j. _____

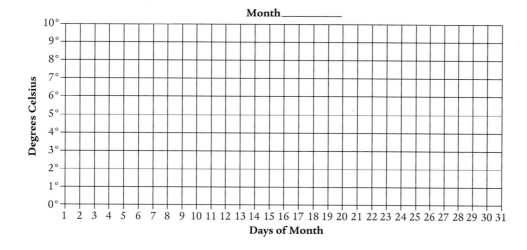

25. Convert the following refrigerator temperatures and log them on the Fahrenheit chart. Note any temperatures out of the safe range.

Date	Degrees C	Degrees F
7/12	1.8°	a. _____
7/13	3.1°	b. _____
7/14	2.8°	c. _____
7/15	3.0°	d. _____
7/16	4.5°	e. _____
7/17	3.2°	f. _____
7/18	3.9°	g. _____
7/19	2.5°	h. _____
7/20	4.1°	i. _____
7/21	4.7°	j. _____

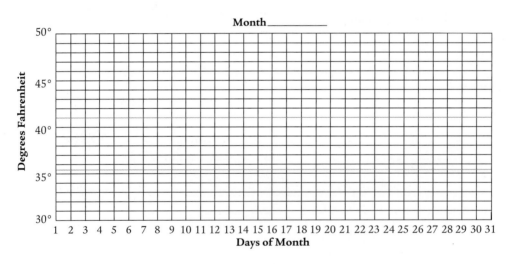

Month_____

Degrees Fahrenheit

Days of Month

Self-check your work in Appendix A.

Convert the given volumes within the household measure system.

1. 3 tsp = _____ fl oz

2. 8 fl oz = _____ tsp

Convert the given volumes between the household measure and metric systems.

3. 8 mL = _____ tsp

4. 8 fl oz = _____ mL

Answer the following questions.

5. How many kilograms does a patient weighing 192 lb weigh?

6. How many 5 mL doses are in a 5 fl oz bottle of antibiotic preparation?

7. How many 3 tsp doses are in 500 mL?

Determine the dose of acetaminophen for each of the following children using the dose table provided.

Acetaminophen			
Age	Dose (mg)	Age	Dose (mg)
0–3 mo	40	6–8 yr	320
4–11 mo	80	9–10 yr	400
1–<2 yr	120	11 yr	480
2–3 yr	160	12–14 yr	640
4–5 yr	240	>14 yr	650

8. 22 lb, 11 months

9. 21 lb, 15 months

Calculate the following using either the dimensional analysis or the ratio-proportion method.

10. Using the following label, how many grams of amoxicillin are in the bottle?

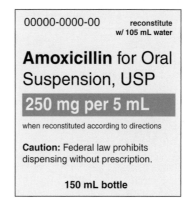

11. Using the following label, how many milligrams of Trileptal are in 1 tbsp?

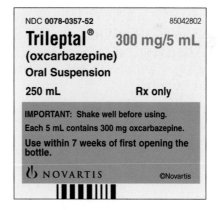

12. Using the following label, how many milligrams of furosemide are contained in 3 mL?

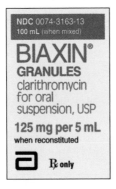

13. Using the following label, how many milligrams of Biaxin are contained in 3 tsp?

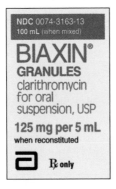

14. Using the drug shown for question 13, if a patient is taking 3 tsp every 12 hours, how many days will the bottle of Biaxin last?

15. How many prednisone 10 mg tablets are needed to fill the following prescription?

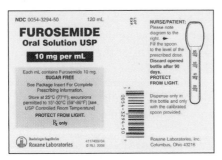

Rx   **Prednisone 10 mg**

Take 80 mg × 2 days

Take 70 mg × 1 day

Take 60 mg × 2 days

Take 50 mg × 1 day

Take 40 mg × 2 days

Take 30 mg × 1 day

Take 20 mg × 2 days

Take 10 mg × 1 day

Take 5 mg × 2 days

Use the label to answer the following questions.

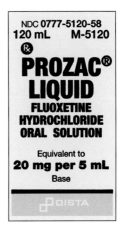

16. How many milligrams are in ½ tsp?

17. How many milligrams are in ¾ tsp?

18. How many milliliters are needed to provide 40 mg?

19. How many milliliters are needed to provide 5 mg?

20. Convert the following temperatures and log them on the Celsius chart.

Date	Degrees F	Degrees C
6/21	43°	a. _____
6/22	40°	b. _____
6/23	41°	c. _____
6/24	38°	d. _____
6/25	39°	e. _____
6/26	40.5°	f. _____
6/27	37°	g. _____

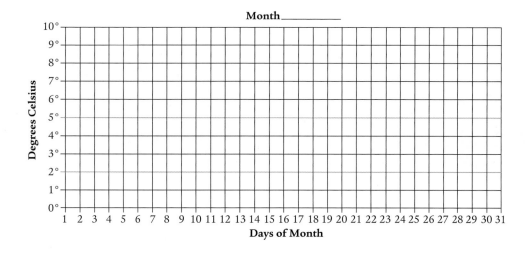

Month_____

Days of Month

Preparing Injectable Medications

6

Learning Objectives

- Calculate the volume to be measured when given a specific dose.
- Calculate the amount of drug in a given volume.
- Identify drugs that use units as a dose designation.
- Calculate the volume of a substance that has an electrolyte as its primary ingredient.
- Calculate the quantity of units in a given concentration and dose.
- Calculate the volume of insulin to be administered.

Preview chapter terms and definitions.

6.1 Intramuscular and Subcutaneous Injections

injection
a method of administering medications in which a syringe with a needle or cannula is used to penetrate through the skin or membrane into the tissue below

infusion
the administration of a large volume of liquid medication given parenterally over a long period

parenteral
administered by injection and not by way of the gastrointestinal system

subcutaneous injection
an injection given into the vascular, fatty layer of tissue under the skin

intramuscular injection
an injection given into the aqueous muscle tissue

intravenous infusion
the injection of fluid into the veins

An **injection** is a method of administering medications in which a syringe with a needle or cannula is used to penetrate through the skin or membrane into the tissue below. An **infusion** is a type of injection in which a large volume of fluid is administered over a long period through a needle or catheter, usually into a vein. Medications given as injections are considered **parenteral,** which literally means occurring outside the intestines. In other words, the medications do not pass through the gastrointestinal system. There are three types of injections: subcutaneous (SC) injections, intramuscular (IM) injections, and intravenous (IV) infusions. All three types of injections are given by healthcare professionals on a regular basis. A **subcutaneous injection** is given into the vascular, fatty layer of tissue under the layers of skin. Most medications given by this route are quickly absorbed. Patients can self-administer medications such as insulin by this route. An **intramuscular injection** is given into the aqueous muscle tissue. Water-soluble medications are absorbed rapidly when given intramuscularly, whereas oil-based medications are absorbed slowly. With proper training, patients can self-administer medications by IM injection, but this route requires more skill and coordination than the subcutaneous route and is often more painful as well. An **intravenous infusion** is given into a vein. This route is used when a large amount of fluid must be administered to a patient. Most IV infusions are administered to inpatients, although the trend of home and office administration of IVs is on the rise.

Medications given by injection are often ordered by milligram, and the pharmacy or nursing staff must select and prepare an appropriate concentration of medication from available stock. The amount of medication is calculated using the same methods used to calculate liquid oral solutions.

When calculating the dose, an estimate should be made so that a syringe with a barrel of the most appropriate size can be selected. Selection of the appropriate syringe largely depends on the variety of syringes available. In most institutional pharmacies, syringes with barrel sizes that will hold a total volume of 1 mL, 3 mL, 5 mL, 10 mL, 20 mL, and 50 mL are available. The syringes are marked to indicate volume using tenths or twentieths of a milliliter. Become familiar with these demarcations before using any syringe to measure a volume.

Ideally, the syringe chosen is one that will provide the most accurate measurement of the needed volume. Typically, the smaller the syringe, the more accurate its measure. With this in mind, the total volume to be prepared should generally fill at least half of the syringe barrel. For example, when measuring 2.8 mL of medication, the selection of the 3 mL or 5 mL syringe would be appropriate, because the 2.8 mL would fill half or more of either syringe. If the 10 mL syringe were chosen for dispensing 2.8 mL, the volume of fluid measured might not be measured as accurately as it would be in the smaller syringes.

Calculating the Volume of an Injectable Solution

The volume of medication to be administered is calculated by both the pharmacy staff and the nursing staff who will administer the medications. Some facilities prepare syringes ahead of time for the nursing staff, but others provide the vial and syringe for the nursing staff to draw up just prior to administration. The following examples will demonstrate how to calculate the volume using the ratio-proportion and dimensional analysis methods. When a small volume (less than 20 mL) is to be administered, it is rounded off to the nearest hundredth, because the measuring devices can measure to this degree of accuracy. Larger volumes are rounded to the tenth or whole milliliter.

Example 6.1.1

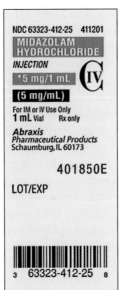

How many milliliters of the medication shown in the label below must be prepared to provide 12.5 mg to a patient?

Solution 1: Using the ratio-proportion method,

$$\frac{x \text{ mL}}{12.5 \text{ mg}} = \frac{1 \text{ mL}}{5 \text{ mg}}$$

$$x \text{ mL} = (12.5 \text{ mg}) \times \frac{1 \text{ mL}}{5 \text{ mg}} = 2.5 \text{ mL}$$

Solution 2: Using the dimensional analysis method,

$$12.5 \text{ mg} \times \frac{1 \text{ mL}}{5 \text{ mg}} = 2.5 \text{ mL}$$

Example 6.1.2

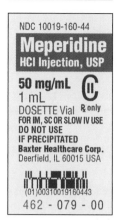

How many milliliters of the medication shown in the label to the left must be prepared to provide 25 mg of meperidine to a patient?

Solution 1: Using the ratio-proportion method,

$$\frac{x \text{ mL}}{25 \text{ mg}} = \frac{1 \text{ mL}}{50 \text{ mg}}$$

$$x \text{ mL} = \frac{(25 \text{ mg}) \times 1 \text{ mL}}{50 \text{ mg}} = 0.5 \text{ mL}$$

Solution 2: Using the dimensional analysis method,

$$25 \text{ mg} \times \frac{1 \text{ mL}}{50 \text{ mg}} = 0.5 \text{ mL}$$

Example 6.1.3

How many milliliters of medication shown in the following label must be prepared to provide 10 mg adenosine?

Solution 1: Using the ratio-proportion method,

$$\frac{x \text{ mL}}{10 \text{ mg}} = \frac{4 \text{ mL}}{12 \text{ mg}}$$

$$x \text{ mL} = \frac{(10 \text{ mg}) \times 4 \text{ mL}}{12 \text{ mg}} = 3.333 \text{ mL, rounded to 3.3 mL}$$

Solution 2: Using the dimensional analysis method,

$$10 \text{ mg} \times \frac{4 \text{ mL}}{12 \text{ mg}} = 3.333 \text{ mL, rounded to 3.3 mL}$$

Calculating the Quantity of Drug in an Injectable Solution

The ratio-proportion and dimensional analysis methods can also be used to determine the amount of drug in an injectable solution. The following examples will demonstrate these calculations.

Example 6.1.4　　How many milligrams of morphine are in 2 mL of the solution shown in the label below?

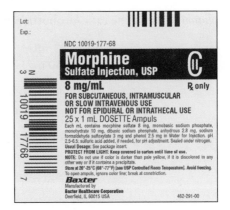

Solution 1: Using the ratio-proportion method,

$$\frac{x \text{ mg}}{2 \text{ mL}} = \frac{8 \text{ mg}}{1 \text{ mL}}$$

$$x \text{ mg} = \frac{(2 \text{ mL}) \times 8 \text{ mg}}{1 \text{ mL}} = 16 \text{ mg}$$

Solution 2: Using the dimensional analysis method,

$$2 \text{ mL} \times \frac{8 \text{ mg}}{1 \text{ mL}} = 16 \text{ mg}$$

Example 6.1.5　　How many milligrams of carboplatin are in 30 mL of the solution shown in the label below?

Solution 1: Using the ratio-proportion method,

$$\frac{x \text{ mg}}{30 \text{ mL}} = \frac{450 \text{ mg}}{45 \text{ mL}}$$

$$x \text{ mg} = \frac{(30 \text{ mL}) \times 450 \text{ mg}}{45 \text{ mL}} = 300 \text{ mg}$$

Solution 2: Using the dimensional analysis method,

$$30 \text{ mL} \times \frac{450 \text{ mg}}{45 \text{ mL}} = 300 \text{ mg}$$

Example 6.1.6

NDC 63323-280-02   28002
FUROSEMIDE
INJECTION, USP
20 mg/2 mL
(10 mg/mL)
For IM or IV Use   Rx only
2 mL Single Dose Vial
Preservative Free
Discard unused portion.
PROTECT FROM LIGHT.
Do not use if discolored.
Abraxis
Pharmaceutical Products
Schaumburg, IL 60173

401803C

LOT/EXP

3   63323-280-02   4

How many milligrams of furosemide are in 6 mL of the solution shown in the label to the left?

Solution 1: Using the ratio-proportion method,

$$\frac{x \text{ mg}}{6 \text{ mL}} = \frac{20 \text{ mg}}{2 \text{ mL}}$$

$$x \text{ mg} = \frac{(6 \text{ mL}) \times 20 \text{ mg}}{2 \text{ mL}} = 60 \text{ mg}$$

Solution 2: Using the dimensional analysis method,

$$6 \text{ mL} \times \frac{20 \text{ mg}}{2 \text{ mL}} = 60 \text{ mg}$$

Calculating Ratio Strength

ratio strength
a means of describing the concentration of a liquid medication based on a ratio such as *a* grams:*b* milliliters

The **ratio strength** *a*:*b* (read as "*a* to *b*") means there are *a* parts of a pure drug in *b* parts of a liquid solution. The units indicated in a ratio strength are *a* grams:*b* milliliters. This is the same unit rule that is used to indicate the percent strength of medications. For example, a 1% solution could be written as 1:100, and the units would be 1 g:100 mL.

Example 6.1.7

How many grams of a drug are present in 500 mL of a 1:200 solution?

Solution 1: Using the ratio-proportion method,

$$\frac{x \text{ g}}{500 \text{ mL}} = \frac{1 \text{ g}}{200 \text{ mL}}$$

$$x \text{ g} = \frac{(500 \text{ mL}) \times 1 \text{ g}}{200 \text{ mL}} = 2.5 \text{ g}$$

Solution 2: Using the dimensional analysis method,

$$500 \text{ mL} \times \frac{1 \text{ g}}{200 \text{ mL}} = 2.5 \text{ g}$$

Example 6.1.8

How many grams of pure drug are in 500 mL of a 1:3000 solution?

Solution 1: Using the ratio-proportion method,

$$\frac{x \text{ g}}{500 \text{ mL}} = \frac{1 \text{ g}}{3000 \text{ mL}}$$

$$x \text{ g} = \frac{(500 \text{ mL}) \times 1 \text{ g}}{3000 \text{ mL}} = 0.1666 \text{ g, rounded to } 0.17 \text{ g}$$

Solution 2: Using the dimensional analysis method,

$$500 \text{ mL} \times \frac{1 \text{ g}}{3000 \text{ mL}} = 0.1666 \text{ g, rounded to } 0.17 \text{ g}$$

Example 6.1.9

How many milligrams of pure drug are in 1.5 mL of a 1:1000 solution of epinephrine?

Solution 1: Using the ratio-proportion method,

$$\frac{x \text{ g}}{1.5 \text{ mL}} = \frac{1 \text{ g}}{1000 \text{ mL}}$$

$$x \text{ g} = \frac{(1.5 \text{ mL}) \times 1 \text{ g}}{1000 \text{ mL}} = 0.0015 \text{ g} = 1.5 \text{ mg}$$

Solution 2: Using the dimensional analysis method,

$$1.5 \text{ mL} \times \frac{1 \text{ g}}{1000 \text{ mL}} = 0.0015 \text{ g} = 1.5 \text{ mg}$$

Example 6.1.10

How many milliliters are needed to provide 20 mg of a drug if the solution available is 1:500?

Begin by converting 20 mg to 0.02 g.

Solution 1: Using the ratio-proportion method,

$$\frac{x \text{ mL}}{0.02 \text{ g}} = \frac{500 \text{ mL}}{1 \text{ g}}$$

$$x \text{ mL} = \frac{(0.02 \text{ g}) \times 500 \text{ mL}}{1 \text{ g}} = 10 \text{ mL}$$

Solution 2: Using the dimensional analysis method,

$$0.02 \text{ g} \times \frac{500 \text{ mL}}{1 \text{ g}} = 10 \text{ mL}$$

6.1 Problem Set

Determine the volume to be prepared for each ordered injectable solution using the labels provided. (Round to the hundredth place.)

1. How many milliliters of solution are needed to provide 50 mg of lidocaine?

2. How many milliliters of solution are needed to provide 350 mg of acyclovir?

3. How many milliliters of solution are needed to provide 80 mg of furosemide?

4. How many milliliters of solution are needed to provide 0.5 mcg of calcitriol?

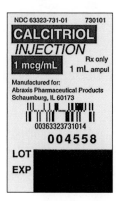

5. How many milliliters of solution are needed to provide 100 mg of diphenhydramine?

6. How many milliliters of solution are needed to provide 30 mg of famotidine?

7. How many milliliters of solution are needed to provide 40 mg of famotidine?

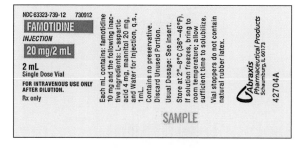

8. How many milliliters of solution are needed to provide 250 mg of ampicillin?

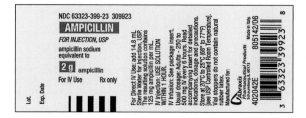

9. How many milliliters of solution are needed to provide 400 mg of azithromycin?

10. How many milliliters of solution are needed to provide 50 mg of cisplatin?

Calculate the quantity of drug in the injectable solution using the provided vial labels.

11. How many milligrams of ketorolac are contained in 0.5 mL?

12. How many milligrams of ketorolac are contained in 1.75 mL?

13. How many milligrams of lidocaine HCl are contained in 3.75 mL?

14. How many milligrams of midazolam HCl are contained in 1.3 mL?

15. How many milligrams of midazolam HCl are contained in 5 mL?

16. How many milligrams of midazolam HCl are contained in 5 mL?

17. How many milligrams of midazolam HCl are contained in 5 mL?

18. How many milligrams of dexamethasone are contained in 8 mL?

19. How many milligrams of ondansetron are contained in 1.5 mL?

20. How many milligrams are contained in 2.5 mL?

Calculate the amount of drug in a ratio solution.

21. How many milligrams are in 2 mL of a 1:1000 solution?

22. How many micrograms are in 1 mL of a 1:5000 solution?

23. How many micrograms are in 1.5 mL of a 1:10,000 solution?

24. How many micrograms are in 1.4 mL of a 1:2000 solution?

25. How many micrograms are in 2.5 mL of a 1:10,000 solution?

Calculate the volume of solution needed for each requested dose.

26. How many milliliters of 1:1000 solution are needed to provide a 500 mg dose?

27. How many milliliters of 1:10,000 solution are needed to provide a 50 mg dose?

28. How many milliliters of 1:300 solution are needed to provide a 600 mg dose?

29. How many milliliters of 1:500 solution are needed to provide a 250 mg dose?

30. How many milliliters of 1:750 solution are needed to provide a 0.01 g dose?

Self-check your work in Appendix A.

6.2 Other Units of Measure

electrolytes
substances such as mineral salts that carry an electrical charge when dissolved in a solution

atomic weight
the weight of a single atom of an element compared to the weight of a single atom of hydrogen

molecular weight
the sum of the atomic weights of all atoms in one molecule of a compound

millimole (mM)
molecular weight expressed in milligrams

milliequivalent (mEq)
the ratio of the weight of a molecule to its valence, used to measure the concentration of electrolytes in a volume of solution; also an amount of medication that will provide the patient with a specific amount (equivalent amount) of an electrolyte

valence
the ability of a molecule to bond, as indicated by its positive or negative charge; represented by a superscript plus or minus sign next to an element's chemical symbol

Although most medications are dosed using the units of the metric system, such as milligrams or grams, doses of some medications are calculated using other units of measure. Some of these substances are as simple as salts, but others are complicated proteins or hormones such as insulin. Other examples include penicillin V, whose unit is based on the number of bacteria affected, and heparin, whose unit is based on the amount of anticoagulant property present. Although these substances do have weights, they will be dosed based on their activity, and the weight will often be disregarded.

Calculating Milliequivalents

Many fluids in pharmacy contain dissolved mineral salts known as **electrolytes.** They are so named because they conduct a charge through the solution when connected to electrodes.

Most electrolyte solutions are measured by milliequivalents, which are related to molecular weight. Molecular weights are based on the atomic weight of common elements. The **atomic weight** of an element is the weight of a single atom of that element compared to the weight of a single atom of hydrogen. The **molecular weight** of a compound is the sum of the atomic weights of all atoms in one molecule of the compound. A **millimole (mM)** is the molecular weight expressed as milligrams.

A **milliequivalent (mEq)** is the ratio of the weight of a molecule to its **valence,** or the likely charge or ability to bond with an equally charged molecule.

$$mEq = \frac{\text{molecular weight}}{\text{valence}}$$

Valence is most familiar as the plus or minus sign next to chemical abbreviations or symbols such as Na^+, Cl^-, or Ca^{++}. The valence of substances used in pharmacy preparations is most commonly plus or minus 1, 2, or 3. Milliequivalents represent both the amount of active substance and the likelihood that the substance, once in the body, will cause a change in the way two compounds are bonded.

Electrolyte solutions and certain drugs, besides being measured by weight at the manufacturer, are also measured in millimoles and milliequivalents. These types of measure are particularly important when working with intravenous solutions. For example, you may be asked to add 28 mEq of sodium chloride to an IV bag. You would then need to calculate the amount of milliliters of sodium chloride solution to add to the IV bag, given an available solution of 4 mEq/mL.

Fortunately, medications commonly used today are standardized, and the calculations needed in the pharmacy will involve determining the volume of a substance that has an electrolyte as its primary ingredient.

Example 6.2.1

You are requested to add 44 mEq of sodium chloride (NaCl) to an IV bag. Sodium chloride is available as a 4 mEq/mL solution. How many milliliters will you add to the bag?

Solution 1: Using the ratio-proportion method,

$$\frac{x \text{ mL}}{44 \text{ mEq}} = \frac{1 \text{ mL}}{4 \text{ mEq}}$$

$$x \text{ mL} = \frac{(44 \text{ mEq}) \times 1 \text{ mL}}{4 \text{ mEq}} = 11 \text{ mL}$$

Solution 2: Using the dimensional analysis method,

$$44 \text{ mEq} \times \frac{1 \text{ mL}}{4 \text{ mEq}} = 11 \text{ mL}$$

Example 6.2.2

A patient needs to take a solution of potassium chloride to replace potassium lost due to diuresis. The available solution is shown in the label below. The physician has indicated that the patient needs 15 mEq. How many milliliters will be prepared for the patient?

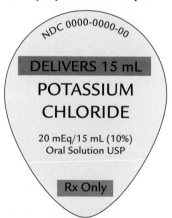

NDC 0000-0000-00

DELIVERS 15 mL

POTASSIUM CHLORIDE

20 mEq/15 mL (10%)
Oral Solution USP

Rx Only

Solution 1: Using the ratio-proportion method,

$$\frac{x \text{ mL}}{15 \text{ mEq}} = \frac{15 \text{ mL}}{20 \text{ mEq}}$$

$$x \text{ mL} = \frac{(15 \text{ mEq}) \times 15 \text{ mL}}{20 \text{ mEq}} = 11.25 \text{ mL, rounded to } 11 \text{ mL}$$

Solution 2: Using the dimensional analysis method,

$$15 \text{ mEq} \times \frac{15 \text{ mL}}{20 \text{ mEq}} = 11.25 \text{ mL, rounded to } 11 \text{ mL}$$

Example 6.2.3

You are instructed to add 20 mEq of potassium chloride to a patient's IV solution bag. Using the multiple dose vial label provided, how many milliliters should be drawn up?

Solution 1: Using the ratio-proportion method,

$$\frac{x \text{ mL}}{20 \text{ mEq}} = \frac{1 \text{ mL}}{2 \text{ mEq}}$$

$$x \text{ mL} = \frac{(20 \text{ mEq}) \times 1 \text{ mL}}{2 \text{ mEq}} = 10 \text{ mL}$$

Solution 2: Using the dimensional analysis method,

$$20 \text{ mEq} \times \frac{1 \text{ mL}}{2 \text{ mEq}} = 10 \text{ mL}$$

Example 6.2.4

You are instructed to add 16 mEq of potassium chloride to a patient's IV bag. Using the single dose vial labels, select the correct vial and then calculate how many milliliters you will prepare.

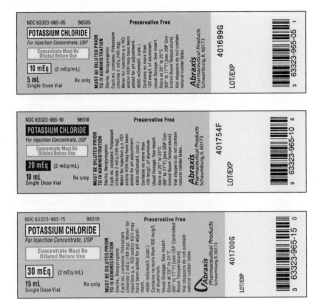

Part I. Analyze the total milliequivalents in each vial in order to choose the correct vial. In the labels shown, the manufacturer has highlighted the milliequivalents in each vial. Since your order calls for 16 mEq, you will select the potassium chloride vial labeled "20 mEq." The total volume is 10 mL.

Part II. Determine the number of milliliters needed to fill the order.

Solution 1: Using the ratio-proportion method,

$$\frac{x \text{ mL}}{16 \text{ mEq}} = \frac{10 \text{ mL}}{20 \text{ mEq}}$$

$$x \text{ mL} = \frac{(16 \text{ mEq}) \times 10 \text{ mL}}{20 \text{ mEq}} = 8 \text{ mL}$$

Solution 2: Using the dimensional analysis method,

$$16 \text{ mEq} \times \frac{10 \text{ mL}}{20 \text{ mEq}} = 8 \text{ mL}$$

Example 6.2.5

You have been instructed to add 15 mL of sodium chloride to a patient's IV bag for dilution. Using the label shown below, calculate how many milliequivalents of sodium chloride will be in 15 mL of solution.

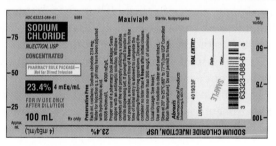

Solution 1: Using the ratio-proportion method,

$$\frac{x \text{ mEq}}{15 \text{ mL}} = \frac{4 \text{ mEq}}{1 \text{ mL}}$$

$$x \text{ mEq} = \frac{(15 \text{ mL}) \times 4 \text{ mEq}}{1 \text{ mL}} = 60 \text{ mEq}$$

Solution 2: Using the dimensional analysis method,

$$15 \text{ mL} \times \frac{4 \text{ mEq}}{1 \text{ mL}} = 60 \text{ mEq}$$

Example 6.2.6   You must add 9 mM of an inorganic phosphate to an IV solution. You have 15 mM/5 mL available. How many milliliters should you add?

Solution 1: Using the ratio-proportion method,

$$\frac{x \text{ mL}}{9 \text{ mM}} = \frac{5 \text{ mL}}{15 \text{ mM}}$$

$$x \text{ mL} = \frac{(9 \text{ mM}) \times 5 \text{ mL}}{15 \text{ mM}} = 3 \text{ mL}$$

Solution 2: Using the dimensional analysis method,

$$9 \text{ mM} \times \frac{5 \text{ mL}}{15 \text{ mM}} = 3 \text{ mL}$$

Calculating Units

unit
the amount of activity associated with a medication that has biological impact on a patient

A number of drugs, including insulin, heparin, corticotropin (ACTH), Factor VIII, penicillin, and some vitamins, are measured in units. A **unit** describes the amount of activity within a unique test system. Drugs that are derived mostly from biological products are expressed in international units, or United States Pharmacopeia (USP) units. Both of these types of units are expressed as "units."

Each drug has a unique biological assay to define its unit of activity. For example, insulin is dosed in units, and the units are based on the amount of glucose that a specific amount of insulin can make available to the cells in a living human being. The degree of activity in this case refers to the insulin's activity. When insulin is prescribed and administered, the dose is based on how much assistance the patient's body will need. Different types and brands of insulin have different weights, but all insulins use a common "unit" of activity. Thus, the weight can be disregarded, and the unit becomes a universal dose for insulin. Insulin syringes are prepared universally and marked according to these standard units. Manufacturers maintain the same concentration of insulin from brand to brand so that the standard insulin syringe will measure out a uniform unit of insulin with a known activity level in the body.

Insulin doses are always calculated in units. Although it is important to know the approximate volume in milliliters, the preparation will most likely involve the use of syringes that are specially marked with units instead of milliliters. Insulin is concentrated

FIGURE 6.1
Standard Insulin Syringe Sizes

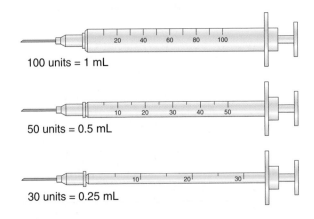

100 units = 1 mL

50 units = 0.5 mL

30 units = 0.25 mL

as "U-100" insulin, which means that there are 100 units in 1 mL (or 100 units/mL). Insulin syringes are available in standard unit sizes as illustrated in Figure 6.1.

Example 6.2.7

A patient is to receive a bolus (concentrated) dose of heparin. If the dose is 7500 units and you have a vial with the label shown below, how many milliliters will you prepare?

Solution 1: Using the ratio-proportion method,

$$\frac{x \text{ mL}}{7500 \text{ units}} = \frac{1 \text{ mL}}{5000 \text{ units}}$$

$$x \text{ mL} = \frac{(7500 \text{ units}) \times 1 \text{ mL}}{5000 \text{ units}} = 1.5 \text{ mL}$$

Solution 2: Using the dimensional analysis method,

$$7500 \text{ units} \times \frac{1 \text{ mL}}{5000 \text{ units}} = 1.5 \text{ mL}$$

Example 6.2.8

A patient is to receive 1000 units/kg of the bacitracin IM indicated on the label below. The patient weighs 15 kg. How many milliliters of bacitracin are needed?

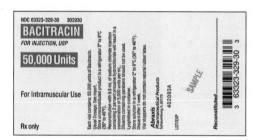

Begin by determining the number of units in a dose, based on the patient's weight of 15 kg.

$$15 \text{ kg} \times \frac{1000 \text{ units}}{1 \text{ kg}} = 15,000 \text{ units}$$

Then, calculate the amount of milliliters needed, using either the ratio-proportion method or the dimensional analysis method.

Solution 1: Using the ratio-proportion method,

$$\frac{x \text{ mL}}{15{,}000 \text{ units}} = \frac{10 \text{ mL}}{50{,}000 \text{ units}}$$

$$x \text{ mL} = \frac{(15{,}000 \text{ units}) \times 10 \text{ mL}}{50{,}000 \text{ units}} = 3 \text{ mL}$$

Solution 2: Using the dimensional analysis method,

$$15{,}000 \text{ units} \times \frac{10 \text{ mL}}{50{,}000 \text{ units}} = 3 \text{ mL}$$

As discussed earlier in this section, insulin is dosed with the concentration of 100 units/mL, and all insulin is dosed and calibrated to the standard U-100 or "unit." In spite of this consistency, many types of insulin products are available. Some insulin products require the patient to withdraw medication from a vial. Other insulin products come in a prefilled syringe or "pen" with a disposable needle on the tip. Only insulin syringes should be used to administer or dispense insulin.

Reading insulin labels can be challenging because labels may have only slight differentiations from one product to another. When preparing an insulin dose or prescription, triple-check the medication's label against the printed label and the ordered medication. Confirm that the NDC numbers match. If the pharmacy is equipped with a bar code scanner, such a device will be helpful in confirming that the correct medication is being used.

The following examples demonstrate the calculation of a volume of insulin in milliliters (vs. standard units). Calculating the volume of insulin in milliliters is helpful when determining how long a vial or pen of insulin will last a patient.

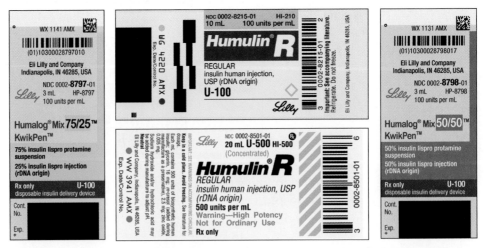

Although it is true for all drug labels, it is especially important to read insulin labels carefully.

Example 6.2.9

A patient is to receive 32 units of regular insulin each morning before breakfast. Insulin comes in a 100 units/mL concentration. How many milliliters will the patient receive with each dose? How many days will the vial last?

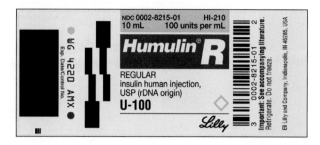

Part I. Calculate the volume the patient will receive with each dose by using either the ratio-proportion method or the dimensional analysis method.

Solution 1: Using the ratio-proportion method,

$$\frac{x \text{ mL}}{32 \text{ units}} = \frac{1 \text{ mL}}{100 \text{ units}}$$

$$x \text{ mL} = \frac{(32 \text{ units}) \times 1 \text{ mL}}{100 \text{ units}} = 0.32 \text{ mL}$$

Solution 2: Using the dimensional analysis method,

$$32 \text{ units} \times \frac{1 \text{ mL}}{100 \text{ units}} = 0.32 \text{ mL}$$

Part II. Using the volume per dose just calculated, determine the number of days a single vial will last. In this example, the patient takes a single dose a day.

Solution 1: Using the ratio-proportion method,

$$\frac{x \text{ days}}{10 \text{ mL}} = \frac{1 \text{ day}}{0.32 \text{ mL}}$$

$$x \text{ mL} = \frac{(10 \text{ mL}) \times 1 \text{ day}}{0.32 \text{ mL}} = 31.25 \text{ days, or } 31 \text{ days}$$

Solution 2: Using the dimensional analysis method,

$$10 \text{ mL} \times \frac{1 \text{ day}}{0.32 \text{ mL}} = 31.25 \text{ days, or } 31 \text{ days}$$

Example 6.2.10   A patient is to receive 49 units of Humulin 70/30 insulin. Insulin comes in a 100 units/mL concentration. How many milliliters will the patient receive in each dose? How many vials will the patient need to last 30 days (1 month)?

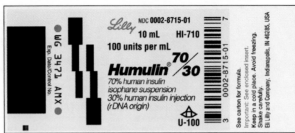

Part I.   Calculate the volume the patient will receive with each dose by using either the ratio-proportion method or the dimensional analysis method.

Solution 1: Using the ratio-proportion method,

$$\frac{x \text{ mL}}{49 \text{ units}} = \frac{1 \text{ mL}}{100 \text{ units}}$$

$$x \text{ mL} = \frac{(49 \text{ units}) \times 1 \text{ mL}}{100 \text{ units}} = 0.49 \text{ mL}$$

Solution 2: Using the dimensional analysis method,

$$49 \text{ units} \times \frac{1 \text{ mL}}{100 \text{ units}} = 0.49 \text{ mL}$$

Part II.   Using the volume per dose just calculated, determine the number of milliliters needed for 30 days.

Solution 1: Using the ratio-proportion method,

$$\frac{x \text{ mL}}{30 \text{ days}} = \frac{0.49 \text{ mL}}{1 \text{ day}}$$

$$x \text{ mL} = \frac{(30 \text{ days}) \times 0.49 \text{ mL}}{1 \text{ day}} = 14.7 \text{ mL}$$

Solution 2: Using the dimensional analysis method,

$$30 \text{ days} \times \frac{0.49 \text{ mL}}{1 \text{ day}} = 14.7 \text{ mL}$$

Since 1 vial = 10 mL, 2 vials will be needed to last 30 days.

Example 6.2.11   Humalog 75/25 KwikPen is useful for patients with busy life styles or those "trying out" a new formula of insulin. How many units are in the KwikPen with the following label? If a patient uses 23 units daily, how many days will this KwikPen last this patient?

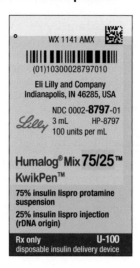

Part I.   Calculate the total number of units in a single pen.

Solution 1: Using the ratio-proportion method,

$$\frac{x \text{ units}}{3 \text{ mL}} = \frac{100 \text{ units}}{1 \text{ mL}}$$

$$x \text{ units} = \frac{(3 \text{ mL}) \times 100 \text{ units}}{1 \text{ mL}} = 300 \text{ units}$$

Solution 2: Using the dimensional analysis method,

$$3 \text{ mL} \times \frac{100 \text{ units}}{1 \text{ mL}} = 300 \text{ units}$$

Part II.   Calculate the number of days a single pen will last using the patient's daily units. Again, you can use either the ratio-proportion method or the dimensional analysis method.

Solution 1: Using the ratio-proportion method,

$$\frac{x \text{ days}}{300 \text{ units}} = \frac{1 \text{ day}}{23 \text{ units}}$$

$$x \text{ days} = \frac{(300 \text{ units}) \times 1 \text{ day}}{23 \text{ units}} = 13.04 \text{ days, or 13 days}$$

Solution 2: Using the dimensional analysis method,

$$300 \text{ units} \times \frac{1 \text{ day}}{23 \text{ units}} = 13.04 \text{ days, or 13 days}$$

6.2 Problem Set

Perform the necessary calculations to answer each of the following. (Round to the hundredth place.)

1. An order requires 30 mEq of potassium phosphate. You have a 4.4 mEq/mL solution available. How many milliliters should you put in the IV bag?

2. An order requires 45 mEq of potassium phosphate. You have 4.4 mEq/mL available. How many milliliters should be put in the IV solution?

3. A prescription states that a patient must take 32 mEq of potassium. The potassium replacement selected has 8 mEq per tablet. How many tablets should the patient need to take?

4. A patient is to use a sugar- and alcohol-free solution of potassium that contains 40 mEq/15 mL. He is to take 30 mEq daily in two equally divided doses. How many milliliters will each dose be?

5. A prescription has been filled for 15 mL Rum-K with breakfast. Rum-K contains 20 mEq/10 mL. How many milliequivalents is the patient taking with each dose?

6. A patient needs to take 30 mEq of potassium orally. The solution on hand has 20 mEq/15 mL. How much should be prepared for the patient?

For questions 7–10, select the vial that is needed to fill each order with the required number of milliequivalents of potassium chloride, and then calculate the volume to be withdrawn from the selected vial for the order.

7. Add 14 mEq potassium chloride to the patient's IV solution.

8. Add 19 mEq potassium chloride to the patient's IV solution.

9. Add 27 mEq potassium chloride to the patient's IV solution.

10. Add 50 mEq potassium chloride to the patient's IV solution.

For each of the following questions, use the label provided to calculate the volume or amount requested.

11. How many milliequivalents of potassium chloride are in 8 mL of the solution?

12. How many milliequivalents of potassium chloride are in 15 mL of the solution?

Use the following label to answer questions 13 and 14.

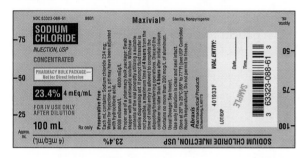

13. The following order is received by the pharmacy. Using a vial with the label shown above, how many milliliters should you add to the bag?

℞ Give 132 mEq of sodium chloride in 100 mL

Infuse at 62 mL/hour

14. An order is received indicating that you should add 120 mEq sodium chloride to an IV bag of D_5W. Using a vial with the label shown above, how many milliliters should you add to the bag?

Use the following label to answer questions 15 and 16.

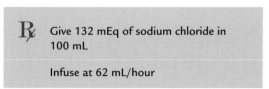

15. A patient is to receive 4 units of oxytocin. Using the vial with the label shown above, how many milliliters will be needed?

16. A patient has received 2.8 mL of the oxytocin solution shown in the label above. How many units is this?

17. A patient is to receive 3500 units heparin, and the following label shows the drug you are to dispense. How many milliliters is this?

18. A patient needs an injection of heparin. An order for 0.43 mL has been prepared. How many units of heparin are in the dose if it contains 20,000 units/0.8 mL?

19. Prepare 24,000 units of heparin from the vial with the label shown below. How many milliliters is this?

20. Prepare 24,000 units of heparin from the vial with the label shown below. How many milliliters is this?

21. Prepare two syringes for a patient on the orthopedic floor. Each syringe should contain 30 mg of Lovenox. How many milliliters will be in each syringe?

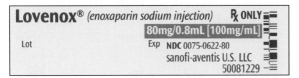

Calculate the following volumes or amount of units.

22. Pen VK (penicillin V–potassium) can be reconstituted to many different concentrations. You are filling an order for 175,000 units and have available a concentration that has already been concentrated to 500,000 units/mL. How many milliliters is the dose?

23. Bicillin CR is given as an intramuscular injection preparation. It comes as 600,000 units/mL, and the dose is 1.5 million units. What is the volume to be administered?

24. A physician has ordered 385,000 units of Pen VK (penicillin V–potassium) for a patient. Your stock preparation has 50,000 units/mL. How many milliliters should the dose be?

25. A patient is to receive Humulin 70/30 insulin at a dose of 45 units at 8:00 every morning. Using the vial with the following label, how many milliliters should be drawn into the syringe?

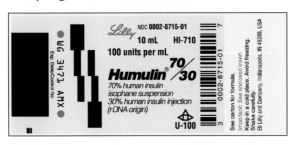

26. A patient uses 18 units of insulin each morning and 10 units at 7 p.m. How long will the vial shown in the following label last?

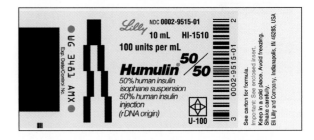

27. A patient uses 20 units of insulin in the morning and 18 units of insulin every evening.

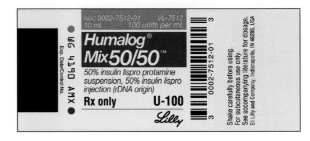

a. How many units total does the patient use daily?

b. How many vials (shown in the label) are needed for 30 days?

28. A patient uses 10 units of Humulin R each morning and 15 units of Humulin 70/30 at lunch and supper. Using the labels below, how many vials of each will the patient need for 30 days?

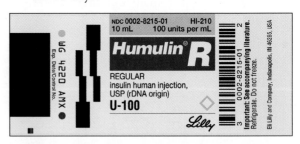

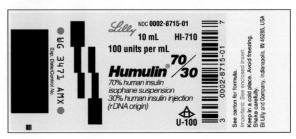

29. A patient uses 0.5 mL daily of Lantus shown in the following label. How many units is this?

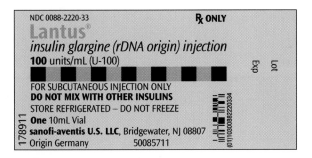

NDC 0088-2220-33   **℞ ONLY**

Lantus®
insulin glargine (rDNA origin) injection
100 units/mL (U-100)

FOR SUBCUTANEOUS INJECTION ONLY
DO NOT MIX WITH OTHER INSULINS
STORE REFRIGERATED – DO NOT FREEZE
One 10mL Vial
sanofi-aventis U.S. LLC, Bridgewater, NJ 08807
Origin Germany   50085711

178911

Lot   Exp

30. Using the label shown below, how long will two vials of Apidra last a patient who uses 20 units twice daily?

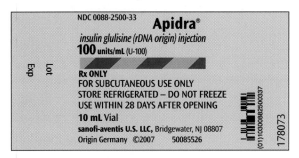

NDC 0088-2500-33   **Apidra®**
insulin glulisine (rDNA origin) injection
100 units/mL (U-100)

Rx ONLY
FOR SUBCUTANEOUS USE ONLY
STORE REFRIGERATED – DO NOT FREEZE
USE WITHIN 28 DAYS AFTER OPENING
10 mL Vial
sanofi-aventis U.S. LLC, Bridgewater, NJ 08807
Origin Germany   ©2007   50085526

Exp   Lot

178073

Self-check your work in Appendix A.

6.3 Solutions Using Powders

powder volume (pv)
the space occupied by dry pharmaceuticals, calculated as the difference between the final volume and the volume of the diluting ingredient, or the diluent volume; the amount of space occupied by lyophilized (freeze-dried) medication in a sterile vial, used for reconstitution

In preparing solutions, although the active ingredient is discussed in terms of weight, it also occupies a certain amount of space. With lyophilized (freeze-dried) pharmaceuticals in a sterile vial that are used for reconstitution, this space is referred to as **powder volume (pv).** It is equal to the difference between the final volume (fv) and the volume of the diluting ingredient, or the diluent volume, (dv), as expressed in the following equation:

$$\text{powder volume} = \text{final volume} - \text{diluent volume}$$

or

$$pv = fv - dv$$

Example 6.3.1

A dry powder antibiotic must be reconstituted for use. The label states that the dry powder occupies 0.5 mL. Using the formula for solving for powder volume, determine the diluent volume (the amount of solvent added). You are given the final volume for three different examples below with the same powder volume.

Final Volume	Powder Volume
(1) 2 mL	0.5 mL
(2) 5 mL	0.5 mL
(3) 10 mL	0.5 mL

$$dv = fv - pv$$
(1) $dv = 2 \text{ mL} - 0.5 \text{ mL} = 1.5 \text{ mL}$
(2) $dv = 5 \text{ mL} - 0.5 \text{ mL} = 4.5 \text{ mL}$
(3) $dv = 10 \text{ mL} - 0.5 \text{ mL} = 9.5 \text{ mL}$

Example 6.3.2

You are to reconstitute 1 g of dry powder. The label states that you are to add 9.3 mL of diluent to make a final solution of 100 mg/mL. What is the powder volume?

Begin by calculate the final volume. The strength of the final solution will be 100 mg/mL. Since you start with 1 g = 1000 mg of powder, for a final volume x of the solution, it will have strength 1000 mg/x mL.

Solution 1: Using the ratio-proportion method,

$$\frac{x \text{ mL}}{1000 \text{ mg}} = \frac{1 \text{ mL}}{100 \text{ mg}}$$

$$x \text{ mL} = \frac{(1000 \text{ mg}) \times 1 \text{ mL}}{100 \text{ mg}} = 10 \text{ mL}$$

Solution 2: Using the dimensional analysis method,

$$1000 \text{ mg} \times \frac{1 \text{ mL}}{100 \text{ mg}} = 10 \text{ mL}$$

Then, using the calculated final volume and the given diluent volume, calculate the powder volume.

$$pv = fv - dv$$

$$pv = 10 \text{ mL} - 9.3 \text{ mL} = 0.7 \text{ mL}$$

Example 6.3.3

A label states that a 5 g quantity of an antibiotic in a bottle should be reconstituted with 8.7 mL saline for injection. The resulting concentration will be 500 mg/mL. What is the powder volume contained in the vial?

First, convert 500 mg to grams.

$$500 \text{ mg} \times \frac{1 \text{ g}}{1000 \text{ mg}} = 0.5 \text{ g}$$

Second, determine the total number of milliliters that will contain the resultant concentration of 0.5 g/mL.

$$\frac{x \text{ mL}}{5 \text{ g}} = \frac{1 \text{ mL}}{0.5 \text{ g}}$$

$$x \text{ mL} = 10 \text{ mL}$$

Third, subtract the diluent volume from the total volume.

$$10 \text{ mL total volume} - 8.7 \text{ mL diluent} = 1.3 \text{ mL powder volume}$$

6.3 Problem Set

Solve the following.

1. You need to make an injectable solution with a final concentration of 375 mg/mL. On hand you have a vial that contains 1.5 g with the instructions to add 3.3 mL. What is the powder volume?

2. The pharmacy must add water to an oral suspension before it can be dispensed to the patient. The dose is to be 250 mg/tsp, and the dry powder is 5 g with a powder volume of 8.6 mL. How much water must you add?

3. An injectable preparation comes packaged as a 1 g vial, and you want a final concentration of 125 mg/2 mL. The vial states that you are to add 14.4 mL diluent. What is the powder volume?

4. The label of a 2 g vial states that you are to add 6.8 mL to get a concentration of 250 mg/mL. What is the powder volume?

5. In question 4, to make a final concentration of 125 mg/mL, how much diluent must you add?

6. The label of a 4 g vial states that you are to add 11.7 mL to get a concentration of 250 mg/mL. What is the powder volume?

7. The label of a 6 g vial says that if you add 12.5 mL of diluent to the vial's contents you will get a concentration of 1 g/2.5 mL. What concentration do you get if you add 2.5 mL?

8. You have added 3.3 mL of diluent to a 1 g vial and now have a final volume of 4 mL. What is the powder volume?

9. How many milliliters of the medication in question 8 do you need for a 100 mg dose?

10. If you add 8.8 mL of diluent to a 2 g vial and get a final concentration of 200 mg/mL, what is the powder volume?

11. A 10 g vial must have 45 mL of diluent added to it. It has a powder volume of 5 mL. How many milligrams will be in each milliliter of the final solution?

12. For an oral suspension, you add 170 mL of fluid and get a final volume of 200 mL. If it contains 8 g of medication, how many milligrams will be in 1 tsp?

13. A 20 g bulk vial label states that if you add 106 mL of diluent, the concentration will be 1 g/6 mL. How much diluent would you add to get a concentration of 1 g/3 mL?

14. You need a concentration of 375 mg/mL. Your vial contains 2 g with instructions to add 3.5 mL of diluent. What is the powder volume?

15. An oral medication requires reconstitution. The dose is 300 mg/tsp. The dry powder is 2.5 g with a volume of 9.6 mL. How much water do you add?

16. A 5 g vial requires that 8.6 mL diluent be added to get a concentration of 250 mg/mL. What is the powder volume?

17. A 10 g vial label says to add 20 mL of diluent to get 1 g per 2.5 mL. What concentration would you get if you added 35 mL?

18. You add 4.3 mL of diluent to a 1 g vial and have a final volume of 5 mL. What is the powder volume?

19. A 5 g vial requires 25 mL to be added. It has a powder volume of 5 mL. How many milligrams are in each milliliter of the final solution?

20. A 20 g vial must have 90 mL of diluent added. It has a powder volume of 10 mL. How many milligrams will be in each milliliter of the final solution?

21. A 3 g vial requires 20 mL of diluent to be added. It has a powder volume of 5 mL. How many milligrams are in each milliliter of the final solution?

22. A pediatric antibiotic requires 67 mL to be added to the bottle for reconstitution. The final volume will be 100 mL. What is the powder volume?

23. If the bottle in question 22 is reconstituted and there are 35 g of active ingredient in the bottle, what will the resulting strength be in milligrams per milliliters?

Solve the following compounding problems.

24. The pharmacy receives the following compound. What is the final concentration in milligrams per milliliters?

> ℞ **Vancomycin Ophthalmic Solution**
>
> 1. Remove and discard 9 mL of fluid from a commercial tears bottle (15 mL).
>
> 2. Add 10 mL SWFI to a vancomycin 500 mg vial. There will be a dry volume of 0.2 mL.
>
> 3. Place 10.2 mL of reconstituted vancomycin into "tears" bottle.

25. The pharmacy receives the following compound.

> **Cephalosporin Intravitreal Ophthalmic Antibiotic Preparation**
>
> 1. Reconstitute a 1 g vial with 4.4 mL of BSS.
>
> 2. Take 1 mL of this and add 9 mL of BSS.
>
> 3. Inject 0.1 mL intravitreally.

a. What concentration is the vial of cephalosporin when you reconstitute it in milligrams per milliliters?

b. What milligram dose is the patient receiving?

Self-check your work in Appendix A.

Determine the volume to prepared for each ordered injectable solution using the labels provided. (Round to the hundredth place.)

1. How many milliliters of solution are needed to provide 2 g of acyclovir?

2. How many milliliters of solution are needed to provide 60 mg of furosemide?

3. How many milliliters of solution are needed to provide 25 mg of diphenhydramine HCl?

4. How many milliliters of solution are needed to provide 10 mg of famotidine?

Calculate the quantity of drug in an injectable solution using the provided vial labels.

5. How many milligrams of ketorolac are contained in 1.4 mL?

6. How many milligrams of lidocaine HCl are contained in 3.1 mL?

7. How many milligrams of midazolam are contained in 0.8 mL?

8. How many milligrams of progesterone are contained in 1.8 mL?

Calculate the quantity of a drug using ratio strength.

9. How many grams are in 600 mL of a 1:200 solution of drug product?

10. How many milligrams are in 5 mL of a 1:5000 solution?

11. How many milligrams are in 0.5 mL of a 1:1000 solution?

12. How many micrograms are in 0.5 mL of a 1:1000 solution? Perform the necessary calculations to answer the following.

Perform the necessary calculations to determine the amount of medication needed to prepare the following orders.

13. Using the following order and the stock solutions of lidocaine and furosemide with the labels shown below, how many milliliters of each solution should be added to the IV bag?

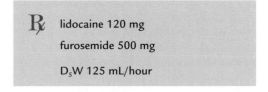

14. Using the following order and the stock solutions of potassium chloride with the label shown below, how many milliliters of potassium chloride will be added to the IV bag?

> ℞ potassium chloride 24 mEq
>
> NS at 100 mL/hour

15. Fill the order below given the following preparations. How much of each is needed?

> ℞ 40 g dextrose 5% (5 g/100 mL)
>
> 40 g dextrose 20% (20 g/100 mL)
>
> sodium chloride 24 mEq
>
> potassium chloride 10 mEq
>
> aminophylline 300 mg
>
> regular insulin 2 units

a. 40 g dextrose using dextrose 5% (5 g/100 mL)

b. 40 g dextrose using dextrose 20% (20 g/100 mL)

c. sodium chloride: 4 mEq/mL

d. potassium chloride: 2 mEq/mL

e. aminophylline: 25 mg/mL

f. insulin: 100 units/mL

16. Fill the given order with the stock solutions with the following labels. How much of each is needed?

> ℞ sodium chloride   18 mEq
>
> potassium chloride   30 mEq
>
> cefazolin   1 g
>
> diphenhydramine   100 mg

a. sodium chloride 4 mEq/mL

b. potassium chloride 40 mEq/20 mL

c. cefazolin 500 mg/mL

d. diphenydramine 50 mg/mL

Calculate the milliliters needed to provide the following quantities of drug. (Round to the nearest hundredth place.)

17. Pen VK (penicillin V–potassium) can be reconstituted to many different concentrations. You are filling an order for 230,000 units and have available a concentration that has already been reconstituted to 500,000 units/mL. How many milliliters is the dose?

18. Prepare 15,000 units of heparin from the vial with the label shown below. How many milliliters is this?

19. How many milliequivalents of sodium chloride are in 3.5 mL of the solution shown in the label below?

20. Prepare two syringes for a patient on the orthopedic floor. Each syringe should contain 35 mg of Lovenox. How many milliliters will be in each vial?

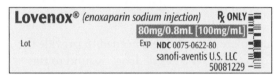

21. A patient is to receive 0.42 mL Lantus daily. Using the label below, how many units is this?

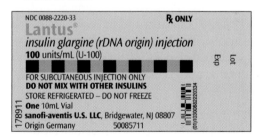

22. A patient uses 18 units of insulin twice daily. How long will the two vials shown in the following label last?

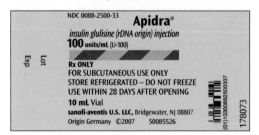

For questions 23 and 24, select the vial that is needed to fill each order with the required number of milliequivalents of potassium chloride, and then calculate the volume to be withdrawn from the selected vial for the order.

23. Add 16 mEq potassium chloride to the patient's IV solution.

24. Add 38 mEq potassium chloride to the patient's IV solution.

Solve the following problems involving powders that are reconstituted.

25. The label of a vial states that it contains 1 g in 10 mL. You know that 9.6 mL were added. What is the powder volume?

26. Your bottle of Amoxil (amoxicillin) says to add 39 mL to the bottle to get a solution of 150 mg/tsp. The total amount in the bottle is 2 g. What is the powder volume?

27. A 10 g vial label states that the concentration is 100 mg/mL if you add 87 mL. How much would you need to add to get a concentration of 50 mg/mL?

28. An oral suspension once reconstituted is to have a dose of 250 mg/tsp, and the dry powder is 4 g with a powder volume of 11.3 mL. How much water must you add?

29. A 30 g vial must have 76 mL added and has a powder volume of 12.6 mL. How many milligrams per milliliter will be in the final solution?

30. A 1 g vial requires 8.9 mL to be added to have a concentration of 100 mg/mL. What is the powder volume?

Preparing Intravenous Medications

7

Learning Objectives

- Describe percentage strength as weight in weight, weight in volume, and volume in volume.
- Calculate the amount of medication in a solution based on a given percentage strength.
- Calculate the percentage strength of medication in a given solution.
- Describe the types of IV sets by drops delivered.

- Calculate IV drop rates and flow rates using various sets.
- Estimate and calculate time for IV administration.
- Calculate rates of IV infusion and IV piggyback infusion.

STUDY PARTNER

Preview chapter terms and definitions.

7.1 Percentage and Ratio Strength

solution
a mixture of two or more substances

solute
the substance dissolved in the liquid solvent in a solution

solvent
the liquid that dissolves the solute in a solution

weight in weight (w/w)
the number of grams of a drug (solute) in 100 g of the final product (solution)

A **solution** is a mixture of two or more substances. Solutions may exist in any of the three states of matter: gas, liquid, or solid. Solutions can also exist in the following combinations of components:

two liquids (example: a mixed drink)
gas in a liquid (example: soda water)
solid in a liquid (example: salt water)
solid in a solid (example: fruit and gelatin in jelly)

In a solution, the substance dissolved in the liquid is called the **solute,** and the liquid is the **solvent.** If both substances are liquids, usually the component representing the greater amount is considered the solvent, and the component representing the smaller amount is the solute. The goal in preparing pharmaceutical solutions is to mix concentrations that result in accurately measured doses.

In general, in comparing two solutions containing the same components, the solution containing the smaller amount of solute is considered dilute. The solution containing the larger amount of solute is considered concentrated. As discussed in Chapter 6, the concentration of one substance dissolved in another substance may be expressed as either a percentage or a ratio strength.

How the concentration of the solute in the solvent is expressed as a percentage strength depends on which is a solid and/or which is a liquid. The concentrations can also be expressed as fractions, as shown in the following list.

$$\text{weight in weight (w/w)} = \text{number of grams of the drug in 100 g of the final product} = \frac{x \text{ g drug}}{100 \text{ g product}}$$

$$\text{weight in volume (w/v)} = \text{number of grams of the drug in 100 mL of the final product} = \frac{x \text{ g drug}}{100 \text{ mL product}}$$

$$\text{volume in volume (v/v)} = \text{number of milliliters of the drug in 100 mL of the final product} = \frac{x \text{ mL drug}}{100 \text{ mL product}}$$

Example 7.1.1

A 9% solution means there are 9 parts of the drug in 100 parts of the solution. Express this percentage strength as weight in weight (w/w), weight in volume (w/v), and volume in volume (v/v).

w/w = 9 g of the drug in 100 g of the final product (or 9 g/100 g)
w/v = 9 g of the drug in 100 mL of the solution (or 9 g/100 mL)
v/v = 9 mL of the drug in 100 mL of the solution (or 9 mL/100 mL)

Example 7.1.2

Express the components of a 1% hydrocortisone cream as a weight-in-weight solution.

A 1% hydrocortisone cream is a compound that contains 1 g of hydrocortisone in each 100 g of 1% hydrocortisone cream.

Example 7.1.3

Express the components of a 5% solution of dextrose in the form of a weight-in-volume solution.

A 5% dextrose solution contains 5 g of dextrose in each 100 mL of D_5W.

Example 7.1.4

Express the components of 70% rubbing alcohol as a volume-in-volume solution.

Seventy percent rubbing alcohol contains 70 mL of pure alcohol in each 100 mL of solution.

The following ratios are important to remember when setting up problems involving solutions. Weight-in-weight problems involve mixing two solids, such as a dry powder and a cream.

$$\text{percentage strength of w/w solution} = \frac{\text{g of active ingredient}}{100 \text{ g final product}} \times 100$$

Weight-in-volume problems involve adding a solid drug to a liquid, such as a powder dissolved in a syrup.

$$\text{percentage strength of w/v solution} = \frac{\text{g of active ingredient}}{100 \text{ mL solution}} \times 100$$

Volume-in-volume problems involve mixing a pure liquid and another liquid, such as pure alcohol or water.

$$\text{percentage strength of v/v solution} = \frac{\text{mL of active ingredient}}{100 \text{ mL solution}} \times 100$$

Intravenous solutions that are given in large quantities are labeled as a percentage strength, such as Dextrose 5%, which is also written as D_5W or D5W. Normal saline (abbreviated as NS) is a solution of water and sodium chloride at 0.9% concentration. Plain water that is germ-free but has no dextrose or sodium chloride added to it is referred to as *sterile water*. The labels below show examples of how intravenous and injectable products are labeled. The striking difference between these labels and to the previous label examples is that there is no milligrams per milliliter designation. When the percentage of concentration is known, that percentage can be used to find the amount of the active ingredient, as demonstrated in the following example.

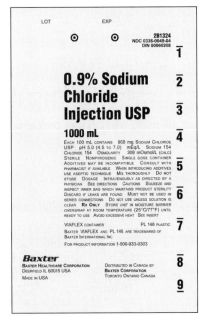

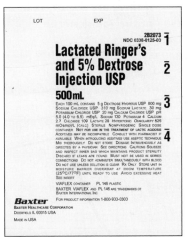

Example 7.1.5   **How many grams of dextrose are in a 1 L of D₅W?**

Note that D_5W means 5% dextrose in water, or a concentration of 5 g/100 mL. Solve this problem by using the ratio-proportion method, but first note that 1 L equals 1000 mL.

$$\frac{x \text{ g}}{1000 \text{ mL}} = \frac{5 \text{ g}}{100 \text{ mL}}$$

$$x \text{ g} = 50 \text{ g}$$

The percentage strength of solid solute in a solution is always calculated in the same manner and is expressed in grams per milliliter. The following formula should be committed to memory and will be used in the following example.

$$\text{percentage of w/v solution} = \frac{\text{grams of solute}}{\text{milliliters of solution}} \times 100$$

The following examples will demonstrate the use of this formula.

Example 7.1.6   **If there are 30 g of dextrose in 500 mL of the solution, what is the percentage strength of the solution?**

Insert the values into the w/v equation.

$$x\% \text{ w/v} = \frac{30 \text{ g}}{500 \text{ mL}} \times 100 = 0.06 \text{ g/mL} \times 100$$

$$x\% \text{ w/v} = 6\% \text{ w/v}$$

This can also be solved by using the ratio-proportion method.

$$\frac{x \text{ g}}{100 \text{ mL}} = \frac{30 \text{ g}}{500 \text{ mL}}$$

$$x \text{ g} = 6 \text{ g, or } 6\% \text{ w/v}$$

Example 7.1.7   **If there are 9 g of fat in 240 mL of milk, what is the percentage strength of the solution?**

Insert the values into the w/v equation.

$$x\% \text{ w/v} = \frac{9 \text{ g}}{240 \text{ mL}} \times 100 = 3.75\% \text{ w/v}$$

This can also be solved by using the ratio-proportion method.

$$\frac{x \text{ g}}{100 \text{ mL}} = \frac{9 \text{ g}}{240 \text{ mL}}$$

$$x \text{ g} = 3.75 \text{ g, or } 3.75\% \text{ w/v}$$

Example 7.1.8

If there are 50 g dextrose in a 2 L oral solution, what is the percentage strength of the solution?

Convert 2 L to milliliters, and insert the values into the w/v equation.

$$x\%\ w/v = \frac{50\ g}{2000\ mL} \times 100 = 2.5\%\ w/v$$

This can also be solved by using the ratio-proportion method.

$$\frac{x\ g}{100\ mL} = \frac{50\ g}{2000\ mL}$$

$$x\ g = 2.5\ g,\ or\ 2.5\%\ w/v$$

Example 7.1.9

If there are 875 mg of medication in a 2 tsp dose, what is the percentage strength of the solution?

Convert 875 mg to grams, and convert 2 tsp to milliliters (1 tsp = 5 mL). Insert the values into the w/v equation.

$$x\%\ w/v = \frac{0.875\ g}{10\ mL} \times 100 = 8.75\%\ w/v$$

This can also be solved by using the ratio-proportion method.

$$\frac{x\ g}{100\ mL} = \frac{0.875\ g}{10\ mL}$$

$$x\ g = 8.75\ g,\ or\ 8.75\%\ w/v$$

The percentage of solution equation can also be applied to weight-in-weight and volume-in-volume solutions, as shown in the following examples.

Example 7.1.10

There are 1250 mg of hydrocortisone in 5 oz of ointment. What is the percentage strength of drug?

Convert both 1250 mg and 5 oz to grams (1 oz = 30 g). Insert the values into the w/w equation.

$$x\%\ w/w = \frac{1.25\ g}{150\ g} \times 100 = 0.83\%\ w/w$$

This can also be solved by using the ratio-proportion method.

$$\frac{x\ g}{100\ g} = \frac{1.25\ g}{150\ g}$$

$$x\ g = 0.83\ g,\ or\ 0.83\%\ w/w$$

Example 7.1.11   A 1 pt beverage contains 120 mL of pure alcohol. What is the percentage strength of alcohol?

Convert 1 pt to milliliters (1 pt = 480 mL). Insert the values into the v/v equation.

$$x\% \text{ v/v} = \frac{120 \text{ mL}}{480 \text{ mL}} \times 100 = 25\% \text{ v/v}$$

This can also be solved by using the ratio-proportion method.

$$\frac{x \text{ mL}}{100 \text{ mL}} = \frac{120 \text{ mL}}{480 \text{ mL}}$$

$$x \text{ mL} = 25 \text{ mL, or } 25\% \text{ v/v}$$

7.1 Problem Set

Express the following as weight-in-weight, weight-in-volume, or volume-in-volume solutions.

1. Express the components of betamethasone dipropionate 0.05% ointment as a weight-in-weight solution.

2. Express the components of furosemide 10 mg/mL and 11.5% alcohol as a weight-in-volume and a volume-in-volume solution, respectively.

3. Express the components of ciclopirox 8% topical solution as a weight-in-volume solution.

Calculate the following.

4. If a patient drinks 8 fl oz of 2% milk, how many grams of fat were consumed?

5. An injection of 1.3 mL lidocaine 2% was given. How many milligrams of lidocaine is this?

6. A dose calls for 2 capsules of 300 mg rifamycin to be given in 1 fl oz of cherry syrup. What is the percentage strength?

Calculate the percentage strength of drug in the following drug formulations.

7.

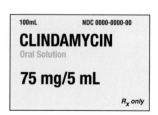

8.

9.

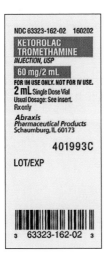

10.

11.

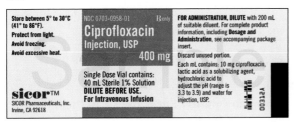

12.

13.

14.

Calculate the amount of drug in milligrams for the following dispensed containers.

15. terconazole 0.8%, 20 g

16. benzoyl peroxide 10%, 30 g cream

17. hydroxypyridinone 0.77%, 45 g

18. ketoconazole 2%, 7 fl oz shampoo

19. permethrin 5%, 60 g cream

20. metronidazole cream 1%, 30 g tube

21. carbamide peroxide 6.5%, 15 mL solution

22. povidone-iodine 7.5%, 4 fl oz cleansing solution

23. lidocaine 1.5%, 10 mL vial

24. ipratropium bromide 0.03%, 30 mL

Calculate the amount of medication in the following doses.

25. You have found a 300 mL bottle of a 7.5% solution on the shelf. If the dose is 1 tsp, how many milligrams are in one dose?

26. How many milligrams are in 1 tbsp of a 0.5% drug product?

27. How many milligrams are in 0.5 mL of a 1:1000 solution?

28. Calculate the percentage strength of dextrose if 45 g are added to 500 mL of sterile water.

29. How many grams of dextrose are needed to make 3500 mL of a 24.5% solution?

30. a. How many grams are in 600 mL of a 1:200 solution of drug product?

    b. What is the percentage strength of the solution?

31. The following compound is" received in the pharmacy. What is the final percentage concentration of tobramycin?

> ℞ **Tobramycin Ophthalmic Solution**
>
> 1. Obtain a 5 mL bottle of tobramycin ophthalmic solution (3 mg/mL).
> 2. Add 2 mL of tobramycin injection (40 mg/mL) to the ophthalmic solution.

32. The following compound is received in the pharmacy.

> ℞ **Aminoglycoside: Gentamicin**
>
> 1. Combine 0.5 mL of gentamicin (4 mg/2 mL) with 0.5 mL BSS.
> 2. Inject 0.1 mL intravitreally.

    a. What is the concentration of the final dilution?

    b. What percentage strength is this concentration?

    c. How many milligrams are to be injected?

How many grams of NaCl are in the following volumes of NS (0.9%)?

33. 100 mL

34. 250 mL

35. 500 mL

36. 1000 mL

37. 2225 mL

How many grams of NaCl are in the following volumes of $\frac{1}{2}$NS (0.45%)?

38. 125 mL

39. 250 mL

40. 750 mL

41. 1800 mL

42. 2600 mL

How many grams of dextrose are in the following volumes of D_5W (5%)?

43. 75 mL

44. 385 mL

45. 525 mL

46. 1350 mL

47. 3000 mL

How many grams of dextrose are in the following volumes of $D_{10}W$ (10%)?

48. 100 mL

49. 450 mL

50. 875 mL

51. 1100 mL

52. 2300 mL

Self-check your work in Appendix A.

7.2 IV Flow Rates

flow rate
the rate, expressed in milliliters per hour or drops per minute, at which medication is flowing through an IV line; also called infusion rate and rate of infusion

The pharmacy staff is responsible for calculating the **flow rate** of a medication to be administered intravenously. This rate is expressed in terms of how many milliliters per hour or drops per minute a patient should receive; it can also be expressed in terms of how much IV fluid should be prepared per shift or per day. The flow rate is often referred to as the infusion rate or rate of infusion.

Physicians typically order the type of IV fluid to be given, any additives required, and the rate at which it should be given as a certain number of milliliters per hour. The nursing staff closely monitors IV fluids to ensure that an appropriate amount of medication is given over the specified time to achieve the intended therapeutic response.

The duration of therapy may be calculated using the following formula.

Safety Note

Round down the duration of therapy to the whole hour.

$$\text{duration of therapy} = \frac{\text{volume of fluid or amount of drug to be infused}}{\text{flow rate}}$$

When calculating the duration of therapy, always round your answer down to the whole hour.

Example 7.2.1

A 1 L IV is running at 125 mL/hour. How often will you send up a new bag?

$$\text{the time the bag will last} = \frac{\text{volume of fluid}}{\text{flow rate}}$$

$$x \text{ hours} = \frac{1000 \text{ mL}}{125 \text{ mL/hour}} = 8 \text{ hours}$$

Using the dimensional analysis method,

$$x \text{ hours} = 1 \text{ L} \times 1000 \text{ mL}/1 \text{ L} \times 1 \text{ hour}/125 \text{ mL} = 8 \text{ hours}$$

Thus, a new bag will be needed every 8 hours.

Example 7.2.2

If an IV is running at 150 mL/hour and three 1 L bags are sent to the floor, how long will these bags last?

$$x \text{ hours} = \text{the time the 3 bags will last}$$

$$x \text{ hours} = \frac{3000 \text{ mL}}{150 \text{ mL/hour}} = 20 \text{ hours}$$

Using the dimensional analysis method,

$$x \text{ hours} = 3 \text{ L} \times 1000 \text{ mL}/1 \text{ L} \times 1 \text{ hour}/150 \text{ mL} = 20 \text{ hours}$$

When an order specifies a volume or amount of drug to be given over a specific period of time, the flow rate (expressed in milliliters per hour) can be calculated using the following formula.

$$\text{flow rate} = \frac{\text{volume of fluid or amount of drug to be infused}}{\text{duration of therapy}}$$

The following examples will demonstrate these calculations.

Example 7.2.3

The following order is sent to the IV room.

> **Medication: Solu-Cortef 300 mg**
> **Fluid volume: 300 mL**
> **Time of infusion: 4 hours**

What volume of fluid is given per hour, and what amount of drug is given per hour?

Part I. Determine the volume of fluid given per hour.

$$300 \text{ mL} \div 4 \text{ hours} = 75 \text{ mL/hour}$$

Part II. Calculate the amount of drug given per hour.

$$300 \text{ mg} \div 4 \text{ hours} = 75 \text{ mg/hour}$$

Example 7.2.4

The following order is sent to the IV room.

> **Medication: cefazolin 500 mg/D5W**
> **Fluid volume: 50 mL**
> **Time of infusion: ½ hour**

What volume of fluid is administered per hour, and what amount of drug is given per hour?

Part I. Determine the volume of fluid given per hour.

$$50 \text{ mL} \div 0.5 \text{ hour} = 100 \text{ mL/hour}$$

Part II. Calculate the amount of drug given per hour.

$$500 \text{ mg} \div 0.5 \text{ hour} = 1000 \text{ mg/hour}$$

7.2 Problem Set

Answer the following questions.

1. A liter IV bag is running at 50 mL/hour. How long will it last?

2. A liter bag of fluid is hung at 7 P.M. and runs at 100 mL/hour. How long will it last?

3. A 500 mL bag of IV fluid is running at 30 mL/hour. How long will it last?

4. If a patient is given 60 mg of medication in 75 mL over 45 minutes, what is the flow rate in milliliters per hour?

5. A patient receives 20,000 units of heparin in an IV of 100 mL over 45 minutes. What is the flow rate in milliliters per hour?

6. A patient is to receive 2 g of medication in 150 mL over 90 minutes. What is the flow rate in milliliters per hour?

7. A physican has ordered 2800 mL every 24 hours. At what rate should the pump be set in milliliters per hour?

8. A patient is to receive 250 mL over 30 minutes. How many milliliters per hour should the pump be set to?

9. If 500 mL is to be administered over 4 hours, what is the infusion rate in milliliters per hour?

10. If 2000 mL is to be administered over 8 hours, what is the infusion rate in milliliters per hour?

11. A fluid volume of 500 mL is to be given over 2 hours. What is the rate in milliliters per hour?

12. A patient has orders for 500 mL $D_5W\frac{1}{2}NS$ and KVO (keep vein open). The flow rate will be 15 mL/hour. How long will the 500 mL IV bag last if no changes are made in the next 24 hours?

13. A patient is to be given 1 L of $D_5W\frac{1}{2}NS$ + 20 mEq KCl at the rate of 125 mL/hour.

    a. How long will a single bag last the patient?

    b. How many 1 L bags will be needed for this patient for the next 24 hours?

14. A patient is receiving lactated Ringer's at 150 mL/hour. A 1 L bag is started at 7 A.M. from the nursing stock drawer. How many additional bags will the patient need to last the rest of this day and until 6 P.M. the following day?

15. A patient is to have three 1 L bags of NS in the next 24 hours. What is the rate in milliliters per hour?

For each rate, determine the quantity of 1 L bags needed for 24 hours. (Rounded up to the nearest 1L bag.)

16. 50 mL/hour _____

17. 75 mL/hour _____

18. 100 mL/hour _____

19. 120 mL/hour _____

20. 125 mL/hour _____

21. 130 mL/hour _____

22. 150 mL/hour _____

23. 175 mL/hour _____

24. 200 mL/hour _____

25. 225 mL/hour _____

Interpret the following prescriptions and provide the requested rates.

26. Medication: Solu-Cortef (hydrocortisone) 250 mg
    Fluid volume: 250 mL
    Time of infusion: 4 hours
    How many (a) milliliters per hour? _____

    (b) milligrams per hour? _____

27. Medication: penicillin G 12 million units
    Fluid volume: 500 mL
    Time of infusion: 12 hours
    How many (a) milliliters per hour? _____

    (b) units per hour? _____

28. Medication: 4:1 (4 mg/mL) lidocaine
    Dose: 6 mg/hour
    How many (a) milliliters per hour? _____

    (b) micrograms per hour? _____

29. Medication: Solu-Medrol
    (methylprednisolone) 250 mg
    Dose: 20 mg/hour
    Fluid volume: 500 mL
    How many (a) milliliters per hour? _____

(b) grams per hour? _____

30. Medication: dopamine 40 mg
    Dose: 1 mg/min
    Fluid volume: 500 mL
    How many (a) milliliters per hour? _____

    (b) milligrams per hour? _____

31. Medication: Intropin (dopamine hydrochloride) 800 mg
    Dose: 12 mcg/kg/min
    Patient weight: 198 lb
    Fluid volume: 500 mL
    How many (a) milliliters per hour? _____

    (b) milligrams per hour? _____

32. Medication: gentamicin 480,000 mcg
    Dose: 4 mcg/kg/min
    Patient weight: 176 lb
    Fluid volume: 750 mL
    How many (a) milliliters per hour? _____

    (b) milligrams per hour? _____

Self-check your work in Appendix A.

7.3 Drop Sets and Infusion Rates

Pharmacy staff and the nursing staff are responsible for calculating the rate of administration for IV fluids in a drops per minute rate (expressed as gtt/min). The nursing staff will use this rate to manually adjust the IV flow at the drop chamber or set the electronic infusion pump at the patient's bedside. The rate in drops per minute can be calculated manually by counting the number of drops of fluid that fall into the drip chamber over a minute. The nurse can then manually adjust the rate up or down by using a clamp on the IV tubing. Most inpatient facilities now use electronic infusion pumps to regulate both the volume and the rate of a patient's IV medication. The rate can be adjusted digitally, while the pump uses a clamp to adjust the rate at which the fluid flows through tubing routed through a chamber in the pump. Pumps can be set to give IV fluids in milliliters per hour or drops per minute.

drop set
the number of drops an IV set takes to make 1 mL; also called drip set

mini-drip set
a drop set at a rate of 60 gtt/mL

Calculating the flow rate in drops per minute is complicated by the variety of IV sets available. Manufacturers produce calibrated IV tube sets that have different size drops. An IV set is identified by the number of drops it takes to make 1 mL. This calibration is referred to as a **drop set** or a drip set. The most common sets are 10, 15, 20, and 60, meaning 10 gtt/mL, 15 gtt/mL, 20 gtt/mL, and 60 gtt/mL, respectively. The drop sizes for the 10, 15, and 20 calibrations produce macrodrops, and the 60 calibration produces microdrops. The 60 gtt/mL set is called a **mini-drip set.** Figure 7.1 illustrates

FIGURE 7.1
IV Drop Sets

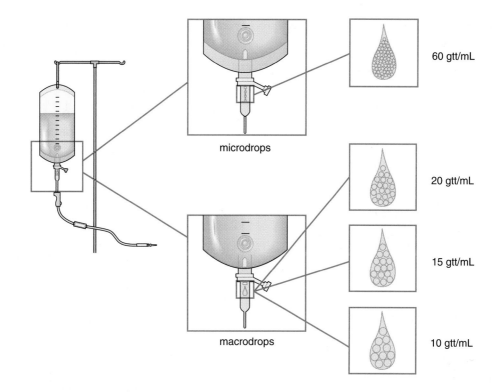

microdrops

60 gtt/mL

20 gtt/mL

15 gtt/mL

macrodrops

10 gtt/mL

these different drop sizes. When an IV is started for a patient, the drop set for the IV set tubing will be printed in prominent type on the outside of the IV set package.

The 10 drop and 15 drop sets are commonly used for adult patients, while the 60 drop set is used for pediatric patients or patients who are critically ill and are being given medications that have a narrow therapeutic window.

To determine the rate in drops per minute at which the IV fluid is to be infused, the volume of fluid, delivery time, and calibration of the administration set must be known. The following formula is used.

Remember

The abbreviation gtt comes from the Latin word *guttae,* which means "drops."

$$x \text{ gtt/min} = \frac{(\text{volume of fluid} \div \text{delivery time}) \times (\text{drop rate of administration set used})}{60 \text{ min/hour}}$$

Safety Note

Round down to a whole drop when a drop per minute calculation results in a partial drop.

The following examples will demonstrate the use of this formula and will also show how the dimensional analysis method can be used to solve these problems. It is common practice to round down in the event a partial drop or minute is calculated. For example, 20.6 gtt/min would be rounded down to 20 gtt/min.

Example 7.3.1

If an IV is running at 60 mL/hour, what is the rate in drops per minute using a 15 drop set?

Solution 1: Insert the values from the problem statement into the formula to determine the drops per minute. Remember that a 15 drop set runs at a rate of 15 gtt/mL.

$$x \text{ gtt/min} = \frac{(\text{volume of fluid} \div \text{delivery time}) \times (\text{drop set rate})}{60 \text{ min/hour}}$$

$$x \text{ gtt/min} = \frac{(60 \text{ mL} \div 1 \text{ hour}) \times (15 \text{ gtt/mL})}{60 \text{ min/hour}} = 15 \text{ gtt/min}$$

(handwritten annotations:)
$$\frac{60 \text{ mL}}{60 \text{ min}}$$
$$\frac{1 \text{ mL}}{\text{min}}$$
$$\frac{15 \text{ gtt}}{\text{mL}}$$

Solution 2: This problem can also be solved using the dimensional analysis method.

$$x \text{ gtt/min} = 60 \text{ mL/hour} \times 15 \text{ gtt/mL} \times 1 \text{ hour/60 min} = 15 \text{ gtt/min}$$

Example 7.3.2

If 500 mg of a drug is to be administered from a 50 mL minibag over 30 minutes using a 15 drop set, how many drops per minute is that?

Solution 1: Begin by identifying the amounts to insert into the equation.

> Volume of fluid = 50 mL
> Fluid delivery time = 30 min = 0.5 hour
> Drop rate of administration set = 15 gtt/mL

Insert the values from the problem statement into the formula to determine the drops per minute rate.

$$x \text{ gtt/min} = \frac{(\text{volume of fluid} \div \text{delivery time}) \times (\text{drop set rate})}{60 \text{ min/hour}}$$

$$x \text{ gtt/min} = \frac{(50 \text{ mL} \div 0.5 \text{ hour}) \times (15 \text{ gtt/mL})}{60 \text{ min/hour}} = 25 \text{ gtt/min}$$

Solution 2: This problem can also be solved using the dimensional analysis method.

$$x \text{ gtt/min} = 50 \text{ mL/0.5 hour} \times 15 \text{ gtt/mL} \times 1 \text{ hour/60 min} = 25 \text{ gtt/min}$$

Example 7.3.3

You are to prepare 750 mg of medication in 75 mL for infusion over 30 minutes, using a 10 drop set. How many drops per minute will that be?

Solution 1: Begin by identifying the amounts to insert into the equation.

> Volume of fluid = 75 mL
> Fluid delivery time = 30 min = 0.5 hour
> Drop rate of administration set = 10 gtt/mL

Insert the values from the problem statement into the formula to determine the drops per minute rate.

$$x \text{ gtt/min} = \frac{(\text{volume of fluid} \div \text{delivery time}) \times (\text{set drop rate})}{60 \text{ min/hour}}$$

$$x \text{ gtt/min} = \frac{(75 \text{ mL} \div 0.5 \text{ hour}) \times (10 \text{ gtt/mL})}{60 \text{ min/hour}} = 25 \text{ gtt/min}$$

Solution 2: This problem can also be solved using the dimensional analysis method.

$$x \text{ gtt/min} = 75 \text{ mL/0.5 hour} \times 10 \text{ gtt/mL} \times 1 \text{ hour/60 min} = 25 \text{ gtt/min}$$

Other calculations are done in the hospital pharmacy to calculate infusion time, amount of liquid to be delivered in an infusion, and amount of drug to be infused.

These problems can be solved by using the dimensional analysis method. The following examples will demonstrate some of these important calculations.

Example 7.3.4

An IV flow rate is set at 50 gtt/min. Using a 10 drop set, what is the flow rate in milliliters per hour?

Solution 1: Using the ratio-proportion method, calculate the amount of milliliters in 50 gtt/min.

$$\frac{x \text{ mL}}{50 \text{ gtt/min}} = \frac{1 \text{ mL}}{10 \text{ gtt/min}}$$

$$x \text{ mL} = 5 \text{ mL/min}$$

Then, determine the number of milliliters delivered in 1 hour, which is equal to 60 minutes.

$$\frac{x \text{ mL}}{60 \text{ min}} = \frac{5 \text{ mL}}{1 \text{ min}}$$

$$x \text{ mL} = 300 \text{ mL}$$

Solution 2: This problem can also be solved by using the dimensional analysis method.

$$x \text{ mL/hour} = 1 \text{ mL}/10 \text{ gtt} \times 50 \text{ gtt/min} \times 60 \text{ min/hour} = 300 \text{ mL/hour}$$

Example 7.3.5

If there is a flow rate of 40 gtt/min using a 15 drop set, how many liters will be delivered over 24 hours?

Solution 1: Calculate the milliliters given each minute.

$$\frac{40 \text{ gtt}}{1 \text{ min}} \times \frac{1 \text{ mL}}{15 \text{ gtt}} = \frac{2.67 \text{ mL}}{1 \text{ min}}$$

Use this rate to determine how many milliliters will be given in an hour.

$$2.67 \text{ mL} \times 60 \text{ min/hour} = 160.2 \text{ mL/hour}$$

Finally, calculate the number of milliliters in a day.

$$160.2 \text{ mL/hour} \times 24 \text{ hours} = 3844.8 \text{ mL, which is converted to } 3.84 \text{ L}$$

Solution 2: This problem can also be calculated using the dimensional analysis method.

$$x \text{ L} = 24 \text{ hours} \times 60 \text{ min/hour} \times 40 \text{ gtt/min} \times 1 \text{ mL}/15 \text{ gtt} \times 1 \text{ L}/1000 \text{ mL}$$
$$= 3.84 \text{ L}$$

Example 7.3.6

If a patient is receiving 20 mEq of KCl in 1 L NS and a 10 drop set is used at a rate of 50 gtt/min, how long will the 1 L bag take to infuse?

Solution 1: Calculate the milliliters given each minute.

$$\frac{50 \text{ gtt}}{1 \text{ min}} \times \frac{1 \text{ mL}}{10 \text{ gtt}} = \frac{5 \text{ mL}}{1 \text{ min}}$$

Use this rate to determine how many milliliters will be given in an hour.

$$5 \text{ mL/min} \times 60 \text{ min/hour} = 300 \text{ mL/hour}$$

Finally, determine how long a 1 L bag will take to infuse at this rate.

$$1000 \text{ mL} \times 1 \text{ hour}/300 \text{ mL} = 3.33 \text{ hours, or 3 hours}$$

Solution 2: This problem can also be solved using the dimensional analysis method.

$$x \text{ hours} = 1 \text{ L} \times 1000 \text{ mL/L} \times 10 \text{ gtt/mL} \times 1 \text{ min/50 gtt} \times 1 \text{ hour/60 min}$$
$$= 3.33 \text{ hours, or 3 hours}$$

Example 7.3.7

A patient is getting $D_{10}W$ infused at 50 mL/hour using a 10 drop set. What is the drops per minute rate, and how many grams of dextrose is the patient receiving per hour?

Calculate the drops per minute using dimensional analysis. Note that the drop set is running at a rate of 10 gtt/mL.

$$x \text{ gtt/min} = 1 \text{ hour/60 min} \times 50 \text{ mL/hour} \times 10 \text{ gtt/mL} = 8.33 \text{ gtt/min},$$
rounded down to 8 gtt/min

Set up a proportion to determine the grams of dextrose the patient is receiving in an hour from the $D_{10}W$ (10 g/100 mL) at a rate of 50 mL/hour.

$$\frac{x \text{ g dextrose}}{50 \text{ mL}} = \frac{10 \text{ g}}{100 \text{ mL}}$$

$$x \text{ g dextrose} = 5 \text{ g}$$

Example 7.3.8

A physician orders 150 mg of a drug in a 50 mL bag over one hour, using a 15 drop set. How many drops per minute will that be, and how many micrograms of the drug will be in each drop?

Calculate the drops per minute, using dimensional analysis.

$$x \text{ gtt/min} = 1 \text{ hour/60 min} \times 50 \text{ mL/hour} \times 15 \text{ gtt/mL}$$
$$= 12.5 \text{ gtt/min, rounded down to 12 gtt/min}$$

Now, set up a proportion to determine the amount of drug that will be contained in each drop.

$$\frac{x \text{ mg}}{1 \text{ mL}} = \frac{150 \text{ mg}}{50 \text{ mL}}$$

$$x \text{ mg} = 3 \text{ mg/mL}$$

This can be expressed as follows.

$$x \text{ mg} = 3 \text{ mg}/15 \text{ gtt} = 0.2 \text{ mg/gtt} = 200 \text{ mcg/gtt}$$

The dimensional analysis method can also be used.

$$x \text{ mcg/gtt} = 1 \text{ mL}/15 \text{ gtt} \times 150 \text{ mg}/50 \text{ mL} \times 1000 \text{ mcg/mg} = 200 \text{ mcg/gtt}$$

Example 7.3.9

A patient is getting 16 mEq KCl in 250 mL D₅W. A 10 drop set is being used. How many milliequivalents are in each drop?

Solution 1: Set up a proportion to determine the number of milliequivalents in 1 mL.

$$\frac{x \text{ mEq}}{1 \text{ mL}} = \frac{16 \text{ mEq}}{250 \text{ mL}}$$

$$x \text{ mEq} = 0.064 \text{ mEq}$$

Convert this to milliequivalents in each drop, using the given drop set.

$$0.064 \text{ mEq/mL} \times 1 \text{ mL}/10 \text{ gtt} = 0.0064 \text{ mEq/gtt}$$

Solution 2: Using the dimensional analysis method,

$$x \text{ mEq/gtt} = 1 \text{ mL}/10 \text{ gtt} \times 16 \text{ mEq}/250 \text{ mL} = 0.0064 \text{ mEq/gtt}$$

7.3 Problem Set

Calculate the following.

1. An IV rate is 10 mL/hour. If a 10 drop set is used, what will the rate be in drops per minute?

2. What is the IV flow rate in drops per minute for a child who is receiving 35 mL/hour using a 60 drop set?

3. A patient is to receive 1 g of medication in 100 mL over one hour using a 10 drop set. What is the rate in drops per minute?

4. A nurse will be administering 500 mg of medication in 50 mL over 30 minutes, using a mini-drip set. What is the flow rate in drops per minute?

5. A patient receives 20,000 units of heparin in an IV of 100 mL over 45 minutes. Using a 15 drop set, what is the drops per minute rate?

6. A physician orders 750 mg of a drug in a 100 mL bag over one hour, using a 15 drop set. How many drops per minute will that be?

7. A patient is to be given 1000 mL of LR at 50 mL/hour. What will the drop rate be for a 15 drop set?

8. A patient is to be given 1750 mL at 95 mL/hour. What will the drop rate be if a 15 drop set is used?

9. A physician orders 500 mg of a drug in 50 mL to be given in 30 minutes. If a 10 drop set is used, what will the drop rate be?

10. A patient is to receive 2 g of medication in a liter of NS over 8 hours. If a 15 drop set is used, what will the drop rate be?

11. A patient is to receive 250 mL over 30 minutes using a 15 drop set. How many drops per minute are to be given?

12. A patient is to receive 120 mL/hour. If a 10 drop set is used, what will the drops per minute rate be?

13. If 500 mL is administered at 30 gtt/min using a 10 drop set, what is the flow rate in milliliters per hour?

14. An IV flow rate is set at 45 gtt/min. If a 15 drop set is used, what is the flow rate in milliliters per hour?

15. If 500 mL is administered at 30 gtt/min using a 10 drop set, what is the flow rate in milliliters per hour?

16. A nurse is to administer 750 mL at 30 gtt/min, using a 15 drop set. What is the infusion rate in milliliters per hour?

17. A patient is getting 24 mEq KCl in 500 mL D_5W. A 10 drop set is being used. How many milliequivalents are in each drop?

18. A patient is to be given 1 L of D_5WNS + 1 mEq KCl at the rate of 125 mL/hour.

   a. What will the drops per minute rate be if a 10 drop set is used?

   b. What will the drops per minute rate be if a 15 drop set is used?

   c. What will the drops per minute rate be if a 60 drop set is used?

19. A patient is receiving 30 mEq of KCl in 1 L NS, and a 15 drop set is used to deliver 23 gtt/min.

   a. How long will the 1 L bag take to infuse?

   b. How many milliequivalents will the patient be receiving each hour?

20. A patient is getting $D_{10}W$ infused at 50 mL/hour using a 10 drop set.

   a. What is the drops per minute rate?

   b. How many grams of dextrose is the patient receiving per hour?

21. A physician orders 400 mg of a drug in a 100 mL bag over one hour, using a 15 drop set.

   a. How many drops per minute will that be?

   b. How many micrograms will be administered per drop?

Self-check your work in Appendix A.

7.4 IV Piggybacks

Sometimes, a patient requires only a small amount of fluid for a short period of time. For example, a physician may order that a small volume of fluid and medication be given over a short period to improve a clinical outcome. Often drugs are given this

IV piggyback (IVPB)
a small volume of fluid and medication that is given intravenously in addition to a primary infusion over a short period of time

way, diluted in IV fluid, in what is called an **IV piggyback (IVPB);** the drug in solution is administered from a separate IV bag but through the main IV line, interrupting or blending with the first IV. This medication can be given as a onetime dose or intermittently throughout the day. For example, an antibiotic might be given in three doses spread throughout a 24 hour period. The same method used to determine a rate for continual administration of IV fluids can be applied to IVPB solutions. When doing the calculation, it is important to include both the initial volume in an IVPB and the volume that may be added via syringe to the IVPB as an admixture.

If the volume of the IVPB is 40 mL or less, typically no changes are made in the flow of the primary IV fluid for adult patients. For amounts greater than 40 mL, however, the flow rate may need to be recalculated to ensure that the patient receives the ordered fluids in the time period specified by the physician. To calculate an adjusted rate in milliliters per hour or drops per minute, the volume remaining in the main IV container is usually checked and then divided by the hours remaining before the next container is to be started.

The following examples demonstrate the basic IVPB calculations.

Example 7.4.1

The physician orders 1 g of cefamandole to be infused every 4 hours. It is available as 250 mg/mL. The order indicates that the medication should be given in 100 mL D$_5$W using a 10 drop set over 45 minutes. What is the rate of infusion?

First, convert 250 mg to grams

$$250 \text{ mg} = 0.25 \text{ g.}$$

Second, determine how much cefamandole is needed from the vial.

$$\frac{x \text{ mL cefamandole}}{1 \text{ g}} = \frac{1 \text{ mL}}{0.25 \text{ g}}$$

$$x \text{ mL} = 4 \text{ mL}$$

Third, determine the total volume of the fluid to be infused.

$$4 \text{ mL} + 100 \text{ mL} = 104 \text{ mL}$$

Finally, determine the infusion rate.

$$x \text{ gtt/min} = \frac{\text{volume of fluid} \times \text{gtt/mL}}{\text{time of infusion}}$$

$$= \frac{104 \text{ mL} \times 10 \text{ gtt/mL}}{45 \text{ min}}$$

$$= 23.1 \text{ gtt/min, rounded down to 23 gtt/min}$$

Example 7.4.2

The order calls for 20 mg of premixed famotidine to be given in 50 mL IVPB Q12 hours. It is to be administered using a 15 drop set and is to be given over 20 minutes. What is the rate of infusion?

$$x \text{ gtt/min} = \frac{\text{volume of fluid} \times \text{gtt/mL}}{\text{time of infusion}}$$

$$= \frac{50 \text{ mL} \times 15 \text{ gtt/mL}}{20 \text{ min}}$$

$$= 37.5 \text{ gtt/min, rounded down to } 37 \text{ gtt/min}$$

Example 7.4.3   **The order calls for 1 g of the premixed drug nafcillin to be given in 100 mL IVPB Q6 hours. Using a 10 drop set, it should be administered over 30 minutes. What is the infusion rate?**

$$x\text{gtt/min} = \frac{100 \text{ mL} \times 10 \text{ gtt/mL}}{30 \text{ min}}$$

$$= 33.3 \text{ gtt/min, rounded down to } 33 \text{ gtt/min}$$

Example 7.4.4   **A patient weighing 148 lb is to receive tobramycin 2 mg/kg/dose in 50 mL IVPB. A 15 drop set has been ordered, and the drug is to be given over 30 minutes. The following label shows the drug to be used. What is the appropriate infusion rate?**

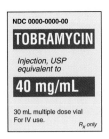

Begin by converting the patient's weight to kilograms.

$$148 \text{ lb} \times 1 \text{ kg}/2.2 \text{ lb} = 67.2727 \text{ kg, rounded to } 67.3 \text{ kg}$$

Then, calculate the tobramycin dose by multiplying the patient's weight in kilograms by the amount per kilogram in the order.

$$67.3 \text{ kg} \times 2 \text{ mg/kg} = 134.6 \text{ mg}$$

Use the dose to calculate the amount of tobramycin concentrate to be added to the bag.

$$\frac{x \text{ mL}}{134.6 \text{ mg}} = \frac{1 \text{ mL}}{40 \text{ mg}}$$

$$x \text{ mL} = 3.4 \text{ mL}$$

Then, determine the total volume to be infused.

$$3.4 \text{ mL concentrate} + 50 \text{ mL} = 53.4 \text{ mL}$$

Finally, determine the infusion rate.

$$x \text{ gtt/min} = \frac{53.4 \text{ mL} \times 15 \text{ gtt}}{\text{mL}/30 \text{ min}}$$

$$= 26.7 \text{ gtt/min, rounded down to } 26 \text{ gtt/min}$$

7.4 Problem Set

Determine the infusion rates in drops per minute for the following orders.

1. Give 50 mL over 15 minutes using a 10 drop set.

   [handwritten: 33.33 gtt/min] *[handwritten: $\frac{50 \text{ mL} \times 10 \text{ gtt/mL}}{15 \text{ min}}$]*

2. Give 100 mL over 20 minutes using a 15 drop set.

   [handwritten: 75 gtt/min] *[handwritten: $\frac{100 \text{ mL} \times 15 \text{ gtt/mL}}{20 \text{ min}}$]*

3. Give 50 mL over 30 minutes using a 15 drop set.

   [handwritten: 25 gtt/min] *[handwritten: $\frac{50 \text{ mL} \times 15 \text{ gtt/mL}}{30 \text{ min}}$]*

4. Give 60 mL over 30 minutes using a 10 drop set.

5. Give 55 mL over 20 minutes using a 15 drop set.

6. Give 63 mL over 15 minutes using a 15 drop set.

7. Give 58 mL over 15 minutes using a 15 drop set

8. Give 61 mL over 25 minutes using a 10 drop set.

Calculate the following doses in milliliters and then determine the infusion rate.

9. Medication order: ceftriaxone 2 g once daily over 20 min
   Available stock: ceftriaxone 2 g in 50 mL premixed; 15 drop set

   [handwritten: $\frac{50 \text{ mL} \times 15 \text{ gtt/mL}}{20 \text{ min}} = 37.5 \text{ gtt/min}$]

10. Medication order: cefotetan 2 g Q12 hours over 30 min
    Available stock: cefotetan 2 g in 50 mL; 10 drop set

    [handwritten: $\frac{50 \text{ mL} \times 10 \text{ gtt/mL}}{30 \text{ min}}$ 16.7667]

11. Medication order: penicillin G 3 million units Q4 hours over 15 min
    Available stock: penicillin G 3 million units in 50 mL premixed; 15 drop set

    [handwritten: 50 gtt/min $\frac{50 \text{ mL} \times 15 \text{ gtt/mL}}{15 \text{ min}}$]

12. Medication order: acyclovir 10 mg/kg Q8 hours over 20 min; patient weighs 169 lb
    Available stock: acyclovir 50 mg/mL; 50 mL minibag; 15 drop set

    [handwritten: 3718 mg   743.6 mL $\frac{743.6 \text{ mL} \times 15 \text{ gtt/mL}}{20 \text{ min}}$ 55.77 gtt/min]

13. Medication order: ceftazolin 2 g Q8 hours over 25 min
    Available stock: cefazolin 2 g in 50 mL premixed; 10 drop set

14. Medication order: cefoperazone 2 g once daily over 30 min
    Available: cefoperazone 2 g in 50 mL premixed; 15 drop set

15. Medication order: cefotetan 1 g once daily over 30 min
    Available stock: cefotetan 1 g in 50 mL premixed; 60 drop set

Self-check your work in Appendix A.

Express the components of the following solutions.

1. Express the components of betaxolol ophthalmic solution 0.25% as a weight-in-volume solution.

2. Express the components of hexachlorophene 3% emulsion as a weight-in-volume solution.

Calculate the following.

3. If there are 500 mg in a 1 tsp dose, what percentage strength is this?

4. If there are 80 g of dextrose in a 1 L IV bag, what is the percentage strength?

Calculate the percentage strength of drug in the following drug formulations.

5.

6.

Calculate the amount of medication in the following doses.

7. How many grams of sodium chloride are in 3 L of NS?

8. How many milligrams are in 1 tsp of an 8% drug product?

Answer the following questions.

9. An IV fluid is running at 125 mL/hour. How long will a liter last?

10. A 100 mL bag is set to run at 150 mL/hour. If it is started at 7 A.M., when will it run out?

11. If 125 mL is to be given over 15 minutes, what is the rate of infusion in milliliters per minute?

12. A patient is receiving NS at 100 mL/hour. If a 1 L bag is started at 10 A.M. upon admission, what time will it run out?

Interpret the following prescriptions and provide the requested rates.

13. Medication: vancomycin 2 g
    Fluid volume: 250 mL
    Time of infusion: 1 hour, 30 min
    How many (a) milliliters per hour? _____

    (b) milligrams per hour? _____

14. Medication: aminophylline 1 g
    Fluid volume: 500 mL
    Time of infusion: 8 hours
    How many (a) milliliters per hour? _____

    (b) milligrams per hour? _____

15. Medication: nitroprusside 50 mg
    Dose: 5 mcg/kg/min
    Patient weight: 143 lb
    Fluid volume: 250 mL
    How many (a) milliliters per hour? _____

    (b) milligrams per hour? _____

Calculate the following.

16. A child is receiving 20 mL/hour with a mini-drip set. How many drops per minute are administered?

17. An IV is to flow at 60 mL/hour using a 10 drop set. How many drops per minute are administered?

18. A physician orders 750 mg of a drug in a 100 mL bag over 30 minutes. Using a 10 drop set, how many drops per minute is that?

19. If there is a flow rate of 24 gtt/min using a 15 drop set, how many liters will be delivered over 24 hours?

20. If a patient is getting an IV solution at 30 gtt/min and a 10 drop set is used, how long will a 1 L bag of NS last?

Determine the infusion rates in drops per minute for the following orders.

21. Give 105 mL over 30 minutes using a 10 drop set.

22. Give 100 mL over 15 minutes using a 10 drop set.

Calculate the following doses in milliliters and then determine the infusion rate.

23. Medication order: ceftriaxone 2 g once daily over 60 min
    Available stock: ceftriaxone 2 g in 50 mL premixed; 60 drop set

24. Medication order: pentamidine 4 mg/kg/dose once daily over 30 min; patient weighs 173 lb
    Available stock: pentamidine 300 mg/ 4 mL; 50 mL minibag; 15 drop set

Using Special Calculations in Compounding

8

Learning Objectives

- Calculate the amount of drug in a final product that has been diluted.
- Calculate the amount of concentrate and diluent needed to make a desired concentration.
- Calculate the amount of two products needed to prepare a desired concentration.
- Determine the least weighable quantity on a balance with a known accuracy and a given margin of error.

- Recognize when a diluent must be added to an ingredient for weighing and measuring purposes.
- Determine the amount of an aliquot in measuring diluted substances.

Preview chapter terms and definitions.

8.1 Concentrations and Dilutions

concentrate
a highly condensed drug product that is diluted prior to administration

dilution
the product obtained when an inactive ingredient, a diluent, is added to a concentrate

diluent
an inactive substance that is added to a concentrate to make it less concentrated; can be a vehicle or a solvent

Pharmaceutical preparations come in different strengths to meet the various dosing needs of patients. A **concentrate** is a highly condensed drug product that most often must be diluted prior to dispensing or administering. A **dilution** is the product obtained when an inactive ingredient, a **diluent,** is added to a concentrate. A diluent, which can be a vehicle or a solvent, is the inactive part of a solution or a mixture and serves to make the resulting solution or mixture less concentrated. A solution results when a solute and solvent mix and the solute is completely dissolved into the solvent. For some drugs, a diluted formulation will have a shorter shelf life than its concentrated form.

Medications may be diluted for several reasons. They are sometimes diluted prior to administration to children, infants, and in older adults to meet the dosing requirements of those patients. Medications may also be diluted so that they can be measured more accurately and easily. For example, volumes less than 0.1 mL are usually considered too small to measure accurately. Therefore, the preparation must be diluted further. Many pharmacies have a policy for how much an injection can be diluted. A rule of thumb is that the required dose should have a volume greater than 0.1 mL and less than 1 mL. Accuracy of weight is dependent on the accuracy of the balance used, as will be discussed later in this chapter.

Antibiotics are often supplied to pharmacies in a concentrated form and must be customized to a patient's weight or medical condition. These drugs are designed to be diluted when they are added to a patient's IV bag, either as a mini-bag or a large volume bag such as the 1 L bag commonly used. Concentrates will often be prominently labeled with a special warning highlighting the need to dilute the concentration.

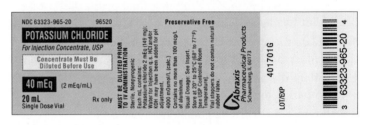

The following examples will demonstrate the two-part method for solving typical dilution problems. For each, the first part uses the ratio-proportion method to solve for the volume of the final product by using a ratio of diluted solution to desired concentration. The second part determines the amount of diluent by subtracting the concentrate from the total volume. Both of these volumes are approximate because they depend on the calibration and accuracy of the measuring devices used.

Although the second part of the calculation problem uses subtraction to determine the amount of diluent added, the amount will actually be determined by adding up to the desired total quantity. The abbreviation QS for "sufficient quantity" is used to describe the process of adding enough of the last ingredient in a compound to reach the desired volume. It is helpful to calculate the necessary amount beforehand so that an adequate supply of medication is available.

Example 8.1.1

Dexamethasone is available as a 4 mg/mL preparation; an infant is to receive 0.35 mg. Prepare a dilution so that the final concentration is 1 mg/mL. How much diluent will you need if the original product is in a 1 mL vial and you dilute the entire vial?

Part I. Determine the volume (in milliliters) of the final product. Since the strength of the dexamethasone is 4 mg/mL, a 1 mL vial will contain 4 mg of the active ingredient. Then, for a final volume x of solution, you will have a concentration of $(4/x)$ mg/mL.

$$\underset{\substack{\textbf{Diluted} \\ \textbf{solution}}}{\frac{x \text{ mL}}{4 \text{ mg}}} = \underset{\substack{\textbf{Desired} \\ \textbf{concentration}}}{\frac{1 \text{ mL}}{1 \text{ mg}}}$$

$$x \text{ mL} = \frac{(4 \cancel{\text{ mg}}) \times 1 \text{ mL}}{1 \cancel{\text{ mg}}}$$

$$x \text{ mL} = 4 \text{ mL final product}$$

Part II. Subtract the volume of the concentrate from the total volume to determine the volume of diluent needed.

4 mL total volume − 1 mL concentrate = 3 mL diluent needed

Therefore, an additional 3 mL of diluent are needed to dilute the original 1 mL of preparation to arrive at a final concentration of 1 mg/mL.

Example 8.1.2

You are instructed to make 1000 mL of a 0.8% w/v solution. You have in stock a concentrate of 95% w/v. How much of the concentrate will you use? How much diluent will be needed?

Part I. Determine how many grams there will be in the final product so that you can determine the strength of the solution.

$$\frac{x \text{ g}}{1000 \text{ mL}} = \frac{0.8 \text{ g}}{100 \text{ mL}}$$

$$x \text{ g} = \frac{(1000 \cancel{\text{ mL}}) \times 0.8 \text{ g}}{100 \cancel{\text{ mL}}}$$

$$x \text{ g} = 8 \text{ g in final product}$$

Next, determine how much of the 95% w/v concentrate will be required to provide the desired number of grams.

$$\frac{x \text{ mL}}{8 \text{ g}} = \frac{100 \text{ mL}}{95 \text{ g}}$$

$$x \text{ mL} = \frac{(8 \cancel{\text{ g}}) \times 100 \text{ mL}}{95 \cancel{\text{ g}}}$$

$$x \text{ mL} = 8.42 \text{ mL concentrate}$$

Part II. Determine how many milliliters of diluent you will need to add to make an 0.8% solution.

1000 mL total volume − 8.42 mL concentrate = 991.58 mL diluent

$$\frac{x \text{ mg}}{240 \text{mL}} = \frac{\text{mg}}{10}$$

Example 8.1.3

You are instructed to make 240 mL of a 0.45% w/v solution. You have a 100% w/v concentrate in stock. How much of the concentrate will you use? How much diluent will be needed?

Part I. Determine the number of grams desired in the final solution.

$$\frac{x \text{ g}}{240 \text{ mL}} = \frac{0.45 \text{ g}}{100 \text{ mL}}$$

$$x \text{ g} = \frac{(240 \text{ mL}) \times 0.45 \text{ g}}{100 \text{ mL}}$$

$$x \text{ g} = 1.08 \text{ g}$$

Next, determine how much of the concentrated solution will be required to provide the desired number of grams.

$$\frac{x \text{ mL}}{1.08 \text{ g}} = \frac{100 \text{ mL}}{100 \text{ g}} = \frac{1 \text{ mL}}{1 \text{ g}}$$

$$x \text{ mL} = 1.08 \text{ mL}$$

Part II. Determine how many milliliters of diluent will be needed.

240 mL total volume − 1.08 mL concentrate = 238.92 mL diluent

Example 8.1.4

You are instructed to make 500 mL of a 1:500 w/v solution. You have in stock a concentrate of 80% w/v. How much of the concentrate will you use? How much diluent will be needed?

Part I. Start by determining how many grams should be in the final solution.

$$\frac{x \text{ g}}{500 \text{ mL}} = \frac{1 \text{ g}}{500 \text{ mL}}$$

$$x \text{ g} = 1 \text{ g}$$

Next, determine how many milliliters of the concentrate will be required to provide the desired number of grams.

$$\frac{x \text{ mL}}{1 \text{ g}} = \frac{100 \text{ mL}}{80 \text{ g}}$$

$$x \text{ mL} = 1.25 \text{ mL}$$

Part II. Now you can determine how many milliliters of diluent will be needed.

500 mL total volume − 1.25 mL concentrate = 498.75 mL diluent

---

Example 8.1.5

You have been instructed to add 2 g of cefazolin to five 1 L bags of NS and 2 g to three 1 L bags of D$_5$W. How many milliliters of the cefazolin solution shown in the label below will you place in each bag and how many milliliters will you need for all of the bags? Assuming you started with a new vial, how much of the vial will remain after you have prepared the orders?

Part I. Determine the amount of cefazolin concentrate for 1 ordered bag, using the label's stated dilution of 1 g/5 mL.

$$\frac{x\text{ mL}}{2\text{ g}} = \frac{5\text{ mL}}{1\text{ g}}$$

$$x\text{ mL} = \frac{(2\text{ g}) \times 5\text{ mL}}{1\text{ g}} = 10\text{ mL}$$

Use the volume of concentrate for 1 bag to determine the total volume of cefazolin concentrate needed to create all of the ordered dilutions.

5 orders + 3 orders = 8 orders

8 orders × 10 mL/order = 80 mL

Part II. Since it is not stated on the label, calculate the volume of cefazolin concentrate in the vial.

$$\frac{x\text{ mL}}{20\text{ g}} = \frac{5\text{ mL}}{1\text{ g}}$$

$$x\text{ mL} = \frac{(20\text{ g}) \times 5\text{ mL}}{1\text{ g}} = 100\text{ mL}$$

Determine the amount of cefazolin concentrate that will be left over after the order is filled.

total vial volume − needed volume = left-over volume

100 mL − 80 mL = 20 mL

8.1 Problem Set

Calculate the amount of concentrate and diluent for each of the following compounds. Round to the hundredth place for this problem set. Remember that the amount measured will be *approximate* due to equipment constraints.

1. Prepare 3 mL of a 10 mg/mL phenobarbital solution from a 65 mg/mL stock solution that comes in a 1 mL vial. How much concentrate and how much diluent are needed to obtain the desired final volume?

2. A drug is supplied as a 40 mg/mL solution in a 50 mL vial. You need to make 10 mL of a 10 mg/mL solution. How much concentrate and diluent will be needed?

3. Folic acid is commonly available as a 5 mg/mL injection. You are to make a preparation that contains 50 mcg/mL in a total volume of 30 mL. How much folic acid and how much diluent must be used?

4. Prepare 10 mL of a 200 mcg/mL folic acid solution by using a 5 mg/mL stock solution. How much folic acid and how much diluent will you need?

5. Prepare 20 mL of a 5 mg/mL tobramycin solution from a 40 mg/mL stock solution. How much tobramycin and how much diluent are needed?

6. Prepare 10 mL of a 50 mg/mL methicillin solution from a stock solution of 250 mg/0.5 mL. How much methicillin and how much diluent are needed?

7. Prepare 20 mL of a 100 mcg/mL vitamin B_{12} solution from a 1 mg/mL stock solution. How much B_{12} and diluent are needed?

8. Prepare 8 mL of a 5 mg/mL hydrocortisone solution from a 100 mg/2 mL stock solution. How many milliliters of hydrocortisone and diluent are needed?

9. Prepare 15 mL of a 50 mg/mL cefazolin dilution from a stock of 1 g/5 mL. How many milliliters of diluent and stock solution will be needed?

10. Prepare one dose of 0.6 mg gentamicin in 2 mL diluted from a stock solution of 20 mg/mL. How much gentamicin and how much diluent are used?

11. A drug comes packaged as 10 mg/mL. Make a preparation totaling 25 mL of 2 mg/mL concentration. How much drug and how much diluent are used?

12. Nafcillin comes packaged as a powder for constitution at 250 mg/mL. Prepare 20 mL of a 25 mg/mL dilution. How many milligrams of the drug and what volume of diluent are needed?

13. Metoclopramide 5 mg/mL is used to make 10 mL of 0.5 mg/mL solution. What volume of drug and how much diluent are required?

14. Prepare 20 mL of a 50 mg/mL drug dilution from a stock of 2 g/5 mL. How many milliliters of diluent and stock drug solution will be needed?

15. Prepare a 10 mcg/mL solution of a drug with a final volume of 3 mL. How many milliliters of stock drug (50 mcg/mL) will be needed?

16. Prepare 5 mL of a 5 mcg/mL dilution from a stock drug of 50 mcg/mL. How much drug and diluent are needed?

17. You receive an order for 100 mL of a 30% hydrochloric acid solution. You have a 90% solution in stock. How many milliliters of concentrate will you need?

18. A patient needs 10 mL of 4 mcg/mL magnesium sulfate solution. You have 10 mcg/mL on hand.

    a. How much concentrate will you need?

    b. How much diluent?

19. You need 5 mL of heparin 100 units/mL. In stock you have 10,000 units/mL in a 20 mL vial.

    a. How much concentrate will you need?

    b. How much diluent?

20. An order calls for 5 mL of 50 mg/mL Terramycin. On hand you have 200 mg/mL Terramycin.

    a. How much concentrate will you need?

    b. How much diluent?

21. A doctor orders 2 mL of 80 mg/mL tobramycin. The pharmacy stocks 160 mg/mL.

    a. How much concentrate will you need?

    b. How much diluent?

22. An IV of 0.45% sodium chloride 1000 mL needs to be infused. The pharmacy carries only 0.9% sodium chloride 1000 mL.

    a. How much concentrate will you need?

    b. How much diluent?

23. You need 50 mL of 5% dextrose for a patient. You have 70% dextrose 1000 mL on hand.

    a. How much concentrate will you need?

    b. How much diluent?

24. A patient needs 35% dextrose 500 mL. The pharmacy has only 70% dextrose 1000 mL.

    a. How much concentrate will you need?

    b. How much diluent?

25. An IV order calls for 300 mL of Liposyn 10%. The only Liposyn in stock is Liposyn 20%.

    a. How much concentrate will you need?

    b. How much diluent?

Calculate the volume of concentrate used in the following orders.

26. You have been instructed to add 1.5 g of vancomycin to a 1 L bag of NS.

a. How many milliliters of the vancomycin solution shown in the label above will you place in the bag?

b. Assuming you have a new vial, how many milliliters will remain in the vial after you have prepared the order?

27. You have been instructed to add 0.5 g of cefazolin to three 1 L bags of NS.

a. How many milliliters of the cefazolin solution shown in the label above will you place in each bag?

b. Assuming you have a new vial, how many milliliters will remain in the vial after you have prepared the order?

28. A patient is to take 8 mg of dexamethasone in four equally divided doses. Each dose is to be diluted to 1 mg/mL strength and given as a bolus injection every 6 hours.

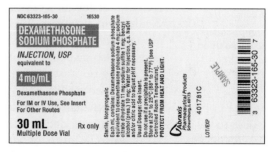

a. How many milliliters of the dexamethasone solution shown in the label above will be required to provide the 8 mg?

b. How many milliliters will be in each of the bolus doses?

29. You have been instructed to add 20 mEq potassium chloride to a 1 L bag of NS and 10 mEq to a 1 L bag of D$_5$W.

a. How many milliliters of the potassium solution shown in the label above will you place in each bag?

b. Assuming you have a new vial, how many milliliters will remain in the vial after you have prepared the orders?

30. You have been instructed to add 2 g of vancomycin to two 1 L bags of NS.

a. How many milliliters of the vancomycin solution above will you place in each bag?

b. Assuming you have a new vial, how many milliliters will remain in the vial after you have prepared the order?

Self-check your work in Appendix A.

8.2 Compound Formulas

compounding
the process of using raw ingredients and/or other prepared ingredients to prepare a drug product for a patient

formula
a written document listing the ingredients and instructions needed to prepare a compound

compounded stock solution
a solution that is prepared in a large amount and kept in stock in the pharmacy to be divided for individual prescriptions

Compounding is the process of using raw ingredients and/or other prepared ingredients to prepare a drug product for a patient. This is similar to making a cake from scratch by using ingredients such as butter, sugar, eggs, flour, and baking powder.

A **formula** is a written document prepared by the pharmacist that lists the ingredients and instructions needed to prepare a compound. Some formulas are intended to prepare a single prescription, and others are intended to prepare a **compounded stock solution,** or a large amount to be divided for individual prescription orders later. Commonly used compounds can be made in advance to have on hand as needed.

Some pharmacies routinely prepare compounded products for physicians who prescribe these special preparations on a regular basis. A pharmacy that prepares these compounds will often have a "recipe" for making a large amount to have on hand over the coming days or weeks. It is not uncommon to prepare a compound that can be divided and dispensed to as many as twenty patients. Preparing compounds in advance can result in cost savings by reducing the labor needed to make the product and can also save time in providing the compound to the patient. Although the Food and Drug Administration prohibits retail pharmacies from mass manufacturing compounded medications, anticipatory compounding is permitted in small quantities when a particular pharmacy is located near a physician's office that routinely orders certain compounded prescriptions.

Pharmacies store formulas in many ways. They may be maintained as a computerized file system or informally in a card file or binder. Some pharmacies also have different formulas for different prescribers, as each prescriber may prefer a slightly different version of a compound.

Enlarging or reducing formulas involves taking the recipe for a particular compounded medication and adjusting the amount of the ingredients meet the needs of the pharmacy's order. This practice is similar to doubling the ingredients in a recipe for cookies in order to make twice as many cookies. Retaining the correct proportion of each ingredient in this process is very important. A cookie made from a doubled batch should have the same ratio of ingredients as a cookie made from a single batch. The same should be true when a formula is doubled in the compounding pharmacy.

Accurate records and documentation of mathematical calculations used in reducing or enlarging a formula are essential. All amounts should be calculated and recorded prior to weighing, measuring, and mixing.

The dispensed compound must match the concentration and the amount ordered. For example, a formula may result in 120 mL of solution, and the patient may need only 20 mL. Or the patient may need 60 g of a cream, and a formula may be written for 15 g. The following examples will demonstrate the calculations for reducing or enlarging formulas.

Example 8.2.1

You need to prepare 100 mL of an iodine solution for a patient. The pharmacy's formula follows.

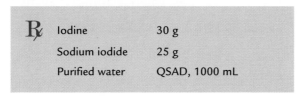

The formula indicates the resulting volume is 1000 mL, and your patient needs 100 mL. So, you will need $\frac{1}{10}$ (i.e., 100 mL desired/1000 mL formula) of each amount. Dividing each ingredient amount by 10 will result in the following:

Iodine	30 g ÷ 10 = 3 g
Sodium iodide	25 g ÷ 10 = 2.5 g
Purified water	1000 mL ÷ 10 = 100 mL

Example 8.2.2

You need to prepare 1 lb of coal tar ointment for a patient. Your formula results in 4 oz (120 g) of ointment.

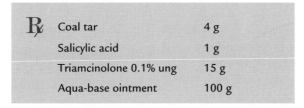

Since 1 lb = 16 oz, you will need to multiply your formula by 4 to obtain the correct amount of coal tar ointment.

Coal tar	4 g × 4 = 16 g
Salicylic acid	1 g × 4 = 4 g
Triamcinolone 0.1% ung	15 g × 4 = 60 g
Aqua-base ointment	100 g × 4 = 400 g

Example 8.2.3   **You need to prepare four syringes for the following order.**

> ℞   Phenol 5% w/v syringes sodium chloride 5 mL

Calculate the amount of phenol needed in each syringe.

$$\frac{x \text{ g}}{5 \text{ mL}} = \frac{5 \text{ g}}{100 \text{ mL}}$$

$$x \text{ g} = 0.25 \text{ g or } 250 \text{ mg/syringe}$$

For four syringes, you will need

$$4 \text{ syringes} \times 250 \text{ mg/syringe} = 1000 \text{ mg phenol}$$

You will also need

$$4 \text{ syringes} \times 5 \text{ mL sodium chloride/syringe} = 20 \text{ mL sodium chloride}$$

8.2 Problem Set

1. Fill the following order by preparing two bags of 500 mL admixture from your stock solutions of lidocaine 20% and furosemide 10 mg/mL. State how much ingredient you should add to the two bags.

> ℞   Lidocaine 2.5 g
>
>   Furosemide 500 mg
>
>   1000 mL D₅W

2. Fill the following order and prepare enough admixture for a 24 hour period. How much of each ingredient will you need to bring into the IV room? Potassium chloride comes packaged as 2 mEq/mL in 15 mL vials.

> ℞   1000 mL NS with 20 mEq potassium chloride
>
>   infuse at 125 mL/hour

3. You are to prepare a 30 g jar of ointment using the following formula. State how much of each ingredient you will need.

> ℞   Coal tar   4 g
>
>   Salicylic acid   1 g
>
>   Triamcinolone 1% ung   15 g
>
>   Aqua-base ointment   100 g
>
>   yields 120 g

4. Use the following formula to prepare 150 vaginal suppositories. How much of each ingredient should you weigh out?

> ℞   Progesterone   2.4 g
>
>   Polyethylene glycol 3350   30 g
>
>   Polyethylene glycol 1000   90 g
>
>   yields 30 vaginal suppositories

5. You need to prepare the following formula for six patients. How much of each ingredient should you measure out?

> ℞ Podophyllum resin 25%
>
> Benzoin tincture QSAD 20 mL

6. You have a prescription for 12 fl oz of Magic Mixture Number 7, and the pharmacy's formula follows. How much of each ingredient should you measure out?

> ℞ **Magic Mixture Number 7**
>
> Tetracycline
>
> 500 mg capsules 16 capsules
>
> Hydrocortisone suspension 15 mL
>
> Lidocaine oral suspension 30 mL
>
> Mylanta suspension QSAD 240 mL

7. Prepare four 15 mL dropper bottles of Otic-caine using the following formula. How much of each ingredient should you measure out?

> ℞ **Otic-caine Drops**
>
> Antipyrine 1.8 g
>
> Benzocaine 0.5 g
>
> Glycerin QSAD 30 mL

8. Tetracycline sclerosing solution is used to reduce the size of cysts that form in the kidneys of renal transplant patients. The following formula is used when making tetracycline sclerosing solution. List the ingredients and amounts needed to make a solution containing 2 g of tetracycline.

> ℞ Tetracycline HCl powder 1 g
>
> Ascorbic acid powder 2.5 g
>
> Sterile saline for injection 10 mL
>
> Instructions
>
> 1. Weigh out powders and mix in a nonsterile glass container.
>
> 2. Add 10 mL sterile saline and swirl to dissolve.
>
> 3. Draw up solution in a 20 mL syringe and push through a 0.22 micron filter.

Self-check your work in Appendix A.

8.3 Alligations

Physicians often prescribe concentrations of medications that are not commercially available, and these prescriptions must be compounded (added together) at the pharmacy. When an ordered concentration is not commercially available, either of two methods may be used to fill the prescription in the pharmacy. The first is to use a concentrated stock solution, as in the examples in the first section of this chapter. This method is used when the amount of concentrate is very small and can be added to the product in a relatively small volume.

The second approach is to combine two different solutions with the same active ingredient in differing strengths. The resulting concentration, which is called an

alligation, will be greater than the weaker strength but less than the stronger strength. For example, 1% and 5% hydrocortisone ointments may be combined to provide a 3% ointment. This method is used when the two quantities needed to prepare the desired concentration are both relatively large.

The amount of each solution is calculated by using the **alligation alternate method.** This calculation is used to determine the proportions of given percentages needed to prepare the desired concentration. The alligation alternate method requires changing the percentages to parts of a proportion and then using the proportion to obtain the amounts of the two ingredients. The answer can then be checked by using the following formula.

$$\text{milliliters} \times \text{percent (expressed as a decimal)} = \text{grams}$$

It is important to note that this formula works for any strength of solution.

The following examples will demonstrate the application of the alligation alternate method.

Example 8.3.1

Prepare 250 mL of dextrose 7.5% w/v using dextrose 5% (D₅W) w/v and dextrose 50% (D₅₀W) w/v. How many milliliters of each will be needed?

Step 1. Set up a box arrangement, and at the upper-left corner, write the percent of the highest concentration (50%) as a whole number. At the lower-left corner, write the percent of the lowest concentration (5%) as a whole number, and in the center, write the desired concentration.

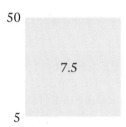

Step 2. Subtract the center number from the upper-left number (note: the smaller from the larger), and put it at the lower-right corner. Now subtract the lower-left number from the center number (again: the smaller from the larger), and put it at the upper-right corner.

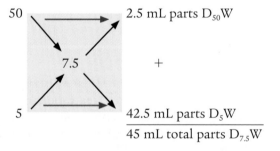

The 2.5 mL represents the number of parts of the 50% solution that will be needed to make the final 7.5% solution, and the 42.5 mL represents the number of parts of the 5% solution that will be needed. The sum of these two numbers, 2.5 mL + 42.5 mL = 45 mL, is the total number of parts of the 7.5% solution. In terms of ratios, the ratio of the 5% solu-

tion to the 7.5% solution is 42.5:45, and the ratio of the 50% solution to the 7.5% solution is 2.5:45. Much less of the 50% solution is needed to make the 7.5% solution.

Step 3. Calculate the volume needed of each dextrose solution.

50% Dextrose

$$\frac{x \text{ mL of } 50\%}{250 \text{ mL}} = \frac{2.5 \text{ mL parts } D_{50}W}{45 \text{ mL total parts } D_{7.5}W}$$

$$x \text{ mL of } 50\% = \frac{(250 \cancel{\text{ mL}}) \times 2.5 \text{ mL parts}}{45 \cancel{\text{ mL}} \text{ total parts } D_{7.5}W}$$

$$x \text{ mL of } 50\% = 13.8888 \text{ mL } D_{50}W, \text{ rounded to } 13.89 \text{ mL}$$

5% Dextrose

$$\frac{x \text{ mL of } 5\%}{250 \text{ mL}} = \frac{42.5 \text{ mL parts } D_5W}{45 \text{ mL total parts } D_{7.5}W}$$

$$x \text{ mL of } 5\% = \frac{(250 \cancel{\text{ mL}}) \times 42.5 \text{ mL parts}}{45 \cancel{\text{ mL}} \text{ total parts } D_{7.5}W}$$

$$x \text{ mL of } 5\% = 236.11 \text{ mL } D_5W$$

Step 4. Add the volumes of the two solutions together. The sum should equal the required volume of dextrose 7.5%.

$$\begin{array}{r} 236.11 \text{ mL} \\ +13.89 \text{ mL} \\ \hline 250.00 \text{ mL} \end{array}$$

Step 5. Check your answer by calculating the amount of solute (dextrose) in all three solutions. The number of grams of solute should equal the sum of the grams of solutes from the 50% solution and the 5% solution, using the following formula.

$$\text{mL} \times \% \text{ (as a decimal)} = g$$

$$250 \text{ mL} \times 0.075 = 18.75 \text{ g}$$
$$13.89 \text{ mL } D_{50}W \times 0.5 = 6.945 \text{ g}$$
$$236.11 \text{ mL } D_5W \times 0.05 = 11.805 \text{ g}$$

$$\begin{array}{r} 11.805 \text{ g} \\ +6.945 \text{ g} \\ \hline 18.750 \text{ g} \end{array}$$

The amounts measured to prepare this prescription will be rounded to the nearest milliliter, 14 mL $D_{50}W$ and 236 mL D_5W.

Example 8.3.2   You are instructed to make 454 g of 3% zinc oxide cream. You have in stock 10% and 1% zinc oxide cream. How much of each percent will you use?

Step 1. We will simplify the step method used in Example 8.3.1 by combining Steps 1 and 2 into a single step and calculating the ratios right at the square, where it is easy to visualize.

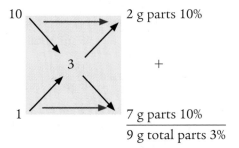

$$10 \qquad 2 \text{ g parts } 10\%$$
$$3 \qquad +$$
$$1 \qquad \frac{7 \text{ g parts } 10\%}{9 \text{ g total parts } 3\%}$$

Step 2. **10% zinc oxide cream**

$$\frac{x \text{ g of } 10\%}{454 \text{ g}} = \frac{2 \text{ g parts } 10\%}{9 \text{ g total parts } 3\%}$$

$$x \text{ g of } 10\% = 101 \text{ g of } 10\% \text{ zinc oxide cream}$$

1% zinc oxide cream

$$\frac{x \text{ g of } 1\%}{454 \text{ g}} = \frac{7 \text{ g parts } 1\%}{9 \text{ g total parts } 3\%}$$

$$x \text{ g of } 1\% = 353 \text{ g of } 1\% \text{ zinc oxide cream}$$

Step 3. Check your work.

$$353 \text{ g} + 101 \text{ g} = 454 \text{ g}$$

Example 8.3.3   You have been instructed to make 30 g of a 6% ointment. You have on hand a 4% and an 8% ointment. How much of each will you use?

Step 1.

$$8 \qquad 2 \text{ g parts } 8\%$$
$$6 \qquad +$$
$$4 \qquad \frac{2 \text{ g parts } 4\%}{4 \text{ g total parts } 6\%}$$

Step 2. **8% ointment**

$$\frac{x \text{ g of } 8\%}{30 \text{ g}} = \frac{2 \text{ g parts } 8\%}{4 \text{ g total parts } 6\%}$$

$$x \text{ g of } 8\% = 15 \text{ g of } 8\% \text{ ointment}$$

4% ointment

$$\frac{x \text{ g of } 4\%}{30 \text{ g}} = \frac{2 \text{ g parts } 4\%}{4 \text{ g total parts } 6\%}$$

$$x \text{ g of } 4\% = 15 \text{ g of } 4\% \text{ ointment}$$

Step 3. Check your work.

$$15 \text{ g} + 15 \text{ g} = 30 \text{ g}$$

alligation medial method
the mathematical calculation used to find the final concentration created when two or more known quantities of known concentrations are compounded

On some occasions, you will have to calculate the final concentration or percentage strength of a mixture that is composed of known quantities and percentage strengths of two or more ingredients. The calculation used is called the **alligation medial method.** The resulting percentage is the "middle" or "medial" strength, as it is somewhere between the strengths of the ingredients. The following example will demonstrate the alligation medial method calculation.

Example 8.3.4

You have been asked to prepare a mixture with the following ingredients: 30 g of 1% hydrocortisone cream, 20 g of 0.5% hydrocortisone ointment, and 10 g of Eucerin cream base. What will be the percentage of hydrocortisone in the final mixture?

Begin by determining the amount of active ingredient (hydrocortisone) in each of the items added to the mixture. Because the Eucerin cream does not contain hydrocortisone, a calculation is not needed for this ingredient. However, it is necessary to calculate the amount of active ingredient in the other two amounts.

30 g of 1% w/w hydrocortisone cream

Solution 1: Using the ratio-proportion method,

$$\frac{x \text{ g}}{30 \text{ g}} = \frac{1 \text{ g}}{100 \text{ g}}$$

$$x \text{ g} = 0.3 \text{ g hydrocortisone}$$

Solution 2: Using the dimensional analysis method,

$$30 \text{ g} \times 1 \text{ g}/100 \text{ g} = 0.3 \text{ g hydrocortisone}$$

20 g of 0.5% w/w hydrocortisone ointment

Solution 1: Using the ratio-proportion method,

$$\frac{x \text{ g}}{20 \text{ g}} = \frac{0.5 \text{ g}}{100 \text{ g}}$$

$$x \text{ g} = 0.1 \text{ g hydrocortisone}$$

Solution 2: Using the dimensional analysis method,

$$20 \text{ g} \times 0.5 \text{ g}/100 \text{ g} = 0.1 \text{ g hydrocortisone}$$

Next, determine the amount of grams in the final mixture.

30 g 1% cream + 20 g 0.5% ointment + 10 g Eucerin = 60 g final mixture

Finally, add the active ingredients and divide by the total quantity to determine the final concentration.

$$\frac{0.3 \text{ g} + 0.1 \text{ g}}{60 \text{ g}} \times 100 = 0.6666\%, \text{ rounded to } 0.7\%$$

Note that the final concentration of 0.7% is between the concentrations of the ingredients. (It is less than 1% and more than 0.5%.)

8.3 Problem Set

Use the alligation alternate method to answer the following problems.

1. Prepare 200 mL of 7.5% dextrose solution using D_5W and $D_{10}W$. How much of each solution will be needed?

2. Prepare 400 mL of D_8W from $D_{20}W$ and sterile water for injection (SWFI). How much of each will be needed? (Note: water is considered to be 0% solution.)

3. Prepare 500 mL of $D_{12.5}W$. You have on hand D_5W, $D_{10}W$, and $D_{20}W$. How much of which two solutions will you need?

4. You must prepare a 250 mL solution of D_6W using SWFI, $D_{10}W$, or $D_{50}W$. How much of which two will you need?

5. Prepare a $D_{7.5}W$ solution beginning with 500 mL of D_5W and adding $D_{50}W$. What will the final volume be, and how much $D_{50}W$ will be used?

6. Prepare 250 mL of 8% dextrose from D_5W and $D_{20}W$. How much of each is needed?

7. Prepare 300 mL of 7.5% dextrose using SWFI and $D_{20}W$. How much of each is needed?

8. Prepare 500 mL of 12.5% dextrose using $D_{10}W$ and $D_{20}W$. How much of each is needed?

9. Prepare 150 mL of 7.5% dextrose from D_5W and $D_{10}W$. How much of each is needed?

10. Prepare 25 mL of 9% dextrose in water. Use D_5W and $D_{20}W$. How much of each fluid is used?

11. A physician has ordered 300 mL of $D_{12.5}W$. You have $D_{10}W$ and $D_{20}W$ available. How much $D_{10}W$ and $D_{20}W$ will you use to prepare 300 mL of $D_{12.5}W$?

> ℞   300 mL $D_{12.5}W$
>
>   KCl 14 mEq

12. Prepare 500 mL of a 15% dextrose solution using D_5W and $D_{50}W$. How much of each solution will be needed?

13. Prepare 100 mL of a 12% dextrose solution using D_5W and $D_{20}W$. How much of each solution will be needed?

14. Prepare 60 g of a 3% cream from a 1% cream and a 10% cream. How many ounces of each cream will you need to weigh out?

15. Prepare 30 g of a 7.5% cream from a 5% and 15% cream. How much of each cream will you need to weigh out?

16. Prepare 1 L of 80% alcohol from 70% and 100%. How much of each do you need to measure out?

17. Prepare 3 L of a 12.5% dextrose solution from D_5W and $D_{50}W$. How much of each solution will be needed?

18. Prepare 100 mL of 5% hydrogen peroxide from a 1.5% and a 30% solution. How much of each solution will be needed?

19. Prepare four 30 g jars of hydrocortisone 3% cream. Use 1% and 5% creams. How much of each cream will be needed?

20. Prepare 2400 g of coal tar ointment 20%. You have on hand coal tar solution and ointment base. How much of each will be needed?

21. Prepare 45 g of 10% zinc oxide using petrolatum and a 20% zinc oxide ointment. How much of each will be needed?

22. Prepare 1 L of 50% alcohol from 70% solution and 15% solution. How much of each solution will be needed?

23. Prepare 1 gallon of a 1:10 solution of bleach using a 2% stable commercial bleach solution and a 100% bleach concentrate. How much of each solution will be needed?

24. Prepare 30 mL of a 1:200 solution by combining a 1:10 and a 1:400 solution. How much of each solution will be needed?

25. Prepare 120 mL of a 1:500 solution by combining a 1:250 and a 1:750 solution. How much of each will be needed?

26. The pharmacy receives the following order, and you have $D_{10}W$ and $D_{20}W$ available.

> ℞ 300 mL $D_{12.5}W$
>
> KCl 14 mEq

a. Calculate the volumes of liquid needed to prepare the order.

b. You will need to prepare three bags of the solution for the next three shifts. How much of each ingredient will you need?

27. The pharmacy receives the following order, and you have the following ingredients to use to fill it: dextrose in 5% and 20%, sodium chloride 4 mEq/mL, potassium chloride 2 mEq/mL, and aminophylline 25 mg/mL.

> ℞ 1000 mL dextrose 8%
>
> Sodium chloride 24 mEq
>
> Potassium chloride 10 mEq
>
> Aminophylline 300 mg

a. Calculate the amount of each solution needed to prepare a 1 L bag.

b. After creating the 1 L bag, you are instructed to prepare a second bag, but this one is to be 500 mL. How much of each ingredient will be needed to create the second bag?

Using the alligation medial method, determine the resulting concentration for each of the following compounds.

28. You have mixed equal parts of a 20% and a 5% benzocaine ointment. What is the resulting concentration?

29. You have mixed 20 mL of a 1:400 solution and 30 L of a 1:150 solution. What is the resulting concentration?

30. You have mixed 30 g of 2% cream into 30 g of 8% cream. What is the resulting concentration?

31. You have mixed 100 g of 8% cream into 200 g of 3% cream. What is the resulting concentration?

32. You have mixed 1 L of solution containing 15% alcohol, 500 mL of solution containing 3% alcohol, and 300 mL of solution containing 70% alcohol. What is the resulting concentration?

33. What is the final percentage strength of a mixture made from 30 mL of 1.5% hydrogen peroxide and 10 mL of 30% hydrogen peroxide?

34. What is the percentage strength of a mixture made from 300 mL of 70% alcohol and 200 mL of 95% alcohol?

35. What is the percentage strength of a mixture made from 100 mL each of 50% alcohol, 70% alcohol, and 95% alcohol?

36. What is the percentage strength of a mixture made from 60 g each of 5% coal tar ung and 10% coal tar ung?

37. What is the percentage strength of a mixture made from 20 g of 50% ichthamol, 10 g of 10% ichthamol, and 60 g of 5% ichthamol?

38. What is the percentage strength of a mixture made from 300 mL of witch hazel containing 14% alcohol, 100 mL of 95% alcohol, and 500 mL of distilled water?

39. What is the percentage strength of a mixture made from 60 g of 20% zinc oxide and 120 g of white petrolatum?

40. What is the percentage strength of a mixture containing 20 mL of 2% lidocaine, 10 mL SWFI, and 5 mL sodium bicarbonate?

Self-check your work in Appendix A.

8.4 Least Measurable Quantity and Aliquot Measurements

At times, you will be handling very small amounts of medications when preparing a compounded prescription in the pharmacy. In these situations, it is essential to know the smallest amount that can be accurately weighed on your balance. The following formula will determine this amount.

$$\frac{100 \times \text{balance sensitivity}}{\text{permissible \% margin of error}} = \text{least weighable quantity}$$

Example 8.4.1

A Class A balance has a sensitivity of 6 mg. The order being prepared may have up to a 3% margin of error. What is the smallest amount that can be accurately weighed?

$$\frac{100 \times \text{balance sensitivity}}{\text{permissible \% margin of error}} = \frac{100 \times 6 \text{ mg}}{3} = 200 \text{ mg}$$

Example 8.4.2

A Class A balance has a sensitivity of 6 mg. The order being prepared may have up to a 1% margin of error. What is the smallest amount that can be accurately weighed?

$$\frac{100 \times \text{balance sensitivity}}{\text{permissible \% margin of error}} = \frac{100 \times 6 \text{ mg}}{1} = 600 \text{ mg}$$

aliquot
a measured portion, fraction, or part of an ingredient that is placed into solution or into a mixture of other ingredients to aid in measuring a very small amount

If a very small amount needs to be weighed and the pharmacy balance does not allow for measuring this dose, an aliquot may be used. An **aliquot** is a measured portion, fraction, or part that is placed into solution or into a mixture of other ingredients. The diluted mixture can then be weighed out, and the desired active ingredient can be measured more accurately.

TABLE 8.1   Steps for Weight Aliquot Measuring

Step 1. Calculate the least weighable quantity (LWQ), based on the sensitivity of your balance and the permissible margin of error. This equation has been given in the text above.

Step 2. Determine the amount of the ordered drug that you will actually weigh out. This amount must be equal to or larger than the least weighable quantity. To calculate the amount of drug to weigh out, multiply the amount of drug ordered by a whole number such as 2, 5, 10, or 20, until you have a weighable amount—that is, an amount greater than the least weighable quantity. The whole number you choose is called a *factor*. The factor chosen is arbitrary, but it must result in an amount greater than the least weighable quantity.

Step 3. Determine the amount of diluent (inert ingredient) to add.
  a. First determine the total amount of mixture (drug + diluent) that will be required. The total amount of mixture is calculated by multiplying the amount of drug weighed out (determined in Step 2) by some factor. The factor does not have to be the same as the one that was used in Step 2, but for convenience it often is.

$$\text{drug weighed out} \times \text{factor} = \text{total amount of mixture}$$

  b. Calculate the amount of diluent needed by subtracting the amount of the drug weighed out (Step 2) from the total amount of mixture.

$$\text{total amount of mixture} - \text{drug weighed out} = \text{diluent}$$

Step 4. Combine the drug and diluent measured in Steps 2 and 3 and mix them well so that the drug is evenly distributed throughout the mixture.

Step 5. Determine the amount of mixture needed to provide the originally ordered amount by using the ratio-proportion method.

$$\frac{x \text{ mg mixture}}{\text{amount of drug ordered}} = \frac{\text{total amount of mixture}}{\text{amount of drug weighed}}$$

(The total amount of mixture was calculated in Step 3a; the amount of drug weighed out was calculated in Step 2.)

For example, if an order calls for a small amount, such as 75 mg, and allows for a very small margin of error, we may not be able to accurately weigh out this amount. The least weighable quantity must be calculated. This quantity is what will be measured. Aliquot measuring can be performed using the steps defined in Table 8.1.

Example 8.4.3

You receive a prescription for 75 mg of antibiotic in 15 mL of Cherry Syrup USP. A 5% margin of error is allowed, and you are to use a Class A balance with a sensitivity of 6 mg. What amount of aliquot mixture will contain the ordered amount of drug?

Step 1. Determine the least weighable quantity.

$$\frac{100 \times \text{balance sensitivity}}{\text{permissible \% margin of error}} = \frac{100 \times 6 \text{ mg}}{5} = 120 \text{ mg}$$

So at least 120 mg of the active ingredient must be weighed. At least this amount must be weighed for the diluent used as well.

Step 2. Determine the amount to be weighed. Because the amount that is to be weighed out has to be equal to or larger than the least weighable quantity, which in this case is 120 mg, multiply the desired amount by 2.

$$75 \text{ mg} \times 2 = 150 \text{ mg}$$

Step 3. Determine the total amount of mixture that will be required and the amount of inert ingredient.

$$150 \text{ mg active ingredient} \times 2 = 300 \text{ mg total mixture}$$

$$300 \text{ mg total} - 150 \text{ mg active ingredient} = 150 \text{ mg inert ingredient}$$

You must weigh 150 mg of the inert ingredient.

Step 4. Determine the total weight of the drug and diluent by restating the equation from Step 3.

$$150 \text{ mg drug} + 150 \text{ mg inert ingredient} = 300 \text{ mg}$$

Step 5. Determine the amount of mixture needed to provide the originally ordered amount.

$$x \text{ mg mixture} = \frac{(75 \text{ mg drug ordered}) \times (300 \text{ mg mixture})}{150 \text{ mg drug}}$$

$$x \text{ mg mixture} = 150 \text{ mg}$$

So a 150 mg aliquot will contain 75 mg of the drug, the ordered amount of drug.

Example 8.4.4

You receive a prescription for 15 mg of antibiotic in 10 mL Cherry Syrup USP. A 3% margin of error is allowed, and you are to use a balance with a sensitivity of 4 mg. What amount of aliquot mixture will contain the ordered amount of drug?

Step 1. Determine the least weighable quantity.

$$\frac{100 \times \text{balance sensitivity}}{\text{permissible \% margin of error}} = \frac{100 \times 4 \text{ mg}}{3} = 133 \text{ mg}$$

So at least 133 mg of the active ingredient must be weighed. At least this amount must be weighed for the diluent used as well.

Step 2. Determine the amount to be weighed.

$$15 \text{ mg} \times 10 = 150 \text{ mg}$$

Step 3. Determine the total amount of mixture that will be required and the amount of inert ingredient.

$$150 \text{ mg active ingredient} \times 10 = 1500 \text{ mg total mixture}$$

$$1500 \text{ mg total} - 150 \text{ mg active ingredient} = 1350 \text{ mg inert ingredient}$$

You must weigh 1350 mg of the inert ingredient.

Step 4. Determine the total weight of the drug and diluent.

$$150 \text{ mg drug} + 1350 \text{ mg diluent} = 1500 \text{ mg}$$

Step 5. Determine the amount of mixture needed to provide the originally ordered amount.

$$x \text{ mg mixture} = \frac{(15 \text{ mg drug ordered}) \times (1500 \text{ mg mixture})}{150 \text{ mg drug}}$$

$$x \text{ mg mixture} = 150 \text{ mg}$$

So a 150 mg aliquot will contain 15 mg of the drug, the ordered amount of drug.

Example 8.4.5

You receive a prescription for 5 mg of antibiotic in 3 mL of normal saline (NS). A 5% margin of error is allowed, and you are to use a Class A balance with a sensitivity of 4 mg. What amount of aliquot mixture will contain the ordered amount of drug?

Step 1. Determine the least weighable quantity.

$$\frac{100 \times \text{balance sensitivity}}{\text{permissible \% margin of error}} = \frac{100 \times 4 \text{ mg}}{5} = 80 \text{ mg}$$

So at least 80 mg of the active ingredient must be weighed. At least this amount must be weighed for the diluent used as well.

Step 2. Determine the amount to be weighed.

$$5 \text{ mg} \times 20 = 100 \text{ mg}$$

Step 3. Determine the total amount of mixture that will be required and the amount of inert ingredient.

$$100 \text{ mg active ingredient} \times 20 = 2000 \text{ mg total mixture}$$

$$2000 \text{ mg total} - 100 \text{ mg active ingredient} = 1900 \text{ mg inert ingredient}$$

You must weigh 1900 mg of the inert ingredient.

Step 4. Determine the total weight of the drug and diluent.

$$100 \text{ mg drug} + 1900 \text{ mg diluent} = 2000 \text{ mg}$$

Step 5. Determine the amount of mixture needed to provide the originally ordered amount.

$$x \text{ mg mixture} = \frac{(5 \text{ mg drug ordered}) \times (2000 \text{ mg mixture})}{100 \text{ mg drug}}$$

$$x \text{ mg mixture} = 100 \text{ mg}$$

So a 100 mg aliquot will contain 5 mg of the drug, the ordered amount of drug.

TABLE 8.2   Steps for Volume Aliquot Measuring

Step 1. Determine the minimum volume that can be measured accurately. This amount will vary because it depends on the size of the syringe or graduated cylinder available.

Step 2. Determine the multiple of the active ingredient that will provide the smallest volume that can be accurately measured.

Step 3. Determine the total volume of the mixture by multiplying the volume of active ingredient by the same multiple (factor) used in Step 2.

Step 4. Determine the amount of diluent needed by subtracting the amount of active ingredient calculated from the mixture total.

Step 5. Determine the amount of mixture needed to provide the originally ordered amount by using the ratio-proportion method.

Aliquot measurement can also be used to prepare pharmaceutical preparations that include very small volumes of liquid. In these situations, it is not necessary to determine the least weighable quantity. Instead, you will consider the available syringes in the pharmacy and determine the minimum amount that can be precisely measured. This is typically a volume that will fill at least one-third to one-half of the syringe barrel or can easily be measured in a properly marked graduated cylinder. Volume aliquot measuring can be performed using the steps listed in Table 8.2.

Example 8.4.6

You receive a prescription for 0.25 mL of a drug. The minimum volume that can be accurately measured in your pharmacy is 1.0 mL. What amount of aliquot mixture will contain the ordered volume of drug?

Safety Note

A trailing zero is appropriate if it is used to communicate the accuracy of a measurement.

Step 1. The minimum volume that can be measured accurately is 1.0 mL. The trailing zero indicates a measurement accuracy to a tenth of a milliliter.

Step 2. Determine the multiple of the active ingredient that will provide the smallest volume that can be accurately measured.

$$0.25 \text{ mL} \times 4 = 1.0 \text{ mL active ingredient}$$

Step 3. Determine the total volume of the mixture.

$$1.0 \text{ mL} \times 4 = 4.0 \text{ mL total mixture}$$

Step 4. Determine the amount of diluent needed.

$$4.0 \text{ mL total} - 1.0 \text{ mL active ingredient} = 3.0 \text{ mL diluent needed}$$

Step 5. Determine the amount of mixture needed to provide the originally ordered amount.

$$\frac{x \text{ mL mixture}}{0.25 \text{ mL drug}} = \frac{4.0 \text{ mL mixture}}{1.0 \text{ mL drug}}$$

$$x \text{ mL mixture} = 1.0 \text{ mL}$$

So a 1.0 mL aliquot will contain the needed ingredient.

Example 8.4.7

You receive a prescription for 0.15 mL of a drug. The minimum volume that can be accurately measured in your pharmacy is 0.5 mL. What amount of aliquot mixture will contain the ordered amount of drug?

Step 1. The minimum volume that can be measured accurately is 0.5 mL. The measurement accuracy is to a tenth of a milliliter.

Step 2. Determine the multiple of the active ingredient that will provide the smallest volume that can be accurately measured.

$$0.15 \text{ mL} \times 4 = 0.6 \text{ mL active ingredient}$$

Step 3. Determine the total volume of the mixture.

$$0.6 \text{ mL} \times 4 = 2.4 \text{ mL total mixture}$$

Step 4. Determine the amount of diluent needed.

$$2.4 \text{ mL total} - 0.6 \text{ mL active ingredient} = 1.8 \text{ mL diluent needed}$$

Step 5. Determine the amount of mixture needed to provide the originally ordered amount.

$$\frac{x \text{ mL mixture}}{0.15 \text{ mL drug}} = \frac{2.4 \text{ mL mixture}}{0.6 \text{ mL drug}}$$

$$x \text{ mL mixture} = 0.6 \text{ mL mixture}$$

So, a 0.6 mL aliquot will contain the needed ingredient.

8.4 Problem Set

Determine the amount of drug, diluent, mixture, and aliquot for each of these aliquot problems using weight. For each problem, first calculate the least weighable quantity; then use the smallest factor possible to calculate the amount of drug to be weighed out. Use the factor given in the problem to calculate the amount of diluent to be added. (*Note: Sometimes these two factors will be the same; sometimes they will not.*)

1. 20 mg Drug A
   3.5% margin of error allowed
   Torsion balance with a sensitivity of 4 mg
   use the multiple 6 for the diluent

   a. least weighable quantity: _____

   b. amount of drug: _____

   c. amount of mixture: _____

   d. amount of diluent: _____

   e. amount of aliquot: _____

2. 5 mg Drug B
   3% margin of error allowed
   Torsion balance with a sensitivity of 5 mg
   use the multiple 35 for the diluent

   a. least weighable quantity: _____

   b. amount of drug: _____

   c. amount of mixture: _____

   d. amount of diluent: _____

   e. amount of aliquot: _____

3. 12 mg Drug C
   5.5% margin of error allowed
   Torsion balance with a sensitivity of 5 mg
   use the multiple 15 for the diluent

   a. least weighable quantity: _____

   b. amount of drug: _____

   c. amount of mixture: _____

   d. amount of diluent: _____

   e. amount of aliquot: _____

4. 25 mg Drug D
   5% margin of error allowed
   Torsion balance with a sensitivity of 6 mg
   use the multiple 6 for the diluent

   a. least weighable quantity: _____

   b. amount of drug: _____

   c. amount of mixture: _____

   d. amount of diluent: _____

   e. amount of aliquot: _____

5. 6 mg Drug E
   4% margin of error allowed
   Torsion balance with a sensitivity of 6 mg
   use the multiple 25 for the diluent

   a. least weighable quantity: _____

   b. amount of drug: _____

   c. amount of mixture: _____

   d. amount of diluent: _____

   e. amount of aliquot: _____

6. 22.5 mg Drug F
   4% margin of error allowed
   Torsion balance with a sensitivity of 4 mg
   use the multiple 5 for the diluent

   a. least weighable quantity: _____

   b. amount of drug: _____

   c. amount of mixture: _____

   d. amount of diluent: _____

   e. amount of aliquot: _____

7. 17.75 mg Drug G
   5% margin of error allowed
   Torsion balance with a sensitivity of 4 mg
   use the multiple 5 for the diluent

   a. least weighable quantity: _____

   b. amount of drug: _____

   c. amount of mixture: _____

   d. amount of diluent: _____

   e. amount of aliquot: _____

8. 18 mg Drug H
   6% margin of error allowed
   Torsion balance with a sensitivity of 5 mg
   use the multiple 5 for the diluent

   a. least weighable quantity: _____

   b. amount of drug: _____

   c. amount of mixture: _____

   d. amount of diluent: _____

   e. amount of aliquot: _____

9. 30 mg Drug J
   5% margin of error allowed
   Torsion balance with a sensitivity of 5 mg
   use the multiple 4 for the diluent

   a. least weighable quantity: _____

   b. amount of drug: _____

   c. amount of mixture: _____

   d. amount of diluent: _____

   e. amount of aliquot: _____

10. 8.75 mg Drug K
    5% margin of error allowed
    Torsion balance with a sensitivity of 3 mg
    use the multiple 7 for the diluent

    a. least weighable quantity: _____

b. amount of drug: _____

c. amount of mixture: _____

d. amount of diluent: _____

e. amount of aliquot: _____

Determine the amount of drug, mixture, diluent, and aliquot for each of these aliquot problems using volume. Use the smallest factor (or multiple) possible to calculate the amount of drug to be measured out. Use the factor given in the problem to calculate the amount of diluent to be added. (Note: Sometimes these two factors will be the same; sometimes they will not.)

11. 0.5 mL Drug L
    1.0 mL is the minimum volume that can be accurately measured
    use the multiple 4 for the diluent

    a. amount of drug: _____

    b. amount of mixture: _____

    c. amount of diluent: _____

    d. amount of aliquot: _____

12. 0.3 mL Drug M
    0.5 mL is the minimum volume that can be accurately measured
    use the multiple 5 for the diluent

    a. amount of drug: _____

    b. amount of mixture: _____

    c. amount of diluent: _____

    d. amount of aliquot: _____

13. 0.75 mL Drug N
    1.0 mL is the minimum volume that can be accurately measured
    use the multiple 5 for the diluent

    a. amount of drug: _____

    b. amount of mixture: _____

    c. amount of diluent: _____

    d. amount of aliquot: _____

14. 0.25 mL Drug O
    1.5 mL is the minimum volume that can be accurately measured
    use the multiple 6 for the diluent

    a. amount of drug: _____

    b. amount of mixture: _____

    c. amount of diluent: _____

    d. amount of aliquot: _____

15. 0.45 mL of Drug P
    1.0 mL is the minimum volume that can be accurately measured
    use the multiple 3 for the diluent

    a. amount of drug: _____

    b. amount of mixture: _____

    c. amount of diluent: _____

    d. amount of aliquot: _____

16. 0.95 mL of Drug Q
    1.5 mL is the minimum volume that can be accurately measured
    use the multiple 2 for the diluent

    a. amount of drug: _____

    b. amount of mixture: _____

    c. amount of diluent: _____

    d. amount of aliquot: _____

17. 0.5 mL of Drug R
    1.0 mL is the minimum volume that can be accurately measured
    use the multiple 4 for the diluent

    a. amount of drug: _____

    b. amount of mixture: _____

    c. amount of diluent: _____

    d. amount of aliquot: _____

18. 0.5 mL of Drug S
    1.0 mL is the minimum volume that can be accurately measured
    use the multiple 5 for the diluent

    a. amount of drug: _____

    b. amount of mixture: _____

    c. amount of diluent: _____

    d. amount of aliquot: _____

19. 0.85 mL of Drug T
    1.5 mL is the minimum volume that can be accurately measured
    use the multiple 2 for the diluent

    a. amount of drug: _____

    b. amount of mixture: _____

    c. amount of diluent: _____

    d. amount of aliquot: _____

20. 0.05 mL of Drug U
    1.0 mL is the minimum volume that can be accurately measured
    use the multiple 20 for the diluent

    a. amount of drug: _____

    b. amount of mixture: _____

    c. amount of diluent: _____

    d. amount of aliquot: _____

    Self-check your work in Appendix A.

Practice Test

1. Prepare 8 mL of hydrocortisone solution with a concentration of 5 mg/mL from 100 mg/2 mL stock.

   a. How many milliliters of hydrocortisone are needed?

   b. How many milliliters of diluent are needed?

2. Prepare 5 mL of a 5 mcg/mL solution from a stock solution of 50 mcg/mL.

   a. How much stock solution is needed?

   b. How many milliliters of diluent are needed?

3. An order calls for a total of 500 mL of a 2% solution. You have a 10% soaking solution on hand.

   a. How much concentrate will you need?

   b. How much diluent?

4. A doctor writes a prescription for 280 mL of a 5 mg/mL solution. The pharmacy carries a 20% solution.

   a. How much concentrate will you need?

   b. How much diluent?

5. You need 50 mL of a 10% boric acid solution. The pharmacy carries only 85% boric acid.

   a. How much concentrate will you need?

   b. How much diluent?

6. A doctor orders 1000 mL of 35% dextrose. Your pharmacy carries only 50% dextrose 1000 mL.

   a. How much concentrate will you need?

   b. How much diluent?

7. A hospital pharmacy has 8.5% Aminosyn on hand. The order calls for 500 mL of 2.5% Aminosyn.

   a. How much of the 8.5% will be used to fill the order?

   b. How much diluent?

8. A patient is to take 6 mg of dexamethasone in two equally divided doses. Each dose is to be diluted to 1 mg/mL strength and given as a bolus injection every 12 hours.

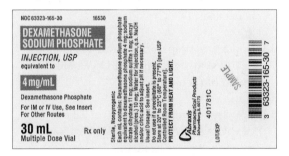

   a. How many milliliters of the dexamethasone solution shown in the label above will be required to provide the 6 mg?

   b. How many milliliters will be in each of the bolus doses?

9. You have been instructed to add 15 mEq potassium chloride to a 1 L bag of NS and 8 mEq to a 1 L bag of D$_5$W.

   a. How many milliliters of the potassium solution shown in the label above will you place in each bag?

   b. Assuming you have a new vial, how much of the vial will remain after you have prepared the orders?

10. You are to prepare five 60 g jars of ointment using the following formula. How much of each ingredient will you need to create the total amount?

R	Coal tar	4 g
	Salicylic acid	1 g
	Triamcinolone 1% ung	15 g
	Aqua-base ointment	100 g

11. You are to prepare 400 mL of 7.5% dextrose solution using D_5W and $D_{10}W$. How much of each solution will be needed?

12. You are to prepare 800 mL of 8% dextrose from D_5W and $D_{20}W$. How much of each is needed?

13. You are to prepare 1000 mL of 7.5% dextrose using SWFI and $D_{20}W$. How much of each is needed?

14. You are to prepare 200 mL of 12.5% dextrose using $D_{10}W$ and $D_{20}W$. How much of each is needed?

15. You are to prepare 500 mL of a 15% dextrose solution using D_5W and $D_{50}W$. How much of each is needed?

16. What fraction of 10% alcohol should be mixed with 70% alcohol to obtain 50% alcohol?

17. A doctor writes an order for a total of 300 mL of 42.5% Liposyn. You have in stock 5% Liposyn and 50% Liposyn. How much of each will you need?

18. You receive an order that calls for 60 g of a 30% ointment. On the shelf you have a 2% and a 50% ointment. How much of each will you use to fill the order?

19. An order calls for 1000 mL of 60% Travasol. On the shelf the pharmacy carries 40% and 70% Travasol. How many milliliters of each will you need to fill the order?

20. An order calls for 30 g of 5% bacitracin ointment. The pharmacy carries only 3% and 10% bacitracin ointment. How many grams of the 3% and 10% ointment will you need to fill the order?

21. What is the percentage strength of a mixture containing 30 mL of 7% iodine and 30 mL of 2% iodine?

22. What is the percentage strength of a mixture containing 30 mL of 70% alcohol, 500 mL of 40% alcohol, and 200 mL of 95% alcohol?

23. A prescription balance with a sensitivity of 6 mg is used to weigh out a substance that is not to have a greater than 5% error. What is the least weighable quantity?

24. Determine the amount of drug, mixture, diluent, and aliquot for the following situation. First, calculate the least weighable quantity; then use the smallest factor possible to calculate the amount of drug to be weighed out. Use the factor given in the problem to calculate the amount of diluent to be added. (These two factors might or might not be the same.)

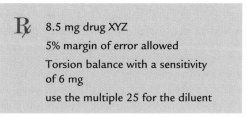

R	8.5 mg drug XYZ
	5% margin of error allowed
	Torsion balance with a sensitivity of 6 mg
	use the multiple 25 for the diluent

a. Least weighable quantity:

b. Amount of drug:

c. Amount of mixture:

d. Amount of diluent:

e. Amount of aliquot:

Using Business Math in the Pharmacy

9

Learning Objectives

- Identify and calculate overhead cost.
- Identify net and gross profit.
- Calculate markup and the markup rate.
- Compute discounts.
- Apply average wholesale price to profit calculations.

- Calculate inventory turnover.
- Calculate depreciation.

Preview chapter terms and definitions.

9.1 Calculations Related to Business

profit
income minus overhead

overhead
the pharmacy's overall cost of doing business; includes salaries, equipment, operating expenses, and rent

All businesses must perform certain accounting operations on a regular basis. Markup, profit, and discounts are calculated every day. Clients are also accustomed to calculating discounts for sales and items on discount. Like any business, the pharmacy must make a **profit;** that is, it must have more receipts than expenses to continue to provide customer services. In addition, the technician needs to understand the importance of overhead as it pertains to monthly bills such as rent, taxes, utilities, and inventory supplies kept on hand.

Overhead

The pharmacy's **overhead** is its general cost of doing business. This is the overall cost for the pharmacy, including salaries, equipment, operating expenses, and rent. Profit equals income minus overhead.

Example 9.1.1

Assume that John's Drug Shop has the following annual overhead expenses:

pharmacist's salary	$60,000.00
two technician salaries ($24,500.00 each)	49,000.00
rent	12,000.00
utilities	5,000.00
software maintenance	1,200.00
liability insurance	3,000.00
business insurance	4,000.00
drug purchases	550,000.00
total overhead	$684,200.00

If a 15% profit is desirable, what amount of income must be received to meet this goal?

Since in this case the profit is to be 15%,

$$\text{overhead} \times 0.15 = \text{profit}$$
$$\$684,200.00 \times 0.15 = \$102,630.00$$

Profit equals incoming receipts minus overhead, so

$$\text{overhead} + \text{profit} = \text{income}$$
$$\$684,200.00 + \$102,630.00 = \$786,830.00$$

When John's Drug Shop has an annual income of $786,830.00, it will be making a 15% profit.

Net Profit

net profit
the difference between the selling price and the overall cost of an item

overall cost
the sum of the cost to purchase the drug from the manufacturer and the cost to dispense the drug

In pharmacy practice, profit is influenced by the selling prices of drugs. For each drug, the **net profit** (the profit calculated in Example 9.1.1) is the difference between the selling price and the overall cost. The **overall cost** is the sum of the cost to purchase the drug from the manufacturer (the pharmacy's purchase price) and the cost to dispense the drug. Cost of dispensing consists of items such as professional handling, which includes processing and recording the prescription, as well as patient consultation.

$$\text{pharmacy's purchase price} + \text{cost to dispense} = \text{overall cost}$$

$$\text{selling price} - \text{overall cost} = \text{profit}$$

$$\text{overall cost} \times \text{desired percent profit} = \text{amount of net profit}$$

Example 9.1.2

A pint bottle of nystatin oral solution costs the pharmacy $20.25. You calculate that it takes $5.10 to dispense the entire contents of one bottle, considering personnel time, pharmacy supplies, shipping, and maintaining the supply. If a 20% profit is the goal for this product, what selling price is required for the pint bottle?

$$\text{pharmacy's purchase price} + \text{cost to dispense} = \text{overall cost}$$
$$\$20.25 + \$5.10 = \$25.35$$

$$\text{overall cost} \times 0.20 = \text{net profit}$$
$$\$25.35 \times 0.20 = \$5.07$$

$$\text{overall cost} + \text{net profit} = \text{selling price}$$
$$\$25.35 + \$5.07 = \$30.42$$

Gross Profit

The difference between the selling price and the pharmacy's purchase price is called **gross profit.** This relation of purchasing and selling does not consider the cost of preparing and dispensing the drug. Thus, the gross profit will always be more than the net profit. Using the example of nystatin oral solution, the gross profit would be $10.17.

$$\text{selling price} - \text{pharmacy's purchase price} = \text{gross profit}$$
$$\$30.42 - \$20.25 = \$10.17$$

Net profit and gross profit are similar to net pay and gross pay. Gross pay is your pay before taxes and other deductions are taken out. Net pay is the amount you "bring home." For example, you may earn $400.00 a week (gross pay) while taking home $325 a week (net pay calculated after deductions are taken).

The **profit margin** is the difference between the cost of doing business (the pharmacy's purchase price, overhead, and preparation) and the selling price or receipts for a product. A negative profit (a loss) occurs when the selling price or receipts for a product is less than the cost of presenting that product for sale.

Like all businesses, pharmacies purchase their products (drugs) at one price from the manufacturer and sell them at a higher price. Although pharmacies are subject to governmental laws and regulations regarding the sale of drugs, markup still plays a part in the pricing system.

The markup is computed as

$$\text{selling price} - \text{purchase price} = \text{markup or gross profit}$$

The **markup rate** is expressed as a percentage and is computed as

$$\frac{\text{markup}}{\text{pharmacy's purchase price}} \times 100 = \text{markup rate}$$

Example 9.1.3

A 30 day supply of an antidiabetic agent sells for $45.00 and costs the pharmacy $30.00. What is the markup? What is the markup rate?

The markup is computed as follows:

$$\text{selling price} - \text{pharmacy's purchase price} = \text{markup or gross profit}$$
$$\$45.00 - \$30.00 = \$15.00$$

The markup rate is

$$\frac{\text{markup}}{\text{pharmacy's purchase price}} \times 100 = \text{markup rate}$$

$$\frac{\$15.00}{\$30.00} \times 100 = 50\%$$

Example 9.1.4   If Zantac 75 in a 12 pack costs the pharmacy $8.35 and the selling price is $10.75, what is the markup? What is the markup rate?

The markup is

$$\text{selling price} - \text{pharmacy's purchase price} = \text{markup or gross profit}$$
$$\$10.75 - \$8.35 = \$2.40$$

The markup rate is

$$\frac{\text{markup}}{\text{pharmacy's purchase price}} \times 100 = \text{markup rate}$$

$$\frac{\$2.40}{\$8.35} \times 100 = 28.7\%$$

Markup rates on brand name drug products are typically lower than markup rates on generic drugs. If a pharmacy marks up a $100 brand name drug by 5%, the cost to the consumer would be $105. The markup rate for generic medications is typically much higher, but the selling prices of these drugs are generally less. For example, a pharmacy may mark up a $15 generic drug 33%, which would result in a $20 charge to the customer but only a $5 profit for the pharmacy. As a result of these markup practices, the percentage of profit from selling generic drugs is often higher than the percentage of profit for the corresponding brand name products. However, the actual money made from the sale of an individual generic drug may not be significant.

A growing trend in retail pharmacies is to sell generic drugs to customers at a flat dollar rate, such as $4 or $7, regardless of a fluctuating cost. A flat rate is a low charge for a certain amount of medication, a supply designed to last a specific number of days. The medications available to customers at a flat rate are typically generic medications with low pharmacy purchase prices. Because the medications are inexpensive for the pharmacy to purchase, the pharmacy is still able to make a profit on the drugs while generating additional sales from other prescriptions the patient may have filled at the same time. Table 9.1 lists examples of medications that are often included in a flat-rate listing. The following example will apply the formulas for markup and markup rate to a flat-rate prescription to illustrate how profitable such rates can be for the pharmacy.

TABLE 9.1   Flat Rate Medications

Medication	Use
amoxicillin	infections
atenolol	hypertension or heart conditions
estradiol	hormone replacement therapy
fluoxetine	depression
levothyroxine	thyroid
loratadine	allergies
metformin	diabetes
naproxen	pain and inflammation
triamcinolone	skin

Example 9.1.5

A retail pharmacy has an advertised $4.00 flat rate price for generic prescriptions. If the pharmacy's purchase price of 30 amoxicillin 250 mg capsules is $1.20, what is the percent profit on a prescription filled and sold for the flat price?

The markup is

$$\text{selling price} - \text{pharmacy's purchase price} = \text{markup or gross profit}$$
$$\$4.00 - \$1.20 = \$2.80$$

The markup rate is

$$\frac{\text{markup}}{\text{cost}} \times 100 = \text{markup rate}$$

$$\frac{\$2.80}{\$1.20} \times 100 = 233.3\%$$

While the percentage profit is high, the dollar amount (gross profit) is still low and does not include other costs to the pharmacy, such as overhead.

Discount

discount
a reduced selling price

Sometimes a manufacturer or a supplier offers an item at a lower price to a pharmacy. This reduced price is a **discount.** Similarly, a pharmacy may offer consumers a discount, or a deduction from what is normally charged, as an incentive to purchase an item.

$$\text{regular selling price} \times \text{discount rate} = \text{discount}$$

$$\text{regular selling price} - \text{discount} = \text{discounted selling price}$$

Discounts are one of the easiest business-related math calculations, probably because we use them nearly each time we go shopping or buy something on sale. For example, a sale that offers 50% off means that items are half price. In such a scenario, the sales price is calculated by multiplying the regular price by 0.5 (or dividing the regular price by two). Most shoppers can do this in their heads, but the following example will formally demonstrate the calculation.

Example 9.1.6

A retail pharmacy has announced a 50%-off sale on all headache products during the two weeks leading up to the tax-filing deadline. The following products are on sale.

    Tylenol, regular selling price $6.99

    Excedrin Migraine, regular selling price $7.89

    Advil, regular selling price $7.29

How much will the customer pay for each drug, and how much will the customer save on each purchase?

Because 50% is equal to 0.5, you can calculate the sale prices by multiplying the regular price by 0.5.

Calculate the Tylenol sales price.

$$\text{total selling price} \times \text{discount rate} = \text{discount}$$
$$\$6.99 \times 0.5 = \$3.495, \text{ rounded to } \$3.50$$

Calculate the Tylenol savings to the customer.

$$\text{total selling price} - \text{discount} = \text{discounted selling price}$$
$$\$6.99 - \$3.50 = \$3.49$$

Calculate the Excedrin Migraine sales price.

$$\text{total selling price} \times \text{discount rate} = \text{discount}$$
$$\$7.89 \times 0.5 = \$3.945, \text{ rounded to } \$3.95$$

Calculate the Excedrin Migraine savings to the customer.

$$\text{total selling price} - \text{discount} = \text{discounted selling price}$$
$$\$7.89 - \$3.95 = \$3.94$$

Calculate the Advil sales price.

$$\text{total selling price} \times \text{discount rate} = \text{discount}$$
$$\$7.29 \times 0.5 = \$3.645, \text{ rounded to } \$3.65$$

Calculate the Advil savings to the customer.

$$\text{selling price} - \text{discount} = \text{discounted selling price}$$
$$\$7.29 - \$3.65 = \$3.64$$

Example 9.1.7

Assume the pharmacy purchases five cases of dermatological cream at $100.00 per case. If the account is paid in full within 15 days, the supplier offers a 15% discount on the purchase. What is the total discounted selling price?

First, calculate the regular selling price.

$$\text{quantity of product} \times \text{purchase price per unit} = \text{regular selling price}$$
$$5 \text{ cases} \times \$100.00 \text{ per case} = \$500.00$$

Next calculate the discount for payment within 15 days.

$$\text{regular selling price} \times \text{discount rate} = \text{discount}$$
$$\$500.00 \times 0.15 = \$75.00$$

Finally to obtain the discounted selling price, subtract the discount from the regular selling price.

$$\text{regular selling price} - \text{discount} = \text{discounted selling price}$$
$$\$500.00 - \$75.00 = \$425.00$$

Example 9.1.8

Jenny's Drug Store offers a 20% discount on a discontinued brand of cough syrup. How much will a $3.45 bottle cost after the discount?

$$\text{regular selling price} \times \text{discount rate} = \text{discount}$$
$$\$3.45 \times 0.20 = \$0.69$$

$$\text{regular selling price} - \text{discount} = \text{discounted selling price}$$
$$\$3.45 - \$0.69 = \$2.76$$

9.1 Problem Set

The Drugs-R-Us Pharmacy has the following overhead expenses. Use this information to answer questions 1 through 3.

pharmacist(s) salary	$135,000.00
technician(s) salary	52,000.00
rent	23,000.00
utilities	6,000.00
computer maintenance	4,000.00
software subscriptions	2,000.00
liability insurance	4,000.00
business insurance	4,000.00
drug purchases	750,000.00

= 980,000.00

1. If an 18% profit is desirable, what must the pharmacy's income be in order to meet this goal?

   1,150,000

2. If the pharmacy's income is $1,401,489.00, what is its percent profit?

   421489   43%

3. If the pharmacy's income is $1,191,692.00, what is its percent profit?

   211692   21.6%

The Key Pharmacy has the following overhead expenses. Use this information to answer questions 4 through 6.

pharmacist salary	$72,000.00
technician salary	52,000.00
rent	13,000.00
utilities	5,500.00
computer maintenance	2,000.00
software subscriptions	1,500.00
liability insurance	4,000.00
business insurance	3,500.00
drug purchases	50,000.00

4. If a 20% profit is desirable, what must the pharmacy's income be in order to meet this goal?

5. If the pharmacy's income is $991,982, what is its percent profit?

6. If the pharmacy's income is $1,248,301, what is its percent profit?

7. The pharmacy calculates that its income for the week was $54,617.53 and that its net profit was $3700.83. The week's drug purchasing costs amounted to $47,422.14. What was the overhead for the week?

8. Corner Pharmacy has a weekly overhead of $13,033.06. If this pharmacy is to make a 22% profit, what must its sales of goods and services amount to each week?

Calculate the dollar amount of net profit and the percent profit (markup rate) for the following individual prescription drug items. (Round to whole percents.) The dispensing fee is $4.25 for each prescription.

9. propranolol 10 mg
   Pharmacy's Purchase Price: $3.96 per 100 tablets
   Dispense: 50 tablets
   Rx Charge: $8.59

10. amoxicillin 250 mg
    Pharmacy's Purchase Price: $8.50 per 500 capsules
    Dispense: 30 capsules
    Rx Charge: $14.80

11. Paxil (paroxetine) 20 mg
    Pharmacy's Purchase Price: $118.50 per
       100 tablets
    Dispense: 30 tablets
    Rx Charge: $45.50

12. furosemide 40 mg
    Pharmacy's Purchase Price: $83.50 per
       500 tablets
    Dispense: 100 tablets
    Rx Charge: $23.16

13. levothyroxine 0.1 mg
    Pharmacy's Purchase Price: $41.20 per
       100 tablets
    Dispense: 90 tablets
    Rx Charge: $41.70

14. cough syrup
    Pharmacy's Purchase Price: $37.50 per
       pint (480 mL)
    Dispense: 8 fl oz bottle
    Rx Charge: $25.34

15. lo-estrogen/progestin oral contraceptive
    Pharmacy's Purchase Price: $62.30 per
       6 packs of 28
    Dispense: 1 pack of 28
    Rx Charge: $17.90

The pharmacy is selling the following items at a discount this week. Calculate the discounted selling price for each.

16. cough syrup, regular selling price
    $5.89 discounted 20%

17. facial tissues, regular selling price
    $1.19 discounted 15%

18. hair dye, regular selling price $7.29
    discounted 30%

19. body lotion, regular selling price $5.69
    discounted 15%

20. baby shampoo, regular selling price
    $3.89 discounted 25%

21. antacid liquid, regular selling price
    $4.26 discounted 30%

22. acetaminophen tablets, regular selling
    price $8.69 discounted 50%

23. toothpaste, regular selling price $2.99
    discounted 40%

Calculate the following and state the answer in dollars or percent as indicated.

24. Antiviral ointment costs a pharmacy $12.50 per tube. The standard markup is 30%. What is the total selling price of a box of 12 tubes?

25. Eyedrops with antihistamine are purchased from the manufacturer cases of 36 drop-dispenser bottles. The pharmacy desires a markup of $1.75 per bottle. The pharmacy's purchase price is $11.60 per case. What is the selling price per bottle?

26. Identify the markup and the selling price of an oral antibiotic suspension that costs the pharmacist $15.60 per bottle if the markup rate is 25%.

27. An asthma tablet costs the pharmacy $24.80 for a month's supply, and the selling price is $30.75. Calculate the markup rate.

28. Calculate the gross profit from a medication that costs the pharmacy $520.00 for 1000 tablets and sells for $650.00.

29. The cost of dispensing the medication in question 28 is $2.05 per 100 tablets. Calculate the net profit for selling one tablet.

The pharmacy where you work has received a drug shipment. Calculate the markup and selling price on each item and the total selling price of all items together.

	Drug	Quantity	Pharmacy's Purchase Price	Markup Rate	Markup	Selling Price
30.	antibiotic oral solution	1200 mL	$120.50	25%	_____	_____
31.	foot powder	12 containers	$24.00	15%	_____	_____
32.	Motrin (ibuprofen)	2000 tablets	$200.00	27%	_____	_____
33.	Band-Aids	10 boxes	$27.50	21%	_____	_____
34.	antibiotic ointment	18 tubes	$67.50	18%	_____	_____
35.	birth control pills	24 packs	$840.00	32%	_____	_____
36.	DiaBeta (glyburide)	600 tablets	$550.00	30%	_____	_____
37.	**Total**	_____	_____	_____	_____	_____

Self-check your work in Appendix A.

9.2 Insurance Reimbursements for Prescriptions

pharmacy benefits management (PBM)
a prescription processing service that manages insurance reimbursement for prescriptions to pharmacies

Reimbursement for prescription and pharmacy services is largely controlled by contracts with insurance companies and is often brokered through a large prescription processing service called **pharmacy benefits management (PBM).** Reimbursement may be calculated based on the pharmacy's purchase price of medications, the average wholesale price, or a set contract established for a list of preferred drugs. The amount of money paid by the PBM for a particular prescription is calculated and approved by the PBM's computer or the pharmacy's computer via an online connection. Rarely is this cost calculated by personnel in the pharmacy. Nevertheless, it is helpful to understand the reimbursement process and the methods used to calculate the charges for medication. Patients are likely to ask questions about charges and reimbursements, so having a basic understanding of the reconciliation process is essential.

Some claims will be reconciled by an individual pharmacy, but others will pass electronically through a PBM or large clearinghouse. These businesses bill the insurance companies under contract and then reimburse the pharmacy periodically for a batch of prescriptions. Reimbursement may be daily, weekly, or monthly. Some large chain pharmacies may even receive a single payment that covers a large number of stores; the individual store does not receive a check from the company, but rather an invoice or memo indicating the amount being reimbursed. Rejections or denials of prescription drug charges will also come back to the pharmacy in this manner. It is not uncommon to receive an initial online approval for a prescription and then later to receive a rejection or denial of the charges.

When considering profit on an individual prescription, the overall cost of the medication is compared to the amount the pharmacy receives for the dispensed drug. The term *profit* in this situation refers only to the pharmacy's purchase price of the drug used, and it does not include the cost of materials, labor, or overhead. The amount that is charged over and above the pharmacy's purchase price of the medication is referred to as the **dispensing fee.** The dispensing fee is meant to cover all related costs to filling a prescription beyond the pharmacy's purchase price of the medication and includes any actual profit gained.

dispensing fee
amount charged over and above the pharmacy's purchase price of the medication; includes profit, cost of materials, cost of labor, and overhead

Average Wholesale Price (AWP) Applications

A pharmacy may potentially receive payment from several different sources. Historically, patients have been responsible for paying for their own medications. More recently, health maintenance organizations and health insurers have become major players in determining the cost of healthcare, including patient medications. The very survival of a pharmacy depends on its ability to contain costs.

average wholesale price (AWP)
the average price that wholesalers charge the pharmacy for a drug; used to determine reimbursement

The **average wholesale price (AWP)** of a drug is an *average* price that wholesalers charge the pharmacy. Usually, third parties reimburse a pharmacy based upon the AWP. Therefore, the pharmacy has an incentive to purchase a drug below its AWP. Drugs are sold below AWP in some situations, such as when volume discounts, set contract prices, or rebates from manufacturers are available.

$$\text{prescription reimbursement} = \text{AWP} \pm \text{percentage} + \text{dispensing fee}$$

Calculating the amount to charge an insurance company or a patient is most often performed by a computer. The pricing information is generally loaded into a computer ahead of time according to the patients' insurance company contracts. The following examples illustrate one of the methods used to calculate the amount billed.

Example 9.2.1

A pharmacy has three drugs with the following AWPs:

> **Drug A, AWP $120**
>
> **Drug B, AWP $80**
>
> **Drug C, AWP $25**

The pharmacy has a markup of 5% and a dispensing fee of $4.00 for each of these drugs. If a patient presents a prescription for each of these drugs, what will be the total billed?

Begin by calculating the amount billed to the patient for each of the individual drugs.

Drug A

$$\text{AWP} + \text{percentage} + \text{dispensing fee} = \text{amount billed}$$
$$\$120 + (\$120 \times .05) + \$4.00 =$$
$$\$120 + \$6 + \$4.00 = \$130$$

Drug B

$$\text{AWP} + \text{percentage} + \text{dispensing fee} = \text{amount billed}$$
$$\$80 + (\$80 \times .05) + \$4.00 =$$
$$\$80 + \$4 + \$4.00 = \$88$$

Drug C

$$AWP + percentage + dispensing\ fee = amount\ billed$$
$$\$25 + (\$25 \times .05) + \$4.00 =$$
$$\$25 + \$1.25 + \$4.00 = \$30.25$$

Next, determine the total amount billed by adding the amounts billed for the three drugs.

$$\$130 + \$88 + \$30.25 = \$248.25$$

Example 9.2.2

A certain tablet comes in a quantity of 60 and has an AWP of $100.00. The pharmacy has an agreement with the supplier to purchase the drug at the AWP minus 15%. The insurer is willing to pay AWP plus 5% plus a $2.00 dispensing fee. A patient on this insurer's plan purchases 30 tablets for $54.50. How much profit does the pharmacy make on this prescription?

Begin by calculating the amount of the discount.

$$\$100.00 \times 0.15 = \$15.00$$

Then calculate the pharmacy's purchase price of the drug.

$$\$100.00 - \$15.00 = \$85.00$$

Therefore, the pharmacy can purchase this drug at $85.00 per 60 tablets. The insurance company will pay the pharmacy AWP + 5%.

$$\$100.00 + (\$100.00 \times 0.05) =$$
$$\$100.00 + \$5.00 = \$105.00$$

At that price, the amount the insurance company will pay to fill a prescription for 30 pills is

$$(\$105.00 \div 2) + \$2\ (dispensing\ fee) =$$
$$\$52.50 + \$2.00 = \$54.50$$

Compare this to the pharmacy's cost of 30 tablets.

$$\$85.00 \div 2 = \$42.50$$

Therefore, the pharmacy's profit on 30 tablets is

$$\$54.50 - \$42.50 = \$12.00$$

Example 9.2.3

Two hundred capsules are purchased at AWP minus 20%, where AWP is $125. The insurer allows a charge of AWP plus 3% per 200 capsules. What is the highest charge per capsule allowed by the insurer? What will be the profit per capsule?

The pharmacy's discounted purchase price of 200 capsules is

$$\$125.00 - (\$125.00 \times 0.20) =$$
$$\$125.00 - \$25.00 = \$100.00$$

Thus, the cost per capsule to the pharmacy is

$$\$100.00 \div 200 = \$0.50/\text{capsule}$$

The insurance company will pay the pharmacy AWP plus 3% per 200 capsules.

$$\$125.00 + (\$125.00 \times 0.03) =$$
$$\$125.00 + \$3.75 = \$128.75$$

Therefore, the pharmacy would be wise to charge patients

$$\$128.75 \div 200 \text{ capsules} = \$0.64/\text{capsule}$$

thereby making a profit of

$$\text{selling price} - \text{pharmacy's purchase price} = \text{profit}$$
$$\$0.64/\text{capsule charge} - \$0.50/\text{capsule} = \$0.14/\text{capsule}$$

Capitation Fee

capitation fee
a form of reimbursement in which the insurer pays the pharmacy a monthly fee to cover all prescriptions needed by a patient during that month

Some insurers use a form of reimbursement in which the pharmacy is paid a monthly fee, called a **capitation fee,** for some patients. The insurer pays the pharmacy the monthly fee whether or not the patients receive prescriptions during that month. The pharmacy in turn must dispense all the patients' prescriptions, even if the pharmacy's purchase price of the medication and the dispensing fee are more than the monthly fee. When profit is considered in terms of capitation fees, the profit refers only to the pharmacy's purchase price of the medication, and dispensing fees are not included unless a pharmacy insurance contract or capitation contract specifically states a dispensing fee should be considered.

Example 9.2.4

The Corner Drug Store receives a monthly capitation fee of $250.00 for John Jones. During April, John fills three prescriptions totaling $198.75. How much profit does the capitation fee provide?

In this case the monthly fee exceeds the sum of the pharmacy's purchase price, yielding a profit for the pharmacy.

$$\$250.00 - \$198.75 = \$51.25$$

Example 9.2.5   Cindy Carver has the same insurance plan as John Jones, with the same capitation fee. During April, Cindy fills four prescriptions at The Corner Drug Store for a total of $301.25. What is the profit margin?

In this case the pharmacy wasn't so fortunate: the pharmacy's purchase price of the prescriptions exceeds the monthly fee, which costs the pharmacy money (expressed as a negative number).

$$\$250.00 - \$301.25 = -\$51.25$$

9.2 Problem Set

Calculate the cost to the pharmacy as AWP less 13%.

1. AWP $48.90 per 60 tablets and dispense 20 tablets

2. AWP $84.07 per 100 tablets and dispense 30 tablets

3. AWP $30.25 per 1000 tablets and dispense 100 tablets

Calculate AWP plus 4% plus a $6.25 per prescription dispensing fee.

4. AWP $120.68 per 500 tablets and dispense 30 tablets

5. AWP $39.78 per 100 capsules and dispense 60 capsules

6. AWP $317.50 per 30 tablets and dispense 20 tablets

For the following problems, the insurer will pay AWP plus 3.5% and a $4.50 per prescription dispensing fee.

7. AWP $71.35 per 100 tablets and dispense 50 tablets

   a. What is the cost of the medication to the pharmacy if the pharmacy pays AWP less 11.5%?

   b. What is the amount the insurance company will pay for the purchase price of the medication?

   c. What will be the total amount billed to the insurance company?

   d. What is the profit?

8. AWP $36.35 per metered dose inhaler (MDI) and dispense 2 MDI

   a. What is the cost of the medication to the pharmacy if the pharmacy pays AWP less 11.5%?

   b. What is the amount the insurance company will pay for the purchase price of the medication?

   c. What will be the total amount billed to the insurance company?

   d. What is the profit?

9. AWP $302.35 per 30 tablets and dispense 10 tablets

   a. What is the cost of the medication to the pharmacy if the pharmacy pays AWP less 11.5%?

   b. What is the amount the insurance company will pay for the purchase price of the medication?

   c. What will be the total amount billed to the insurance company?

   d. What is the profit?

10. AWP $117.35 per 50 capsules and dispense 6 capsules

    a. What is the cost of the medication to the pharmacy if the pharmacy pays AWP less 11.5%?

    b. What is the amount the insurance company will pay for the purchase price of the medication?

    c. What will be the total amount billed to the insurance company?

    d. What is the profit?

11. AWP $85.35 per 80 g tube and dispense 15 g jar

    a. What is the cost of the medication to the pharmacy if the pharmacy pays AWP less 11.5%?

    b. What is the amount the insurance company will pay for the purchase price of the medication?

    c. What will be the total amount billed to the insurance company?

    d. What is the profit?

Calculate the profit for the following.

12. Mountain Health Maintenance pays a capitation fee of $310.00 per month. Six patients on this plan bring in prescriptions during July. The pharmacy's drug costs for the prescriptions (but not the costs of dispensing the drugs) are as follows:

Patient #1: $15.75, $106.50, $27.80
Patient #2: $210.00
Patient #3: $47.50, $105.25, $160.00, $52.60
Patient #4: $150.00, $210.00, $76.00
Patient #5: $10.50, $28.00, $62.50
Patient #6: $210.00, $210.00, $17.00

    a. What is the total capitation?

    b. What is the pharmacy's cost for all of the prescriptions?

    c. Was the pharmacy's gross profit positive or negative?

    d. What was the gross profit?

13. In the preceding question, assume that all drugs were purchased at AWP and that, instead of a capitation fee, the pharmacy was allowed AWP plus 3% and a $2.00 dispensing fee for each drug dispensed.

    a. How much would the pharmacy have received from the insurer?

    b. Is the gross profit more or less than with capitation?

    c. How much more or less?

14. Jackson HMO pays a capitation fee of $275.00 per month to OWL Pharmacy. OWL Pharmacy serves ten of Jackson's clients. The pharmacy fills prescriptions for five of these clients during the month of June. The pharmacy's costs for these prescriptions are as follows:

Patient JES: $89.63
Patient LMS: $126.54 (total cost for 2 prescriptions)
Patient SMJ: $420.45 (total cost for 5 prescriptions)
Patient EMJ: $117.50
Patient BAG: $46.75

The other five clients did not get any prescriptions during the month of June.

    a. What is the capitation received?

    b. What was the cost to the pharmacy for the above prescriptions?

    c. How much was the pharmacy's loss or gain in serving Jackson HMO's patients?

15. Baker HMO pays a capitation fee of $275.00 per month to OWL Pharmacy. OWL Pharmacy serves twelve of Baker's clients. The pharmacy filled prescriptions for five of these clients during the month of May. The pharmacy's costs for these prescriptions are as follows:

Patient KGE: $78.26, $75.23, $25.48
Patient PAD: $128.46, $21.86
Patient THN: $61.89, $41.20
Patient WER: $16.50, $5.80, $3.87, $21.67
Patient REW: $58.24

The other seven clients did not get any prescriptions during the month of May.

a. What is the capitation received?

b. What was the cost to the pharmacy for the above prescriptions?

c. How much was the pharmacy's loss or gain in serving Baker HMO's patients?

16. Blue Care HMO pays a capitation fee of $225.00 per month to Key Pharmacy. Key Pharmacy serves forty of Blue Care's clients. During the month of May, twelve patients had prescriptions filled at a total cost of $1867.50 plus $60.00 in dispensing costs.

a. What is the capitation received?

b. What was the cost to the pharmacy for the above prescriptions (including dispensing costs)?

c. How much was the pharmacy's loss or gain in serving Blue Care HMO's patients?

17. Insurance-R-Us HMO pays a capitation fee of $210.00 per month to Phicks Pharmacy. Phicks Pharmacy serves forty-two of the HMO's clients. During the month of September, twenty-three patients had thirty-one prescriptions filled at a total cost to the pharmacy of $2389.00 plus $4.25 per prescription in dispensing costs.

a. What is the capitation received?

b. What was the cost to the pharmacy for the above prescriptions (including dispensing costs)?

c. How much was the pharmacy's loss or gain in serving the HMO's patients?

Self-check your work in Appendix A.

9.3 Inventory Applications

inventory
a listing of all items that are available for sale in a business

inventory value
the total value of the drugs and merchandise in stock in the pharmacy on a given day

An **inventory** is a listing of all items that are available for sale in a business. **Inventory value** is defined as the total value of the drugs and merchandise in stock on a given day. Pharmacies must maintain a record of drugs and other supplies and merchandise purchased and sold to know when to reorder and when to adjust inventory levels of each item.

Space must be allocated to maintain inventory. Other considerations include shelving design and refrigeration. Keeping medications on the shelf is a cost to a pharmacy, and a large inventory can hinder cash flow. To minimize the shelf space needed and control costs, a pharmacy should try to manage its inventory so that medications arrive shortly before they are dispensed and sold. Nevertheless, a pharmacy may need to keep some slow-moving drugs in stock as a service to a few customers.

Managing Inventory

Today, most inventory records are computerized. Each time drugs are purchased, the quantity and price are entered into the computer database. As customers buy the drugs, the computer system automatically adjusts the inventory record. Pharmacies usually establish an inventory range for each item, that is, a maximum and a minimum number of units to have on hand. When the inventory drops to the minimum level, the item is purchased to restock the supply. This predetermined order point and the order quantity are based on the historical use of each drug.

Example 9.3.1

The maximum inventory level for ampicillin capsules is 1000 capsules. At the end of the day, the computer prints a list of items to be reordered; the list indicates an inventory level of 75 ampicillin capsules. How many capsules should be ordered to restock the inventory to maximum? If the drug wholesaler supplies ampicillin in bottles of 25, 100, 250, and 500 capsules, how many of each bottle size will fill the order (assuming that you begin with one bottle containing 500 capsules)?

To replenish the ampicillin inventory to the maximum level (1000), first determine how much the present level differs.

$$1000 \text{ capsules} - 75 \text{ capsules} = 925 \text{ capsules}$$

Then the idea is to purchase the 925 capsules in bottles of 500, 250, 100, and 25. It is good business practice to purchase the smallest possible number of bottles because large-quantity containers are usually a more economical purchase.

$$500 \text{ capsules} + 250 \text{ capsules} + 100 \text{ capsules} + 25 \text{ capsules} = 925 \text{ capsules}$$
$$\quad\text{1 bottle} \qquad\quad \text{1 bottle} \qquad\quad \text{1 bottle} \qquad\quad \text{3 bottles}$$

Example 9.3.2

The inventory of Zantac 150 mg is to be maintained at a minimum of 240 tablets and a maximum of 300 tablets. If 15 tablets are left on the shelf at the end of the day, how many bottles will be ordered to meet the inventory minimum? Zantac 150 mg is commercially available in a bottle containing 60 tablets.

Begin by determining the difference between the current inventory and the minimum inventory.

$$240 \text{ tablets} - 15 \text{ tablets} = 225 \text{ tablets}$$

Therefore, it will take at least 225 tablets to bring the inventory up to the minimum level for Zantac 150. But the tablets must be ordered in bottles of 60.

$$225 \text{ tablets} \div 60 \text{ tablets/bottle} = 3.75 \text{ bottles}$$

Rounding up, four bottles must be ordered.

Example 9.3.3

The inventory of propranolol 10 mg is to be maintained at a minimum of 300 tablets and a maximum of 1500 tablets. If 212 tablets are left on the shelf at the end of the day, how many bottles will you order to meet the inventory minimum? Propranolol is available in bottles containing 100 tablets, 500 tablets, and 1000 tablets. You normally order the largest-size bottle.

Begin by determining the minimum number of tablets that need to be ordered.

$$300 \text{ tablets} - 212 \text{ tablets} = 88 \text{ tablets}$$

[handwritten: ORDER Largest Bottle any way if it does NOT exceed max!]

Although either of the smaller-sized bottles will work, it is common business practice to order the same package size. Therefore, even though it significantly surpasses the minimum, you will order one bottle of 1,000 propranolol. The resulting inventory will still be within the acceptable range and will not exceed 1500 tablets.

Example 9.3.4

You would like to replenish the lip balm that is kept on the pharmacy counter by the cash register, and you need 18 tubes to fill the container. When you look in the wholesale catalog, it states that the lip balm is $10.20/dozen. How much should you order?

You will order 2 dozen—or 24 tubes of lip balm.

As part of maintaining inventory, it is also important to economize when purchasing stock medications. A purchaser can save money by buying in bulk, and it is usually more economical to buy a larger rather than a smaller amount of a drug. When making drug purchases, balance the optimal inventory level with the available bulk containers (such as bottles containing 100, 500, or 1000 tablets). The larger the container, usually the lower the cost per tablet (or other unit). The best deal per tablet will be purchased unless the particular item is used infrequently. If the drug item is used infrequently, a large bulk container may expire before it is used, and the medication will be destroyed. Cost savings is lost in such an instance. The following example will illustrate a calculation commonly performed when comparing bulk pricing and cost per unit.

Example 9.3.5

An antibiotic is available in the following stock bottle sizes for the prices indicated.

100 capsules/bottle, $2.80 *[handwritten: $0.028]*

500 capsules/bottle, $12.10 *[handwritten: .0242]*

1000 capsules/bottle, $25.30 *[handwritten: .0253]*

Which container provides the best price per capsule, and what is the price per capsule?

Divide each amount by the number of capsules in the bulk container to determine a per capsule cost.

$$\$2.80/\text{bottle} \div 100 \text{ capsules/bottle} = \$0.028/\text{capsule}$$
$$\$12.10/\text{bottle} \div 500 \text{ capsules/bottle} = \$0.0242/\text{capsule}$$
$$\$25.30/\text{bottle} \div 1000 \text{ capsules/bottle} = \$0.0253/\text{capsule}$$

The 500 count bottle is the best value purchase for this medication at 2.4 cents per tablet.

Days' Supply

days' supply
a method of inventory management that tries to keep inventory value approximately equal to the cost to the pharmacy of the products sold in a certain number of days; calculated as the value of inventory divided by the average daily cost of products sold

Often today's pharmacies have $75,000.00 to $200,000.00 in inventory sitting on the shelves as drug products. If a large chain has ten stores in a particular region, the amount of money in goods sitting on the shelf adds up very quickly. Large companies often set goals for lowering the inventory in order to improve cash flow. One method used to set inventory goals for a pharmacy is called **"days' supply,"** which refers to making the value of the inventory approximately equal to the cost to the pharmacy of the products sold in a certain number of days. A common number is in the 25–35 day range. For example, if a pharmacy has a goal of "30 days' supply," its goal is to keep the value of the inventory equal to the total cost to the pharmacy of the products sold in 30 days.

Sometimes, a pharmacy does not know the best number of days to use as a goal in calculating costs. It does know the current inventory value, however, and can easily calculate average daily costs (weekly costs ÷ 7 days). With this information, the pharmacy can determine how many days it will take (what is referred to as "days' supply") for the average daily product costs to equal the value of the inventory. Then the pharmacy can revise the goal as necessary.

$$\text{number of days' supply} = \frac{\text{value of inventory}}{\text{average daily cost of products sold}}$$

Example 9.3.6

Tom's Pharmacy has a total inventory value of $103,699.00. It had sales last week of $37,546.00, and the cost to the pharmacy of the products sold was $28,837.00. What should the pharmacy's days' supply be in order to keep its inventory value stable?

Tom's average daily product costs were

$$\$28,837.00 \div 7 \text{ days} = \$4120.00 \text{ (rounded)}$$

Now, according to the above formula, dividing the value of the inventory by the average daily product costs approximately equals the number of days' supply:

$$\text{number of days' supply} = \frac{\$103,699.00}{\$4120.00} = 25$$

Thus, in 25 days, Tom will have sold products approximately equal to the value of his inventory.

Example 9.3.7

Lisa's Pharmacy has a total inventory value of $176,989.00. Last week it had sales of $45,813.00, and the cost to the pharmacy of the products sold came to $36,592.00. Lisa's goal for the number of days' supply is 29, but she's currently over her goal. How many days' supply is she over, and how much inventory value does this represent?

The average daily product costs were

$$\$36,592.00 \div 7 \text{ days} = \$5227.00 \text{ (rounded)}$$

At the present time, the number of days' supply for the pharmacy is

$$\frac{\$176,989.00}{\$5227.00} = 34$$

Therefore, it takes 34 days for costs to equal the inventory value. In other words, Lisa is 5 days over.

$$5 \times \$5227.00 = \$26,135.00$$

If Lisa can reduce her inventory by this amount, she will have met her goal of 29 days' supply.

Turnover Rate

If a pharmacy does not maintain computerized inventory, it must perform a physical inventory count at intervals, usually annually or semiannually. The physical inventory value is then used to determine the average inventory as follows.

$$\text{average inventory} = \frac{\text{beginning inventory} + \text{present inventory}}{2}$$

Knowing the average inventory allows a pharmacy to calculate the number of times its inventory was repurchased during a cycle (usually a year).

Dividing total annual purchases of inventory by the average inventory value gives the **turnover rate,** or the number of times the amount of goods in inventory was sold during the year. It is calculated as follows.

turnover rate
the number of times the amount of goods in inventory is sold during a year; calculated by dividing total annual purchases of inventory by the average inventory value

$$\text{turnover rate} = \frac{\text{annual purchases of inventory}}{\text{average inventory value}}$$

Knowing this number can help the pharmacist determine if the average inventory level should be increased or decreased, as extra costs may be associated with high or low inventories. Thus, if a pharmacy has an average inventory value of $25,250.00 and annual inventory purchases of $75,000.00, the amount of goods in inventory will turn over 2.97 times, or approximately three times in a year.

$$\text{turnover rate} = \frac{\$75,000.00}{\$25,250.00} = 2.97$$

Example 9.3.8
A pharmacy does a quarterly inventory count and has an average inventory value of $100,000.00. Annual inventory purchases are $500,000.00. What is the turnover rate?

$$\text{turnover rate} = \frac{\$500,000.00}{\$100,000.00} = 5$$

Depreciation

Depreciation is an allowance made to account for the decreasing value of an asset. Properties owned by the pharmacy are called assets. They are put into two broad categories: current and long-term assets. The assets that can be consumed or converted into cash within one year are current assets, and those that cannot are long-term assets, usually buildings and equipment.

Buildings and equipment lose value due to use, obsolescence, and the passage of time. The straight-line depreciation method of calculating depreciation uses the total cost, the estimated life of the property (in years), and the disposal value in the following formula.

$$\text{annual depreciation} = \text{total cost} - \text{disposal value/estimated life}$$

Example 9.3.9
Rafael's Drug Shop buys a compact car for drug deliveries to customers. The cost of the car is $9000.00. Its estimated useful life is five years, and the disposal value is $1200.00. What is the annual depreciation?

$$\text{annual depreciation} = \$9000.00 - \frac{\$1200.00}{5} = \frac{\$7800.00}{5}$$

$$= \$1560$$

9.3 Problem Set

Calculate the number of packages that need to be reordered for each item.

Drug	Package Size	Minimum # Units	Maximum # Units	Current Inventory	Reorder
1. tetracycline 250 mg cap	500	120	700	80	_____
2. amoxicillin 500 mg cap	500	240	1000	118	_____
3. amoxicillin 250 mg cap	500	240	1000	180	_____
4. cefaclor 500 mg tab	60	20	120	35	_____
5. cefprozil 250 mg tab	100	40	150	28	_____
6. cefprozil 500 mg tab	50	20	75	24	_____

Drug	Package Size	Minimum # Units	Maximum # Units	Current Inventory	Reorder
7. metronidazole 500 mg tab	50	30	120	12	_____
8. azithromycin 250 mg cap	30	18	60	36	_____
9. doxycycline 50 mg cap	50	30	150	42	_____

The current inventory of topical products on the shelf is often checked due to compounding needs, special orders, and poor computer tracking of dispensed partial containers of dermal products. For this reason, reordering of topical products must be monitored, even with computer-generated orders. The technician has checked the shelf and found the following. Calculate the number of packages that need to be reordered for each item.

Drug	Package Size	Minimum # Units	Maximum # Units	Current Inventory	Reorder
10. triamcinolone 0.25% cream	15 g	2	4	1	_____
	80 g	2	4	0	_____
11. triamcinolone 0.1% ung	15 g	1	2	1	_____
	60 g	1	2	1	_____
	80 g	1	2	0	_____
12. triamcinolone 0.1% lotion	60 mL	1	2	1	_____
13. fluocinolone 0.025% cream	15 g	1	2	1	_____
	60 g	1	2	1	_____
14. fluocinolone 0.025% ung	60 g	1	2	0 tubes and 1 order waiting	_____
15. desoximetasone 0.25% cream	15 g	1	2	0	_____
	60 g	1	2	0	_____
	4 oz	1	2	1	_____
16. desoximetasone 0.05% gel	15 g	1	1	0 on shelf and 1 order waiting	_____
	60 g	1	1	0	_____
17. halobetasol 0.05% cream	15 g	1	2	1	_____
	45 g	1	2	1	_____
18. fluocinonide 0.05% cream	15 g	1	2	1	_____
	30 g	2	4	1	_____
	60 g	2	4	2	_____
	120 g	1	2	0	_____

Calculate the number of packages that need to be reordered for each item.

Drug	Package Size	Minimum # Units	Maximum # Units	Current Inventory	Reorder
19. fluocinonide 0.05% gel	15 g	1	1	1	_____
	30 g	1	3	2	_____
	60 g	1	3	0	_____
20. fluocinonide 0.05% ung	15 g	1	2	1	_____
	30 g	1	2	1	_____
	60 g	1	2	1 partial	_____
	120 g	1	2	1	_____
21. fluocinonide 0.05% soln	20 mL	1	1	0	_____
	60 mL	1	3	1 partial	_____
22. ramipril 5 mg cap	100	120	240	64	_____
23. verapamil 120 mg SR	100	80	240	52	_____
24. verapamil 240 mg SR	100	120	360	30	_____
25. nicardipine 60 mg SR	60	120	240	20	_____
26. captopril 50 mg tab	100	150	300	76	_____
27. furosemide 40 mg tab	1000	240	1500	134	_____
28. doxazosin 2 mg tab	100	80	240	83	_____
29. atenolol 50 mg tab	1000	240	1500	107	_____
30. atenolol 100 mg tab	100	150	300	111	_____
31. nifedipine 60 mg tab	300	120	625	12 & 2 Rx for 60 pending	_____
32. nifedipine 90 mg tab	100	120	300	63	_____
33. lisinopril 5 mg tab	100	90	260	110	_____
34. lisinopril 10 mg tab	1000	240	1500	146	_____
35. lisinopril 20 mg tab	100	180	250	145	_____
36. lisinopril 40 mg tab	100	90	220	152	_____

37. Review the inventory list below and calculate the necessary purchases to reestablish maximum inventory. Write your answers in the "Purchased" column.

John's Drug Shop Inventory

Drug	Maximum Level	Dispensed Today	Minimum Level	Current Inventory	Purchased
a. Eucerin cream, jars	10	1	3	3	_____
b. Ampicillin, capsules	4500	500	4000	2400	_____
c. Eyedrops, bottles	24	4	4	4	_____
d. Nystatin oral solution	1000 mL	100 mL	200 mL	400 mL	_____
e. Sterile saline	600 mL	315 mL	100 mL	75 mL	_____

38. Adam's Pharmacy has a total inventory value of $183,445.00. Last week the pharmacy had sales of $47,293.00, and the cost to the pharmacy for the products sold came to $38,207.00. Adam's goal is to have a days' supply of 28 days.

   a. How many days' supply does Adam have?

   b. How much is he over or under his goal in dollars?

39. Corbin's Pharmacy has a total inventory value of $123,490.00. Last week the pharmacy had sales of $34,829.00, and the cost to the pharmacy for the products sold came to $26,504.00. Corbin's goal is to have a days' supply of 26 days.

   a. How many days' supply does Corbin have?

   b. How much is he over or under his goal in dollars?

40. Karen's Pharmacy has $147,210.00 in inventory. She is currently at her goal of 24 days' supply. What was her approximate cost of products sold last week?

41. Scott's Pharmacy had sales of $51,280.00 last week. What must his daily sales average be this week in order to make $5000.00 more than last week?

42. Bob's Pharmacy has an inventory of $213,840.00. Last week's sales were $63,910.00. What was the percent profit if the cost of last week's sales was $48,891.00?

43. Teri's Pharmacy has an inventory of $164,590.00. Last week's sales, which totaled $58,223.00, brought in a 21% profit. Now Teri's days' supply goal is 31 days.

   a. What was the cost to the pharmacy of the product sold last week?

   b. What is the pharmacy's days' supply?

   c. How much is the value of the days' supply above or below the goal in dollars?

44. Kathy's Pharmacy has an inventory of $184,520.00. Her cost of sales last week was $28,223.00, and she made a 26% profit. Her days' supply goal is 34 days.

   a. What was the amount sold last week?

   b. What is the pharmacy's days' supply?

   c. How much is the value of the days' supply above or below goal in dollars?

45. If a pharmacy's average inventory for the last year was $132,936.00 and the annual cost total was $1,612,000.00, what was the turnover rate?

46. If a pharmacy's average inventory for the last year was $156,200.00 and the annual cost total was $1,768,000.00, what was the turnover rate?

Calculate the turnover rate for the following drugs sold at Adam's Pharmacy.

Drug	Average Inventory	Annual Purchases	Turnover Rate
47. metformin 500 mg	$520.00	$20,800.00	_____
48. divalproex 250 mg	$178.00	$5760.00	_____
49. citalopram 40 mg	$360.00	$7213.00	_____
50. raloxifene 60 mg	$320.00	$5060.00	_____
51. montelukast chewtab 4 mg	$385.00	$6000.00	_____

52. John's Drug Shop purchases $52,500.00 of antibiotics annually. The pharmacy does an inventory count twice annually, and its average inventory of antibiotics is $5000.00. What is the pharmacy's turnover rate for antibiotics?

53. The pharmacy has a new cash register system. The system cost $8294.00 and should last six years. Its disposal value is $2138.00. What is the annual depreciation?

54. The hospital pharmacy just purchased two new biological safety hoods at $18,350.00 each. Each should last 12 years if maintained properly. The disposal value is $1567.00 each. What is the annual depreciation?

Self-check your work in Appendix A.

Practice Test

The OWL Pharmacy has the following over-head expenses.

pharmacist(s) salary	$126,000.00
technician(s) salary	38,000.00
rent	12,000.00
utilities	7,000.00
computer maintenance	1,500.00
software subscriptions	1,500.00
liability insurance	2,500.00
business insurance	3,000.00
drug purchases	425,000.00

1. If a 25% profit is desirable, what must the pharmacy's income be in order to meet this goal?

2. If the pharmacy's income is $1,401,750.00, what is its percent profit?

Calculate the dollar amount of net profit and the percent profit (markup rate) for the following individual prescription drug items. (Round to whole percents.) The dispensing fee is $5.24 for each prescription.

3. Pepcid (famotidine) 40 mg tablets
   Cost: $84.30 per 30 tablets
   Dispense: 30 tablets
   Rx Charge: $95.00

   a. What is the net profit?

   b. What is the percent profit (markup rate) rounded to the nearest whole number?

4. Acetaminophen/codeine # 3
   Cost: $32.50 per 500 count bottle
   Dispense: 40 tablets
   Rx Charge: $8.95

   a. What is the net profit?

   b. What is the percent profit (markup rate) rounded to the nearest whole percent?

Calculate the following and state the answers in dollars and cents.

5. John's Drug Shop purchases five cases of dermatological cream at $100.00 per case. The invoice specifies a 15% discount if the account is paid in full within 15 days. What is the discounted price?

6. There are 24 tubes of cream per case in question 9. You are to mark each tube up by 20% based on the pharmacy's discounted purchase price. What will the selling price be per tube?

Use the following directions for questions 7 to 12 found on the next page.

The pharmacy accountant wants items tabulated as to percent profit. Calculate the markup and percent profit of each of the following items. (Round to whole percents.)

Item	Pharmacy's Purchase Price	Selling Price	Markup	% Profit
7. amoxicillin	$0.14	$0.28	_____	_____
8. nasal spray	$1.45	$2.15	_____	_____
9. fungal ointment	$3.25	$4.15	_____	_____
10. analgesic tablets	$0.10	$0.15	_____	_____
11. contraceptive foam	$1.35	$5.75	_____	_____
12. nitroglycerin tablets	$8.50	$14.95	_____	_____

Calculate the cost to the pharmacy as AWP less 12%.

13. AWP $94.45 per 120 g tube and dispense 30 g

14. AWP $12.50 per 1 pint liquid and dispense 120 mL

Calculate AWP plus 3% plus a $5.75 per prescription dispensing fee.

15. AWP $21.35 per 30 g tube and dispense 30 g tube

16. AWP $90.32 per pint liquid and dispense 6 fl oz

Calculate the profit for the following.

17. A prescription is written for a tube of ointment. The AWP is $62.00. Smith's Pharmacy purchases the tube at AWP, and Jones's Pharmacy purchases the tube at AWP minus 10%. The insurer will reimburse at AWP plus 2% plus a $1.50 dispensing fee. How much profit does each pharmacy make?

18. A prescription is written for a bottle of cough medication. The AWP is $18.75. McDougall Pharmacy purchases the cough syrup at a cost of $4.00. The pharmacy sells the cough syrup for AWP minus 10% plus $6.00 dispensing fee. How much profit does the pharmacy make?

Calculate the following and express the amounts in dollars and cents.

19. Grant County HMO pays a capitation fee of $195.00 per month to OWL Pharmacy. OWL Pharmacy serves seventeen of the HMO's clients. During the month of June, twelve patients had prescriptions filled at a total cost of $867.50 plus $60 in dispensing costs.

a. What is the capitation received?

b. What is the cost to the pharmacy for the above prescriptions?

c. How much did the pharmacy lose or gain in serving the Grant County HMO patients?

20. Delaware County HMO pays a capitation
fee of $120 per month to Eppley
Pharmacy. The pharmacy serves forty-
six county HMO employees and their
families. During the month of March, the
pharmacy filled prescriptions for twenty-
one patients at a cost of $1428 plus $128
dispensing fees.

a. What was the capitation received?

b. What was the cost to the pharmacy for
the prescriptions?

c. How much did Eppley Pharmacy lose or
gain in serving the HMO patients?

Calculate the number of packages that need to
be reordered for each item.

Drug	Package Size	Minimum # Units	Maximum # Units	Current Inventory	Reorder
21. nicardipine 30 mg SR	60	120	240	18	_____
22. captopril 25 mg tab	100	150	300	60	_____
23. metoprolol 50 mg tab	1000	120	1500	83	_____
24. metoprolol 100 mg	1000	120	2000	341	_____

Calculate the requested value.

25. Down-the-Street Pharmacy does inventory
three times annually, and the average
inventory value is $125,825.00. Annual
purchases of inventory total $188,737.50.
What is the turnover rate?

26. ServU Pharmacy has an inventory
program in the computer system, and the
average value of the inventory is calculated
daily. It is $114,900. Annual purchases
of inventory total $546,210. What is the
turnover rate?

27. The pharmacy has a van for home
deliveries, and its total cost was
$18,452.00. Its disposal value is
$12,208.00. It has an estimated life
of three years. What is the annual
depreciation?

28. The pharmacy has some lab equipment
that cost $1478.00. Its disposal value is
$850.00, and its estimated life is eight
years. What is the annual depreciation?

Understanding the Apothecary System

Learning Objectives

- Identify symbols and measures of the apothecary system.

- Use the apothecary system to solve medication problems.

- Identify approximately equivalent apothecary and metric units and convert measurements between the two systems.

Preview chapter terms and definitions.

10.1 Apothecary Volume and Weight Equivalences

apothecary system
literally the system used by an apothecary, a system of measurement used in pharmacy prior to the metric system; units of measure include minims, fluidrams, scruples, grains, ounces, and pounds

The **apothecary system,** literally the system used by an apothecary, is one of the oldest systems of measurement. The units of measure in this system are denoted with the special symbols shown in Table 10.1. The apothecary system uses fractions, as opposed to decimals, and because this system is less accurate than the metric system, its use is declining in the United States.

Table 10.2 shows the equivalences of the basic measures of volume and weight for the apothecary system. Note that in two instances—the ounce and the dram—the same names are used for measures of both volume and weight. To avoid confusion, always use the word *fluid* when referring to volume measure. Note that whereas in the household system, *fluid ounce* is written as two words, in the apothecary system, *fluidounce* is written as one word, as is *fluidram*.

Safety Note

Do not confuse ounces and drams in the weight and volume systems. Be sure to use the word *fluid* or the symbol *f* when referring to volume.

TABLE 10.1 Apothecary Symbols

Volume		Weight	
Unit of Measure	Symbol	Unit of Measure	Symbol
minim	ℳ	grain	gr
fluidrachm, fluidram	f ℨ	scruple	℈
fluidounce	f	drachm, dram	ℨ
		ounce	℥
		pound	℔ (or #)

Remember

apothecary
pound (℔) =
12 oz
household
pound (lb) =
16 oz

TABLE 10.2   Equivalent Units of Measure in the Apothecary System

Volume	Weight
60 ♏ = 1 f ʒ	20 gr = 1 ℈
6 f ʒ = 1 f ℥ *	3 ℈ = 1 ʒ
16 f ℥ = 1 pt	8 ʒ = 1 ℥
2 pt = 1 qt	12 ℥ = 1 ℔ (or #)†
4 qt = 1 gallon	

* There are actually 8 f ʒ in 1 f ℥, but pharmacies use 6 f ʒ because convention dictates that 1 f ʒ = 1 tsp = 5 mL.

† The apothecary pound equals 12 ℥, but the household pound equals 16 oz and is the more commonly used equivalence.

Converting between Apothecary Units of Measure for Volume

In a practical sense, volumes are no longer measured in fluidrams or minims. The metric system is the most prevalent system of measurement. Measuring a pint of fluid would most likely be measured as a pint or milliliter using a container that has markings for both metric and apothecary systems. However, the following examples will demonstrate how to convert volume units of measure within the apothecary system using equivalents shown in Table 10.2.

Example 10.1.1

How many fluidrams are in 3 pt?

A pint equals 16 f ℥; therefore,

$$3 \text{ pt} = 3 \times 16 \text{ f ℥} = 48 \text{ f ℥}$$

Each fluidounce contains 6 f ʒ; therefore,

$$48 \text{ f ℥} = 48 \times 6 \text{ f ʒ} = 288 \text{ f ʒ}$$

In this case, each unit was replaced by its equivalence for the next smallest unit, until the required unit was reached.

Example 10.1.2

Reduce 7160 ♏ to the smallest possible number of all of the larger units.

Each fluidram contains 60 ♏. Dividing 7160 by 60 gives 119 with a remainder (r.) of 20; therefore,

$$7160 \text{ ♏} = 119 \text{ f ʒ, } 20 \text{ ♏}$$

Note that the remainder is the smaller unit. A fluidounce contains 6 f ʒ; since 119 is greater than 6, we can convert 119 f ʒ to fluidrams. Dividing 119 by 6 gives 19 r.5; therefore,

$$119 \text{ f ʒ} = 19 \text{ f ℥, } 5 \text{ f ʒ}$$

A pint contains 16 f℥; since 19 is greater than 16, we can convert 19 f℥ to pints. Dividing 19 by 16 gives 1 r.3; therefore,

$$19 \text{ f℥} = 1 \text{ pt, } 3 \text{ f℥}$$

Each quart contains 2 pt, which is greater than the amount we have, so no other units can be replaced. Putting it all together,

$$7160 \ ♏ = 1 \text{ pt, } 3 \text{ f℥, } 5 \text{ fℨ, } 20 \ ♏$$

Converting between Apothecary Units of Measure for Weight

As discussed in Chapter 8, quantities that are measured and weighed in the pharmacy for special compounds are weighed in metric units. In a practical sense, grains are the only quantity still relevant in the apothecary weight units. The following examples will demonstrate calculations using grains.

Example 10.1.3

You have 6 ℥ of a dry powder. How many 2 ℨ doses can you make from this?

There are 8 ℨ in an ounce, so

$$6 ℥ \times \frac{8 ℨ}{℥} = 48 ℨ$$

Then determine the number of doses.

$$48 ℨ \div 2 ℨ/\text{dose} = 24 \text{ doses}$$

Therefore, 24 doses of 2 ℨ each can be made from 6 ℥ of dry powder.

Example 10.1.4

Reduce 10,000 gr to the smallest possible number of all of the larger units.

A scruple is equal to 20 gr, and $10,000 \div 20 = 500$, so

$$10,000 \text{ gr} = 500 \ ℈$$

A dram is equal to 3 ℈, and $500 \div 3 = 166$ r.2, so

$$500 \ ℈ = 166 \ ℨ, 2 \ ℈$$

An ounce is equal to 8 ℨ, and $166 \div 8 = 20$ r.6, so

$$166 \ ℨ = 20 \ ℥, 6 \ ℨ$$

Finally, a pound is equal to 12 ℥, and $20 \div 12 = 1$ r.8, so

$$20 \ ℥ = 1 \ ℔, 8 \ ℥$$

Putting it all together,

$$10{,}000 \text{ gr} = 1 \text{ ℔}, 8 \text{ ℥}, 6 \text{ ʒ}, 2 \text{ ℈}$$

Example 10.1.5   **Convert 68 ℥ to grains.**

$$68 \text{ ℥} \times \frac{3 \text{ ℈}}{1 \text{ ℥}} = 204 \text{ ℈}$$

$$204 \text{ ℈} \times \frac{20 \text{ gr}}{1 \text{ ℈}} = 4080 \text{ gr}$$

Example 10.1.6   **Convert 1 ℔ to grains.**

$$1 \text{ ℔} \times \frac{12 \text{ ℥}}{1 \text{ ℔}} = 12 \text{ ℥}$$

$$12 \text{ ℥} \times \frac{8 \text{ ʒ}}{1 \text{ ℥}} = 96 \text{ ʒ}$$

$$96 \text{ ʒ} \times \frac{3 \text{ ℈}}{1 \text{ ʒ}} = 288 \text{ ℈}$$

$$288 \text{ ℈} \times \frac{20 \text{ gr}}{1 \text{ ℈}} = 5760 \text{ gr}$$

10.1 Problem Set

Convert the following.

1. Convert 6 gal to apothecary fluidounces.

2. Convert 1 f℥, 3 f ʒ, 7 ♏ to just minims.

3. Convert 479 f ʒ to the smallest possible of all of the larger apothecary units.

4. How many drams are equivalent to 1 ℔, 6 ℥?

5. Reduce 6000 gr to the smallest number of all of the larger apothecary units.

6. How many fluidrams are equal to 3 qt?

7. Change 10 ℥, 2 ʒ, 1 ℈ to grains.

8. Convert 6 pt to fluidrams.

9. Convert 15 ℔ to ounces.

10. Convert 12 f ʒ to fluidounces.

Self-check your work in Appendix A.

10.2 Conversions between the Apothecary and Metric Systems

To convert metric measurements to apothecary units and vice versa, you need to know the equivalent measures shown in Table 10.3. This table also provides equivalences in the **avoirdupois system** and the household system. As a general rule, convert all quantities to the metric system as soon as possible in the conversion process to make the conversion as accurate as possible. Metric units are readily comparable from one unit to the next, and unlike the apothecary and household systems, the metric system uses only 10-based conversion factors, which are easier to use in calculations.

Converting Fluidounces

When converting from fluidounces to milliliters in pharmacy calculations, it is common practice to round up; for example, round 29.57 mL up to 30 mL. In this chapter, use 30 mL when converting from fluidounces.

A special discrepancy to keep in mind is the difference between the true volume of a fluidram and the commonly used volume. Before the household system was created, 1 f℥ = 3.75 mL and 8 f℥ = 1 f℥. When the household system was formed, 1 f℥ became synonymous with 1 tsp or 5 mL, thus changing the equivalence to 6 f℥ = 1 f℥. Therefore, Table 10.3 states that there are 6 f℥ per 1 f℥ and 1 f℥ = 5 mL. In this chapter, you will use these conversions.

As Chapter 5 explained, it is common practice to round a household fluid ounce (29.57 mL) up to 30 mL. When measuring this amount, this estimation is often

TABLE 10.3   Apothecary, Avoirdupois, Household, and Metric System Equivalents

	Apothecary	Avoirdupois	Household	Metric
Volume				
	16.23 ℳ			1 mL
	1 f℥		1 tsp	5 mL*
	6 f℥ or 1 f℥		6 tsp or 2 tbsp	30 mL (29.57 mL)†
	1 pt		1 pt	480 mL†
	1 qt		1 qt	960 mL
	1 gallon		1 gallon	3840 mL
Weight				
	1 gr			65 mg††
		1 oz		30 g (28.35 g)
			1 oz	30 g
	1 ℥ or 8 ℈			30 g (31.1 g)
	1 ℔			373.2 g
		1 lb	1 lb	454 g

* There are actually 3.75 mL in 1 f℥. However, convention dictates that 1 f℥ = 1 tsp = 5 mL.

† There are actually 29.57 mL in 1 f℥, but 30 mL is usually used. When packaging a pint, companies will typically include 473 mL, rather than the full 480 mL.

†† Many manufacturers use 60 mg instead of 65 mg as the equivalent for 1 gr.

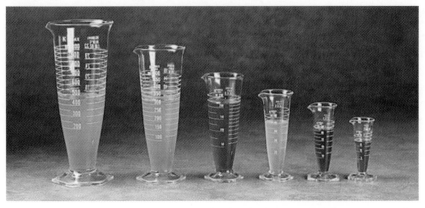

Dual-scale graduated cylinders like these, showing both metric and drams, are used to measure volume in the pharmacy.

appropriate because the volume differs by such a small amount. When measuring multiple fluid ounces that have been rounded up to 30 mL, however, the discrepancy becomes far more apparent. For example, if asked to measure a pint (16 fl oz), one would measure roughly 480 mL. This becomes problematic because 29.57 mL multiplied by 16 is equal to only 473.12 mL, not 480 mL. Most stock bottles are labeled 473 mL, yet pharmacies bill according to the estimation of 480 mL and measure out fluid ounces in 30 mL increments. For the purposes of this chapter, use the rounded 30 mL and 480 mL values.

Example 10.2.1

Convert 1 gallon, 12 f℥ to milliliters.

Begin solving this problem by noting that according to Table 10.3, 1 gallon = 3840 mL. The value of 12 f℥ can be converted to milliliters in two ways.

Solution 1: Using the ratio-proportion method,

$$\frac{x \text{ mL}}{12 \text{ f℥}} = \frac{30 \text{ m}}{1 \text{ f℥}}$$

$$x \text{ mL} = 360 \text{ mL}$$

Solution 2: Using the dimensional analysis method,

$$12 \text{ f℥} \times \frac{30 \text{ mL}}{1 \text{ f℥}} = 360 \text{ mL}$$

Add the milliliter equivalent of 1 gallon and 12 f℥.

$$3840 \text{ mL} + 360 \text{ mL} = 4200 \text{ mL}$$

Example 10.2.2

Convert 2 pt to milliliters.

Solution 1: Using the ratio-proportion method,

$$\frac{x \text{ mL}}{2 \text{ pt}} = \frac{480 \text{ mL}}{1 \text{ pt}}$$

$$x \text{ mL} = 960 \text{ mL}$$

> **Remember**
>
> Two pints is approximately equal to 1000 mL or 1 L.
> 1 pint =
>   480 mL
> 2 pints =
>   960 mL

Solution 2: Using the dimensional analysis method,

$$2 \text{ pt} \times \frac{480 \text{ mL}}{1 \text{ pt}} = 960 \text{ mL}$$

Example 10.2.3

Convert 6 f ʒ to milliliters.

Solution 1: Using the ratio-proportion method,

$$\frac{x \text{ mL}}{6 \text{ f}ʒ} = \frac{30 \text{ mL}}{1 \text{ f}ʒ}$$

$$x \text{ mL} = 180 \text{ mL}$$

Solution 2: Using the dimensional analysis method,

$$6 \text{ f}ʒ \times \frac{30 \text{ mL}}{1 \text{ f}ʒ} = 180 \text{ mL}$$

Example 10.2.4

Convert ³⁄₄ gallon to milliliters.

Begin by converting the fraction to a decimal.

$$³⁄₄ \text{ gallon} = 0.75 \text{ gallon}$$

Solution 1: Using the ratio-proportion method,

$$\frac{x \text{ mL}}{0.75 \text{ gallon}} = \frac{3840 \text{ mL}}{1 \text{ gallon}}$$

$$x \text{ mL} = 2880 \text{ mL}$$

Solution 2: Using the dimensional analysis method,

$$0.75 \text{ gallon} \times \frac{3840 \text{ mL}}{1 \text{ gallon}} = 2880 \text{ mL}$$

Example 10.2.5

Convert 8 f ʒ to fluidrams.

First, convert fluidounces to milliliters.
Solution 1: Using the ratio-proportion method,

$$\frac{x \text{ mL}}{8 \text{ f}ʒ} = \frac{30 \text{ mL}}{1 \text{ f}ʒ}$$

$$x \text{ mL} = 240 \text{ mL}$$

Solution 2: Using the dimensional analysis method,

$$8 \text{ f} \text{℥} \times \frac{30 \text{ mL}}{1 \text{ f} \text{℥}} = 240 \text{ mL}$$

Second, convert milliliters to fluidrams.
Solution 1: Using the ratio-proportion method,

$$\frac{x \text{ f} \text{℥}}{240 \text{ mL}} = \frac{1 \text{ f} \text{℥}}{5 \text{ mL}}$$

$$x \text{ f} \text{℥} = 48 \text{ f} \text{℥}$$

Solution 2: Using the dimensional analysis method,

$$240 \text{ mL} \times \frac{1 \text{ f} \text{℥}}{5 \text{ mL}} = 48 \text{ f} \text{℥}$$

Converting Ounces

Remember

Round the value of 1 ounce in all three systems to 30 g.

Many prescribers are accustomed to writing prescription orders in ounces of medication, in both liquid and solid forms. As mentioned earlier, however, the metric system is considered to be a more accurate system and is becoming the system of choice in the United States. Also, many pharmacy computer systems are programmed to accept amounts only in metric units. Therefore, another calculation performed frequently is the conversion of ounces to grams. According to Table 10.3, the apothecary ounce equals 31.1 g, the avoirdupois ounce equals 28.35 g, and the household ounce equals 30 g. In all three cases, it is common practice to round to 30 g.

Example 10.2.6

You have 14 ℥ of a dry chemical. What is the equivalent weight in grams?

Solution 1: Using the ratio-proportion method,

$$\frac{x \text{ g}}{14 \text{℥}} = \frac{30 \text{ g}}{1 \text{℥}}$$

$$x \text{ g} = 420 \text{ g}$$

Solution 2: Using the dimensional analysis method,

$$14 \text{℥} \times \frac{30 \text{ g}}{1 \text{℥}} = 420 \text{ g}$$

Example 10.2.7

Convert 23 ℥ to grams.

Solution 1: Using the ratio-proportion method,

$$\frac{x \text{ g}}{23 \text{℥}} = \frac{30 \text{ g}}{1 \text{℥}}$$

$$x \text{ g} = 690 \text{ g}$$

Solution 2: Using the dimensional analysis method,

$$23\,\text{₹} \times \frac{30\ \text{g}}{1\,\text{₹}} = 690\ \text{g}$$

Example 10.2.8

Convert 2 lb (avoirdupois) to grams.

Solution 1: Using the ratio-proportion method,

$$\frac{x\ \text{g}}{2\ \text{lb}} = \frac{454\ \text{g}}{1\ \text{lb}}$$

$$x\ \text{g} = 908\ \text{g}$$

Solution 2: Using the dimensional analysis method,

$$2\ \text{lb} \times \frac{454\ \text{g}}{1\ \text{lb}} = 908\ \text{g}$$

Converting Grains

grain
the smallest unit of measure in the apothecary system that is used with any frequency in pharmacy

A **grain** is the smallest unit of weight in the apothecary system that is used with any frequency in the pharmacy. Even so, this unit of measure is used on only a handful of labels for medications such as nitroglycerin, and the converted dose in milligrams appears on the same label. Nevertheless, the value of a grain can differ. In Table 10.3, the grain is equal to 65 mg, but many other references use 60 mg instead. Most pharmacists use the 65 mg conversion.

Example 10.2.9

How many grams are in 32 gr?

Begin by noting the equivalency stated in Table 10.3, and converting the value to grams.

$$1\ \text{gr} = 65\ \text{mg} = 0.065\ \text{g}$$

Solution 1: Using the ratio-proportion method,

$$\frac{x\ \text{g}}{32\ \text{g}} = \frac{0.065\ \text{g}}{1\ \text{gr}}$$

$$x\ \text{g} = 2.08\ \text{g}$$

Solution 2: Using the dimensional analysis method,

$$32\ \text{gr} \times \frac{0.065\ \text{g}}{1\ \text{gr}} = 2.08\ \text{g}$$

Example 10.2.10   How many grains are in a 325 mg aspirin tablet?

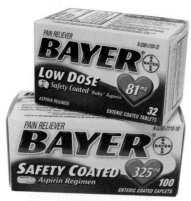

Aspirin is most frequently used in the 81 mg and 325 mg strengths.

Solution 1: Using the ratio-proportion method,

$$\frac{x \text{ gr}}{325 \text{ mg}} = \frac{1 \text{ gr}}{65 \text{ mg}}$$

$$x \text{ gr} = 5 \text{ gr}$$

Solution 2: Using the dimensional analysis method,

$$325 \text{ mg} \times \frac{1 \text{ gr}}{65 \text{ mg}} = 5 \text{ gr}$$

A prescription for a 5 gr aspirin tablet may be written as "gr V aspirin."

10.2 Problem Set

Convert the following values to the units indicated.

1. 3 qt = _____ mL

2. 300 mL = _____ f ℥

3. 75 mL = _____ f ℥

4. 120 mL = _____ f ℥

5. 15 mL = _____ f ℥

6. 6 pt = _____ mL = _____ f ℥

7. 60 mL = _____ f ℥ = _____ f ℥

8. 180 mL = _____ f ℥ = _____ f ℥

9. 3 pt = _____ f ℥ = _____ mL

10. 8 f ℥ = _____ mL = _____ f ℥

Convert the following values to milliliters.

11. ½ f ℥

12. 1 f ℥

13. 2 f ℥

14. 3 f ℥

15. 4 f ℥

16. 5 f ℥

17. 6 f ℥

18. 7 f ℥

19. 8 f ℥

20. 9 f ℥

21. 10 f ℥

22. 11 f ℥

23. 12 f ℥

24. 13 f ℥

25. 14 f ℥

26. 15 f ℥

27. 16 f ℥

28. 1 pt

29. 2 pt

30. 3 pt

Convert the following values to apothecary fluid-ounces.

31. 240 mL

32. 180 mL

33. 45 mL

34. 90 mL

35. 10 mL

36. 30 mL

37. 360 mL

38. 50 mL

39. 1000 mL

40. 500 mL

41. 960 mL

42. 480 mL

43. 15 mL

44. 60 mL

45. 5 mL

46. 150 mL

47. 120 mL

48. 210 mL

49. 100 mL

50. 200 mL

Calculate the following doses. Round to the hundredth place.

51. A drug is available as 5 gr/f ʒ, and the order is for 20 mL. How many milligrams will that be?

52. A drug is available as 0.45 g/f ʒ. The order is for 15 mg. How many milliliters will that be?

53. A medicine is available as 40 mcg/mL, and the order is for 0.4 g. How many fluidrams will that be?

54. You receive an order for ½ gr of medication, and you have on hand tablets of 10 mg, 5 mg, and 2.5 mg strengths. What is the smallest number of tablets you can dispense? What strengths will they be?

55. A drug is available as 1.2 g/f ʒ. If you prepare a dose of 300 mg, how many fluidrams will you need?

56. You are to prepare a dose of ¹⁄₅₀ gr. You have available tablets of 650 mcg, 300 mcg, and 150 mcg. What is the least number of tablets you can use (and which tablets) to make up the dose?

57. A medication is packaged as 20 gr/f ʒ. How many milligrams are in a teaspoonful of this medication?

58. An order requests 600 mg, and the medication is available as 8 gr/f ʒ. How many milliliters will be needed?

59. You receive an order for 45 gr of medication; you have a concentration of 1 g/tbsp available. How many milliliters should you measure out?

60. A preparation is available as 500 mg/tsp. The pharmacist asks you to measure out 46.296 gr. How many milliliters should you measure out?

61. You have in your pharmacy a dry powder that you are to package in 1 oz packets (avoirdupois). How many grams will you need to make 25 doses of 1 f ʒ each?

62. You are to make a gallon of cough preparation that will have 1 gr of active ingredient per teaspoonful. How many grams of active ingredient will you need?

63. You have just finished making a pint of a preparation that has $\frac{1}{10}$ gr/mL. How many milligrams of active ingredient did you use?

64. You have just finished a bulk manufacturing task in which you put 617.28 gr of active ingredient in 4 L of solution. If the usual dose is 1 tbsp, how many milligrams of medication are in each dose?

65. Instructions with a medication call for taking 1 cup (8 f ʒ) of medication each day. If there is $\frac{1}{5}$ gr/mL in the medication, how many grams of active ingredient will the patient get daily?

66. A medication order is for 10 gr total. How many 325 mg tablets should you dispense?

67. An order for 3 gr of medication is sent in. You have 5 mg tablets. How many tablets should be dispensed?

68. You prepare a bulk medication of 3 ℔, but you are to dispense in grams. How many grams do you have?

69. You are to prepare 500 mg of a medication that comes in a concentration of 4 gr/f ʒ. How many milliliters will you need?

70. The order received is for 50 gr of medication. The stock solution is 0.75 g/tbsp. How many milliliters should you measure out?

71. A medication is available in a concentration of 44 mg/f ʒ. You are to prepare 132 mg. How many fluidrams is that?

72. You are to make $\frac{1}{2}$ gallon of a medication that will have 2 g of active ingredient per teaspoonful. How many milligrams of active ingredient will you need?

73. You have 2 L of solution with 60 gr of active ingredient. If a dose is 1 tbsp, how many milligrams are in a dose?

74. You are to make suppositories that have 2 gr of the active ingredient in each. If you have 4.16 g of the active ingredient, how many suppositories can be made?

Nitro-stat tablets are available in the following strengths. In milligrams, what are the strengths of the four doses? Round to the tenths place.

75. $\frac{1}{400}$ gr

76. $\frac{1}{200}$ gr

77. $\frac{1}{150}$ gr

78. $\frac{1}{100}$ gr

79. If the patient uses the maximum of three tablets in the prescription below, how many milligrams has he used?

℞   Nitro-stat $\frac{1}{150}$ gr

Disp: #100

Sig: I tab SL q5 min prn angina

(max 3 tab, then go to hospital, if symptoms not relieved)

Store in original container.

Self-check your work in Appendix A.

Practice Test

Additional Practice Questions

Convert the following.

1. 1.5 gallon = _____ pt

2. 1 qt = _____ pt

3. 12 f ℨ = _____ f ℨ

4. 2½ pt = _____ mL

5. 360 mL = _____ f ℨ

6. 150 mL = _____ f ℨ

7. 500 mL = _____ f ℨ

8. 750 mL = _____ f ℨ

9. 3 pt = _____ mL

10. 150 mL = _____ f ℨ

11. 20 mL = _____ f ℨ

12. 2 pt = _____ f ℨ

13. 40 f ℨ = _____ mL

14. 8 f ℨ = _____ f ℨ

Answer the following questions.

15. How many fluidrams are in 3 qt, 1 pt?

16. A drug is available as ½ gr/f ℨ. If the patient is to receive ¼ gr, how many milliliters will that be?

17. A medication is available as 10 gr/15 mL, and the patient is to receive 30 g. How many fluidounces will you give?

18. A drug is packaged as 36 mg/mL, and you are to give 1.62 g. What volume will that be in fluidounces?

19. How many 0.325 g tablets will you dispense for an order requesting 20 gr?

20. A medication is packaged as 22 mg/f ℨ, and you are to dispense 132 mg. How many fluidrams will you need?

Appendix A
Problem Set Answers

Chapter 1

1.1 Problem Set

1. $\frac{1}{2}$

2. $\frac{3}{8}$

3. $\frac{2}{1}$

4. $\frac{2}{6}$

5. $\frac{1}{10}$

6. $1\frac{14}{15}$

Work:

Solution 1.

Create common denominators:

$\frac{5}{6} \times \frac{10}{10} = \frac{50}{60}, \frac{7}{10} \times \frac{6}{6} = \frac{42}{60}, \frac{2}{5} \times \frac{12}{12} = \frac{24}{60};$

Add the numerators:

$\frac{50}{60} + \frac{42}{60} + \frac{24}{60} = \frac{116}{60};$

Simplify:

$\frac{116}{60} = 1\frac{56}{60} = 1\frac{14}{15}$

Solution 2.

Create common denominators:

$\frac{5}{6} \times \frac{5}{5} = \frac{25}{30}, \frac{7}{10} \times \frac{3}{3} = \frac{21}{30}, \frac{2}{5} \times \frac{6}{6} = \frac{12}{30};$

Add the numerators:

$\frac{25}{30} + \frac{21}{30} + \frac{12}{30} = \frac{58}{30};$

Simplify:

$\frac{58}{30} = \frac{29}{15} = 1\frac{14}{15}$

7. $1\frac{37}{96}$

Work:

Create common denominators:

$\frac{21}{32} \times \frac{3}{3} = \frac{63}{96}, \frac{1}{12} \times \frac{8}{8} = \frac{8}{96}, \frac{31}{48} \times \frac{2}{2} = \frac{62}{96};$

Add the numerators:

$\frac{63}{96} + \frac{8}{96} + \frac{62}{96} = \frac{133}{96};$

Simplify:

$\frac{133}{96} = 1\frac{37}{96}$

8. $\frac{1}{4}$

9. $6\frac{7}{10}$

10. $2\frac{1}{5}$

11. $\frac{9}{10}$

12. $\frac{2}{5}$

13. $\frac{1}{12}$

Work:

$\dfrac{\frac{1}{2}}{6} = \frac{1}{2} \div 6 = \frac{1}{2} \times \frac{1}{6} = \frac{1}{12}$

14. 0.2

15. 0.05

16. 4.5

17. 0.3

18. 0.005

19. 0.002

20. 1.8

21. 0.04

22. 0.008

23. 3 tablets

Work:

Create common denominators:

$\frac{1}{4}, \frac{1}{2} \times \frac{2}{2} = \frac{2}{4}, 1\frac{1}{2} = \frac{3}{2} \times \frac{2}{2} = \frac{6}{4}, \frac{3}{4}$

Add the numerators:

$\frac{1}{4} + \frac{2}{4} + \frac{6}{4} + \frac{3}{4} = \frac{12}{4}$

Simplify:

$^{12}\!/_4 = 3$

24. 2 tablets containing $^1\!/_{100}$ g in each tablet

Work:

$2 \times {}^1\!/_{100} = {}^2\!/_{100} = {}^1\!/_{50}$

Because the denominator is smaller, $^1\!/_{50} > {}^1\!/_{150}$

25. $\dfrac{375 \text{ grains} \times 1 \text{ unit dose}}{^1\!/_4 \text{ grain}} = 375 \times 4$

$= 1500 \text{ containers}$

26. 3 bags

Work:

Create common denominators:

$^1\!/_2 \times {}^{10}\!/_{10} = {}^{10}\!/_{20}, \; {}^4\!/_5 \times {}^4\!/_4 = {}^{16}\!/_{20}, \; {}^1\!/_4 \times {}^5\!/_5 = {}^5\!/_{20},$

$2^1\!/_2 = {}^5\!/_2 \times {}^{10}\!/_{10} = {}^{50}\!/_{20};$

Add the numerators:

$^{10}\!/_{20} + {}^{16}\!/_{20} + {}^5\!/_{20} + {}^{50}\!/_{20} = {}^{81}\!/_{20};$

Simplify:

$^{81}\!/_{20} = 4^1\!/_{20}$ lb sugar needed

Sugar is sold in bags of 2 lb/bag; 2 bags would = 4 lb sugar (2 × 2 lb = 4 lb), and we need $^1\!/_{20}$ lb more than that, so 3 bags are needed. 3 bags × 2 lb/bag = 6 lb; 6 lb total − 4 $^1\!/_{20}$ lb needed = 1 $^{19}\!/_{20}$ lb left over.

27. 1 bag

Work: Since we need 4 $^1\!/_{20}$ lb sugar (problem 24), one 5 lb bag will provide the sugar needed.

1.2 Problem Set

1. 10

2. 5

3. 624

4. 2050

5. 48

6. XVII

7. LXVII

8. MCMXCV or MVM

9. 4.1

10. 0.6

11. 2.02

12. 0.017

13. 0

14. 6

15. 3

16. hundreds

17. hundredth

18. thousandth

19. ones

20. tenth

21. 68,000 (move decimal to the right 4 places)

22. 1,870,000 (move decimal to the right 6 places)

23. 10,300,000 (move decimal to the right 7 places)

24. 0.00084 (move decimal to the left 4 places)

25. 0.00768 (move decimal to the left 3 places)

26. 0.00006239 (move decimal to the left 5 places)

27. 3.29×10^{-9}

28. 3.9×10^{11}

29. 3.8×10^{-3}

30. 5.2×10^{16}

31. 3.779×10^6

32. 2.02×10^{-10}

33. 157.5 tablets (158 tablets, to the next whole tablet)

34. a. 10 grain

   b. 1 daily

   c. 100 tablets

35. a. $^1\!/_2$ grain

   b. 2 grains or 4 tablets daily

   c. 28 tablets

   d. 25 days

36. a. 28 tablets

    b. 7 days

37. a. 5 tablets daily

    b. 150 tablets

    c. 20 days

1.3 Problem Set

1. 784.36

2. 0.9

3. 1.88

4. 2.729

5. 14.373

6. 3.0983

7. 11.998

8. 467.42

9. 450

10. 1.846

11. 1.333

12. 3.87

13. 0.14

14. 0.08

15. 0.196

16. 0.049

17. 34.907 (34.9)

18. 1.395 (1.4)

19. a. 3 tablet/dose × 0.25 mg/tablet
       = 0.75 mg/dose

    b. 0.75 mg/dose × 4 doses/day = 3 mg

    c. 3 tablets/dose × 4 doses/day × 14 days
       = 168 tablets

    d. no; 168 tablets − 100 tablets = 68 tablets;
       the patient will need 68 more tablets

    e. alprazolam 0.25 mg #100/$14.95 + $7.59
       = $22.54

20. a. 0.25 mg/tablet × 4 tablets /dose
       = 1 mg/dose

    b. $17.46 × 1.25 = $21.825, rounded to
       $21.83

    c. $23.87 × 0.5 = $11.935, rounded to
       $11.94

    d. 50 tablets × 1 day/4 tablets = 12.5 days

21. a. 1000 mL × 1 bottle/120 mL
       = 8.33 bottles, rounded to 8 bottles

    b. 120 mL/bottle × 8 bottles = 960 mL;
       1000 mL − 960 mL = 40 mL

22. 8.5 mL/dose × 2 doses/day × 2 days
    = 34 mL

    5.75 mL/dose × 2 doses/day × 5 days
    = 57.5 mL

    34 mL + 57.5 mL = 91.5 mL

23. a. $47

    b. $15

    c. $4

24. a. $70.08

    b. $111.64

25. a. 89.5%

    b. 85.0%

    c. 92.2%

1.4 Problem Set

1. 200 + 700 + 300 + 600 = 1800; (100 ÷ 2) ×
   4 = 200; 1800 + 200 = 2000 estimate, 1915
   actual

2. 100; (100 ÷ 2) × 4 = 200; 100 + 200 = 300
   estimate, 275 actual

3. 10 + 10 + 10 = 30; (10 ÷ 2) × 4 = 20; 30 +
   20 = 50 estimate, 54.11 actual

4. 90 + 10 + 40 + 10 = 150; (10 ÷ 2) × 4 =
   20; 150 + 20 = 170 estimate, 170.42 actual

5. 20 estimate, 20.82 actual

6. $7 estimate, $6.38 actual

7. $12 estimate, $12.25 actual

8. $5 estimate, $5.19 actual

9. $82 estimate, $81.71 actual

10. $50 estimate, $50.58 actual

11. 56,000 estimate, 52,060.8 actual

12. 1400 estimate, 1407.3 actual

13. 1) Round to 600 and 15, ignoring the 3 decimals. 2) 600 × 15 = 9000. 3) Put 3 decimals back, so answer is 9. Actual is 8.976.

14. 1) Round to 5000 and 1, ignoring 1 decimal. 2) 5000 × 1 = 5000. 3) Put decimal back, or 500. Actual is 444.1068.

15. 120,000 estimate, 111,294 actual

16. 9000 estimate, 11,402.3 actual

17. 10 estimate, 10.28 actual

18. 300 estimate, 321.70 actual

19. 75 estimate, 73 actual

20. 200 estimate, 191.87 actual

21. 100 ÷ 10 = 10 estimate, 8.79 actual

22. food dye $2 estimate + sugar $8 estimate + soda $1 estimate + cherry $2 estimate + bleach $2 estimate + water $4 estimate = $19 estimate, $19.10 actual

23. 3 mL + 8 mL + 2 mL + 4 mL = 17 mL estimate, therefore use 30 mL vial

24. 1720 mL IV fluids + 150 mL juice + 130 mL coffee = 2000 mL estimate

25. 800 mL + 200 mL + 300 mL + 3000 mL = 4300 mL estimate

1.5 Problem Set

1. 6

2. 2

3. 2

4. 3

5. 1

6. 4

7. 2

8. 1

9. 8

10. 1

11. 42.8

12. 100.0

13. 0.0427

14. 18.4

15. 0.00392

16. 0.35, 2 significant figures

17. 0.06, 1 significant figure

18. 1.99, 3 significant figures

19. 0.01, 1 significant figure

20. 1.03, 3 significant figures

21. 63.8

22. 30

23. 163

24. a. 1.784 g to 1.78 g

    b. 3.2 g

    c. 3.2 g + 1.78 g + 2.46 g + 5.87 g = 13.31 g; 13.31 g ÷ 0.125 g = 106.48 capsules; 0.48 of a capsule × 0.125 g = 0.06 g

25. a. 21.65 mg × 45 doses = 974.25 mg

    b. 3 significant figures

Chapter 2

2.1 Problem Set

1. $^3/_7$

2. $^8/_6 = ^4/_3 = 1^1/_3$

3. $^3/_4$

4. $^4/_6 = ^2/_3$

5. $^1/_7$

6. 2:3

7. 6:8 = 3:4

8. 5:10 = 1:2

9. 1:9

10. 1:10,000

11. 1 tablet:40 mg or 40 mg:1 tablet

12. 300 mg:5 mL or 5 mL:300 mg

13. 250 mg:5 mL or 5 mL:250 mg

14. The dose of $\frac{1}{2}$ tablet is multiplied by the ratio of 500 mg/tablet.

40 mg ÷ 2 = 20 mg (or x mg/$\frac{1}{2}$ tablet = 40 mg/1 tablet; x mg = 20 mg)

15. The dose of 10 mL is multiplied by the ratio of 300 mg/5 mL.

300 mg × 2 = 600 mg (or x mg/10 mL = 300 mg/5 mL; x mg = 600 mg)

16. The dose of 15 mL is multiplied by the ratio of 250 mg/5 mL.

250 mg × 3 = 750 mg (or x mg/15 mL = 250 mg/5 mL; x mg = 750 mg)

17. 10 g, 1000 mL, 1 g (or x g/100 mL = 10 g/1000 mL; x g = 1 g)

18. 1 g, 100 mL, 5 g (or x g/500 mL = 1 g/100 mL; x g = 5 g)

19. 1 g, 250 mL, 4 g (or x g/1000 mL = 1 g/250 mL; x g = 4 g)

20. 1 g, 1000 mL, 0.5 g (or x g/50 mL = 1 g/1000 mL; x g = 0.05 g)

2.2 Problem Set

1. 6 ÷ 7 = 0.857, rounded to 0.86, 0.86 × 100 = 86%

2. 5 ÷ 12 = 0.416, rounded to 0.42, 0.42 × 100 = 42%

3. 1 ÷ 4 = 0.25, 0.25 × 100 = 25%

4. 2 ÷ 3 = 0.666, rounded to 0.67, 0.67 × 100 = 67%

5. 0.5 ÷ 10 = 0.05, 0.05 × 100 = 5%

6. 2 ÷ 3 = 0.666, rounded to 0.67, 0.67 × 100 = 67%

7. 1.5 ÷ 4.65 = 0.3225, rounded to 0.323, 0.323 × 100 = 32.3%

8. 1 ÷ 250 = 0.004, 0.004 × 100 = 0.4%

9. 1 ÷ 10,000 = 0.0001, 0.001 × 100 = 0.01%

10. 1 ÷ 6 = 0.166, rounded to 0.17, 0.17 × 100 = 17%

11. 50% = $^{50}/_{100}$ = $^5/_{10}$ = $\frac{1}{2}$

12. 2% = $^2/_{100}$ = $^1/_{50}$

13. 6% 100 = 0.06

14. 12.5% 100 = 0.125

15. 126% 100 = 1.26

16. 20 × 0.05 = 1

17. 60 × 0.20 = 12

18. 63 × 0.19 = 11.97

19. 70 × 1.10 = 77

20. 50 × 0.002 = 0.1

21. 1:3, 0.33

22. $^1/_{40}$, 0.025

23. 50%, 1:2

24. 1%, $^1/_{100}$

25. $^9/_{10}$, 9:10

26. $^2/_3$ or $^{67}/_{100}$; 2:3 or 67:100

27. 0.2%, 0.002

28. $^{0.09}/_{20}$, 0.09:20

29. $^1/_{20}$, 0.05

30. 1:5, 0.2

31. $^1/_{10,000}$ = 0.0001 × 100 = 0.01% solution

32. $^1/_{20}$ = 0.05 × 100 = 5% solution

33. $^1/_{25}$ = 0.04 × 100 = 4% solution

34. $^1/_{800}$ = 0.00125 × 100 = 0.125% solution

35. $^1/_{10}$ = 0.1 × 100 = 10% solution

2.3 Problem Set

1. 5

2. 0.07843, rounded to 0.08

3. 4.5

4. 0.1

5. 0.16

6. 5.7692, rounded to 5.77

7. 54.4

8. 242.6666, rounded to 242.67

9. 25.9411, rounded to 25.94

10. 16

11. 44.3571, rounded to 44.36

12. 21.3870, rounded to 21.39

13. 78.3333, rounded to 78.33

14. 10.7307, rounded to 10.73

15. 77.3636, rounded to 77.36

16. $x\%/100 = 72\%/254$, $x\% = 28.3464\%$, rounded to 28.35%

17. $x/100\% = 44/90\%$, $x = 48.8888$, rounded to 48.89

18. $x/100\% = 100/44\%$, $x = 227.2727$, rounded to 227.27

19. $x/100\% = 34/28\%$, $x = 121.4285$, rounded to 121.43

20. $x\%/100 = 24.5\%/45$, $x\% = 54.4444\%$, rounded to 54.44%

21. x g/100 mg = 1 g/1000 mg; x g = 0.1 g

22. x g/247 mg = 1 g/1000 mg; x g = 0.247 g

23. x g/1420 mg = 1 g/1000 mg; x g = 1.42 g

24. x g/495 mg = 1 g/1000 mg; x g = 0.495 g

25. x g/3781 mg = 1 g/1000 mg; x g = 3.781 g

26. x mg/0.349 g = 1000 mg/1 g; x mg = 349 mg

27. x mg/1.5 g = 1000 mg/1 g; x mg = 1500 mg

28. x mg/0.083 g = 1000 mg/1 g; x mg = 83 mg

29. x mg/0.01 g = 1000 mg/1 g; x mg = 10 mg

30. x mg/2.1 g = 1000 mg/1 g; x mg = 2100 mg

31. x kg/6.3 lb = 1 kg/2.2 lb; x kg = 2.863 kg, rounded to 2.9 kg

32. x kg/15 lb = 1 kg/2.2 lb; x kg = 6.818 kg, rounded to 6.8 kg

33. x kg/97 lb = 1 kg/2.2 lb; x kg = 44.090 kg, rounded to 44.1 kg

34. x kg/115 lb = 1 kg/2.2 lb; x kg = 52.272 kg, rounded to 52.3 kg

35. x kg/186 lb = 1 kg/2.2 lb; x kg = 84.545 kg, rounded to 84.5 kg

36. x lb/7.5 kg = 2.2 lb/1 kg; x lb = 16.5 lb

37. x lb/3.6 kg = 2.2 lb/1 kg; x lb = 7.92 lb, rounded to 7.9 lb

38. x lb/79.2 kg = 2.2 lb/1 kg; x lb = 174.24 lb, rounded to 174.2 lb

39. x lb/90 kg = 2.2 lb/1 kg; x lb = 198 lb

40. x lb/0.5 kg = 2.2 lb/1 kg; x lb = 1.1 lb

41. x mL/100 mg = 1 mL/50 mg, x mL = 2 mL

42. x tablets/375 mg = 1 tablet/125 mg, x tablets = 3 tablets

43. x mL/300 mg = 1 mL/20 mg, x mL = 15 mL

44. x folders/$15.00 = 100 folders/$7.40, x folders = 202.7 folders; 200 folders can be purchased (2 boxes of 100 folders)

45. x mL/10,000 units = 15 mL/250,000 units, x mL = 0.6 mL

46. x mL/60 mg = 1 mL/40 mg, x mL = 1.5 mL

47. x mL/60 mg = 4 mL/40 mg, x mL = 6 mL

48. x mL/300 mg = 10 mL/500 mg, x mL = 6 mL

49. x mL/30 mg = 1 mL/5 mg, x mL = 6 mL

50. x mL/30 mg = 1 mL/20 mg, x mL = 1.5 mL

51. x mg/5 mL = 20 mg/2 mL, x mg = 50 mg

52. x mL/80 mg = 2 mL/20 mg, x mL = 8 mL

53. x mL/50 mg = 2 mL/20 mg, x mL = 5 mL

54. x mL/12.5 mg = 2 mL/20 mg, x mL = 1.25 mL

55. x mg/3.5 mL = 20 mg/2 mL, x mg = 35 mg

2.4 Problem Set

1. 189 mg −185 mg = 4 mg; (4 mg/185 mg) × 100 = 2.162%, rounded to 2.16%

2. 500 mg − 476 mg = 24 mg; (24 mg/500 mg) × 100 = 4.8%

3. 1507 mg − 1200 mg = 307 mg; (307 mg/1200 mg) × 100 = 25.583%, rounded to 25.58%

4. 15 mg − 12.5 mg = 2.5 mg; (2.5 mg/15 mg) × 100 = 16.666%, rounded to 16.67%

5. 415 mcg − 400 mcg = 15 mcg; (15 mcg/400 mcg) × 100 = 3.75%

6. 6.3 mL − 5 mL = 1.3 mL; (1.3 mL/5 mL) × 100 = 26%

7. 15 mL – 13 mL = 2 mL; (2 mL/15 mL) × 100 = 13.333%, rounded to 13.33%

8. 20 mL – 15 mL = 5 mL; (5 mL/15 mL) × 100 = 33.333%, rounded to 33.33%

9. 1.5 L – 1.45 L = 0.05 L; (0.05L/1.5 L) × 100 = 3.333%, rounded to 3.33%

10. 726 mL – 700 mL = 26 mL; (26 mL/700 mL) × 100 = 3.714%, rounded to 3.71%

11. 0.03 × 3 mL = 0.09 mL; because 3 mL – 2.6 mL = 0.4 mL, the difference is *not* within a percentage of error of 3%

12. 0.03 × 12.5 mL = 0.375; because 12.5 mL – 12.1 mL = 0.4 mL, the difference is *not* within a percentage of error of 3%

13. 0.03 × 1.8 mL = 0.054 mL; because 1.8 mL – 1.5 mL = 0.3 mL, the difference is *not* within a percentage of error of 3%

14. 0.03 × 3.2 mL = 0.096 mL; because 3.2 mL – 3.29 mL = −0.09 mL, the difference is within a percentage of error of 3%

15. 0.06 × 150 mg = 9 mg; because 150 mg – 149 mg = 1 mg, the difference is within a percentage of error of 6%

16. 0.06 × 200 mg = 12 mg; because 200 mg – 192 mg = 8 mg, the difference is within a percentage of error of 6%

17. 0.06 × 30 mg = 1.8 mg; because 30 mg – 31.5 mg = −1.5 mg, the difference is within a percentage of error of 6% (or 1.5 mg < 1.8 mg)

18. 0.06 × 454 mg = 27.24 mg; because 454 mg – 450 mg = 4 mg, the difference is within a percentage of error of 6%

19. 200 mL × 0.005 = 1 mL; 200 mL – 1 mL = 199 mL; 200 mL + 1 mL = 201 mL; the acceptable range is 199 mL to 201 mL

20. 10.3 mL × 0.0075 = 0.07725 mL, rounded to 0.08 mL; 10.3 mL – 0.08 mL = 10.22 mL; 10.3 mL + 0.08 mL = 10.38 mL; the acceptable range is 10.22 mL to 10.38 mL

21. 830 mL × 0.02 = 16.6 mL; 830 mL – 16.6 mL = 813.4 mL; 830 mL + 16.6 mL = 846.6 mL; the acceptable range is 813.4 mL to 846.6 mL

22. 18 g × 0.0015 = 0.027 g, rounded to 0.03 g; 18 g – 0.03 g = 17.97 g; 18 g + 0.03 g = 18.03 g; the acceptable range is 17.97 g to 18.03 g

23. 750 mg × 0.004 = 3 mg; 750 mg − 3 mg = 747 mg; 750 mg + 3 mg = 753 mg; the acceptable range is 747 mg to 753 mg

24. 100 mg × 0.2 = 20 mg; so the range of accuracy is 80 mg (100 mg − 20 mg) to 120 mg (100 mg + 20 mg)

25. 500 mg × 0.12 = 60 mg; so the range of vitamin C contained in the tablet is 440 mg (500 mg − 60 mg) to 560 mg (500 mg + 60 mg)

Chapter 3

3.1 Problem Set

1. Number does not meet standard validity tests. J is not an appropriate initial letter for the DEA number of a medical doctor. Checksum calculation: 2 + 6 + 8 = 16; (1 + 9 + 7) × 2 = 34; 16 + 34 = 50; last digit of checksum matches last digit (0).

2. The number meets standard validity tests. M is an appropriate initial letter for the DEA number of a mid-level practitioner; G is the first letter of the prescriber's last name. Checksum calculation: 3 + 8 + 6 = 17; (0 + 1 + 5) × 2 = 12; 17 + 12 = 29; last digit of checksum matches last digit (9).

3. Number does not meet standard validity tests. B is an appropriate initial letter for the DEA number of a primary practitioner; H is the first letter of the prescriber's last name. Checksum calculation: 9 + 9 + 0 = 18; (9 + 8 + 7) × 2 = 48; 18 + 48 = 66; last digit of sum (6) does not match checksum digit (0).

4. Number does not meet standard validity tests. A is an appropriate initial letter for the DEA number of a primary practitioner; L is the first letter of the prescriber's last name. Checksum calculation: 6 + 3 + 6 = 15; (2 + 0 + 1) × 2 = 6; 15 + 6 = 21; Last digit of sum (1) does not match checksum digit (8).

5. Number does not meet standard validity tests. The second letter (D) of the DEA number does not match the first letter of the physician's last name (L). Checksum

calculation: 7 + 3 + 2 = 12; (6 + 8 + 2) × 2 = 32; 12 + 33 = 44; last digit of checksum matches last digit (4).

6. Number meets standard validity tests. B is an appropriate initial letter for the DEA number of a primary practitioner; P is the first letter of the prescriber's last name. Checksum calculation: 4 + 1 + 2 = 7; (4 + 2 + 0) × 2 = 12; 7 + 12 = 19; last digit of checksum matches last digit (9).

7. Number meets standard validity tests. A is an appropriate initial letter for the DEA number of a primary practitioner; P is the first letter of the prescriber's last name. Checksum calculation: 3 + 5 + 4 = 12; (0 + 1 + 9) × 2 = 20; 12 + 20 = 32; last digit of checksum matches last digit (2).

8. Number meets standard validity tests. M is an appropriate initial letter for the DEA number of a mid-level practitioner; W is the first letter of the prescriber's last name. Checksum calculation: 2 + 6 + 2 = 10; (8 + 4 + 2) × 2 = 28; 10 + 28 = 38; last digit of checksum matches last digit (8).

9. b. 0.25% acetic acid is correct answer. Calculation: x g/100 mL = 1 g/400 mL; x g = 0.25 g

10. c. isoproterenol 1:200 solution is correct answer. Calculation: x g/100 mL = 0.005 g/mL; x g = 0.5 g, or 0.5%, a 1:200 solution

11. Brand/trade name: Epivir
Generic name: lamivudine
Dosage form: oral solution
Strength: 10 mg/mL
Total quantity: 240 mL
Storage requirement(s): room temperature (77 °F), in tightly closed bottles
Manufacturer: GlaxoSmithKline
NDC number: 0173-0471-00

12. Brand/trade name: Prozac
Generic name: fluoxetine
Dosage form: pulvules or capsules
Strength: 20 mg
Total quantity: 100 capsules
Storage requirement(s): room temperature (59–86 °F)
Manufacturer: Eli Lilly & Company (Dista)
NDC number: 077-3105-02

13. Brand/trade name: Diovan
Generic name: valsartan
Dosage form: tablets
Strength: 80 mg
Total quantity: 90 tablets
Storage requirement(s): room temperature (77 °F)
Manufacturer: Novartis
NDC number: 0078-0358-34

14. Brand/trade name: Diovan HCT
Generic name: valsartan and hydrochlorothiazide
Dosage form: tablets
Strength: 160 mg and 12.5 mg
Total quantity: 90 tablets
Storage requirement(s): room temperature (77 °F)
Manufacturer: Novartis
NDC number: 0078-0315-34

15. Brand/trade name: Trileptal
Generic name: oxcarbazepine
Dosage form: oral suspension
Strength: 300 mg/5 mL
Total quantity: 250 mL
Storage requirement(s): room temperature (77 °F), in original container
Manufacturer: Novartis
NDC number: 0078-0357-52

16. Brand/trade name: Restoril
Generic name: temazepam
Dosage form: capsule
Strength: 7.5 mg
Total quantity: 100 capsules
Storage requirement(s): room temperature
Manufacturer: Mallinckrodt
NDC number: 0406-9915-01

17. 20 tablets; XX is Roman numeral for 20

18. 3 capsules/day × 10 days = 30 capsules

19. 48 tablets. Determine number of tablets needed for each part of the prescription: 4 tablets/dose × 2 doses/day × 2 days = 16 tablets; 3 tablets/dose × 2 doses/day × 2 days = 12 tablets; 4 tablets/dose × 1 dose/day × 2 days = 8 tablets; 3 tablets/dose × 1 dose/day × 2 days = 6 tablets; 2 tablets/dose × 1 dose/day × 2 days = 4 tablets; 1 tablet/dose × 1 dose/day × 2 days = 2 tablets. Add the subtotals to determine the total

number to dispense: 16 tablets + 12 tablets + 8 tablets + 6 tablets + 4 tablets + 2 tablets = 48 tablets.

20. 1 oz/day × 7 days/week = 7 oz for a one week supply

21. 150 capsules; #CL = Roman numeral C (100) plus Roman numeral L (50)

3.2 Problem Set

1. bid = twice a day

2. DAW = dispense as written

3. IM = intramuscular

4. IV = intravenous

5. mL = milliliter

6. NKA = no known allergy

7. npo = nothing by mouth

8. q3 h = every 3 hours

9. qid = four times a day

10. tid = three times a day

11. A route of administration is the way the drug is to be given to the patient.

12. Oral, injection, rectal, topical

13. IM = intramuscular; IV = intravenous; po = by mouth

14. bid = twice a day; qid = four times a day; q2 h = every 2 hours, etc.

15. see Table 3.3

16. Take two capsules by mouth four times a day as needed for itching.

17. Apply one patch every night at bedtime and remove every morning. (Note that hs is a dangerous abbreviation.)

18. Apply one-half inch of ointment every six hours.

19. Take two tablets by mouth three times a day before meals.

20. Take one-half tablet twice a day.

21. Instill two drops into the right eye every four hours.

22. Take one tablet with a glass of water one-half hour before breakfast every seven days.

Chapter 4

4.1 Problem Set

1. mcg

2. mg

3. L

4. g

5. kg

6. m

7. cm

8. mL

9. cc

10. dL

11. 0.6 g

12. 50 kg

13. 0.4 mg

14. 0.04 L

15. 4.2 g

16. 0.005 g

17. 0.06 g

18. 2.6 L

19. 0.03 L

20. 0.02 mL

21. 13,333 doses

Work: 5 kg = 5000 g = 5,000,000 mg

  5,000,000 mg available ÷ 375 mg = 13,333.33 doses, rounded to 13,333 doses

22. a. 2 tablets/dose × 2 doses/day = 4 tablets/day; 30 tablets available ÷ 4 tablets/day = 7.5 days

  b. 4 tablets/day × 30 days/month = 120 tablets/month; 120 tablets/month × 0.05 mg/tablet = 6 mg/month

23. 0.9 g/day ÷ 3 doses/day = 0.3 g/dose

24. a. 1.2 g/day ÷ 4 doses/day = 0.3 g/dose

  b. Convert to milligrams, 0.3 g/dose × 1000 mg/1 g = 300 mg/dose
  Only the 300 mg tablets can be used.

25. a. x g/100 mL = 1 g/1000 mL, x g = 0.1 g or 0.1%

   b. August 31, 2011

4.2 Problem Set

1. x mg/1964 mcg = 1 mg/1000 mcg; x mg = 1.964 mg

2. x g/418 mg = 1 g/1000 mg; x g = 0.418 g

3. x mcg/651 mg = 1000 mcg/1 mg; x mcg = 651,000 mcg

4. x mcg/0.84 mg = 1000 mcg/1 mg; x mcg = 840 mcg

5. x mcg/0.012 g = 1,000,000 mcg/1 g; x mcg = 12,000 mcg

6. x g/9,213,406 mcg = 1 g/1,000,000 mcg; x g = 9.213406 g

7. x g/284 mg = 1 g/1000 mg; x g = 0.284 g

8. x mg/9382.5 mcg = 1 mg/1000 mcg; x mg = 9.3825 mg

9. x g/12,321 mcg = 1 g/1,000,000 mcg; x g = 0.012321 g

10. x kg/184 g = 1 kg/1000 g; x kg = 0.184 kg

11. 52 mL × 1 L/1000 mL = 0.052 L

12. 2.06 g × 1000 mg/1 g = 2060 mg

13. 16 mg × 1000 mcg/1 mg = 16,000 mcg

14. 256 mg × 1 g/1000 mg = 0.256 g

15. 2,703,000 mcg × 1 g/1,000,000 mcg = 2.703 g

16. 6.9 L × 1000 mL/1 L = 6900 mL

17. 62.5 mg × 1 g/1000 mg = 0.0625 g

18. 15 kg × 1000 g/1 kg = 15,000 g

19. 2,785,000 mcg × 1 g/1,000,000 mcg = 2.785 g

20. 8.234 mg × 1000 mcg/1 mg = 8234 mcg

21. 2 kg × 1,000,000 mg/1 kg = 2,000,000 mg; or x mg/2 kg = 1,000,000 mg/1 kg, x mg = 2,000,000 mg

22. 21 L × 1000 mL/1 L = 21,000 mL; or x mL/21 L = 1000 mL/1 L, x mL = 21,000 mL

23. 576 mL × 1 L/1000 mL = 0.576 L; or x L/576 mL = 1 L/1000 mL, x L = 0.576 L

24. 823 kg × 1,000,000 mg/1 kg = 823,000,000 mg; or x mg/823 kg = 1,000,000 mg/1 kg, x mg = 823,000,000 mg

25. 27 mcg × 1 mg/1000 mcg = 0.027 mg; or x mg/27 mcg = 1 mg/1000 mcg, x mg = 0.027 mg

26. 5000 mcg × 1 mg/1000 mcg = 5 mg; or x mg/5000 mcg = 1 mg/1000 mcg, x mg = 5 mg

27. 20 mcg × 1 mg/1000 mcg = 0.02 mg; or x mg/20 mcg = 1 mg/1000 mcg, x mg = 0.02 mg

28. 4.624 mg × 1000 mcg/1 mg = 4624 mcg; or x mcg/4.624 mg = 1000 mcg/1 mg, x mcg = 4624 mcg

29. 3.19 g × 1000 mg/1 g = 3190 mg; or x mg/3.19 g = 1000 mg/1 g, x mg = 3190 mg

30. 8736 mcg × 1 mg/1000 mcg = 8.736 mg; or x mg/8736 mcg = 1 mg/1000 mcg, x mg = 8.736 mg

31. 830 mL × 1 L/1000 mL = 0.83 L; or x L/830 mL = 1 L/1000 mL, x L = 0.83 L

32. 0.94 L × 1000 mL/1 L = 940 mL; or x mL/0.94 L = 1000 mL/1 L, x mL = 940 mL

33. 1.84 g × 1000 mg/1 g = 1840 mg; or x mg/1.84 g = 1000 mg/1 g, x mg = 1840 mg

34. 560 mg × 1 g/1000 mg = 0.56 g ; or x g/560 mg = 1 g/1000 mg, x g = 0.56 g

35. 1200 mcg × 1 mg/1000 mcg = 1.2 mg; or x mg/1200 mcg = 1 mg/1000 mcg, x mg = 1.2 mg

36. 125 mcg × 1 mg/1000 mcg = 0.125 mg; or x mg/125 mcg = 1 mg/1000 mcg, x mg = 0.125 mg

37. 0.275 mg × 1000 mcg/1 mg = 275 mcg; or x mcg/0.275 mg = 1000 mcg/1 mg, x mcg = 275 mcg

38. 480 mL × 1 L/1000 mL = 0.48 L; or x L/480 mL = 1 L/1000 mL, x L = 0.48 L

39. 239 mg × 1 g/1000 mg = 0.239 g; or x g/239 mg = 1 g/1000 mg, x g = 0.239 g

40. 1500 mg $\times$ 1 g/1000 mg = 1.5 g; or
    x g/1500 mg = 1 g/1000 mg, x g = 1.5 g

41. a. 2 tsp/dose $\times$ 5 mL/tsp $\times$ 2 doses/day =
       20 mL/day

    b. 20 mL/day $\times$ 7 days/course of treatment
       = 140 mL/course of treatment

    c. 20 mL/day $\times$ 125 mg/5 mL $\times$
       1 g/1000 mg = 0.5 g

    d. Since each bottle contains 100 mL, two
       bottles will be needed (200 mL − 140 mL
       = 60 mL to be discarded).

42. (1) Convert 1.5 g to milligrams: x mg/1.5 g =
    1000 mg/1 g, x mg = 1500 mg.
    (2) Determine number of capsules: 1500 mg
    $\times$ 1 capsule/250 mg = 6 capsules

43. a. Convert the prescribed dose to grams,
       1000 mg = 1 g. Since one vial contains 5 g,
       there are five 1 g doses in one vial.

    b. x days/5 doses $\times$ 1 day/2 doses, x days =
       2.5 days

4.3 Problem Set

1. x tablets/30 mg = 1 tablet/7.5 mg, x tablets
   = 4 tablets

2. x mL/20 mg = 2 mL/25 mg, x mL = 1.6 mL

3. x mL/125 mg = 5 mL/100 mg, x mL =
   6.25 mL, rounded to 6.3 mL

4. x mL/4 mg = 1 mL/5 mg, x mL = 0.8 mL

5. x capsules/1750 mg = 1 capsule/250 mg,
   x capsule = 7 capsules

6. x mL/18 mg = 5 mL/25 mg, x mL = 3.6 mL

7. x mL/400 mg = 5 mL/200 mg, x mL =
   10 mL

8. a. x mL/1000 mg = 5 mL/250 mg, x mL =
      20 mL

    b. x mL/75 mg = 1 mL/15 mg, x mL = 5 mL

    c. x tablets/500 mg = 1 tablet/1000 mg,
       x tablets = 0.5 tablet; 0.5 tablet/dose $\times$
       3 doses/day = 1.5 tablets/day

9. Convert 10 mg to 10,000 mcg;
   x mL/10,000 mcg = 1 mL/40 mcg, x mL =
   250 mL

10. x mg/2 mL = 40 mg/1 mL, x mg = 80 mg

11. Convert 400 mcg to 0.4 mg; x mL/1 mg =
    1 mL/0.4 mg, x mL = 2.5 mL

12. x mcg/1.2 mL = 400 mcg/1 mL, x mcg =
    480 mcg

13. Convert 80 mg to 80,000 mcg; x mcg/0.63 mL
    = 80,000 mcg/15 mL, x mcg = 3360 mcg

14. 1.05 kg = 1050 g = 1,050,000 mg;
    x capsules/1,050,000 mg = 1 capsule/35 mg,
    x capsules = 30,000 capsules

15. x doses/880 mg = 2 doses/80 mg, x dose =
    22 doses

16. Convert 1600 mg to
    1,600,000 mcg; x mcg/4 mL =
    1,600,000 mcg/560 mL, x mcg =
    11,428.571 mcg, rounded to 11,428.6 mcg

17. Convert 10 mg to 10,000 mcg;
    x mL/10,000 mcg = 1 mL/40 mcg, x mL =
    250 mL

18. x mL/2000 units = 1 mL/5000 units, x mL =
    0.4 mL

19. x mL/20 mg = 1 mL/10 mg, x mL = 2 mL

20. x mg/3.5 mL = 10 mg/1 mL, x mg = 35 mg

21. x mg/12.5 mL = 50 mg/5 mL, x mg =
    125 mg

22. x mL/100 mg = 5 mL/50 mg, x mL = 10 mL

23. 0.5 mL $\times$ 10 mg/1 mL = 5 mg

24. 0.8 mL $\times$ 10 mg/1 mL = 8 mg

25. x mL/150 mg = 5 mL/300 mg, x mL = 2.5 mL

26. Since 0.5 g = 500 mg, x mL/500 mg =
    5 mL/300 mg, x mL = 8.33 mL, rounded to
    8.3 mL

27. 50 mg $\times$ 1 mL/75 mg = 0.6666 mL, rounded
    to 0.7 mL

28. x mg/0.8 mL = 75 mg/1 mL, x mg = 60 mg

29. x mL/100 mg = 5 mL/125 mg, x mL = 4 mL

30. x mg/7.5 mL = 125 mg/5 mL, x mg =
    187.5 mg

31. x mL/20 mg = 5 mL/12.5 mg, x mL = 8 mL

32. x mL/50 mg = 5 mL/12.5 mg, x mL = 20 mL

33. a. Since 150 mg × 1 capsule/25 mg = 6 capsules, 150 mg × 1 capsule/50 mg = 3 capsules, and 150 mg × 1 capsule/75 mg = 2 capsules, the 75 mg/capsule product will result in the fewest capsules taken per day, 2 capsules.

    b. 2 capsules/day × 7 days/week = 14 capsules/week

34. a. 500 mg/dose × 4 doses/day = 2000 mg/day; 2000 mg × 5 mL/250 mg = 40 mL

    b. 50 mg × 1 tablet/25 mg = 2 tablets

    c. 8 mEq × 15 mL/20 mEq = 6 mL

    d. 200 mg/dose × 3 doses/day = 600 mg/day; 600 mg × 5 mL/100 mg = 30 mL

4.4 Problem Set

See page 283 for answers 1–4 of figure Nomogram for Estimating Body Surface Area of Children.

1. 0.405 m², rounded to 0.41 m²

2. 0.565 m², rounded to 0.57 m²

3. 0.89 m²

4. 0.71 m²

See page 284 for answers 5–10 of figure Nomogram for Estimating Body Surface Area of Adults.

5. 1.275 m², rounded to 1.28 m²

6. 1.75 m²

7. 1.72 m²

8. 1.96 m²

9. 1.49 m²

10. 2.15 m²

11. 56 kg × 0.5 mg/kg = 28 mg

12. 87 kg × 125 mg/kg = 10,875 mg per day; for each dose, 10,875 mg/day ÷ 6 doses/day = 1812.5 mg/dose

13. 1.4 kg × 4 mL/kg = 5.6 mL

14. a. 80 kg × 0.625 mg/kg = 50 mg

    b. 50 mg ÷ 3 doses = 16.6666 mg/dose, rounded to 16.67 mg/dose

15. 6 kg × 5 mg/kg/day = 30 mg/day; 30 mg/day ÷ 2 doses/day = 15 mg/dose

16. 68.64 kg × 125 mg/kg/day = 8580 mg/day

17. 10 kg × 10 mg/kg/day = 100 mg/day; 1 day = 24 hours; 100 mg/day = 100 mg/24 hours; 100 mg/24 hours ÷ 2 = 50 mg/12 hours

18. 1.1 m² × 25 mg/m² = 27.5 mg; 27.5 mg/day ÷ 2 doses/day = 13.75 mg/dose

19. 0.67 m² × 0.75 mg/m² = 0.5025 mg, rounded to 0.50 mg

20. 0.85 m² × 100 mg/m² = 85 mg

21. 0.71 m² × 250 mg/m² = 177.5 mg

22. 0.83 m² × 3.3 mg/m² = 2.739 mg, rounded to 2.74 mg

23. 0.74 m² × 2 mg/m² = 1.48 mg. The physician has ordered a dose higher than the recommended dose. See page 285 of figure Nomogram for Estimating Body Surface Area of Children.

24. 0.48 m² × 3.3 mg/m² = 1.584 mg. The physician has ordered a dose higher than the recommended dose. See page 286 for answers.

25. 0.47 m² × 250 mg/m² = 117.5 mg. The physician has ordered a dose higher than the recommended dose. See page 287 for answers.

26. 40.9 kg × 50 mg/kg/day = 2045 mg/day is the recommended dose; order is 300 mg × 3 doses/day = 900 mg/day, which is under the recommended dose per day.

27. a. 36.4 kg × 50 mg/kg = 1820 mg

    b. 36.4 kg × 100 mg/kg = 3640 mg

    c. 250 mg × 3 doses/day = 750 mg/day, which is under the minimum recommended dose

    d. 250 mg/dose × 50 mL/500 mg = 25 mL/dose

28. a. 5.45 kg × 20 mg/kg = 109 mg

    b. 5.45 kg × 40 mg/kg = 218 mg

    c. 125 mg × 3 doses/day = 375 mg, which is higher than the maximum recommended dose

    d. 125 mg/dose × 5 mL/125 mg = 5 mL/dose

Problem Set 4.4, answers for questions 1–4
Nomogram for Estimating Body Surface Area of Children

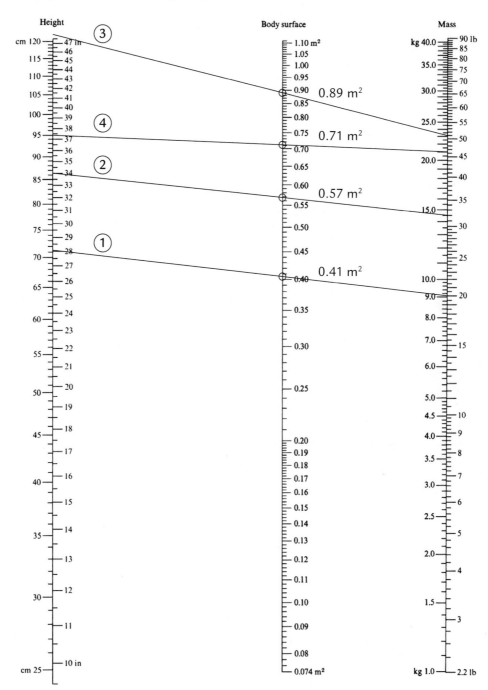

Problem Set 4.4, answers for questions 5–10
Nomogram for Estimating Body Surface Area of Adults

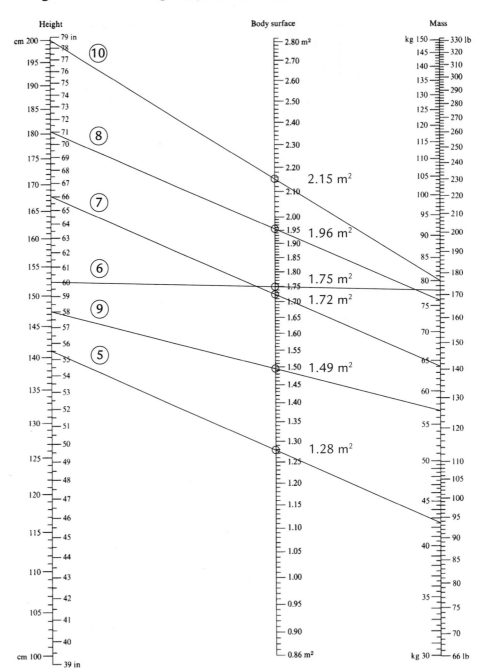

Problem Set 4.4, answer for question 23
Nomogram for Estimating Body Surface Area of Children

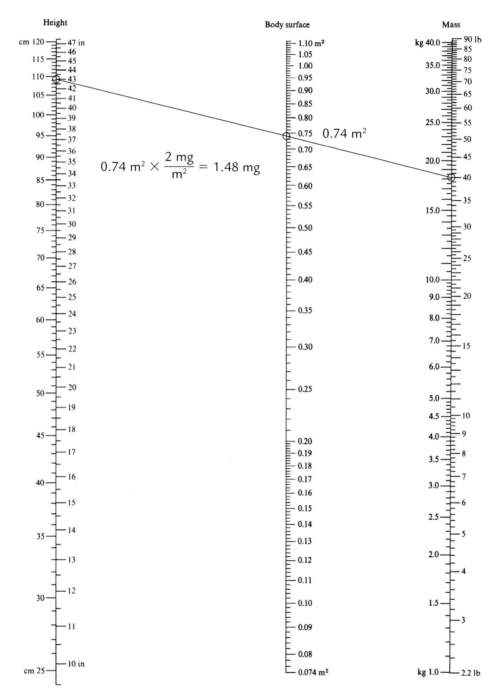

$$0.74 \text{ m}^2 \times \frac{2 \text{ mg}}{\text{m}^2} = 1.48 \text{ mg}$$

Problem Set 4.4, answer for question 24
Nomogram for Estimating Body Surface Area of Children

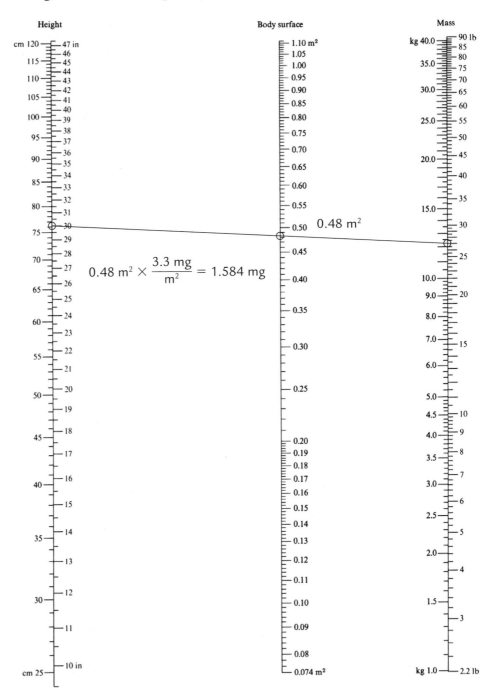

Problem Set 4.4, answer for question 25
Nomogram for Estimating Body Surface Area of Children

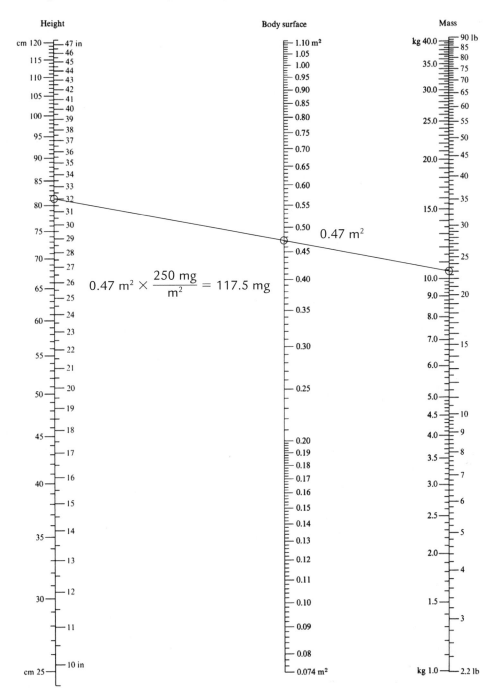

$$0.47 \text{ m}^2 \times \frac{250 \text{ mg}}{\text{m}^2} = 117.5 \text{ mg}$$

29. a. 11.8 kg × 0.5 mg/kg = 5.9 mg

    b. 11.8 kg × 1 mg/kg = 11.8 mg

    c. 10 mL × 12 mg/5 mL = 24 mg

    d. No, it is not a safe dose. It is higher than 11.8 mg, the maximum recommended dose.

30. a. 9.32 kg × 5 mg/kg = 46.6 mg; 24 hours/day × 1 dose/8 hours = 3 doses/day; 46.6 mg × 3 doses/day = 139.8 mg/day

    b. 9.32 kg × 10 mg/kg = 93.2 mg; 24 hours/day × 1 dose/6 hours = 4 doses/day; 93.2 mg × 4 doses/day = 372.8 mg/day

    c. 125 mg/dose × 3 doses/day = 375 mg/day, which is higher than the maximum recommended dose

    d. 125 mg × 5 mL/100 mg = 6.25 mL

31. a. 50 kg × 25 mg/kg = 1250 mg

    b. 50 kg × 50 mg/kg = 2500 mg

    c. 500 mg × 2 doses/day = 1000 mg/day, which is under the minimum recommended dose

    d. 500 mg × 5 mL/250 mg = 10 mL

32. a. 28.6 kg × 10 mg/kg = 286 mg

    b. 28.6 kg × 15 mg/kg = 429 mg

    c. It is within the recommended range.

    d. 325 mg × 5 mL/160 mg = 10.156 mL, rounded to 10.16 mL

33. a. [8 years/(8 years + 12 years)] × 600 mg = 240 mg

    b. 68 lb/150 lb × 600 mg = 271.99 mg, rounded to 272 mg

Chapter 5

5.1 Problem Set

1. 8 cups × 1 pt/2 cups = 4 pt

2. 3 pt × 2 cups/1 pt = 6 cups; 6 cups × 8 fl oz/1 cup = 48 fl oz

3. 1 pt × 2 cups/1 pt = 2 cups; 2 cups × 8 fl oz/1 cup = 16 fl oz; 16 fl oz × 2 tbsp/1 fl oz = 32 tbsp

4. 3 qt × 2 pt/1 qt = 6 pt; 6 pt × 2 cups/1 pt = 12 cups; 12 cups × 8 fl oz/1 cup = 96 fl oz

5. 28 tsp × 1 tbsp/3 tsp = 9.333 tbsp, rounded to 9.33 tbsp; 9.33 tbsp × 1 fl oz/2 tbsp = 4.665 fl oz, rounded to 4.67 fl oz

6. 1 pt × 1 qt/2 pt = 0.5 qt or 1/2 qt

7. 6 cups × 8 fl oz/1 cup = 48 fl oz; 48 fl oz × 2 tbsp/1 fl oz = 96 tbsp; 96 tbsp × 3 tsp/1 tbsp = 288 tsp

8. 80 mL = 5.3 tbsp, about 5 1/3 tbsp

9. 6 fl oz = 180 mL

10. 90 mL = 3 fl oz

11. 800 mL = 1.67 pt

12. 53 mL = 10.6 tsp, about 10 2/3 tsp

13. 35 mL = 7 tsp

14. 10 L = 10,000 mL; 10,000 mL × 1 gal/3840 mL = 2.604 gal, rounded to 2.6 gal

15. 4 tbsp = 60 mL

16. 15 mL × 1 tsp/5 mL = 3 tsp

17. 720 mL × 1 pt/480 mL = 1.5 pt, or 1½ pt

18. 30 tsp × 5 mL/1 tsp = 150 mL

19. 120 mL × 1 fl oz/30 mL = 4 fl oz

20. ½ gal = 0.5 gal × 3840 mL/1 gal = 1920 mL

21. 2 L = 2000 mL; 2000 mL × 1 pt/480 mL = 4.166 pt, rounded to 4.2 pt

22. 3 tbsp × 15 mL/1 tbsp = 45 mL

23. 1 fl oz × 30 mL/1 fl oz = 30 mL

24. 2 fl oz × 30 mL/1 fl oz = 60 mL

25. 3 fl oz × 30 mL/1 fl oz = 90 mL

26. 4 fl oz × 30 mL/1 fl oz = 120 mL

27. 5 fl oz × 30 mL/1 fl oz = 150 mL

28. 6 fl oz × 30 mL/1 fl oz = 180 mL

29. 7 fl oz × 30 mL/1 fl oz = 210 mL

30. 8 fl oz × 30 mL/1 fl oz = 240 mL

31. 12 fl oz × 30 mL/1 fl oz = 360 mL

32. 16 fl oz × 30 mL/1 fl oz = 480 mL

33. 2 oz × 30 g/1 oz = 60 g

34. 1.5 oz × 30 g/1 oz = 45 g

35. 8 oz × 30 g/1 oz = 240 g

36. 906 g × 1 lb/454 g = 1.995 lb, rounded to 2 lb

37. 30 g × 1 lb/454 g = 0.0660 lb, rounded to 0.07 lb, 1/16 lb

38. 0.8 oz × 30 g/1 oz = 24 g

39. 3.5 lb × 1 kg/2.2 lb = 1.59 kg, rounded to 1.6 kg

40. 14 lb × 1 kg/2.2 lb = 6.364 kg, rounded to 6.4 kg

41. 42 lb × 1 kg/2.2 lb = 19.09 kg, rounded to 19 kg

42. 97 lb × 1 kg/2.2 lb = 44.09 kg, rounded to 44 kg

43. 112 lb × 1 kg/2.2 lb = 50.909 kg, rounded to 50.9 kg

44. 165 lb × 1 kg/2.2 lb = 75 kg

45. 178 lb × 1 kg/2.2 lb = 80.909 kg, rounded to 80.9 kg

46. 247 lb × 1 kg/2.2 lb = 112.27 kg, rounded to 112 kg

47. 2 pt = 960 mL and 6 fl oz = 180 mL, so total milliliters = 960 mL + 180 mL = 1140 mL; 1140 mL × 1 dose/5 mL = 228 doses

48. 3 cups = 24 fl oz, 24 fl oz = 720 mL; 720 mL × 1 dose/10 mL = 72 doses

49. 12 bottles × 16 fl oz = 192 fl oz, 192 fl oz = 5760 mL; 5760 mL × 1 dose/15 mL = 384 doses

50. 5 fl oz = 150 mL; 150 mL × 1 dose/5 mL = 30 doses

51. 1 pt = 480 mL; 480 mL × 1 dose/15 mL = 32 doses

52. 1.5 fl oz = 45 mL, 45 mL × 3 times/day = 135 mL/day

53. 8 fl oz = 240 mL; 240 mL × 1 dose/7.5 mL = 32 doses

54. ½ tsp × 5 mL/1 tsp × 10 mg/1 mL = 25 mg

55. 4 fl oz × 30 mL/1 fl oz = 120 mL; 120 mL × 10 mg/1 mL = 1200 mg; 1200 mg × 1 day/20 mg = 60 days

56. 10 mg/day × 1 mL/1 mg = 10 mL/1 day; 10 mL/1 day × 1 tsp/5 mL = 2 tsp/1 day

57. 200 mL × 1 tsp/5 mL = 40 tsp; 40 tsp × 1 day/1 tsp = 40 days

58. Conversions: 180 lb × 1 kg/2.2 lb = 81.8181 kg, rounded to 81.8 kg; 2 tsp × 5 mL/1 tsp = 10 mL

    81.8 kg × 10 mL/68 kg = 12.029411 mL, rounded to 12 mL

    300 mL × 1 dose/12 mL = 25 doses

59. Conversions: 52 lb × 1 kg/2.2 lb = 23.636 kg, rounded to 23.6 kg; 1 tsp × 5 mL/1 tsp = 5 mL; 4 fl oz × 30 mL/1 fl oz = 120 mL

    23.6 kg × 5 mL/20 kg = 5.9 mL

    120 mL × 1 dose/5.9 mL = 20.3389 doses, or 20 full doses

60. Conversions: 172 lb × 1 kg/2.2 lb = 78.181 kg, rounded to 78.2 kg; 2 tbsp × 15 mL/1 tbsp = 30 mL; 12 fl oz × 30 mL/1 fl oz = 360 mL

    78.2 kg × 30 mL/50 kg = 46.92 mL, rounded to 46.9 mL

    360 mL × 1 dose/46.9 mL = 7.6759 doses, or 7 full doses

5.2 Problem Set

1. 243 mg

2. 324 mg

3. 405 mg

4. 648 mg

5. 6 lb × 1 kg/2.2 lb = 2.727 kg, rounded to 2.73 kg; per day range is 6.6 mg to 16.4 mg (rounded from 6.552 mg and 16.38 mg)

6. 1 lb = 16 oz, so 7 lb 12 oz = (16 oz × 7) + 12 oz = 124 oz, and 124 oz / 16 oz = 7.75 lb; 7.75 lb × 1 kg/2.2 lb = 3.52 kg; per day range is 8.4 mg (rounded from 8.448 mg) to 21.1 mg

7. 23 lb × 1 kg/2.2 lb = 10.454 kg, rounded to 10.45 kg; per day range is 37.6 mg to 50.2 mg (rounded from 50.16 mg)

8. 18 lb × 1 kg/2.2 lb = 8.181 kg, rounded to 8.18 kg; per day range is 24.5 mg to 29.5 mg (rounded from 29.448 mg)

9. 5 mL × 80 mg/15 mL = 26.67 mg

10. 60 mg × 5 mL/120 mg = 2.5 mL or ½ tsp

11. 240 mL × 24 mg/5 mL = 1152 mg or 1.152 g

12. 120 mL × 65 mg/15 mL = 520 mg

13. 10 mL × 2500 mg/60 mL = 420 mg (rounded from 416.67 mg)

14. 15 mL × 260 mg/600 mL = 6.5 mg

15. 600 mL × 25 mg/5 mL = 3000 mg = 3 g

16. Note that the prescribed dose is given in tablespoonsful and the question asks for the number of milligrams in a teaspoonful. 5 mL × 30 mg/15 mL = 10 mg

17. 480 mL × 40 mg/1 mL = 19,200 mg or 19.2 g

18. a. 150 mL × 1 dose/3.75 mL = 40 doses; 40 doses × 1 day/3 doses = 13.3 days

    b. 3.75 mL/dose × 3 doses/day = 11.25 mL/day × 10 days = 112.5 mL; 150 mL − 112.5 mL = 37.5 mL

19. a. 1 tsp = 5 mL; 10 mL/day × 14 days = 140 mL; 150 mL bottle selected

    b. 150 mL − 140 mL = 10 mL

20. 1 tbsp = 15 mL and 12 fl oz/bottle = 360 mL/bottle; 15 mL/dose × 3 doses/day = 45 mL/day; 360 mL/bottle × 1 day/45 mL = 8 days/bottle

21. 2 tsp = 10 mL and 1 tbsp = 15 mL, so 25 mL/1 2-day total; 300 mL × 1 2-day unit/25 mL = 12 2-day units, or 24 days

22. 600 mL × 25 mg/15 mL = 1000 mg or 1 g

23. 12 fl oz/bottle = 360 mL/bottle and 1 fl oz × 4 doses/day = 30 mL × 4 doses/day = 120 mL/day; 120 mL/day × 14 days/treatment = 1680 mL/treatment; 1680 mL/treatment × 1 bottle/360 mL = 4.666 bottles, or a total of 5 bottles to be purchased

24. (4 tablets × 2/day) + (3 tablets × 2/day) + (1 tablet × 1/day) = 15 tablets

25. 24 hr/day × 1 dose/3 hr = 8 doses/day; 8 doses/day × 10 days = 80 doses; 80 doses × (1 mL/dose × 2 cheeks) = 160 mL

26. a. 12 fl oz/bottle = 360 mL/bottle, 1 tsp/dose = 5 mL/dose; 360 mL/bottle × 25 mg/5 mL = 1800 mg/bottle

    b. 9 g = 9000 mg; 9000 mg/therapy × 1 bottle/1800 mg = 5 bottles; 5 bottles − 1 initial bottle = 4 refills

27. 2 tsp/dose = 10 mL/dose; 3 doses/day × 10 mL/dose = 30 mL/day; 30 mL/day × 15 days/treatment = 450 mL/treatment; 450 mL/treatment × 1 fl oz/30 mL = 15 fl oz/treatment

28. 2 tbsp/dose = 30 mL/dose; 3 doses/day × 30 mL/dose = 90 mL/day; 20 days/treatment × 90 mL/day = 1800 mL/treatment

29. 1 tsp = 5 mL

    Child 1: 5 mL/dose × 3 doses/day = 15 mL/day, 15 mL/day × 4 days = 60 mL

    Child 2: 10 mL/dose × 3 doses/day = 30 mL/day, 30 mL/day × 4 days = 120 mL

    60 mL + 120 mL = 180 mL

    Since 1 bottle = 4 fl oz, 4 fl oz/bottle × 30 mL/1 fl oz = 120 mL/bottle

    The mother will need 2 bottles, or 240 mL.

30. Child 1: x mg/5 mL = 25 mg/5 mL, x mg = 25 mg

    Child 2: x mg/10 mL = 25 mg/5 mL, x mg = 50 mg

31. ¾ tsp = 0.75 tsp; 0.75 tsp × 5 mL/tsp = 3.75 mL; 3.75 mL × 187 mg/5 mL = 140.25 mg

32. 1½ tsp = 1.5 tsp; 1.5 tsp × 5 mL/tsp = 7.5 mL; 7.5 mL × 187 mg/5 mL = 280.5 mg

33. 125 mg × 5 mL/187 mg = 3.3422 mL, rounded to 3.34 mL

34. 500 mg × 5 mL/187 mg = 13.3689 mL, rounded to 13.37 mL

35. a. 180 g ÷ 3 equal parts = 60 g of each

    b. 180 g × 1 oz/30 g = 6 oz; use a 6 oz jar

    c. 1/3/XX + 6 months = 7/3/XX

36. 12 fl oz bottle × 30 mL/1 fl oz = 360 mL;
    360 mL × 1 syringe/60 mL = 6 syringes

5.3 Problem Set

1. $(0° − 32°) ÷ 1.8 = −17.777$ °C, rounded to −17.8 °C

2. $(23° − 32°) ÷ 1.8 = −5$ °C

3. $(36° − 32°) ÷ 1.8 = 2.222$ °C, rounded to 2.2 °C

4. $(40° − 32°) ÷ 1.8 = 4.444$ °C, rounded to 4.4 °C

5. $(64° − 32°) ÷ 1.8 = 17.777$ °C, rounded to 17.8 °C

6. $(72° − 32°) ÷ 1.8 = 22.222$ °C, rounded to 22.2 °C

7. $(98.6° − 32°) ÷ 1.8 = 37$ °C

8. $(100.5° − 32°) ÷ 1.8 = 38.055$ °C, rounded to 38.1 °C

9. $(102.8° − 32°) ÷ 1.8 = 39.333$ °C, rounded to 39.3 °C

10. $(105° − 32°) ÷ 1.8 = 40.555$ °C, rounded to 40.6 °C

11. $(1.8 × −15°) + 32 = 5$ °F

12. $(1.8 × 18°) + 32 = 64.4$ °F

13. $(1.8 × 27°) + 32 = 80.6$ °F

14. $(1.8 × 31°) + 32 = 87.8$ °F

15. $(1.8 × 38°) + 32 = 100.4$ °F

16. $(1.8 × 40°) + 32 = 104$ °F

17. $(1.8 × 49°) + 32 = 120.2$ °F

18. $(1.8 × 63°) + 32 = 145.4$ °F

19. $(1.8 × 99.8°) + 32 = 211.64$ °F, rounded to 211.6 °F

20. $(1.8 × 101.4°) + 32 = 214.52$ °F, rounded to 214.5 °F

21. $(1.8 × 130°) + 32 = 266$ °F

22. a. $(1.8 × −20°) + 32 = −4$ °F

    b. 2/1/07 + 6 months = August 1, 2007

23. $(300° − 32°) ÷ 1.8 = 148.888$ °C, rounded to 148.9 °C

24. a. 2.3 °C, see chart below

    b. 3.2 °C

    c. 3.9 °C

    d. 2.1 °C

    e. 2.7 °C

    f. 1.6 °C, too cold

    g. 2.4 °C

    h. 2.7 °C

    i. 1.9 °C, too cold

    j. 3.8 °C

Problem Set 5.3, chart for question 24

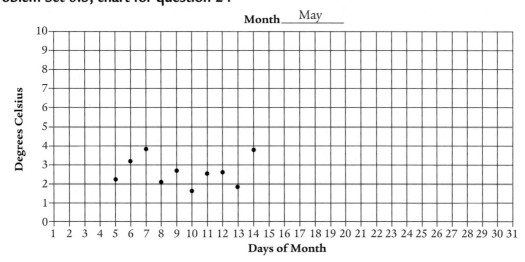

Month ____May____

Problem Set 5.3, chart for question 25

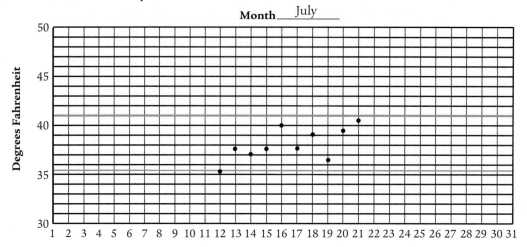

25. a. 35.2 °F, too cold, see chart above

b. 37.6 °F

c. 37 °F

d. 37.4 °F

e. 40.1 °F

f. 37.8 °F

g. 39 °F

h. 36.5 °F

i. 39.4 °F

j. 40.5 °F

Chapter 6

6.1 Problem Set

1. x mL/50 mg = 1 mL/10 mg; x mL = 5 mL

2. x mL/350 mg = 10 mL/500 mg; x mL = 7 mL

3. x mL/80 mg = 10 mL/100 mg; x mL = 8 mL

4. x mL/0.5 mcg = 1 mL/0.5 mcg; x mL = 0.5 mL

5. x mL/100 mg = 1 mL/50 mg; x mL = 0.5 mL

6. x mL/30 mg = 20 mL/200 mg; x mL = 3 mL

7. x mL/40 mg = 2 mL/20 mg; x mL = 4 mL

8. x mL/250 mg = 1 mL/125 mg; x mL = 2 mL

9. x mL/400 mg = 5 mL/500 mg; x mL = 4 mL

10. x mL/50 mg = 100 mL/100 mg; x mL = 50 mL

11. x mg/0.5 mL = 15 mg/1 mL; x mg = 7.5 mL

12. x mg/1.75 mL = 60 mg/2 mL; x mg = 52.5 mg

13. x mg/3.75 mL = 20 mg/1 mL; x mg = 75 mg

14. x mg/1.3 mL = 2 mg/2 mL; x mg = 1.3 mg

15. x mg/5 mL = 50 mg/10 mL; x mg = 25 mg

16. x mg/5 mL = 25 mg/5 mL; x mg = 12.5 mg

17. x mg/5 mL = 10 mg/10 mL; x mg = 5 mg

18. x mg/8 mL = 10 mg/1 mL; x mg = 80 mg

19. x mg/1.5 mL = 4 mg/2 mL; x mg = 3 mg

20. x mg/2.5 mL = 50 mg/1 mL; x mg = 125 mg

21. x g/2 mL = 1 g/1000 mL; x g = 0.002 g = 2 mg

22. x g/1 mL = 1 g/5000 mL; x g = 0.0002 g = 0.2 mg = 200 mcg

23. x g/1.5 mL = 1 g/10,000 mL; x g = 0.00015 g = 0.15 mg = 150 mcg

24. x g/1.4 mL = 1 g/2000 mL; x g = 0.0007 g = 0.7 mg = 700 mcg

25. x mg/2.5 mL = 1 g/10,000 mL; x mg = 0.00025 g = 0.25 mg = 250 mcg

26. Convert 500 mg to 0.5 g; x mL/0.5 g = 1000 mL/1 g; x mL = 500 mL

27. Convert 50 mg to 0.05 g; x mL/0.05 g = 10,000 mL/1 g; x mL = 500 mL

28. Convert 600 mg to 0.6 g; x mL/0.6 g = 300 mL/1 g; x mL = 180 mL

29. Convert 250 mg to 0.25 g; x mL/0.25 g = 500 mL/1 g; x mL = 125 mL

30. x mL/0.01 g = 750 mL/1 g; x mL = 7.5 mL

6.2 Problem Set

1. x mL/30 mEq = 1 mL/4.4 mEq; x mL = 6.81818 mL, rounded to 6.82 mL

2. x mL/45 mEq = 1 mL/4.4 mEq; x mL = 10.22727 mL, rounded to 10.23 mL

3. x tablets/32 mEq = 1 tablet/8 mEq; x tablets = 4 tablets

4. x mL/30 mEq = 15 mL/40 mEq; x mL = 11.25 mL; 11.25 mL ÷ 2 doses = 5.625 mL, rounded to 5.63 mL

5. x mEq/15 mL = 20 mEq/10 mL; x mEq = 30 mEq

6. x mL/30 mEq = 15 mL/20 mEq; x mL = 22.5 mL

7. Select the 20 mEq vial

    x mL/14 mEq = 1 mL/2 mEq; x mL = 7 mL

8. Select the 20 mEq vial

    x mL/19 mEq = 1 mL/2 mEq; x mL = 9.5 mL

9. Select the 30 mEq vial

    x mL/27 mEq = 1 mL/2 mEq; x mL = 13.5 mL

10. Select the 10 mEq vial and the 40 mEq vial

    x mL/50 mEq = 1 mL/2 mEq; x mL = 25 mL

11. x mEq/8 mL = 30 mEq/15 mL; x mEq = 16 mEq

    or x mEq/8 mL = 2 mEq/1 mL; x mEq = 16 mEq

12. x mEq/15 mL = 40 mEq/20 mL; x mEq = 30 mEq

    or x mEq/15 mL = 2 mEq/1 mL; x mEq = 30 mEq

13. x mL/132 mEq = 1 mL/4 mEq; x mL = 33 mL

14. x mL/120 mEq = 1 mL/4 mEq; x mL = 30 mL

15. x mL/4 units = 1 mL/10 units; x mL = 0.4 mL

16. x units/2.8 mL = 10 units/1 mL; x units = 28 units

17. x mL/3500 units = 1 mL/1000 units; x mL = 3.5 mL

18. x units/0.43 mL = 20,000 units/0.8 mL; x units = 10,750 units

19. x mL/24,000 units = 1 mL/10,000 units; x mL = 2.4 mL

20. x mL/24,000 units = 1 mL/5000 units; x mL = 4.8 mL

21. x mL/30 mg = 0.8 mL/80 mg; x mL = 0.3 mL

22. x mL/175,000 units = 1 mL/500,000 units; x mL = 0.35 mL

23. x mL/1,500,000 units = 1 mL/600,000 units; x mL = 2.5 mL

24. x mL/385,000 units = 1 mL/50,000 units; x mL = 7.7 mL

25. x mL/45 units = 1 mL/100 units; x mL = 0.45 mL

26. Calculate morning dose: x mL/18 units = 1 mL/100 units; x mL = 0.18 mL

    Calculate evening dose: x mL/10 units = 1 mL/100 units; x mL = 0.1 mL

    Add morning and evening doses: 0.18 mL/morning + 0.1 mL/evening = 0.28 mL/day

    Since the vial shown on the label contains 10 mL, calculate time for 10 mL vial to last: x days/10 mL vial = 1 day/0.28 mL; x days = 35.714 days, rounded to 35 days

27. a. Add morning and evening units: 20 units + 18 units = 38 units/day

    b. x mL/38 units = 1 mL/100 units; x mL = 0.38 mL. Calculate the number of days of therapy in a 10 mL vial: 10 mL ÷ 0.38 mL = 26.3 days, rounded down to 26 days for 1 vial. Therefore, 2 vials will be needed for 30 days of therapy.

28. Humulin R: 10 units/dose × 1 dose/day × 30 days = 300 units

    Humulin 70/30 Mix: 15 units/dose × 2 doses/day × 30 days = 900 units

x mL/450 units = 1 mL/100 units; x mL = 4.5 mL of each, so one vial of each is needed

29. x units/0.5 mL = 100 units/1 mL; x units = 50 units

30. 20 units/dose × 2 doses/day = 40 units/day

x days/40 units = 1 mL/100 units; x mL = 0.4 mL are used daily

x days/20 mL = 1 day/0.4 mL; x days = 50 days

6.3 Problem Set

1. Convert 375 mg to 0.375 g.

x mL/1.5 g = 1 mL/0.375 g; x mL = 4 mL

4 mL final volume − 3.3 mL diluent volume = 0.7 mL powder volume

2. Convert 250 mg to 0.25 g, and note that 1 tsp = 5 mL.

x mL/5 g = 5 mL/0.25 g; x mL = 100 mL final volume

100 mL final volume − 8.6 mL powder volume = 91.4 mL diluent volume

3. Convert 1 g to 1000 mg.

x mL/1000 mg = 2 mL/125 mg; x mL = 16 mL final volume

16 mL final volume − 14.4 mL diluent = 1.6 mL powder volume

4. Convert 250 mg to 0.25 g.

x mL/2 g = 1 mL/0.25 g; x mL = 8 mL final volume

8 mL final volume − 6.8 mL diluent = 1.2 mL powder volume

5. Convert 125 mg to 0.125 g.

x mL/2 g = 1 mL/0.125 g; x mL = 16 mL final volume

Using the powder volume calculated in #4, 16 mL final volume − 1.2 mL powder volume = 14.8 mL diluent volume

6. Convert 250 mg to 0.25 g.

x mL/4 g = 1 mL/0.25 g; x mL = 16 mL final volume

16 mL final volume − 11.7 mL diluent = 4.3 powder volume

7. a. x mL/6 g = 2.5 mL/1 g; x mL = 15 mL final volume; 15 mL final volume − 12.5 mL diluent volume = 2.5 mL powder volume

   b. 2.5 mL powder volume + 2.5 mL diluent volume = 5 mL final volume; 6 g/5mL = 1.2 g/mL = 1200 mg/mL

8. 4 mL final volume − 3.3 mL diluent = 0.7 mL powder volume

9. Using the information from #8, 1 g/4 mL, and converting 1 g to 1000 mg: x mL/100 mg = 4 mL/1000 mg; x mL = 0.4 mL

10. x mL/2 g = 1 mL/0.2 g, x mL = 10 mL final volume; 10 mL final volume − 8.8 mL diluent = 1.2 mL powder volume

11. Convert 10 g to 10,000 mg; 45 mL DV + 5 mL PV = 50 mL FV; x mg/1 mL = 10,000 mg/50 mL; x mg = 200 mg, so there will be 200 mg/mL

12. Convert 8 g to 8000 mg, and remember 1 tsp = 5 mL. x mg/5 mL = 8000 mg/200 mL; x mg = 200 mg, so there are 200 mg/5 mL or 200 mg/tsp

13. a. x mL/20 g = 6 mL/1 g, x mL = 120 mL FV; 120 mL FV − 106 mL DV = 14 mL PV

    b. x mL/20 g = 3 mL/1 g, x mL = 60 mL FV; 60 mL FV − 14 mL PV = 46 mL DV

14. Convert 2 g to 2000 mg; x mL/2000 mg = 1 mL/375 mg, x mL = 5.3 mL FV; 5.3 mL FV − 3.5 mL DV = 1.8 mL PV

15. Convert 2.5 g to 2500 mg; x mL/2500 mg = 5 mL/300 mg, x mL = 41.7 mL FV; 41.7 mL FV − 9.6 mL PV = 32.1 mL DV

16. Convert 5 g to 5000 mg; x mL/5000 mg = 1 mL/250 mg, x mL = 20 mL FV; 20 mL FV − 8.6 mL DV = 11.4 mL PV

17. x mg/10 g = 2.5 mL/1 g, x mL = 25 mL FV; 25 mL FV − 20 mL DV = 5 mL PV; 5 mL PV + 35 mL new DV = 40 mL FV; 10 g/40 mL = 0.25 g/mL or 250 mg/mL

18. 5 mL FV − 4.3 mL DV = 0.7 mL PV

19. 25 mL DV + 5 mL PV = 30 mL FV; convert 5 g to 5000 mg; x mg/1 mL = 5000 mg/30 mL, x mg = 167 mg, so 167 mg/mL

20. 90 mL DV + 10 mL PV = 100 mL FV; convert 20 g to 20,000 mg; x mg/1 mL = 20,000 mg/100 mL; x mg = 200 mg, so 200 mg/mL

21. 20 mL DV + 5 mL PV = 25 mL FV; convert 3 g to 3000 mg; x mg/1 mL = 3000 mg/25 mL; x mg = 120 mg, so 120 mg/mL

22. 100 mL FV − 67 mL DV = 33 mL PV

23. Convert 35 g to 35,000 mg; x mg/1 mL = 35,000 mg/100 mL, x mg = 350 mg, so 350 mg/mL

24. (1) 15 mL − 9 mL = 6 mL in bottle; (2) 10 mL + 0.2 mL = 10.2 mL vancomycin; (3) 10.2 mL vancomycin + 6 mL bottle = 16.2 mL FV; x mg/1 mL = 500 mg/16.2 mL; x mg = 30.8641 mg, rounded to 31 mg, so 31 mg/mL

25. a. x mg/1 mL = 1000 mg/4.4 mL; x mg = 227 mg, so 227 mg/mL; 1 mL + 9 mL = 10 mL, so 227 mg/10 mL, which is simplified to 22.7 mg/mL

    b. x mg /0.1 mL = 22.7 mg/1 mL = 2.27 mg

Chapter 7

7.1 Problem Set

1. There are 0.05 g betamethasone in 100 g of ointment.

2. There are 10 mg of furosemide in 1 mL of solution and 11.5 mL of alcohol in each 100 mL of solution.

3. There are 8 g of ciclopirox in 100 mL of solution.

4. 8 fl oz = 240 mL, so x g/240 mL = 2 g/100 mL; x g = 4.8 g

5. x g/1.3 mL = 2 g/100 mL; x g = 0.026 g = 26 mg

6. 2 capsules × 300 mg = 600 mg or 0.6 g and 1 fl oz = 30 mL, so x g/100 mL = 0.6 g/30 mL; x g = 2 g, or 2% w/v

7. x g/100 mL = 0.075 g/5 mL; x g = 1.5 g; therefore, there is 1.5% w/v

8. x g/100 mL = 0.04 g/4 mL; x g = 1 g; therefore, there is 1% w/v

9. x g/100 mL = 0.06 g/2 mL; x g = 3 g; therefore, there is 3% w/v

10. x g/100 mL = 0.025 g/5 mL; x g = 0.5 g; therefore, there is 0.5% w/v

11. x g/100 mL = 0.4 g/40 mL; x g = 1 g; therefore, there is 1% w/v

12. x g/100 mL = 20 g/100 mL; x g = 20 g; therefore, there is 20% w/v

13. x g/100 mL = 0.04 g/1 mL; x g = 4 g; therefore, there is 4% w/v

14. x g/100 mL = 0.02 g/1 mL; x g = 2 g; therefore, there is 2% w/v

15. x g/20 g = 0.8 g/100 g; x g = 0.16 g, which equals 160 mg

16. x g/30 g = 10 g/100 g; x g = 3 g, which equals 3000 mg

17. x g/45 g = 0.77 g/100 g; x g = 0.3465 g, which equals 346.5 mg

18. 7 fl oz = 210 mL, so x g/210 mL = 2 g/100 mL; x g = 4.2 g, which equals 4200 mg

19. x g/60 g = 5 g/100 g; x g = 3 g, which equals 3000 mg

20. x g/30 g = 1 g/100 g; x g = 0.3 g, which equals 300 mg

21. x g/15 mL = 6.5 g/100 mL; x g = 0.975 g, which equals 975 mg

22. 4 fl oz = 120 mL, so x g/120 mL = 7.5 g/100 mL; x g = 9 g, which equals 9000 mg

23. x g/10 mL = 1.5 g/100 mL; x g = 0.15 g, which equals 150 mg

24. x g/30 mL = 0.03 g/100 mL; x g = 0.009 g, which equals 9 mg

25. 1 tsp equals 5 mL, so x g/5 mL = 7.5 g/100 mL; x g = 0.375 g, which equals 375 mg

26. 1 tbsp equals 15 mL, so x g/15 mL = 0.5 g/100 mL; x g = 0.075 g, which equals 75 mg

27. x g/0.5 mL = 1 g/1000 mL; x g = 0.0005 g, which equals 0.5 mg

28. x g/100 mL = 45 g/500 mL; x g = 9 g, therefore, there is 9% w/v

29. x g/3500 mL = 24.5 g/100 mL; x g = 857.5 g

30. a. x g/600 mL = 1 g/200 mL; x g = 3 g

   b. x g/100 mL = 1 g/200 mL; x g = 0.5 g, or 0.5% w/v

31. (1) x mg/5 mL = 3 mg/1 mL; x mg = 15 mg

   (2) x mg/2 mL = 40 mg/1 mL; x mg = 80 mg

   (3) 15 mg + 80 mg = 95 mg

   (4) x g/100 mL = 0.095 g/7 mL; x g = 1.357 g, rounded to 1.4 g; therefore, there is 1.4% w/v

32. a. x mg/0.5 mL = 4 mg/2 mL; x mg = 1 mg; 0.5 mL + 0.5 mL = 1 mL; 1 mg/mL

   b. x g/100 mL = 0.001 g/1 mL; x g = 0.1 g, or 0.1% w/v

   c. x mg/0.1 mL = 1 mg/1 mL; x mg = 0.1 mg

33. x g/100 mL = 0.9 g/100 mL; x g = 0.9 g

34. x g/250 mL = 0.9 g/100 mL; x g = 2.25 g

35. x g/500 mL = 0.9 g/100 mL; x g = 4.5 g

36. x g/1000 mL = 0.9 g/100 mL; x g = 9 g

37. x g/2225 mL = 0.9 g/100 mL; x g = 20.025 g, rounded to 20 g

38. x g/125 mL = 0.45 g/100 mL; x g = 0.5625 g, rounded to 0.56 g

39. x g/250 mL = 0.45 g/100 mL; x g = 1.125 g, rounded to 1.13 g

40. x g/750 mL = 0.45 g/100 mL; x g = 3.375 g, rounded to 3.38 g

41. x g/1800 mL = 0.45 g/100 mL; x g = 8.1 g

42. x g/2600 mL = 0.45 g/100 mL; x g = 11.7 g

43. x g/75 mL = 5 g/100 mL; x g = 3.75 g

44. x g/385 mL = 5 g/100 mL; x g = 19.25 g

45. x g/525 mL = 5 g/100 mL; x g = 26.25 g

46. x g/1350 mL = 5 g/100 mL; x g = 67.5 g

47. x g/3000 mL = 5 g/100 mL; x g = 150 g

48. x g/100 mL = 10 g/100 mL; x g = 10 g

49. x g/450 mL = 10 g/100 mL; x g = 45 g

50. x g/875 mL = 10 g/100 mL; x g = 87.5 g

51. x g/1100 mL = 10 g/100 mL; x g = 110 g

52. x g/2300 mL = 10 g/100 mL; x g = 230 g

7.2 Problem Set

1. 1000 mL ÷ 50 mL/hour = 20 hours

2. 1000 mL ÷ 100 mL/hour = 10 hours, or 7 p.m. to 5 a.m.

3. 500 mL ÷ 30 mL/hour = 16.67 hours, rounded down to 16 hours

4. 45 min = 0.75 hour; 75 mL ÷ 0.75 hour = 100 mL/hour

   dimensional analysis: 60 min/hour × 75 mL/45 min = 100 mL/hour

5. 100 mL ÷ 0.75 hour = 133 mL/hour

6. 150 mL ÷ 1.5 hours = 100 mL/hour

7. 2800 mL ÷ 24 hours = 116 mL/hour

8. 30 min = 0.5 hour; 250 mL ÷ 0.5 hour = 500 mL/hour

9. 500 mL ÷ 4 hours = 125 mL/hour

10. 2000 mL ÷ 8 hours = 250 mL/hour

11. 500 mL ÷ 2 hours = 250 mL/hour

12. 500 mL ÷ 15 mL/hour = 33 hours

13. a. 1000 mL ÷ 125 mL/hour = 8 hours

   b. 24 hours ÷ 8 hours/bag = 3 bags

14. 1000 mL ÷ 150 mL/hour = 6.67 hours, rounded down to 6 hours; 7 a.m. today until 6 p.m. the next day = 35 hours; 35 hours × 1 bag/6 hours = 6 bags until 6 p.m. the next day; therefore, dose = 5 additional bags needed

15. 3000 mL ÷ 24 hours = 125 mL/hour

16. 50 mL/hour × 24 hours = 1200 mL, or 2 bags

17. 75 mL/hour × 24 hours = 1800 mL, or 2 bags

18. 100 mL/hour × 24 hours = 2400 mL, or 3 bags

19. 120 mL/hour × 24 hours = 2880 mL, or 3 bags

20. 125 mL/hour × 24 hours = 3000 mL, or 3 bags

21. 130 mL/hour × 24 hours = 3120 mL, or 4 bags

22. 150 mL/hour × 24 hours = 3600 mL, or 4 bags

23. 175 mL/hour × 24 hours = 4200 mL, or 5 bags

24. 200 mL/hour × 24 hours = 4800 mL, or 5 bags

25. 225 mL/hour × 24 hours = 5400 mL, or 6 bags

26. a. 250 mL ÷ 4 hours = 62.5 mL/hour

    b. 250 mg ÷ 4 hours = 62.5 mg/hour

27. a. 500 mL ÷ 12 hours = 41.7 mL/hour

    b. 12,000,000 units ÷ 12 hours = 1,000,000 units/hour

28. a. x mL/6 mg = 1 mL/4 mg; x mL = 1.5 mL, or 1.5 mL/hour

    dimensional analysis: 6 mg/hour × 1 mL/4 mg = 1.5 mL/hour

    b. x mcg/6 mg = 1000 mcg/1 mg; x mcg = 6000 mcg/hour

29. a. x mL/20 mg = 500 mL/250 mg; x mL = 40 mL/hour

    dimensional analysis: 20 mg/hour × 500 mL/250 mg = 40 mL/hour

    b. 20 mg/hour = 0.02 g/hour

30. a. x mL/1 mg = 500 mL/40 mg; x mL = 12.5 mL, and 12.5 mL/min × 60 min/hour = 750 mL/hour

    dimensional analysis: 60 min/hour × 1 mg/min × 500 mL/40 mg = 750 mL/hour

    b. 1 mg/min × 60 min/hour = 60 mg/hour

31. a. 198 lb × 1 kg/2.2 lb = 90 kg

    90 kg × 12 mcg/kg = 1080 mcg

    x mL/1080 mcg = 500 mL/800,000 mcg; x mL = 0.675 mL

    0.675 mL/min × 60 min/hour = 40.5 mL/hour

dimensional analysis: 60 min/hour × 1.08 mg/min × 500 mL/800 mg = 40.5 mL/hour

    b. 1080 mcg/min × 60 min/hour = 64,800 mcg/hour, which equals 64.8 mg/hour

32. a. 176 lb × 1 kg/2.2 lb = 80 kg

    80 kg × 4 mcg/kg = 320 mcg/min

    x mL/320 mcg = 750 mL/480,000 mcg; x mL = 0.5 mL

    0.5 mL/min × 60 min/hour = 30 mL/hour

    dimensional analysis: 60 min/hour × 320 mcg/min × 750 mL/480,000 mcg = 30 mL/hour

    b. 320 mcg/min × 60 min/hour = 19,200 mcg/hour, which equals 19.2 mg/hour

7.3 Problem Set

1. 10 mL/hour × 10 gtt/mL × 1 hour/60 min = 1.67 gtt/min

2. 35 mL/hour × 60 gtt/mL × 1 hour/60 min = 35 gtt/min

3. 100 mL/60 min × 10 gtt/mL = 16.67 gtt/min, rounded down to 16 gtt/min

4. 50 mL/30 min × 60 gtt/mL = 100 gtt/min

5. 100 mL/45 min × 15 gtt/mL = 33.3333 gtt/min, rounded to 33 gtt/min

6. 100 mL/60 min × 15 gtt/mL = 25 gtt/min

7. 50 mL/60 min × 15 gtt/mL = 12.5 gtt/min, rounded down to 12 gtt/min

8. 95 mL/60 min × 15 gtt/mL = 23.75 gtt/min, rounded down to 23 gtt/min

9. 50 mL/30 min × 10 gtt/mL = 16.67 gtt/min, rounded down to 16 gtt/min

10. 1000 mL/480 min × 15 gtt/mL = 31.25 gtt/min, rounded down to 31 gtt/min

11. 250 mL/30 min × 15 gtt/mL = 125 gtt/min

12. 120 mL/60 min × 10 gtt/mL = 20 gtt/min

13. 30 gtt/min × 1 mL/10 gtt × 60 min/hour = 180 mL/hour

14. 45 gtt/min × 1 mL/15 gtt × 60 min/hour = 180 mL/hour

15. 30 gtt/min × 1 mL/10 gtt × 60 min/hour = 180 mL/hour

16. 30 gtt/min × 1 mL/15 gtt × 60 min/hour = 120 mL/hour

17. a. x mEq/mL = 24 mEq/500 mL; x mEq = 0.048 mEq

    b. 0.048 mEq/10 gtt = 0.0048 mEq/gtt

18. a. 125 mL/60 min × 10 gtt/mL = 20.83 gtt/min, rounded down to 20 gtt/min

    b. 125 mL/60 min × 15 gtt/mL = 31.25 gtt/min, rounded down to 31 gtt/min

    c. 125 mL/60 min × 60 gtt/mL = 125 gtt/min

19. a. 23 gtt/min × 1 mL/15 gtt = 1.53 mL/min; 1.53 mL/min × 60 min/hour = 91.8 mL/hour; 1000 mL × 1 hour/91.8 mL = 10.89 hours, or almost 11 hours

    b. 30 mEq/1000 mL × 1 mL/15 gtt = 0.002 mEq/gtt

    0.002 mEq/gtt × 23 gtt/min = 0.046 mEq/min

    0.046 mEq/min × 60 min/hour = 2.76 mEq/hour

    dimensional analysis: 1 hour × 60 min/hour × 23 gtt/min × 1 mL/15 gtt × 30 mEq/1000 mL = 2.76 mEq/hour

20. a. 50 mL/60 min × 10 gtt/mL = 8.33 gtt/min, rounded down to 8 gtt/min

    b. x g dextrose/50 mL = 10 g/100 mL; x g dextrose = 5 g, or 5 g per hour

21. a. 100 mL/60 min × 15 gtt/mL = 25 gtt/min

    b. x mcg/mL = 400,000 mcg/100 mL; x mcg = 4000 mcg

    4000 mcg/15 gtt = 266.7 mcg/gtt

7.4 Problem Set

1. (50 mL × 10 gtt/mL) ÷ 15 min = 33.3333 gtt/min, rounded to 33 gtt/min

2. (100 mL × 15 gtt/min) ÷ 20 min = 75 gtt/min

3. (50 mL × 15 gtt/min) ÷ 30 min = 25 gtt/min

4. (60 mL × 10 gtt/min) ÷ 30 min = 20 gtt/min

5. (55 mL × 15 gtt/min) ÷ 20 min = 41.25 gtt/min, rounded down to 41 gtt/min

6. (63 mL × 15 gtt/min) ÷ 15 min = 63 gtt/min

7. (58 mL × 15 gtt/min) ÷ 15 min = 58 gtt/min

8. (61 mL × 10 gtt/min) ÷ 25 min = 24.4 gtt/min, rounded down to 24 gtt/min

9. a. 2 g in 50 mL

   b. (50 mL × 15 gtt/mL) ÷ 20 min = 37.5 gtt/min, rounded down to 37 gtt/min

10. a. 2 g in 50 mL

    b. (50 mL × 10 gtt/mL) ÷ 30 min = 16.7 gtt/min, rounded down to 16 gtt/min

11. a. 3 million units in 50 mL

    b. (50 mL × 15 gtt/mL) ÷ 15 min = 50 gtt/min

12. a. 169 lb ÷ 2.2 lb/kg = 76.8 kg

    10 mg/kg × 76.8 kg = 768 mg

    x mL/768 mg = 1 mL/50 mg; x mL = 15.36 mL

    15.36 mL + 50 mL bag = 65.36 mL

    b. 15 gtt/mL × 65.36 mL/20 min = 49.02 gtt/min, rounded down to 49 gtt/min

13. a. 2 g in 50 mL

    b. (50 mL × 10 gtt/mL) ÷ 25 min = 20 gtt/min

14. a. 2 g in 50 mL

    b. (50 mL × 15 gtt/mL) ÷ 30 min = 25 gtt/min

15. a. 1 g in 50 mL

    b. (50 mL × 60 gtt/mL) ÷ 30 min = 100 gtt/min

Chapter 8

8.1 Problem Set

1. x mg/3 mL = 10 mg/1 mL; x mg = 30 mg needed

   x mL/30 mg = 1 mL/65 mg; x mL = 0.4615 mL concentrate, rounded to 0.46 mL concentrate

3 mL total volume − 0.46 mL concentrate = 2.54 mL diluent

2. x mg/10 mL = 10 mg/1 mL; x mg = 100 mg needed

x mL/100 mg = 1 mL/40 mg; x mL = 2.5 mL concentrate

10 mL total volume − 2.5 mL concentrate = 7.5 mL diluent

3. x mcg/30 mL = 50 mcg/1 mL; x mcg = 1500 mcg needed = 1.5 mg needed

x mL/1.5 mg = 1 mL/5 mg; x mL = 0.3 mL concentrate

30 mL total volume − 0.3 mL concentrate = 29.7 mL diluent

4. x mcg/10 mL = 200 mcg/1 mL; x mcg = 2000 mcg needed = 2 mg needed

x mL/2 mg = 1 mL/5 mg; x mL = 0.4 mL concentrate

10 mL total volume − 0.4 mL concentrate − 9.6 mL diluent

5. x mg/20 mL = 5 mg/1 mL; x mg = 100 mg needed

x mL/100 mg = 1 mL/40 mg; x mL = 2.5 mL concentrate

20 mL total volume − 2.5 mL concentrate = 17.5 mL diluent

6. x mg/10 mL = 50 mg/1 mL; x mg = 500 mg needed

x mL/500 mg = 0.5 mL/250 mg; x mL = 1 mL concentrate

10 mL total volume − 1 mL concentrate = 9 mL diluent needed

7. x mcg/20 mL = 100 mcg/1 mL; x mcg = 2000 mcg needed

x mL/2000 mcg = 1 mL/1000 mcg; x mL = 2 mL concentrate

20 mL total volume − 2 mL concentrate = 18 mL diluent needed

8. x mL/8 mL = 5 mg/1 mL; x mL = 40 mg

x mL/40 mg = 2 mL/100 mg; x mL = 0.8 mL concentrate

8 mL total volume − 0.8 mL concentrate = 7.2 mL diluent

9. x mg/15 mL = 50 mg/1 mL; x mg = 750 mg cefazolin

x mL/750 mg = 5 mL/1000 mg; x mL = 3.75 mL concentrate

15 mL total volume − 3.75 mL concentrate = 11.25 mL diluent

10. x mL/0.6 mg = 1 mL/20 mg; x mL = 0.03 mL concentrate

2 mL total volume − 0.03 mL concentrate = 1.97 mL diluent

11. x mg/25 mL = 2 mg/1 mL; x mg = 50 mg

x mL/50 mg = 1 mL/10 mg; x mL = 5 mL concentrate

25 mL total volume − 5 mL concentrate = 20 mL diluent

12. x mg/20 mL = 25 mg/1 mL; x mg = 500 mg

x mL/500 mg = 1 mL/250 mg; x mL = 2 mL concentrate

20 mL total volume − 2 mL concentrate = 18 mL diluent

13. x mg/10 mL = 0.5 mg/1 mL; x mg = 5 mg

x mL/5 mg = 1 mL/5 mg; x mL = 1 mL concentrate

10 mL total volume − 1 mL concentrate = 9 mL diluent

14. x mg/20 mL = 50 mg/1 mL; x mg = 1000 mg

x mL/1000 mg = 5 mL/2000 mg; x mL = 2.5 mL concentrate

20 mL total volume − 2.5 mL concentrate = 17.5 mL diluent

15. x mcg/3 mL = 10 mcg/1 mL; x mcg = 30 mcg

x mL/30 mcg = 1 mL/50 mcg; x mL = 0.6 mL concentrate

3 mL total volume − 0.6 mL concentrate = 2.4 mL diluent

16. x mcg/5 mL = 5 mcg/1 mL; x mcg = 25 mcg

x mL/25 mcg = 1 mL/50 mcg; x mL = 0.5 mL concentrate

5 mL total volume − 0.5 mL = 4.5 mL diluent

17. x g/100 mL total volume = 30 g/100 mL; x g = 30 g in final product

x mL/30 g = 100 mL/90 g; x mL = 33.333 mL concentrate, rounded to 33.33 mL concentrate

18. a. x mcg/10 mL = 4 mcg/1 mL; x mcg = 40 mcg

x mL/40 mcg = 1 mL/10 mcg; x mL = 4 mL concentrate

b. 10 mL total volume − 4 mL concentrate = 6 mL diluent

19. a. x units/5 mL = 100 units/1 mL; x units = 500 units

x mL/500 units = 1 mL/10,000 units; x mL = 0.05 mL concentrate

b. 5 mL total volume − 0.05 mL concentrate = 4.95 mL diluent

20. a. x mg/5 mL = 50 mg/1 mL; x mg = 250 mg needed

x mL/250 mg = 1 mL/200 mg; x mL = 1.25 mL concentrate

b. 5 mL total volume − 1.25 mL concentrate = 3.75 mL diluent

21 a. x mg/2 mL = 80 mg/1 mL; x mg = 160 mg tobramycin needed

x mL/160 mg = 1 mL/160 mg; x mL = 1 mL concentrate

b. 2 mL total volume − 1 mL concentrate = 1 mL diluent

22. a. x g/1000 mL = 0.45 g/100 mL; x g = 4.5 g

x mL/4.5 g = 100 mL/0.9 g; x mL = 500 mL concentrate

b. 1000 mL total volume − 500 mL concentrate = 500 mL diluent

23. a. x g/50 mL = 5 g/100 mL; x g = 2.5 g dextrose needed

x mL/2.5 g = 100 mL/70 g; x mL = 3.57 mL concentrate

b. 50 mL total volume − 3.57 mL concentrate = 46.43 mL diluent

24. a. x g/500 mL = 35 g/100 mL; x g = 175 g dextrose needed

x mL/175 g = 100 mL/70 g; x mL = 250 mL concentrate

b. 500 mL total volume − 250 mL concentrate = 250 mL diluent

25. a. x g/300 mL = 10 g/100 mL; x g = 30 g needed

x mL/30 g = 100 mL/20 g; x mL = 150 mL concentrate

b. 300 mL total volume − 150 mL concentrate = 150 mL diluent

26. a. x mL/1.5 g = 10 mL/1 g; x mL = 15 mL

b. 100 mL total − 15 mL used = 85 mL remains

27. a. x mL/0.5 g = 5 mL/1 g; x mL = 2.5 mL

b. 100 mL total − 2.5 mL = 97.5 mL remains

28. a. x mL/8 mg = 1 mL/4 mg; x mL = 2 mL

b. 2 mL/dose ÷ 4 doses = 0.5 mL

29. a. x mL/20 mEq = 1 mL/2 mEq; x mL = 10 mL

b. 20 mL total − 10 mL used = 10 mL remains

30. a. x mL/2 g = 10 mL/0.5 g; x mL = 40 mL

b. 100 mL total − 40 mL used = 60 mL remains

8.2 Problem Set

1. Divide all ingredients by 2.

1000 mL D_5W ÷ 2 = 500 mL D_5W per bag

2.5 g lidocaine ÷ 2 = 1.25 g

x mL/1.25 g = 100 mL/20 g; x mL = 6.25 mL lidocaine per bag

500 mg furosemide ÷ 2 = 250 mg

x mL/250 mg = 1 mL/10 mg; x mL = 25 mL furosemide per bag

2. 125 mL/hour × 24 hour = 3000 mL

20 mEq potassium × 3 bags = 60 mEq potassium concentrate

x mL/60 mEq = 1 mL/2 mEq; x mL = 30 mL potassium total

30 mL total × vial/15 mL = 2 vials needed

3. 120 g ÷ 30 g = 4 (so divide the formula by 4), or

4 g ÷ 4 = 1 g coal tar

1 g ÷ 4 = 0.25 g salicylic acid

15 g ÷ 4 = 3.75 g triamcinolone 1% ung

100 g ÷ 4 = 25 g aqua-base ointment

alternatively,

x g/4 g coal tar = 30 g/120 g; x g = 1 g coal tar

x g/1 g salicylic acid = 30 g/120 g; x g = 0.25 g salicylic acid

x g/15 g triamcinolone 1% ung = 30 g/120 g; x g = 3.75 g triamcinolone 1% ung

x g/100 g aqua-base ointment = 30 g/120 g; x g = 25 g aqua-base ointment

4. 150 vaginal suppositories ÷ 30 = 5, so multiply the formula by 5

2.4 g progesterone × 5 = 12 g progesterone

30 g PEG 3350 × 5 = 150 g PEG 3350

90 g PEG 1000 × 5 = 450 g PEG 1000

5. x g/20 mL = 25 g/100 mL; x g = 5 g resin concentrate

20 mL total volume − 5 mL resin concentrate = 15 mL benzoin diluent

6 patients × 5 mL = 30 mL resin concentrate

6 patients × 15 mL diluent = 90 mL diluent

6. 12 fl oz = 30 mL/fl oz = 360 mL total volume

x capsules/16 capsules tetracycline = 360 mL/240 mL; x capsules = 24 capsules tetracycline

x mL/15 mL hydrocortisone = 360 mL/240 mL; x mL = 22.5 mL hydrocortisone

x mL/30 mL lidocaine = 360 mL/240 mL; x mL = 45 mL lidocaine

QSAD 360 mL total volume, approximately 292 mL

7. This solution uses the ratio-proportion method. However, simple multiplication can also be used, as in Example 8.2.2.

4 droppers × 15 mL/dropper = 60 mL and the formula makes 30 mL

x g/1.8 g antipyrine = 60 mL/30 mL; x g = 3.6 g antipyrine

x g/0.5 g benzocaine = 60 mL/30 mL; x g = 1 g benzocaine

x g/30 mL glycerine = 60 mL/30 mL; x g = 60 mL glycerine

8. Multiply each ingredient by 2 to get 2 g tetracycline HCl powder, 5 g ascorbic acid powder, 20 mL sterile saline for injection.

8.3 Problem Set

1.

10		2.5 mL parts 10%
	7.5	44 tol
5		2.5 mL parts 5%
		5 mL total parts 7.5%

x mL $D_{10}W$/200 mL = 2.5 mL parts/5 mL total parts; x mL = 100 mL $D_{10}W$

x mL D_5W/200 mL = 2.5 mL parts/5 mL total parts; x mL = 100 mL D_5W

2.

20		8 mL parts $D_{20}W$
	8	
0		12 mL parts SWFI
		20 mL total parts 8%

x mL $D_{20}W$/400 mL = 8 mL parts/20 mL total parts; x mL = 160 mL $D_{20}W$

x mL/400 mL = 12 mL parts/20 mL total parts; x mL = 240 mL SWFI

3.

20		7.5 mL parts $D_{20}W$
	12.5	
5		7.5 mL parts D_5W
		15 mL total parts $D_{12.5}W$

x mL $D_{20}W/500$ mL = 7.5 mL parts/15 mL total parts; x mL = 250 mL $D_{20}W$

x mL $D_5W/500$ mL = 7.5 mL parts/15 mL total parts; x mL = 250 mL D_5W

Or

20		2.5 mL parts $D_{20}W$
	12.5	
10		7.5 mL parts $D_{10}W$
		10 mL total parts $D_{12.5}W$

x mL $D_{20}W/500$ mL = 2.5 mL parts/10 mL total parts; x mL = 125 mL $D_{20}W$

x mL $D_{10}W/500$ mL $\times$ 7.5 mL parts/10 mL total parts; x mL = 375 mL $D_{10}W$

4.

50		6 mL parts $D_{50}W$
	6	
0		44 mL parts SWFI
		50 mL total parts D_6W

x mL $D_{50}W/250$ mL = 6 mL parts/50 mL parts; x mL = 30 mL $D_{50}W$

x mL SWFI/250 mL = 44 mL parts/50 mL total parts; x mL = 220 mL SWFI

Or

10		6 mL parts $D_{10}W$
	6	
0		4 mL parts SWFI
		10 mL total parts D_6W

x mL $D_{10}W/250$ mL = 6 mL parts/10 mL total parts; x mL = 150 mL $D_{10}W$

x mL SWFI/250 mL = 4 mL parts/10 mL total parts; x mL = 100 mL SWFI

5.

50		2.5 mL parts $D_{50}W$
	7.5	
5		42.5 mL parts D_5W
		45 mL total parts $D_{7.5}W$

x mL $D_{50}W/500$ mL D_5W = 2.5 mL parts $D_{50}W/42.5$ mL parts D_5W; x mL = 29.411 mL, rounded to 29.4 mL $D_{50}W$ must be added

original volume + milliliters of $D_{50}W$ added = final volume; 500 mL + 29.4 mL = 529.4 mL

6.

20		3 mL parts $D_{20}W$
	8	
5		12 mL parts D_5W
		15 mL total parts D_8W

x mL $D_{20}W/250$ mL = 3 mL parts/15 mL total parts; x mL = 50 mL $D_{20}W$

x mL $D_5W/250$ mL = 12 mL parts/15 mL total parts; x mL = 200 mL D_5W

7.

20		7.5 mL parts $D_{20}W$
	7.5	
0		12.5 mL parts SWFI
		20 mL total parts $D_{7.5}W$

x mL $D_{20}W/300$ mL = 7.5 mL parts/20 mL total parts; x mL = 112.5 mL $D_{20}W$

x mL SWFI/300 mL = 12.5 mL parts/20 mL total parts; x mL = 187.5 mL SWFI

8.

20		2.5 mL parts $D_{20}W$
	12.5	
10		7.5 mL parts $D_{10}W$
		10 mL total parts $D_{12.5}W$

x mL $D_{20}W/500$ mL = 2.5 mL parts/10 mL total parts; x mL = 125 mL $D_{20}W$

x mL $D_{10}W/500$ mL = 7.5 mL parts/10 mL total parts; x mL = 375 mL $D_{10}W$

9.

10		2.5 mL parts $D_{10}W$
	7.5	
5		2.5 mL parts D_5W
		5 mL total parts $D_{7.5}W$

x mL $D_{10}W$/150 mL = 2.5 mL parts/5 mL total parts; x mL = 75 mL $D_{10}W$

x mL D_5W/150 mL = 2.5 mL parts/5 mL total parts; x mL = 75 mL D_5W

10.

20		4 mL parts $D_{20}W$
	9	
5		11 mL parts D_5W
		15 mL total parts D_9W

x mL $D_{20}W$/25 mL = 4 mL parts/15 mL total parts; x mL = 6.6666 mL $D_{20}W$, rounded to 6.7 mL $D_{20}W$

x mL D_5W/25 mL = 11 mL parts/15 mL total parts; x mL = 18.3333 mL D_5W, rounded to 18.3 mL D_5W

11.

20		2.5 mL parts $D_{20}W$
	12.5	
10		7.5 mL parts $D_{10}W$
		10 mL total parts $D_{12.5}W$

x mL $D_{20}W$/300 mL = 2.5 mL parts/10 mL total parts; x mL = 75 mL $D_{20}W$

x mL $D_{10}W$/300 mL = 7.5 mL parts/10 mL total parts; x mL = 225 mL $D_{10}W$

12.

50		10 mL parts $D_{50}W$
	15	
5		35 mL parts D_5W
		45 mL total parts $D_{15}W$

x mL $D_{50}W$/500 mL = 10 mL parts/45 mL total parts; x mL = 111.111 mL $D_{50}W$, rounded to 111.1 mL $D_{50}W$

x mL D_5W/500 mL = 35 mL parts/45 mL total parts; x mL = 388.888 mL D_5W, rounded to 388.9 mL D_5W

13.

20		7 mL parts $D_{20}W$
	12	
5		8 mL parts D_5W
		15 mL total parts $D_{12}W$

x mL $D_{20}W$/100 mL = 7 mL parts/15 mL total parts; x mL = 46.666 mL $D_{20}W$, rounded to 46.7 mL $D_{20}W$

x mL D_5W/100 mL = 8 mL parts/15 mL total parts; x mL = 53.333 mL D_5W, rounded to 53.3 mL D_5W

14.

10		2 oz parts 10%
	3	
1		7 oz parts 1%
		9 oz total parts 3%

x oz 10%/2 oz = 2 oz parts/9 oz total parts; x oz = 0.444 oz 10%, rounded to 0.44 oz

x oz 1%/2 oz = 7 oz parts/9 oz total parts; x oz = 1.555 oz 1%, rounded to 1.56 oz

15.

15		2.5 g parts 15%
	7.5	
5		7.5 g parts 5%
		10 g total parts 7.5%

x g 15%/30 g = 2.5 g parts/10 g total parts; x g = 7.5 g 15%

x g 5%/30 g = 7.5 g parts/10 g total parts; x g = 22.5 g 5%

16.

100		10 mL parts 100%
	80	
70		20 mL parts 70%
		30 mL total parts 80%

x mL 100%/1000 mL = 10 mL parts/30 mL total parts; x mL = 333.333 mL 100%, rounded to 333 mL 100%

x mL 70%/1000 mL = 20 mL parts/30 mL total parts; x mL = 666.666 mL 70%, rounded to 667 mL 70%

17.

50		7.5 mL parts $D_{50}W$
	12.5	
5		37.5 mL parts D_5W
		45 mL total parts $D_{12.5}W$

x mL $D_{50}W$/3000 mL = 7.5 mL parts/45 mL total parts = 500 mL $D_{50}W$

x mL D_5W/3000 mL = 37.5 mL parts/45 mL total parts; x mL = 2500 mL D_5W

18.

30		3.5 mL parts 30%
	5	
1.5		25 mL parts 1.5%
		28.5 mL total parts 5%

x mL 30%/100 mL = 3.5 mL parts/28.5 mL total parts; x mL = 12.280701 mL 30%, rounded to 12.3 mL 30%

x mL 1.5%/100 mL = 25 mL parts/28.5 mL total parts; x mL = 87.719298 mL 1.5%, rounded to 87.7 mL 1.5%

19.

5		2 g parts 5%
	3	
1		2 g parts 1%
		4 g total parts 3%

x g 5%/120 g = 2 g parts/4 g total parts; x g = 60 g 5%

x g 1%/120 g = 2 g parts/4 g total parts; x g = 60 g 1%

20.

100		20 g parts coal tar solution
	20	
0		80 g parts ointment base
		100 g total parts 20% aligation ointment

x g ointment base/2400 g = 80 g parts/100 g total parts; x g = 1920 g ointment base

x g coal tar solution/2400 g = 20 g parts/100 g total parts; x g = 480 g coal tar solution

21.

20		10 g parts 20% zinc
	10	
0		10 g parts petrolatum
		20 g total parts 10% alligation ointment

x g 20% zinc/45 g = 10 g parts/20 g total parts; x g = 22.5 g 20% zinc

x g petrolatum/45 g = 10 g parts/20 g total parts; x g = 22.5 g petrolatum

22.

70		35 mL parts 70%
	50	
15		20 mL parts 15%
		55 mL total parts 50%

x mL 70%/1000 mL = 35 mL parts/55 mL total parts; x mL = 636.3636 mL 70%, rounded to 636.4 mL 70%

x mL 15%/1000 mL = 20 mL parts/55 mL total parts; x mL = 363.636 mL 15%, rounded to 363.6 mL 15%

23. Note: 1 gallon = 3840 mL

100		8 mL parts 100%
	10	
2		90 mL parts 2%
		98 mL total parts 10%

x mL 100%/3840 mL = 8 mL parts/98 mL total parts; x mL = 313.46938 mL 100%, rounded to 313.5 mL 100%

x mL 2%/3840 mL = 90 mL parts/98 mL total parts; x mL = 3526.5306 mL 2%, rounded to 3526.5 mL 2%

24.

10		0.25 mL parts 10% (1:10)
	0.5	
0.25		9.5 mL parts 0.25% (1:400)
		9.75 mL total parts 0.5%

x mL 1:10/30 mL = 0.25 mL parts/9.75 mL total parts; x mL = 0.7692 mL 1:10, rounded to 0.8 mL 1:10

x mL 1:400/30 mL = 9.5 mL parts/9.75 mL total parts; x mL = 29.2307 mL 1:400, rounded to 29.2 mL 1:400

25.

0.4		0.07 mL parts 1:250
	0.2	
0.13		0.2 mL parts 1:750
		0.27 mL total parts 0.2% aligation solution

x mL 1:250/120 mL = 0.07 mL parts/0.27 mL total parts; x mL = 31.111 mL 1:250, rounded to 31.1 mL 1:250

x mL 1:750/120 mL = 0.2 mL parts/0.27 mL total parts; x mL = 88.888 mL 1:750, rounded to 88.9 mL 1:750

26. a.

20		2.5 mL parts $D_{20}W$
	12.5	
10		7.5 mL parts $D_{10}W$
		10 mL total parts $D_{12.5}W$

x mL $D_{20}W$/300 mL = 2.5 mL parts/10 mL total parts; x mL = 75 mL $D_{20}W$

x mL $D_{10}W$/300 mL = 7.5 mL parts/10 mL total parts; x mL = 225 mL $D_{10}W$

b. 225 mL $D_{10}W$/bag × 3 bags = 675 mL $D_{10}W$

75 mL $D_{20}W$/bag × 3 bags = 225 mL $D_{20}W$

27.

20		3 mL parts $D_{20}W$
	8	
5		12 mL parts D_5W
		15 mL total parts D_8W

x mL $D_{20}W$/1000 mL = 3 mL parts/15 mL total parts; x mL = 200 mL $D_{20}W$

x mL D_5W/1000 mL = 12 mL parts/15 mL total parts; x mL = 800 mL D_5W

24 mEq × 1 mL/4mEq = 6 mL sodium chloride

10 mEq × 1 mL/2mEq = 5 mL potassium chloride

300 mg × 1 mL/25 mg = 12 mL aminophylline

500 mL bag will require dividing each by 2
400 mL D_5W
100 mL $D_{20}W$
3 mL sodium chloride

2.5 mL potassium chloride
6 mL aminophylline

28. The concentration is 12.5%. To solve this problem, determine what value is exactly between 20% and 5%.

20% − 5% = 15%
15% ÷ 2 = 7.5%
5% + 7.5% = 12.5%
20% − 7.5% = 12.5%

29. 1:400 = 0.0025
20 mL × 0.0025 g/mL = 0.05 g

1:150 = 0.0067
30 L = 30,000 mL
30,000 mL × 0.0067 g/mL = 201 g

30,000 mL + 20 mL = 30,020 total volume
0.05 g + 201 g = 201.05 g total active ingredients, rounded to 201 g
(30,020)(x) = 201 g
x = 0.0067 = 0.67%

30. x g/30 g = 2 g/100 g; x g = 0.6 g of 2%

x g/30 g = 8 g/100 g; x g = 2.4 g of 8%

0.6 g of 2% + 2.4 g of 8% = 3 g total weight of active ingredient

30 g of 2% + 30 g of 8% = 60 g total weight of cream

3 g/60 g × 100 = 5%

31. x g/100 g = 8 g/100 g; x g = 8 g of 8%

x g/200 g = 3 g/100 g; x g = 6 g of 3%

8 g of 8% + 6 g of 3% = 14 g total weight of active ingredient

100 g of 8% + 200 g of 3% = 300 g total weight

14 g/300 g × 100 = 4.666%, rounded to 4.7%

32. 1000 mL of 15% + 500 mL of 3% + 300 mL of 70% = 1800 mL total volume

amount of alcohol in 1000 mL of 15% alcohol solution: 15% × 1000 mL = 150 mL

amount of alcohol in 500 mL of 3% alcohol solution: 3% × 500 mL = 15 mL

amount of alcohol in 300 mL of 70% alcohol solution: 70% × 300 mL = 210 mL

150 mL + 15 mL + 210 mL = 375 mL active ingredients, total alcohol in the 1800 mL

375 mL/1800 mL × 100 = 20.83%

33. hydrogen peroxide 1.5%: x g/30 mL = 1.5 g/100 mL; x g = 0.45 g active ingredient

hydrogen peroxide 30%: x g/10 mL = 30 g/100 mL; x g = 3 g active ingredient

total volume: 30 mL + 10 mL = 40 mL

(0.45 g + 3 g)/40 mL × 100 = 8.625%, rounded to 8.6%

34. alcohol 70%: x g/300 mL = 70 g/100 mL; x g = 210 g active ingredient

alcohol 95%: x g/200 mL = 95 g/100 mL; x g = 190 g active ingredient

total volume: 300 mL + 200 mL = 500 mL

(210 g + 190 g)/500 mL × 100 = 80%

35. alcohol 50%: x g/100 mL = 50 g/100 mL; x g = 50 g active ingredient

alcohol 70%: x g/100 mL = 70 g/100 mL; x g = 70 g active ingredient

alcohol 95%: x g/100 mL = 95 g/100 mL; x g = 95 g active ingredient

total volume: 100 mL + 100 mL + 100 mL = 300 mL

(50 g + 70 g + 95 g)/300 mL × 100 = 71.666%, rounded to 71.7%

36. coal tar ung 5%: x g/60 g = 5 g/100 g; x g = 3 g active ingredient

coal tar ung 10%: x g/60 g = 10 g/100 g; x g = 6 g active ingredient

total amount: 60 g + 60 g = 120 g

(3 g + 6 g)/120 g × 100 = 7.5%

37. ichthamol 50%: x g/20 g = 50 g/100 g; x g = 10 g active ingredient

ichthamol 10%: x g/10 g = 10 g/100 g; x g = 1 g active ingredient

ichthamol 5%: x g/60 g = 5 g/100 g; x g = 3 g active ingredient

total amount: 20 g + 10 g + 60 g = 90 g

(10 g + 1 g + 3 g)/90 g × 100 = 15.555%, rounded to 15.6%

38. witch hazel 14%: x g/300 mL = 14 g/100 mL; x = 42 g active ingredient

alcohol 95%: x g/100 mL = 95 g/100 mL; x g = 95 g active ingredient

total volume: 300 mL + 100 mL + 500 mL = 900 mL

(42 g + 95 g)/900 mL × 100 = 15.2222%, rounded to 15.2%

39. zinc oxide 20%: x g/60 g = 20 g/100 g; x g = 12 g active ingredient

total amount: 60 g + 120 g = 180 g

12 g/180 g × 100 = 6.6666%, rounded to 6.7%

40. lidocaine 2%: x g/20 mL = 2 g/100 mL; x g = 0.4 g active ingredient

total volume: 20 mL + 10 mL + 5 mL = 35 mL

0.4 g/35 mL × 100 = 1.14285%, rounded to 1.1%

8.4 Problem Set

1. a. (100 × 4 mg) ÷ 3.5 = 114.28 mg, rounded to 114 mg
   b. 20 mg × 6 = 120 mg
   c. 120 mg × 6 = 720 mg
   d. 720 mg − 120 mg = 600 mg
   e. x mg mixture/20 mg = 720 mg/120 mg; (20 × 720) ÷ 120 mg; x mg = 120 mg

2. a. (100 × 5 mg) ÷ 3 = 166.66 mg, rounded to 167 mg
   b. 5 mg × 34 = 170 mg
   c. 170 mg × 35 = 5950 mg
   d. 5950 mg − 170 mg = 5780 mg
   e. x mg mixture/5 mg = 5950 mg/170 mg; (5 × 5950) ÷ 170 mg; x mg = 175 mg

3. a. (100 × 5 mg) ÷ 5.5 = 90.90 mg, rounded to 91 mg
   b. 12 mg × 8 = 96 mg
   c. 96 mg × 15 = 1440 mg
   d. 1440 mg − 96 mg = 1344 mg

e. x mg mixture/12 mg = 1440 mg/96 mg;
(12 × 1440) ÷ 96 mg;
x mg = 180 mg

4. a. (100 × 6 mg) ÷ 5 = 120 mg
   b. 25 mg × 5 = 125 mg
   c. 125 mg × 6 = 750 mg
   d. 750 mg − 125 mg = 625 mg
   e. x mg mixture/25 mg = 750 mg/125 mg;
   (25 × 750) ÷ 125 mg;
   x mg = 150 mg

5. a. (100 × 6 mg) ÷ 4 = 150 mg
   b. 6 mg × 25 = 150 mg
   c. 150 mg × 25 = 3750 mg
   d. 3750 mg − 150 mg = 3600 mg
   e. x mg mixture/6 mg = 3750 mg/150 mg;
   (6 × 3750) ÷ 150 mg;
   x mg = 150 mg

6. a. (100 × 4 mg) ÷ 4 = 100 mg
   b. 22.5 mg × 5 = 112.5 mg
   c. 112.5 mg × 5 = 562.5 mg
   d. 562.5 mg − 112.5 mg = 450 mg
   e. x mg mixture/22.5 mg =
   562.5 mg/112.5 mg;
   (22.5 × 562.5) ÷ 112.5 mg;
   x mg = 112.5 mg

7. a. (100 × 4 mg) ÷ 5 = 80 mg
   b. 17.75 mg × 5 = 88.75 mg
   c. 88.75 mg × 5 = 443.75 mg
   d. 443.75 mg − 88.75 mg = 355 mg
   e. x mg mixture/17.75 mg =
   443.75 mg/88.75 mg;
   (17.75 × 443.75) ÷ 88.75 mg;
   x mg = 88.75 mg

8. a. (100 × 5 mg) ÷ 6 = 83.33 mg, rounded to
   83 mg
   b. 18 mg × 7 = 126 mg
   c. 126 mg × 5 = 630 mg
   d. 630 mg − 126 mg = 504 mg
   e. x mg mixture/18 mg = 630 mg/126 mg;
   (18 × 630) ÷ 126 mg;
   x mg = 90 mg

9. a. (100 × 5 mg) ÷ 5 = 100 mg
   b. 30 mg × 4 = 120 mg
   c. 120 mg × 4 = 480 mg
   d. 480 mg − 120 mg = 360 mg
   e. x mg mixture/30 mg = 480 mg/120 mg;
   (30 × 480) ÷ 120 mg;
   x mg = 120 mg

10. a. (100 × 3 mg) ÷ 5 = 60 mg
    b. 8.75 mg × 7 = 61.25 mg
    c. 61.25 mg × 7 = 428.75 mg
    d. 428.75 mg − 61.25 mg = 367.5 mg
    e. x mg mixture/8.75 mg =
    428.75 mg/61.25 mg;
    (8.75 × 428.75) ÷ 61.25 mg;
    x mg = 61.25 mg

11. a. 0.5 mL × 2 = 1.0 mL
    b. 1.0 mL × 4 = 4.0 mL
    c. 4.0 mL − 1.0 mL = 3.0 mL
    d. x mL mixture/0.5 mL = 4.0 mL/1.0 mL;
    (0.5 × 4.0) ÷ 1.0;
    x mL = 2.0 mL

12. a. 0.3 mL × 2 = 0.6 mL
    b. 0.6 mL × 5 = 3.0 mL
    c. 3.0 mL − 0.6 mL = 2.4 mL
    d. x mL mixture/0.3 mL = 3.0 mL/0.6 mL;
    (0.3 × 3.0) ÷ 0.6;
    x mL = 1.5 mL

13. a. 0.75 mL × 2 = 1.5 mL
    b. 1.5 mL × 5 = 7.5 mL
    c. 7.5 mL − 1.5 mL = 6.0 mL
    d. x mL mixture/0.75 mL = 7.5 mL/1.5 mL;
    (0.75 × 7.5) ÷ 1.5;
    x mL = 3.75 mL

14. a. 0.25 mL × 6 = 1.5 mL
    b. 1.5 mL × 6 = 9.0 mL
    c. 9.0 mL − 1.5 mL = 7.5 mL
    d. x mL mixture/0.25 mL = 9.0 mL/1.5 mL;
    (0.25 × 9.0) ÷ 1.5;
    x mL = 1.5 mL

15. a. 0.45 mL × 3 = 1.35 mL
    b. 1.35 × 3 = 4.05 mL
    c. 4.05 mL − 1.35 mL = 2.7 mL
    d. x mL mixture/0.45 mL =
    4.05 mL/1.35 mL;
    (0.45 × 4.05) ÷ 1.35;
    x mL = 1.35 mL

16. a. 0.95 mL × 2 = 1.9 mL
    b. 1.9 mL × 2 = 3.8 mL
    c. 3.8 mL − 1.9 mL = 1.9 mL
    d. x mL mixture/0.95 mL = 3.8 mL/1.9 mL;
    (0.95 × 3.8) ÷ 1.9;
    x mL = 1.9 mL

17. a. 0.5 mL × 2 = 1.0 mL
    b. 1.0 mL × 4 = 4.0 mL
    c. 4.0 mL − 1.0 mL = 3.0 mL

d. x mL mixture/0.5 mL = 4.0 mL/1.0 mL;
   (0.5 × 4.0) ÷ 1.0;
   x mL = 2.0 mL

18. a. 0.5 mL × 2 = 1.0 mL
    b. 1.0 mL × 5 = 5.0 mL
    c. 5.0 mL − 1.0 mL = 4.0 mL
    d. x mL mixture/0.5 mL = 5.0 mL/1.0 mL;
       (0.5 × 5.0) ÷ 1.0;
       x mL = 2.5 mL

19. a. 0.85 mL × 2 = 1.7 mL
    b. 1.7 mL × 2 = 3.4 mL
    c. 3.4 mL − 1.7 mL = 1.7 mL
    d. x mL mixture/0.85 mL = 3.4 mL/1.7 mL;
       (0.85 × 3.4) ÷ 1.7;
       x mL= 1.7 mL

20. a. 0.05 mL × 20 = 1.0 mL
    b. 1.0 mL × 20 = 20.0 mL
    c. 20.0 mL − 1.0 mL = 19.0 mL
    d. x mL mixture/0.05 mL = 20.0 mL/1.0 mL;
       (0.05 × 20) ÷ 1.0;
       x mL = 1.0 mL

Chapter 9

9.1 Problem Set

1. $135,000.00 + $52,000.00 + $23,000.00
   + $6000.00 + $4000.00 + $2000.00 +
   $4000.00 + $4000.00 + $750,000.00 =
   $980,000.00 overhead;
   $980,000.00 × 0.18 = $176,400.00 profit;
   $980,000.00 + $176,400.00 = $1,156,400.00

2. $1,401,489.00 − $980,000.00 = $421,489.00
   profit;
   ($421,489.00 ÷ $980,000.00) × 100 = 43%

3. $1,191,692.00 − $980,000.00 = $211,692.00
   profit;
   ($211,692.00 ÷ $980,000.00) × 100 = 21.6%,
   rounded to 22%

4. $72,000.00 + $52,000.00 + $13,000.00
   + $5500.00 + $2000.00 + $1500.00 +
   $4000.00 + $3500.00 + $50,000.00 =
   $203,500; $203,500 × 0.2 = $40,700.00
   profit;
   $203,500.00 + $40,700.00 = $244,200.00

5. $991,982.00 − $203,500.00 = $788,482.00;
   ($788,482.00 ÷ $203,500) × 100 = 387.5%,
   rounded to 388%

6. $1,248,301.00 − $203,500.00 =
   $1,044,801.00;
   ($1,044,801.00 ÷ $203,500.00) × 100 =
   513.4%, rounded to 513%

7. $54,617.53 − $3700.83 = $50,916.70

8. $13,033.06 × 0.22 = $2867.27 profit;
   $13,033.06 + $2867.27 = $15,900.33

9. a. $3.96 ÷ 2 = $1.98/50 tablets; $1.98 +
      $4.25 = $6.23 overall cost;
      $8.59 − $6.23 = $2.36 net profit

   b. ($2.36 ÷ $6.23) × 100 = 37.9%, rounded
      to 38%

10. a. ($8.50 ÷ 500) × 30 = $0.51; $0.51 +
       $4.25 = $4.76;
       $14.80 − $4.76 = $10.04

    b. ($10.04 ÷ $4.76) × 100 = 210.9%,
       rounded to 211%

11. a. ($118.50 ÷ 100) × 30 = $35.55; $35.55 +
       $4.25 = $39.80;
       $45.50 − $39.80 = $5.70

    b. ($5.70 ÷ $39.80) × 100 = 14%

12. a. ($83.50 ÷ 500) × 100 = $16.70; $16.70 +
       $4.25 = $20.95;
       $23.16 − $20.95 = $2.21

    b. ($2.21 ÷ $20.95) × 100 = 10.5%, rounded
       to 11%

13. a. ($41.20 ÷ 100) × 90 = $37.08; $37.08 +
       $4.25 = $41.33;
       $41.70 − $41.33 = $0.37

    b. ($0.37 ÷ $41.33) × 100 = 0.9%

14. a. ($37.50 ÷ 480 mL) × 240 = $18.75;
       $18.75 + $4.25 = $23.00;
       $25.34 − $23.00 = $2.34

    b. ($2.34 ÷ $23.00) × 100 = 10%

15. a. $62.30 ÷ 6 = $10.38; $10.38 + $4.25 =
       $14.63;
       $17.90 − $14.63 = $3.27

    b. ($3.27 ÷ $14.63) × 100 = 22%

16. $5.89 × 0.2 = $1.18;
    $5.89 − $1.18 = $4.71

17. $1.19 × 0.15 = $0.18;
    $1.19 − $0.18 = $1.01

18. $7.29 × 0.3 = $2.19;
    $7.29 − $2.19 = $5.10

19. $5.69 × 0.15 = $0.85;
    $5.69 − $0.85 = $4.84

20. $3.89 × 0.25 = $0.97;
    $3.89 − $0.97 = $2.92

21. $4.26 × 0.3 = $1.28;
    $4.26 − $1.28 = $2.98

22. $8.69 × 0.5 = $4.35;
    $8.69 − $4.35 = $4.34

23. $2.99 × 0.4 = $1.20;
    $2.99 − $1.20 = $1.79

24. $12.50 × 0.3 = $3.75;
    $12.50 + $3.75 = $16.25;
    $16.25 × 12 tubes = $195.00

25. $111.60 ÷ 36 = $3.10/bottle;
    $3.10 + $1.75 = $4.85

26. $15.60 × 0.25 = $3.90 markup; $15.60 +
    $3.90 = $19.50

27. $30.75 − $24.80 = $5.95;
    ($5.95 ÷ $24.80) × 100% = 24%

28. $650.00 − $520.00 = $130.00

29. Selling price: $650.00 ÷ 1000 tablets =
    $0.65/tablet

    Pharmacy's purchase price: $520.00 ÷ 1000
    tablets = $0.52/tablet

    Cost to dispense: $2.05 ÷ 100 tablets =
    $0.02/tablet;
    $0.65 − $0.54 = $0.11 net profit

30. $120.50 × 0.25 = $30.13 markup; $120.50 +
    $30.13 = $150.63 selling price

31. $24.00 × 0.15 = $3.60 markup; $24.00 +
    $3.60 = $27.60 selling price

32. $200.00 × 0.27 = $54.00 markup; $200.00 +
    $54.00 = $254.00 selling price

33. $27.50 × 0.21 = $5.78 markup; $27.50 +
    $5.78 = $33.28 selling price

34. $67.50 × 0.18 = $12.15 markup; $67.50 +
    $12.15 = $79.65 selling price

35. $840.00 × 0.32 = $268.80 markup; $840.00
    + $268.80 = $1108.80 selling price

36. $550.00 × 0.3 = $165.00 markup; $550.00 +
    $165.00 = $715.00 selling price

37. $150.63 + $27.60 + $254.00 + $33.28 +
    $79.65 + $1108.80 + $715.00 = $2368.96

9.2 Problem Set

1. ($48.90 ÷ 60) × 20 = $16.30; $16.30 × 0.13
    = $2.12;
    $16.30 − $2.12 = $14.18

2. ($84.07 ÷ 100) × 30 = $25.22; $25.22 × 0.13
    = $3.28;
    $25.22 − $3.28 = $21.94

3. ($30.25 ÷ 1000) × 100 = $3.03; $3.03 × 0.13
    = $0.39;
    $3.03 − $0.39 = $2.64

4. ($1204.68 ÷ 500) × 30 = $7.24; $7.24 × 0.04
    = $0.29;
    $7.24 + $0.29 + $6.25 = $13.78

5. ($39.78 ÷ 100) × 60 = $23.87; $23.87 × 0.04
    = $0.95;
    $23.87 + $0.95 + $6.25 = $31.07

6. ($317.50 ÷ 30) × 20 = $211.67; $211.67 ×
    0.04 = $8.47;
    $211.67 + $8.47 + $6.25 = $226.39

7. a. ($71.35 ÷ 100) × 50 = $35.68; $35.68 ×
    0.115 = $4.10;
    $35.68 − $4.10 = $31.58

    b. $35.68 × 0.035 = $1.25;
    $1.25 + $35.68 = $36.93

    c. $35.68 + $1.25 + $4.50 = $41.43

    d. $41.43 − $31.58 = $9.85

8. a. $36.35 × 2 = $72.70;
    $72.70 × 0.115 = $8.36;
    $72.70 − $8.36 = $64.34

    b. $72.70 × 0.035 = $2.54;
    $2.54 + $72.70 = $75.24

    c. $72.70 + $2.54 + $4.50 = $79.74

    d. $79.74 − $64.34 = $15.40

9. a. ($302.35 ÷ 30) × 10 = $100.78; $100.78
    × 0.115 = $11.59; $100.78 − $11.59 =
    $89.19

    b. $100.78 × 0.035 = $3.53;
    $3.53 + $100.78 = $104.31

c. $100.78 + $3.53 + $4.50 = $108.81

d. $108.81 − $89.19 = $19.62

10. a. ($117.35 ÷ 50) × 6 = $14.08; $14.08 × 0.115 = $1.62;
$14.08 − $1.62 = $12.46

b. $14.08 × 0.035 = $0.49;
$0.49 + $14.08 = $14.57

c. $14.08 + $0.49 + $4.50 = $19.07

d. $19.07 − $12.46 = $6.61

11. a. ($85.35 ÷ 80) × 15 = $16.00; $16.00 × 0.115 = $1.84;
$16.00 − $1.84 = $14.16

b. $16.00 × 0.035 = $0.56;
$0.56 + $16.00 = $16.56

c. $16.00 + $0.56 + $4.50 = $21.06

d. $21.06 − $14.16 = $6.90

12. a. $310.00 × 6 = $1860.00

b. $15.75 + $106.50 + $27.80 + $210.00 + $47.50 + $105.25 + $160.00 + $52.60 + $150.00 + $210.00 + $76.00 + $10.50 + $28.00 + $62.50 + $210.00 + $210.00 + $17.00 = $1699.40

c. positive

d. $1860.00 − $1699.40 = $160.60

13. a. $1699.40 × 0.03 = $50.98;
$2.00 × 17 = $34.00;
$1699.40 + $50.98 + $34.00 = $1784.38

b. less

c. $160.60 gross profit with capitation − $50.98 gross profit without capitation = $109.62 (disregard $34.00 dispensing fee because the gross profit calculation includes only the cost of the drugs)

14. a. $275.00 × 10 = $2750.00

b. $89.63 + $126.54 + $420.45 + $117.50 + $46.75 = $800.87

c. $2750.00 − $800.87 = $1949.13

15. a. $275.00 × 12 = $3300.00

b. $78.26 + $75.23 + $25.48 + $128.46 + $21.86 + $61.89 + $41.20 + $16.50 + $5.80 + $3.87 + $21.67 + $58.24 = $538.46

c. $3300.00 − $538.46 = $2761.54

16. a. $225.00 × 40 = $9000.00

b. $1867.50 + $60.00 = $1927.50

c. $9000.00 − $1927.50 = $7072.50

17. a. $210.00 × 42 = $8820.00

b. $4.25 × 31 = $131.75;
$131.75 + $2389.00 = $2520.75

c. $8820.00 − $2520.75 = $6299.25

9.3 Problem Set

1. (700 − 80) ÷ 500 = 1

2. (1000 − 118) ÷ 500 = 1.764, rounded down to 1

3. (1000 − 180) ÷ 500 = 1.64, rounded down to 1

4. 0

5. (150 − 28) ÷ 100 = 1

6. 0

7. (120 − 12) ÷ 50 = 2

8. 0

9. 0

10. 3, 4

11. 1, 1, 2

12. 1

13. 1, 1

14. 3

15. 2, 2, 1

16. 2, 1

17. 1, 1

18. 1, 3, 2, 2

19. 0, 1, 3

20. 1, 1, 2, 1

21. 1, 3

22. 1

23. 1

24. 3

25. 3

26. 2

27. 1

28. 0

29. 1

30. 1

31. 2

32. 2

33. 0

34. 1

35. 1

36. 0

37. 7, 2100, 20, 0, 525

38. a. $38,207.00 ÷ 7 = $5458.14; $183,445.00 ÷ $5458.14 = 33.6 days, rounded to 34 days

   b. 6 × $5458.14 = $32,748.84 over his goal

39. a. $26,504.00 ÷ 7 = $3786.29; $123,490.00 ÷ $3786.29 = 32.6 days, rounded to 33 days

   b. 7 × $3786.29 = $26,504.03 over his goal

40. $147,210.00 ÷ 24 days = $6133.75/day; $6133.75 × 7 days = $42,936.25

41. $51,280.00 + $5000.00 = $56,280.00; $56,280.00 ÷ 7 = $8040.00

42. $63,910.00 − $48,891.00 = $15,019.00; ($15,019.00 ÷ $48,891.00) × 100 = 30.7%, rounded to 31%

43. a. $58,223.00 × 0.21 = $12,226.83; $58,223.00 − $12,226.83 = $45,996.17

   b. $45,996.17 ÷ 7 = $6570.88; $164,590.00 ÷ $6570.88 = 25 days

   c. 31 days − 25 days = 6 days; 6 days × $6570.88 = $39,425.28 below

44. a. $28,223.00 × 0.26 = $7337.98; $28,223.00 + $7337.98 = $35,560.98

   b. $184,520.00 ÷ $4031.86 = 45.8 days, rounded to 46 days

c. 46 days − 34 days = 12 days; 12 days × $4031.86 = $48,382.32 above

45. $1,612,000.00 ÷ $132,936.00 = 12.1 times

46. $1,768,000.00 ÷ $156,200.00 = 11.3 times

47. $20,800.00 ÷ $520.00 = 40 times

48. $5760.00 ÷ $178.00 = 32.4 times

49. $7213.00 ÷ $360.00 = 20

50. $5060.00 ÷ $320.00 = 15.8 times

51. $6000.00 ÷ $385.00 = 15.6 times

52. $52,500.00 ÷ $5000.00 = 10.5 times

53. ($8294.00 − $2138.00) ÷ 6 = $1026.00

54. ($18,350.00 − $1567.00) ÷ 12 = $1398.58 each

Chapter 10

10.1 Problem Set

1. 6 gal × 4 qt/1 gal × 2 pt/1 qt × 16 f ʒ/1 pt = 768 f ʒ

2. 1 f ʒ × 6 f ʒ/1 f ʒ × 60 ♏ /1 f ʒ = 360 ♏; 3 f ʒ × 60 ♏/1 f ʒ = 180 ♏; 360 ♏ + 180 ♏ + 7 ♏ = 547 ♏

3. a. 479 f ʒ × 1 f ʒ/6 f ʒ = 79 r.5, or 79 f ʒ, 5f ʒ

   b. 79 f ʒ × 1 pt/16 f ʒ = 4 pt r.15, or 4 pt, 15 f ʒ

   c. so 479 f ʒ = 4 pt, 15 f ʒ, 5 f ʒ

4. 1 ℔ × 12 ʒ/1 ℔ × 8 ʒ/1 ʒ = 96 ʒ; 6 ʒ × 8 ʒ/1 ʒ = 48 ʒ; 48 ʒ + 96 ʒ = 144 ʒ

5. a. 6000 gr × 1 ℈/20 gr = 300 ℈

   b. 300 ℈ × 1 ʒ/3 ℈ = 100 ʒ

   c. 100 ʒ × 1 ʒ/8 ʒ = 12 ʒ, r.4 ʒ

   d. 12 ʒ × 1 ℔/12 ʒ = 1 ℔, so 6000 gr = 1 ℔, 4 ʒ

6. 3 qt × 2 pt/1 qt × 16 f ʒ/1 pt × 6 f ʒ/1 f ʒ = 576 f ʒ

7. 10 ʒ × 8 ʒ/1 ʒ × 3 ℈/1 ʒ × 20 gr/1 ℈ = 4800 gr; 2 ʒ × 3 ℈/1 ʒ × 20 gr/1 ℈ = 120 gr; 1 ℈ × 20 gr/1 ℈ = 20 gr; 4800 gr + 120 gr + 20 gr = 4940 gr

8. 6 pt × 16 f ʒ/1 pt × 6 f ʒ /1 f ʒ = 576 f ʒ

9. 15 ℔ × 12 ℥/1 ℔ = 180 ℥

10. 12 f ℥ × 1 f ℥/6 f ℥ = 2 f ℥

10.2 Problem Set

1. 3 qt × 960 mL/1 qt = 2880 mL

2. 300 mL × 1 f ℥/30 mL = 10 f ℥

3. 75 mL × 1 f ℥/5 mL = 15 f ℥

4. 120 mL × 1 f ℥/30 mL = 4 f ℥

5. 15 mL × 1 f ℥/30 mL = 0.5 f ℥, expressed as ½ f ℥

6. 6 pt × 480 mL/1 pt = 2880 mL; 2880 mL × 1 f ℥/5 mL = 576 f ℥

7. 60 mL × 1 f ℥/30 mL = 2 f ℥; 2 f ℥ × 6 f ℥/1 f ℥ = 12 f ℥

8. 180 mL × 1 f ℥/30 mL = 6 f ℥; 6 f ℥ × 6 f ℥/1 f ℥ = 36 f ℥

9. 3 pt × 480 mL/1 pt × 1 f ℥/30 mL = 48 f ℥; 48 f ℥ × 30 mL/1 f ℥ = 1440 mL

10. 8 f ℥ × 30 mL/1 f ℥ = 240 mL; 240 mL × 1 f ℥/5 mL = 48 f ℥

11. ½ f ℥ × 30 mL/1 f ℥ = 15 mL

12. 1 f ℥ × 30 mL/1 f ℥ = 30 mL

13. 2 f ℥ × 30 mL/1 f ℥ = 60 mL

14. 3 f ℥ × 30 mL/1 f ℥ = 90 mL

15. 4 f ℥ × 30 mL/1 f ℥ = 120 mL

16. 5 f ℥ × 30 mL/1 f ℥ = 150 mL

17. 6 f ℥ × 30 mL/1 f ℥ = 180 mL

18. 7 f ℥ × 30 mL/1 f ℥ = 210 mL

19. 8 f ℥ × 30 mL/1 f ℥ = 240 mL

20. 9 f ℥ × 30 mL/1 f ℥ = 270 mL

21. 10 f ℥ × 30 mL/1 f ℥ = 300 mL

22. 11 f ℥ × 30 mL/1 f ℥ = 330 mL

23. 12 f ℥ × 30 mL/1 f ℥ = 360 mL

24. 13 f ℥ × 30 mL/1 f ℥ = 390 mL

25. 14 f ℥ × 30 mL/1 f ℥ = 420 mL

26. 15 f ℥ × 30 mL/1 f ℥ = 450 mL

27. 16 f ℥ × 30 mL/1 f ℥ = 480 mL

28. 1 pt × 480 mL/1 pt = 480 mL

29. 2 pt × 480 mL/1 pt = 960 mL

30. 3 pt × 480 mL/1 pt = 1440 mL

31. 240 mL × 1 f ℥/30 mL = 8 f ℥

32. 180 mL × 1 f ℥/30 mL = 6 f ℥

33. 45 mL × 1 f ℥/30 mL = 1.5 f ℥, expressed as 1½ f ℥

34. 90 mL × 1 f ℥/30 mL = 3 f ℥

35. 10 mL × 1 f ℥/30 mL = 0.33 f ℥, expressed as ⅓ f ℥

36. 30 mL × 1 f ℥/30 mL = 1 f ℥

37. 360 mL × 1 f ℥/30 mL = 12 f ℥

38. 50 mL × 1 f ℥/30 mL = 1.67 f ℥, expressed as 1⅔ f ℥

39. 1000 mL × 1 f ℥/30 mL = 33.33 f ℥, expressed as 33⅓ f ℥

40. 500 mL × 1 f ℥/30 mL = 16.67 f ℥, expressed as 16⅔ f ℥

41. 960 mL × 1 f ℥/30 mL = 32 f ℥

42. 480 mL × 1 f ℥/30 mL = 16 f ℥

43. 15 mL × 1 f ℥/30 mL = 0.5 f ℥, expressed as ½ f ℥

44. 60 mL × 1 f ℥/30 mL = 2 f ℥

45. 5 mL × 1 f ℥/30 mL = 0.17 f ℥, expressed as ⅙ f ℥

46. 150 mL × 1 f ℥/30 mL = 5 f ℥

47. 120 mL × 1 f ℥/30 mL = 4 f ℥

48. 210 mL × 1 f ℥/30 mL = 7 f ℥

49. 100 mL × 1 f ℥/30 mL = 3.33 f ℥, expressed as 3⅓ f ℥

50. 200 mL × 1 f ℥/30 mL = 6.67 f ℥, expressed as 6⅔ f ℥

51. 5 gr × 65 mg/1 gr = 325 mg; 1 f ℥ = 5 mL; 20 mL × 325 mg/5 mL = 1300 mg

52. 0.45 g = 450 mg, 1 f ℥ = 30 mL; 15 mg × 30 mL/450 mg = 1 mL

53. 40 mcg = 0.00004 g, 1 mL × 1 f ℥/5 mL = 0.2 f ℥; 0.4 g × 0.2 f ℥/0.00004 g = 2000 f ℥

54. $\frac{1}{2}$ gr $\times$ 65 mg/1 gr = 32.5 mg, so three 10 mg tablets and one 2.5 mg tablet

55. 1.2 g = 1200 mg, 1 f℥ = 6 f𝔡; 300 mg $\times$ 6 f𝔡 /1200 mg = 1.5 f℥

56. $\frac{1}{50}$ gr = 0.02 gr, 0.02 gr $\times$ 65 mg/1 gr = 1.3 mg; 1.3 mg = 1300 mcg, so two 650 mcg tablets

57. 20 gr $\times$ 65 mg/1 gr = 1300 mg; x mg/5 mL = 1300 mg/30 mL, x mg = 216.67 mg

58. 8 gr $\times$ 65 mg/1 gr = 520 mg; x mL/600 mg = 5 mL/520 mg, x mL = 5.77 mL

59. 45 gr $\times$ 65 mg/1 gr = 2925 mg; x mL/2925 mg = 15 mL/1000 mg, x mL = 43.88 mL

60. 46.296 gr $\times$ 65 mg/1 gr = 3009.24 mg; x mL/3009.24 mg = 5 mL/500 mg, x mL = 30.09 mL

61. 1 oz = 30 g; x g/25 doses = 30 g/1 dose, x g = 750 g

62. 1 gallon = 3840 mL; x g/3840 mL = 0.065 g/5 mL = 49.92 g

63. 1 pt = 480 mL, 1/10 gr = 0.1 gr; 0.1 gr $\times$ 65 mg/1 gr = 6.5 mg; x mg/480 mL = 6.5 mg/1 mL, x mg = 3120 mg

64. 617.28 gr $\times$ 65 mg/1 gr = 40,123.2 mg; x mg/15 mL = 40,123.2 mg/4000 mL, x mg = 150.46 mg

65. $\frac{1}{5}$ gr = 0.2 gr, 0.2 gr $\times$ 65 mg/1 gr = 13 mg = 0.013 g; 1 cup = 240 mL; x g/240 mL = 0.013 g/1 mL, x g = 3.12 g

66. 10 gr $\times$ 65 mg/1 gr = 650 mg; x tablets/650 mg = 1 tablet/325 mg, x tablets = 2 tablets

67. 3 gr $\times$ 65 mg/1 gr = 195 mg; x tablets/195 mg = 1 tablet/5 mg, x tablets = 39 tablets

68. x g/3 ℔ = 373.2 g/1 ℔, x g = 1119.6 g

69. 4 gr $\times$ 65 mg/1 gr = 260 mg; x mL/500 mg = 5 mL/260 mg, x mL = 9.62 mL

70. 50 gr $\times$ 65 mg/1 gr = 3250 mg = 3.25 g; x mL/3.25 g = 15 mL/0.75 g, x mL = 65 mL

71. x f℥/132 mg = 1 f℥/44 mg, x f℥ = 3 f℥

72. $\frac{1}{2}$ gallon = 1920 mL; x mg/1920 mL = 2000 mg/5 mL, x mg = 768,000 mg

73. 60 gr $\times$ 65 mg/1 gr = 3900 mg; x mg/15 mL = 3900 mg/2000 mL, x mg = 29.25 mg/dose

74. 2 gr $\times$ 65 mg/1 gr = 130 mg; 4160 mg $\times$ 1 supp/130 mg = 32 suppositories

75. $\frac{1}{400}$ gr = 0.0025 gr; 0.0025 gr $\times$ 65 mg/1 gr = 0.1625 mg, rounded to 0.2 mg

76. $\frac{1}{200}$ gr = 0.005 gr, 0.005 gr $\times$ 65 mg/1 gr = 0.325 mg, rounded to 0.3 mg

77. $\frac{1}{150}$ gr = 0.00666 gr, rounded to 0.0067 gr; 0.0067 gr $\times$ 65 mg/1 gr = 0.4355 mg, rounded to 0.4 mg

78. $\frac{1}{100}$ gr = 0.01, 0.01 gr $\times$ 65 mg/1 gr = 0.65 mg, rounded to 0.7 mg

79. $\frac{1}{150}$ gr = 0.00666 gr, rounded to 0.0067 gr; 0.0067 gr $\times$ 65 mg/1 gr = 0.4355 mg, rounded to 0.4 mg; 0.4 mg $\times$ 3 = 1.2 mg

Appendix B

Additional Practice with Fractions and Percents

B.1 Working with Fractions

Change each of the mixed numbers to improper fractions.

1. $3\frac{1}{4}$

2. $5\frac{1}{2}$

3. $6\frac{1}{8}$

4. $5\frac{3}{4}$

5. $6\frac{7}{8}$

6. $8\frac{11}{12}$

7. $9\frac{13}{16}$

8. $12\frac{1}{4}$

9. $13\frac{2}{3}$

10. $14\frac{5}{6}$

Change each of the improper fractions to mixed numbers.

11. $\frac{55}{7}$

12. $\frac{75}{8}$

13. $\frac{95}{3}$

14. $\frac{89}{12}$

15. $\frac{125}{9}$

16. $\frac{139}{3}$

17. $\frac{147}{5}$

18. $\frac{269}{6}$

19. $\frac{409}{8}$

20. $\frac{293}{5}$

Reduce the following fractions to their lowest terms.

21. $\frac{2}{6}$

22. $\frac{2}{10}$

23. $\frac{4}{10}$

24. $\frac{8}{12}$

25. $\frac{9}{15}$

26. $\frac{8}{18}$

27. $\frac{8}{26}$

28. $\frac{48}{64}$

29. $\frac{52}{76}$

30. $\frac{75}{180}$

31. $\frac{60}{380}$

32. $\dfrac{85}{120}$

33. $\dfrac{96}{128}$

34. $\dfrac{72}{108}$

35. $\dfrac{75}{195}$

36. $\dfrac{88}{220}$

37. $\dfrac{81}{135}$

38. $\dfrac{156}{252}$

39. $\dfrac{85}{135}$

40. $\dfrac{270}{285}$

Add the following fractions.

41. $\dfrac{1}{2} + \dfrac{2}{3} =$

42. $\dfrac{3}{4} + \dfrac{7}{8} =$

43. $\dfrac{1}{3} + \dfrac{2}{7} =$

44. $\dfrac{5}{6} + \dfrac{7}{8} + \dfrac{2}{3} =$

45. $\dfrac{5}{7} + \dfrac{1}{5} + \dfrac{3}{10} =$

46. $\dfrac{1}{4} + \dfrac{7}{12} + \dfrac{1}{2} + \dfrac{7}{8} =$

47. $\dfrac{5}{16} + \dfrac{1}{4} + \dfrac{9}{24} =$

48. $4\dfrac{1}{2} + 2\dfrac{2}{3} =$

49. $9\dfrac{3}{4} + 7\dfrac{7}{8} =$

50. $5\dfrac{7}{8} + 2\dfrac{1}{3} =$

51. $12\dfrac{1}{6} + 13\dfrac{1}{4} =$

52. $8\dfrac{1}{3} + 5\dfrac{5}{6} + 13\dfrac{5}{8} + 19\dfrac{9}{16} =$

Subtract the following fractions.

53. $\dfrac{1}{2} - \dfrac{1}{4} =$

54. $\dfrac{3}{4} - \dfrac{1}{8} =$

55. $\dfrac{4}{9} - \dfrac{1}{3} =$

56. $\dfrac{5}{8} - \dfrac{1}{3} =$

57. $\dfrac{5}{12} - \dfrac{1}{8} =$

58. $\dfrac{2}{3} - \dfrac{1}{16} =$

59. $\dfrac{6}{7} - \dfrac{2}{3} =$

60. $\dfrac{11}{16} - \dfrac{5}{12} =$

61. $8\dfrac{3}{4} - 2\dfrac{1}{4} =$

62. $7\dfrac{1}{2} - 2\dfrac{1}{4} =$

63. $15\dfrac{2}{3} - 7\dfrac{1}{8} =$

64. $32\dfrac{3}{5} - 7\dfrac{3}{8} =$

65. $63\dfrac{5}{6} - 17\dfrac{7}{16} =$

66. $13\dfrac{1}{2} - 8\dfrac{3}{4} =$

67. $29\dfrac{1}{3} - 13\dfrac{3}{8} =$

68. $37\dfrac{2}{9} - 21\dfrac{1}{3} =$

Multiply the following fractions and reduce to lowest terms. Rewrite as a mixed number if necessary.

69. $\dfrac{2}{3} \times \dfrac{5}{12} =$

70. $\dfrac{5}{9} \times \dfrac{4}{8} =$

71. $\dfrac{3}{16} \times \dfrac{4}{5} =$

72. $\dfrac{7}{8} \times \dfrac{2}{3} =$

73. $\dfrac{7}{12} \times 18 =$

74. $\dfrac{5}{9} \times 21 =$

Multiply the following mixed numbers.

75. $3\dfrac{1}{2} \times 8\dfrac{1}{4} =$

76. $9\dfrac{3}{8} \times 11\dfrac{5}{6} =$

77. $15\dfrac{4}{7} \times 6\dfrac{5}{14} =$

78. $2\dfrac{1}{2} \times 3\dfrac{2}{3} \times 2\dfrac{5}{6} =$

79. $6\dfrac{1}{8} \times 5\dfrac{1}{4} \times 3\dfrac{3}{16} =$

80. $5\dfrac{2}{3} \times 3\dfrac{1}{4} \times 8\dfrac{7}{12} =$

Solve the following word problems using fractions.

81. A man pays $3000.00 for a microcomputer with an annual maintenance fee that is $\frac{1}{5}$ of the purchase price. How much is the annual maintenance fee for this microcomputer?

82. There were 10,240 persons attending a rock concert, and $\frac{2}{5}$ of the audience was female. How many girls and women attended the concert?

83. A jigsaw puzzle contains 5240 pieces. Ralph estimates that the puzzle is $\frac{5}{8}$ completed. How many pieces have been put in place?

84. A jigsaw puzzle contains 905 pieces. Sue estimates the puzzle is $\frac{2}{3}$ completed. How may pieces are not yet placed in the puzzle?

Divide the following mixed numbers and fractions.

85. $3\dfrac{1}{2} \div \dfrac{3}{4} =$

86. $2\dfrac{1}{3} \div \dfrac{5}{6} =$

87. $5\dfrac{1}{4} \div \dfrac{3}{8} =$

88. $6\dfrac{7}{8} \div \dfrac{5}{16} =$

89. $5\dfrac{1}{2} \div 2 =$

90. $16\dfrac{5}{9} \div 3 =$

91. $3\dfrac{1}{2} \div 1\dfrac{3}{4} =$

92. $15\dfrac{7}{8} \div 5\dfrac{9}{16} =$

Find the following.

93. $\dfrac{9}{10}$ of 650

94. $\dfrac{4}{5}$ of 785

95. $\dfrac{3}{8}$ of 248

96. $\dfrac{5}{6}$ of 66

97. $\dfrac{3}{4}$ of 76

98. $\dfrac{5}{7}$ of 56

99. $\dfrac{2}{3}$ of 780

100. $\dfrac{1}{12}$ of 144

Solve the following word problems.

101. An automobile travels 240 miles in $5\frac{1}{2}$ hours. How many miles/hour does the automobile travel?

102. An automobile travels $210\frac{6}{10}$ miles and uses $16\frac{2}{10}$ gallons of gasoline. What is the mileage in miles/gallon?

103. A student is able to transfer $84\frac{3}{4}$ credits and $271\frac{1}{5}$ quality points into another school. The student's grade point average is the number of quality points divided by the number of credits received. What is the student's grade point average based on the transfer of credits into the new school?

104. An auditorium has 31,437 square feet of seating space. Each seat will take $3\frac{1}{2}$ square feet. How many seats will fill the seating space?

B.2 Working with Percents

Convert each of the following percents to a decimal and a reduced fraction. The first problem is completed as an example.

Percent	Decimal Equivalent	Fractional Equivalent
20%	0.2	$\frac{20}{100} = \frac{1}{5}$
105. 30%		
106. 5%		
107. 8%		
108. 15%		

Compute the amount for each of the following problems, rounding to two decimal places.

109. 52% of $520.00

110. 3% of $1640.00

111. 20% of $1840.00

112. $\frac{1}{2}$ % of 3640.00

113. $4\frac{1}{2}$% of $764.00

114. 8% of $514.85

115. 7% of $316.38

116. $17\frac{3}{4}$% of $42.00

Solve the following word problems.

117. Last year a musical production was attended by 15,500 persons. This year's attendance was 92% of last year's attendance. How many attended this year?

118. The Monroe City Council voted to impose a 2% tax on personal incomes. If the average income in Monroe is $14,514.00, what is the average tax levied on each taxpayer?

119. Binford Peeples makes $820.00/week. If he receives a raise of 8%, find the amount of (a) his raise and (b) his new salary.

120. Bert Brown and Clara Johnson are partners in a business that has an annual profit of $64,500.00. Mr. Brown receives 47% of the net profit, and Ms. Johnson receives 53%. How much did (a) Mr. Brown and (b) Ms. Johnson receive?

121. Randy Schwartz purchased a condominium for $85,500.00. The depreciation allowance, for tax purposes, is 5% per year. How much is the annual depreciation allowance for the condominium?

122. Roxanne Adams owned a bond worth $2000.00 that paid interest at $8\frac{1}{2}\%$/year. How much interest did she earn the first year?

The salaries and merit raise indexes for six employees are shown below. Multiply each salary amount by its raise index rate to get the new salary amount.

123. Salary $1500.00
     Raise Index   108%
     New Salary $ _____

124. Salary $1450.00
     Raise Index   109%
     New Salary $ _____

125. Salary $1670.00
     Raise Index $110\frac{1}{2}\%$
     New Salary $ _____

126. Salary $1548.00
     Raise Index $112\frac{1}{2}\%$
     New Salary $ _____

127. Salary $1476.00
     Raise Index $104\frac{3}{4}\%$
     New Salary $ _____

128. Salary $1950.00
     Raise Index   111%
     New Salary $ _____

Solve the following word problems.

129. Dr. Ernest Bishop has a gross earned income of $120,000.00. Of this amount, 42% represents income from patients who paid cash for their medical services, and 58% represents income from patients who charged their medical services. How much of his gross earned income is from (a) cash patients and (b) charge patients?

130. The building owned by Brodnex Jewelry Store has an assessed value of $220,000.00 for property tax purposes. Tax rates are as follows: city, 3.6%; county, 5.3%; and special business, 2.5%. How much tax is owed on the building for (a) city, (b) county, and (c) special business taxes?

131. Bill White owns a house valued at $120,000.00 and furniture worth $25,000.00. The house is insured at 80% of its value, and the furniture at 65% of its value. For how much are (a) the house and (b) the furniture insured? Assuming that the above amounts represent realistic values, (c) how much would Mr. White lose if the house and furniture were completely destroyed by fire?

132. Canty Importers' sales during the first year of operation came to $250,000.00. Second-year sales have been projected to be 125% of first-year sales, while third-year sales have been projected to be 130% of second-year sales. What are the projected sales for (a) the second year and (b) the third year?

133. The Wilson Florist Shop's delivery truck used 2600 L of gasoline last year. By purchasing a more fuel-efficient truck, the company would realize an estimated 7% savings in gasoline. Assuming this is true, (a) how much gasoline would be saved next year, and (b) how much gasoline would be used next year?

134. Connie Gaines gets a monthly salary of $2,400.00. Deductions are made as follows: payroll taxes, 28%; credit union, 8%; and savings account, $12\frac{1}{2}\%$. How much is deducted from her check for (a) payroll taxes, (b) credit union, and (c) savings account?

Appendix C

Additional Practice with Compounding

C.1 Pediatric Safety

Many patients, especially pediatric patients, require a dose that must be customized according to the weight of the patient. Manufacturers often provide a recommended dosage range for use in children based on the child's weight, and the pharmacy technician will usually check prescription orders against the manufacturer's recommended range. Doing this helps the pharmacy and nursing staff to verify that the dose being prescribed and administered is correct and safe. Many facilities have rounding protocols for calculations involving pediatric patients that specify how to round a patient's weight, amounts in milligrams or micrograms, and the volume of fluid to be administered to a pediatric patient. For purposes of Problem Set C.1, patients' weights under 10 lb, expressed either in kilograms or in pounds, should be rounded to the hundredth place; patients' weights of 10 lb or more should be rounded to the tenth place. Medication doses should be rounded to the hundredth place. Devices that measure to a greater degree of accuracy are available for administration of medication to pediatric patients.

C.1 Problem Set

1. You receive the following order for a pediatric patient weighing 60 lb. The drug can be given at a range of 15–20 mg/kg/day in 8–12 hour intervals. Is it safe for this child to receive this dose?

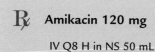

  ℞ **Amikacin 120 mg**

    IV Q8 H in NS 50 mL

2. You receive the following order for a pediatric patient weighing 47 lb. The drug can be given at a range of 7.5–12 mg/kg/day in intervals every 8 hours. Is it safe for this child to receive this dose?

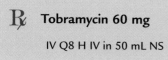

  ℞ **Tobramycin 60 mg**

    IV Q8 H IV in 50 mL NS

3. You receive the following order for a 10-day-old patient weighing 3.1 lb. The following chart indicates the dose information for gentamicin. Is it safe for this child to receive this dose?

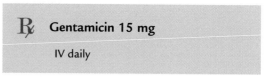

  ℞ **Gentamicin 15 mg**

    IV daily

Gentamicin Dose Information

Weight (in kg)	Dose	Interval	Days Old
<1.2	2.5 mg/kg/day	Q24 H	No age limit
1.2–2	2.5 mg/kg/day	Q18 H	<7
>2	2.5 mg/kg/day	Q12 H	<7
>2	2.5 mg/kg/day	Q8 H	>7

4. You receive the following order for a 9-day-old patient weighing 2.5 lb. The following chart indicates the dose information for vancomycin. Is it safe for this child to receive this dose?

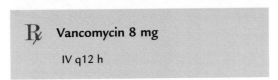

Vancomycin 8 mg

IV q12 h

Vancomycin Dose Information

Weight (in kg)	Dose	Interval	Days Old
<1.2	15 mg/kg/dose	Q24 H	No age limit
1.2–2	15 mg/kg/dose	Q18 H	<7
1.2–2	15 mg/kg/dose	Q12 H	>7
>2	15 mg/kg/dose	Q12 H	<7
>2	15 mg/kg/dose	Q8 H	>7

C.2 Total Parenteral Nutrition

As a pharmacy technician working in the IV room, you will be asked to apply many of the math skills you have learned. One of the most challenging types of calculations involves Total Parenteral Nutrition (TPN). TPN is used for patients who cannot take in and absorb nutrients through the gastrointestinal tract. Patients who are critically ill for a long period of time may receive TPN. These patients need very precise nutritional replacement due to the fragile state of their metabolic homeostasis.

The main ingredients of TPN include carbohydrates (dextrose), protein components (amino acids), fats (lipids), and sterile water for injection (SWFI). Electrolytes such as potassium, medication, multivitamins (MVI), and trace elements are also included. It is important to remember that stock electrolyte solutions contain more than one electrolyte. For example, potassium always comes paired with another electrolyte (chloride, acetate, or phosphate), and the potassium cannot be separated from its pair (you cannot remove just the potassium from a vial containing 5 mL potassium chloride). Sodium also comes in a pair, as sodium acetate.

Most TPN orders are written for 1 L of solution. Some orders may state a specific volume of an ingredient, but others may state a flow rate and duration that must be used to calculate a volume. When only the duration and flow rate are given, the total volume must be determined prior to calculating the volume of any component.

Pharmacy staff often use a customized grid or table to assist in determining the amounts of individual components in the TPN solution. Figure C.1 shows such a grid, which will be the basis for Example C.1 and Problem Set C.2. The column on the left of the grid lists the individual components typically ordered in a TPN solution. The top row indicates the pharmaceutical products available in the pharmacy to provide the ordered nutrients.

The steps in Table C.1 are used in balancing the quantities of the individual components within the TPN grid. The first four steps in Table C.1 balance the electrolytes—potassium chloride (KCl), potassium acetate, sodium phosphate (NaPO$_4$), sodium acetate—beginning with KCl. Potassium is the first electrolyte balanced because potassium must remain within a very narrow range in the blood or the heart may be affected. If a member of the pharmacy staff asks the prescriber to change an electrolyte because the electrolyte solutions do not balance, potassium is the one that will rarely change. Example C.1 illustrates the use of the grid in Figure C.1 and the steps in Table C.1.

FIGURE C.1 TPN Components grid

| TPN Ingredients | Pharmacy Stock | | | | | | | | |
	potassium chloride (KCl)	potassium acetate	sodium phosphate (NaPO₄)	sodium acetate	calcium gluconate	magnesium sulfate	Pepcid	insulin	Total
potassium (K)	_____	_____	_____	_____	_____	_____	_____	_____	_____
sodium (Na)	_____	_____	_____	_____	_____	_____	_____	_____	_____
chloride (Cl)	_____	_____	_____	_____	_____	_____	_____	_____	_____
phosphate (PO₄)	_____	_____	_____	_____	_____	_____	_____	_____	_____
acetate	_____	_____	_____	_____	_____	_____	_____	_____	_____
calcium (Ca)	_____	_____	_____	_____	_____	_____	_____	_____	_____
magnesium (Mg)	_____	_____	_____	_____	_____	_____	_____	_____	_____
multivitamins (MVI)	_____	_____	_____	_____	_____	_____	_____	_____	_____
trace	_____	_____	_____	_____	_____	_____	_____	_____	_____
insulin	_____	_____	_____	_____	_____	_____	_____	_____	_____
Pepcid	_____	_____	_____	_____	_____	_____	_____	_____	_____

TABLE C.1 Steps to Balance TPN Components

1. Record the potassium and chloride needed, and indicate the total of each in the far-right column.
2. Record the potassium and acetate needed, and indicate the total of each in the far-right column.
3. Record the sodium and acetate needed, and indicate the total of each in the far-right column.
4. Record the sodium and phosphate needed, and indicate the total of each in the far-right column.
5. Record the calcium, magnesium, and other minerals needed, and indicate the total of each in the far-right column.
6. Check all of the totals in the far-right column to confirm that the amounts match the order.
7. Calculate the volume of each component needed based on the pharmacy's available solutions.
8. Calculate the dextrose, amino acids, fat emulsion, and sterile water for injection as needed to provide the bulk of the volume for the TPN.

Example C.1   The pharmacy receives the following TPN order.

> ℞ Total TPN volume: 2.5 L
>
> | dextrose | 23% | PO$_4$ | 80 mEq/L |
> |---|---|---|---|
> | amino acids | 11.5 g | acetate | 40 mEq/L |
> | K | 80 mEq/L | MVI | 10 mL/day |
> | Na | 100 mEq/L | trace | 1 mL/day |
> | Cl | 60 mEq/L | Humulin R | 73 units/day |
> | Mg | 18 mEq/L | Pepcid | 60 mg/day |
> | Ca | 15 mEq/L | | |

You have the following stock solutions in the pharmacy.

amino acids	15%	potassium chloride	2 mEq/mL
calcium gluconate	0.48 mEq/mL	potassium phosphate	4.4 mEq/mL
dextrose	70%	sodium acetate	2 mEq/mL
Humulin R insulin	100 units/mL	sodium chloride	4 mEq/mL
lipids	20%	sodium phosphate	4 mEq/mL
magnesium sulfate	4 mEq/mL	sterile water for injection	
Pepcid	10 mg/mL	Zantac	25 mg/mL
potassium acetate	2 mEq/mL		

Balance the quantities of the individual components to determine the ingredients of the final TPN solution.

Step 1. According to the order, we need 80 mEq K. The order also includes 60 mEq Cl, so we can add only 60 mEq KCl. Therefore, we enter 60 mEq in both the potassium box and the chloride box to correspond with 60 mEq KCl. Note that we still need an additional 20 mEq K as the order requires a total of 80 mEq K.

Pharmacy Stock

TPN Ingredients	KCl	potassium acetate	NaPO$_4$	sodium acetate	calcium gluconate	magnesium sulfate	Pepcid	insulin	Total
K	60 mEq	____	____	____	____	____	____	____	60 mEq
Na	____	____	____	____	____	____	____	____	____
Cl	60 mEq	____	____	____	____	____	____	____	60 mEq
PO$_4$	____	____	____	____	____	____	____	____	____
acetate	____	____	____	____	____	____	____	____	____
Ca	____	____	____	____	____	____	____	____	____
Mg	____	____	____	____	____	____	____	____	____
MVI	____	____	____	____	____	____	____	____	____
trace	____	____	____	____	____	____	____	____	____
insulin	____	____	____	____	____	____	____	____	____
Pepcid	____	____	____	____	____	____	____	____	____

Step 2. The order also requests 40 mEq acetate. Since potassium comes as acetate, we should add 20 mEq in both boxes.

Pharmacy Stock

TPN Ingredients	KCl	potassium acetate	NaPO$_4$	sodium acetate	calcium gluconate	magnesium sulfate	Pepcid	insulin	Total
K	60 mEq	20 mEq	_____	_____	_____	_____	_____	_____	80 mEq
Na	_____	_____	_____	_____	_____	_____	_____	_____	_____
Cl	60 mEq	_____	_____	_____	_____	_____	_____	_____	60 mEq
PO$_4$	_____	_____	_____	_____	_____	_____	_____	_____	_____
acetate	_____	20 mEq	_____	_____	_____	_____	_____	_____	20 mEq
Ca	_____	_____	_____	_____	_____	_____	_____	_____	_____
Mg	_____	_____	_____	_____	_____	_____	_____	_____	_____
MVI	_____	_____	_____	_____	_____	_____	_____	_____	_____
trace	_____	_____	_____	_____	_____	_____	_____	_____	_____
insulin	_____	_____	_____	_____	_____	_____	_____	_____	_____
Pepcid	_____	_____	_____	_____	_____	_____	_____	_____	_____

Step 3. We cannot use the sodium chloride to fill the order for 100 mEq Na because the ordered amount of chloride has already been included in the TPN solution. However, the pharmacy stock includes sodium acetate, so add 20 mEq to the sodium acetate box.

Pharmacy Stock

TPN Ingredients	KCl	potassium acetate	NaPO$_4$	sodium acetate	calcium gluconate	magnesium sulfate	Pepcid	insulin	Total
K	60 mEq	20 mEq	_____	_____	_____	_____	_____	_____	80 mEq
Na	_____	_____	_____	20 mEq	_____	_____	_____	_____	20 mEq
Cl	60 mEq	_____	_____	_____	_____	_____	_____	_____	60 mEq
PO$_4$	_____	_____	_____	_____	_____	_____	_____	_____	_____
acetate	_____	20 mEq	_____	20 mEq	_____	_____	_____	_____	40 mEq
Ca	_____	_____	_____	_____	_____	_____	_____	_____	_____
Mg	_____	_____	_____	_____	_____	_____	_____	_____	_____
MVI	_____	_____	_____	_____	_____	_____	_____	_____	_____
trace	_____	_____	_____	_____	_____	_____	_____	_____	_____
insulin	_____	_____	_____	_____	_____	_____	_____	_____	_____
Pepcid	_____	_____	_____	_____	_____	_____	_____	_____	_____

Step 4. The order includes a total of 100 mEq Na. In the previous step, we used 20 mEq, so we have 80 mEq left to fill. The order also requests 80 mEq PO$_4$, so we can add 80 mEq NaPO$_4$ to the chart.

Pharmacy Stock

TPN Ingredients	KCl	potassium acetate	NaPO$_4$	sodium acetate	calcium gluconate	magnesium sulfate	Pepcid	insulin	Total
K	60 mEq	20 mEq	——	——	——	——	——	——	80 mEq
Na	——	——	80 mEq	20 mEq	——	——	——	——	100 mEq
Cl	60 mEq	——	——	——	——	——	——	——	60 mEq
PO$_4$	——	——	80 mEq	——	——	——	——	——	80 mEq
acetate	——	20 mEq	——	20 mEq	——	——	——	——	40 mEq
Ca	——	——	——	——	——	——	——	——	——
Mg	——	——	——	——	——	——	——	——	——
MVI	——	——	——	——	——	——	——	——	——
trace	——	——	——	——	——	——	——	——	——
insulin	——	——	——	——	——	——	——	——	——
Pepcid	——	——	——	——	——	——	——	——	——

Step 5. Now add calcium, magnesium, MVI, trace, insulin, and Pepcid to the chart, based on the original order.

Pharmacy Stock

TPN Ingredients	KCl	potassium acetate	NaPO$_4$	sodium acetate	calcium gluconate	magnesium sulfate	Pepcid	insulin	Total
K	60 mEq	20 mEq	——	——	——	——	——	——	80 mEq
Na	——	——	80 mEq	20 mEq	——	——	——	——	100 mEq
Cl	60 mEq	——	——	——	——	——	——	——	60 mEq
PO$_4$	——	——	80 mEq	——	——	——	——	——	80 mEq
acetate	——	20 mEq	——	20 mEq	——	——	——	——	40 mEq
Ca	——	——	——	——	80 mEq	——	——	——	80 mEq
Mg	——	——	——	——	——	80 mEq	——	——	80 mEq
MVI	——	——	——	——	——	——	10 mL	——	10 mL
trace	——	——	——	——	——	——	1 mL	——	1 mL
insulin	——	——	——	——	——	——	——	73 units	73 units
Pepcid	——	——	——	——	——	——	60 mg	——	60 mg

Step 6. Check the totals against the original order to confirm that the amounts match.

TPN Ingredients	Total
K	80 mEq
Na	100 mEq
Cl	60 mEq
PO$_4$	80 mEq
acetate	40 mEq
Ca	80 mEq
Mg	80 mEq
MVI	10 mL
trace	1 mL
insulin	73 units
Pepcid	60 mg

Step 7. Determine how many milliliters of each electrolyte solution are needed to fill the order. According to the order, we need to make a total of 2.5 L of the TPN solution. For each element that is ordered per liter, determine the amount needed for 1 L, and then determine the final volume based on the total order volume of 2.5 L.

KCl: x mL/60 mEq = 1 mL/2 mEq, x mL= 30 mL;
x mL/2.5 L = 30 mL/1 L, x mL= 75 mL
potassium acetate: x mL/20 mEq = 1 mL/2 mEq, x mL = 10 mL;
x mL/2.5 L = 10 mL/1 L, x mL = 25 mL
NaPO$_4$: x mL/80 mEq = 1 mL/4 mEq, x mL = 20 mL;
x mL/2.5 L = 20 mL/1 L, x mL = 50 mL
sodium acetate: x mL/20 mEq = 1 mL/2 mEq, x mL = 10 mL;
x mL/2.5 L = 10 mL/1 L, x mL = 25 mL
calcium gluconate: x mL/15 mEq = 1 mL/0.48 mEq, x mL = 31.25 mL;
x mL/2.5 L = 31.25 mL/1 L, x mL = 78.13 mL
MgSO$_4$: x mL/18 mEq = 1 mL/4 mEq, x mL = 4.5 mL;
x mL/2.5 L = 4.5 mL/1 L, x mL = 11.25 mL

The Pepcid and Humulin R insulin orders are per day, not per liter.

Pepcid: x mL/60 mg = 1 mL/10 mg, x mL = 6 mL
Humulin: x mL/73 units = 1 mL/100 units, x mL = 0.73 mL

The MVI and trace orders were also per day, but the order indicates a specific volume.

MVI: 10 mL
trace: 1 mL

Step 8. Calculate the amounts of dextrose, amino acids, and sterile water for injection that are required. Use an alligation to calculate the amount of dextrose needed for 1 L, and then adjust the amount for the 2.5 L total volume.

70		23 mL parts
	23	
0		47 mL parts
		70 mL total

x mL/1000 mL = 23 mL parts/70 mL total parts; x mL = 328.571 mL, rounded to 328.6 mL

x mL/2.5 L = 328.6 mL/1 L, x mL= 821.5 mL

Calculate the amount of amino acids needed:

x mL/11.5 g = 100 mL/15 g, x mL = 76.6666 mL, rounded to 76.7 mL

x mL/2.5 L = 76.7 mL/1 L, x mL= 191.75 mL, rounded to 191.8 mL

Calculate the amount of sterile water for injection by subtracting the volume of dextrose and amino acids from the total volume.

2500 mL total volume – (821.5 mL dextrose + 191.8 mL amino acids) = 1486.7 mL

C.2 Problem Set

Round to the tenth place in solving the following problems.

5. You have received the following TPN order.

$\mathrm{R}_{\!x}$ TPN 1.5 L			SO4	10 mEq	
dextrose	35%		Ca	30 mEq	
amino acids		7.5%	Mg	10 mEq	
K	50 mEq		gluconate	30 mEq	
Na	100 mEq		Humulin R		60 units/day
Cl	110 mEq		MVI	10 mL/day	
PO4	40 mEq		trace	1 mL/day	

The pharmacy stock consists of the following.

amino acids	15%	potassium chloride	2 mEq/mL
calcium gluconate	0.48 mEq/mL	potassium phosphate	4.4 mEq/mL
dextrose	70%	sodium acetate	2 mEq/mL
Humulin R insulin	100 units/mL	sodium chloride	4 mEq/mL
lipids	20%	sodium phosphate	4 mEq/mL
magnesium sulfate	4 mEq/mL	sterile water for injection	
Pepcid	10 mg/mL	Zantac	25 mg/mL
potassium acetate	2 mEq/mL		

Balance the TPN components.

TPN Ingredients	KCl	NaCl	NaPO$_4$	calcium gluconate	magnesium sulfate	regular insulin	MVI	trace	Total
K	___	___	___	___	___	___	___	___	___
Na	___	___	___	___	___	___	___	___	___
Cl	___	___	___	___	___	___	___	___	___
PO$_4$	___	___	___	___	___	___	___	___	___
SO$_4$	___	___	___	___	___	___	___	___	___
Ca	___	___	___	___	___	___	___	___	___
Mg	___	___	___	___	___	___	___	___	___
gluconate	___	___	___	___	___	___	___	___	___
regular insulin	___	___	___	___	___	___	___	___	___
MVI	___	___	___	___	___	___	___	___	___
trace	___	___	___	___	___	___	___	___	___

Pharmacy Stock (column header above calcium gluconate / magnesium sulfate / regular insulin / MVI / trace / Total)

6. You need to run the following TPN order at 42 mL/hour, and you need to make a bag that will contain enough fluid to last for 24 hours.

R℞			
dextrose	20%	Ca	12 mEq/L
amino acids	10 g	PO4	30 mEq/L
lipids	5 g	acetate	40 mEq/L
K	40 mEq/L	MVI	10 mL/day
Na	90 mEq/L	trace	1 mL/day
Cl	60 mEq/L	Zantac	100 mg/day
Mg	15 mEq/L		

The pharmacy's stock includes the following.

amino acids	15%	potassium chloride	2 mEq/mL
calcium gluconate	0.48 mEq/mL	potassium phosphate	4.4 mEq/mL
dextrose	70%	sodium acetate	2 mEq/mL
Humulin R insulin	100 units/mL	sodium chloride	4 mEq/mL
lipids	20%	sodium phosphate	4 mEq/mL
magnesium sulfate	4 mEq/mL	sterile water for injection	
Pepcid	10 mg/mL	Zantac	25 mg/mL
potassium acetate	2 mEq/mL		

Balance the TPN components.

Pharmacy Stock

TPN Ingredients	KCl	NaCl	NaPO$_4$	sodium acetate	calcium gluconate	magnesium sulfate	MVI	trace	Zantac	Total
K	___	___	___	___	___	___	___	___	___	___
Na	___	___	___	___	___	___	___	___	___	___
Cl	___	___	___	___	___	___	___	___	___	___
Mg	___	___	___	___	___	___	___	___	___	___
Ca	___	___	___	___	___	___	___	___	___	___
PO$_4$	___	___	___	___	___	___	___	___	___	___
acetate	___	___	___	___	___	___	___	___	___	___
MVI	___	___	___	___	___	___	___	___	___	___
trace	___	___	___	___	___	___	___	___	___	___
Zantac	___	___	___	___	___	___	___	___	___	___

7. You have a TPN order that needs to be infused at 84 mL/hour. You need to make a bag that will last 24 hours.

℞	dextrose	18%	Ca	12 mEq/L
	amino acids	9 g	PO4	40 mEq/L
	lipids	10 g	acetate	40 mEq/L
	K	60 mEq/L	MVI	10 mL/day
	Na	120 mEq/L	trace	1 mL/day
	Cl	100 mEq/L	Humulin R	65 units/day
	Mg	10 mEq/L	Zantac	150 mg/day

The pharmacy has the following stock ingredients.

amino acids	15%	potassium chloride	2 mEq/mL
calcium gluconate	0.48 mEq/mL	potassium phosphate	4.4 mEq/mL
dextrose	70%	sodium acetate	2 mEq/mL
Humulin R insulin	100 units/mL	sodium chloride	4 mEq/mL
lipids	20%	sodium phosphate	4 mEq/mL
magnesium sulfate	4 mEq/mL	sterile water for injection	
Pepcid	10 mg/mL	Zantac	25 mg/mL
potassium acetate	2 mEq/mL		

Balance the TPN components.

TPN Ingredients	KCl	NaCl	NaPO$_4$	sodium acetate	calcium gluconate	magnesium sulfate	MVI	trace	regular Zantac	insulin	Total
K	___	___	___	___	___	___	___	___	___	___	___
Na	___	___	___	___	___	___	___	___	___	___	___
Cl	___	___	___	___	___	___	___	___	___	___	___
Mg	___	___	___	___	___	___	___	___	___	___	___
Ca	___	___	___	___	___	___	___	___	___	___	___
PO$_4$	___	___	___	___	___	___	___	___	___	___	___
acetate	___	___	___	___	___	___	___	___	___	___	___
MVI	___	___	___	___	___	___	___	___	___	___	___
trace	___	___	___	___	___	___	___	___	___	___	___
insulin	___	___	___	___	___	___	___	___	___	___	___
Zantac	___	___	___	___	___	___	___	___	___	___	___

8. You receive the following TPN order that is to be infused at a rate of 125 mL/hour. You need to make a bag that will last 24 hours.

R	dextrose	25%	Ca	10 mEq/L
	amino acids	12.5 g	PO4	60 mEq/L
	lipids	15 g	acetate	30 mEq/L
	K	110 mEq/L	MVI	10 mL/day
	Na	60 mEq/L	trace	1 mL/day
	Cl	80 mEq/L	Pepcid	40 mg/day
	Mg	12 mEq/L		

The pharmacy has the following stock ingredients.

amino acids	15%	potassium chloride	2 mEq/mL
calcium gluconate	0.48 mEq/mL	potassium phosphate	4.4 mEq/mL
dextrose	70%	sodium acetate	2 mEq/mL
Humulin R insulin	100 units/mL	sodium chloride	4 mEq/mL
lipids	20%	sodium phosphate	4 mEq/mL
magnesium sulfate	4 mEq/mL	sterile water for injection	
Pepcid	10 mg/mL	Zantac	25 mg/mL
potassium acetate	2 mEq/mL		

Balance the TPN components.

TPN Ingredients	KCl	potassium acetate	NaPO₄	calcium gluconate	magnesium sulfate	MVI	trace	Pepcid	Total
K	___	___	___	___	___	___	___	___	___
Na	___	___	___	___	___	___	___	___	___
Cl	___	___	___	___	___	___	___	___	___
Mg	___	___	___	___	___	___	___	___	___
Ca	___	___	___	___	___	___	___	___	___
PO₄	___	___	___	___	___	___	___	___	___
acetate	___	___	___	___	___	___	___	___	___
MVI	___	___	___	___	___	___	___	___	___
trace	___	___	___	___	___	___	___	___	___
Pepcid	___	___	___	___	___	___	___	___	___

9. You receive the following TPN order that is to be infused at a rate of 100 mL/hour. You need a bag that will last 24 hours.

℞	dextrose	22%	Ca	8 mEq/L
	amino acids	13 g	PO4	60 mEq/L
	lipids	10 g	acetate	40 mEq/L
	K	120 mEq/L	MVI	10 mL/day
	Na	40 mEq/L	trace	1 mL/day
	Cl	60 mEq/L	Humulin R	85 units/day
	Mg	10 mEq/L	Pepcid	60 mg/day

The pharmacy has the following stock ingredients.

amino acids	15%	potassium chloride	2 mEq/mL
calcium gluconate	0.48 mEq/mL	potassium phosphate	4.4 mEq/mL
dextrose	70%	sodium acetate	2 mEq/mL
Humulin R insulin	100 units/mL	sodium chloride	4 mEq/mL
lipids	20%	sodium phosphate	4 mEq/mL
magnesium sulfate	4 mEq/mL	sterile water for injection	
Pepcid	10 mg/mL	Zantac	25 mg/mL
potassium acetate	2 mEq/mL		

Balance the TPN components.

TPN Ingredients	KCl	sodium acetate	KPO$_4$	calcium gluconate	magnesium sulfate	MVI	regular trace	insulin	Pepcid	Total
K	____	____	____	____	____	____	____	____	____	____
Na	____	____	____	____	____	____	____	____	____	____
Cl	____	____	____	____	____	____	____	____	____	____
Mg	____	____	____	____	____	____	____	____	____	____
Ca	____	____	____	____	____	____	____	____	____	____
PO$_4$	____	____	____	____	____	____	____	____	____	____
acetate	____	____	____	____	____	____	____	____	____	____
MVI	____	____	____	____	____	____	____	____	____	____
trace	____	____	____	____	____	____	____	____	____	____
regular insulin	____	____	____	____	____	____	____	____	____	____
Pepcid	____	____	____	____	____	____	____	____	____	____

C.3 Critical Care IV Medications

Pharmacy technicians may prepare critical care IV medications for cardiac care patients. In addition to accurately mixing medications, IV technicians will need to be able to calculate IV rates in order to determine how long a bag of medication will last. The following problems are examples of these types of calculations. Round to the tenth place.

C.3 Problem Set

10. You receive the following order and are directed to mix a 24 hour supply for the CCU. The doctor wants it mixed in 500 mL of dextrose. You have amiodarone 50 mg/mL vials in stock.

> ℞ **Amiodarone 150 mg**
>
> IV stat, then 1 mg/min for 6 hours, then 0.5 mg/min for remaining 24 hours (maximum 2.2 g/day)

a. How many milliliters of amiodarone will you need to add to the bag?

b. What will the IV rate be in milliliters per hour for the stat dose?

c. What will the IV rate be in milliliters per hour for the first 6 hours?

d. What will the IV rate be in milliliters per hour for the remaining 24 hours?

11. The following order for a nitroglycerin drip for a patient weighing 190 lb comes to your pharmacy. You have stock bottles of NTG 25 mg/250 mL in the pharmacy.

> ℞ **NTG 0.6 mcg/kg/min for 10 min**
>
> If no improvement, increase by 0.2 mcg/kg/min every 3 to 5 min up to a maximum of 200 mcg/min, until patient improves.

a. What will the starting IV rate be in milliliters per hour for this patient?

b. What will the IV rate be in milliliters per hour, if you have to increase the rate three times?

c. What will the IV rate be in milliliters per hour if the final rate is 2 mcg/kg/min?

d. Assuming the final rate is used, how long will the bottle last?

12. You receive an order for a dopamine drip for a 160 lb patient. It is to be infused at 3 mcg/kg/min. The rate can be increased by 2 mcg/kg/min every 30 minutes to achieve the desired response. You need to make a bag that contains 250 mg/100 mL. Dopamine comes as 50 mg/mL vials.

a. How many milliliters of dopamine will you have to add to the bag?

b. What will the starting IV rate be in milliliters per hour?

c. If the doctor tells you to increase the rate by 8 mcg/kg/min, what will the new IV rate be in milliliters per hour?

d. Assuming that the increased rate is used, how many bags will you have to make for a 24 hour supply?

13. A recently ventilated patient who weighs 175 lb receives the following orders.

> ℞ **vecuronium 0.8 mcg/kg/min**
>
> **midazolam 0.2 mg/kg/hour**

Your hospital has standard bags that you mix for these orders: vecuronium 100 mg in 100 mL NS and midazolam 100 mg in 250 mL of NS. Vecuronium comes as 20 mg/mL vials, and midazolam comes as 5 mg/mL vials.

a. How many milliliters of vecuronum will you have to add to each bag?

b. What will the rate be in milliliters per hour for the vecuronium?

c. How long will the bag of vecuronium last?

d. How many bags will you have to make a day?

e. How many milliliters of midazolam will you have to add to each bag?

f. What will the rate be in milliliters per hour for the midazolam?

g. How long will the bag of midazolam last?

h. How many bags will you have to make a day?

C.4 IV Epidurals

Another type of IV you may have to prepare is an epidural. These orders are usually written as percents. When making them, it is important to remember the 10% rule: if the total volume you need to add to an IV bag is greater than 10% of the volume of the bag it is being added to, remove the volume of fluid you are adding. For example, if you have to add 250 mL to a 1000 mL bag, you will need to remove 250 mL of fluid from the bag before adding the 250 mL of fluid because 250 mL is greater than 10% of 1000 mL (100 mL). If needed, apply the 10% rule to the problems that follow.

C.4 Problem Set

14. You receive the following epidural order.

Ḃ	morphine	0.008%
	bupivacaine	0.12%
	NS	250 mL bag

You have the following stock solutions.

bupivacaine   1%
morphine   10 mg/10 mL vial
NS   250 mL bag

a. What volume of each ingredient will be added to the NS bag?

b. Does the 10% rule apply? If so, how much saline will be removed?

15. You receive the following epidural order.

Ḃ	bupivacaine	0.06%
	morphine	0.016%
	NS	250 mL bag

You have the following stock solutions.

bupivacaine   0.75% solution
morphine sulfate   50 mg/25 mL solution
NS   250 mL bag

a. What volume of each ingredient will be added to the NS bag?

b. Does the 10% rule apply? If so, how much saline will be removed?

C.5 Pediatric Parenterals

Other IV calculation problems you may encounter in the pharmacy involve pediatric and newborn dosing. As described in the first section on pediatric safety, you may have to determine if a dose is within a safe range for your patient. Like the pediatric medications discussed earlier, many pediatric and neonatal IV doses are given in chart form. It is important to be able to use a chart to determine if a dose is appropriate for a particular patient.

When determining doses for newborn patients, most hospitals recommend not rounding until the last step in the calculation. This is because many of the medications for these patients have a narrow therapeutic range. If the calculation involves three or four steps, rounding at each step could result in an overdose. Follow this general rule throughout Problem Set B.5 and also follow the instructions on rounding for pediatric patients used in Problem Set B.1.

C.5 Problem Set

16. You receive the following order for a 3-day-old patient weighing 2 lb. Using the reference tables provided, is this dose safe?

> ℞ Loading dose of morphine 0.15 mg IM q2 h prn pain, then morphine 0.025 mg/hour IV prn pain for 3 days

17. You receive the following order for a pediatric patient weighing 14 lb. Using the reference tables provided, is this dose safe?

> ℞ Bolus IV dose of fentanyl 0.01 mg, then IV of 0.3 mg/hour in a 60 mL syringe with a concentration of 1 mg/10 mL

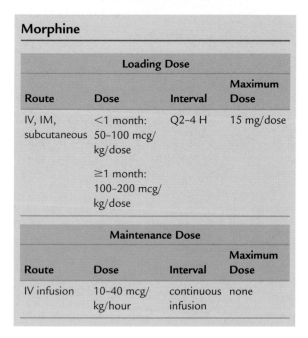

Morphine

| | **Loading Dose** | | |
Route	**Dose**	**Interval**	**Maximum Dose**
IV, IM, subcutaneous	<1 month: 50–100 mcg/ kg/dose	Q2–4 H	15 mg/dose
	≥1 month: 100–200 mcg/ kg/dose		

| | **Maintenance Dose** | | |
Route	**Dose**	**Interval**	**Maximum Dose**
IV infusion	10–40 mcg/ kg/hour	continuous infusion	none

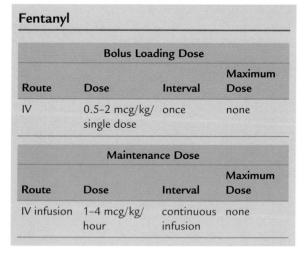

Fentanyl

| | **Bolus Loading Dose** | | |
Route	**Dose**	**Interval**	**Maximum Dose**
IV	0.5–2 mcg/kg/ single dose	once	none

| | **Maintenance Dose** | | |
Route	**Dose**	**Interval**	**Maximum Dose**
IV infusion	1–4 mcg/kg/ hour	continuous infusion	none

C.6 Topical Compounds

Extemporaneous compounding is a function of the pharmacy because not all drugs are available in every dosage form. Therefore, the pharmacy must sometimes create the necessary form based on a prescriber's instructions. Prescribers may indicate exactly how much of each drug is to be mixed to create the required compound in a recipe format, as well as how much should be dispensed to the patient.

C.6 Problem Set

18. The following order is received in the pharmacy. Your pharmacy has pure chemicals available. How much of each ingredient will you need to make the compound?

> ℞ **Muscle Rub**
>
> | methyl salicylate (aq) | 5% |
> | menthol | 15% |
> | camphor | 2% |
> | white petrolatum | 10% |
> | vanishing cream QSAD | 30 g |

19. The following order is received in the pharmacy.

> ℞ **Antioxident Cream**
>
> | vitamin C | 20% |
> | vitamin E | 5% |
> | vitamin A | 2.5% |
> | glycerin | 10% |
> | unibase QSAD | 1 oz |

You have the following ingredients in stock:

> pure vitamin C powder
> vitamin E oil, 50%
> vitamin A oil, 25%
> pure glycerin
> unibase

How much of each ingredient will you need to make the cream?

20. You receive the following order in the pharmacy:

> ℞ **Demerol Suppositories**
>
> | PEG 300 | 40% |
> | PEG 4500 | 50% |
> | demerol | 10% |
>
> Dispense and make 12 suppositories.

Your mold is calibrated so that each suppository weighs 4 g, and demerol is available as 25 mg/mL in 10 mL vials.

a. How much of each ingredient will you need to make the requested number of suppositories?

b. How many milligrams of demerol will be in each suppository?

21. You receive the following order in the pharmacy. You have pure chemicals in stock. How much of each ingredient will you need to make the lip balm?

> ℞ **Medicated Lip Balm**
>
> | camphor | 1% |
> | menthol | 1% |
> | glycerin | 3% |
> | white wax | 8% |
> | white petrolatum QSAD | 2 oz |

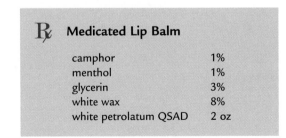

Appendix D

Measures and Conversions

Metric

Volume
1 L = 1000 mL
1 mL = 1 cc

Weight
1 g = 1000 mg
1 mg = 1000 mcg

Household

Volume
1 gallon = 4 quarts
1 qt = 2 pt
1 pt = 2 cups = 16 fl oz
1 fl oz = 2 tbsp = 6 tsp

Weight
1 lb = 16 oz

Length
1 yard = 3 feet
1 foot = 12 inches

Conversions

	Household	Apothecary	Metric
Volume	1 qt = 32 fl oz		0.96 L
	1 pint = 16 fl oz		480 mL *
	1 cup = 8 fl oz		240 mL
	2 tbsp = 1 fl oz	6 f℈ = 1 f℥	30 mL *
	1 tbsp	3 f℈	15 mL
	1 tsp	1 f℈	5 mL †
		1 ♏	0.0625 mL
Weight	2.2 lb		1 kg
	1 lb		454 g
	1 oz	8 ℈	30 g
Length	1 inch		2.5 cm

* There are actually less than 30 mL in 1 fl oz, but 30 mL is usually used. When packaging a pint, companies will typically include 473 mL, rather than the full 480 mL, thus saving money over time.

† There are actually 3.75 mL in an apothecary f℈. However, convention dictates that 1 f℈ = 5 mL = 1 tsp.

Glossary

A

accuracy the correctness of a number in its representation of a given value

aliquot a measured portion, fraction, or part of an ingredient that is placed into solution or into a mixture of other ingredients to aid in measuring a very small amount

alligation alternate method the mathematical calculation used to determine the amounts of two or more dilutions of differing strengths that will be mixed to prepare a product of a desired strength and quantity

alligation medial method the mathematical calculation used to find the final concentration created when two or more known quantities of known concentrations are compounded

alligation the concentration obtained when two or more solutions of different strengths are combined

apothecary system literally the system used by an apothecary, a system of measurement used in pharmacy prior to the metric system; units of measure include minims, fluidrams, scruples, grains, ounces, and pounds

Arabic numbers a numbering system that uses numeric symbols to indicate a quantity, fractions, and decimals; uses the numerals 0, 1, 2, 3, 4, 5, 6, 7, 8, and 9

atomic weight the weight of a single atom of an element compared to the weight of a single atom of hydrogen

average wholesale price (AWP) the average price that wholesalers charge the pharmacy for a drug; used to determine reimbursement

avoirdupois system an alternative system of measurement used in pharmacy prior to the metric system

B

body surface area (BSA) a measurement related to a patient's weight and height, expressed in meters squared (m²), and used to calculate patient-specific doses of medications

brand name the name under which the manufacturer markets a drug; a registered trademark of the manufacturer; also known as the trade name

C

capitation fee a form of reimbursement in which the insurer pays the pharmacy a monthly fee to cover all prescriptions needed by a patient during that month

Celsius a thermometric scale in which 100 degrees is the boiling point of water and 0 degrees is the freezing point of water

Clark's Rule a formula used to determine an appropriate pediatric dose by using the child's weight in pounds and the normal adult dose; weight in lb/150 lb × adult dose = the pediatric dose

common denominator a number into which each of the unlike denominators of two or more fractions can be divided evenly

complex fraction a fraction in which both the numerator and the denominator are fractions

compounded stock solution a solution that is prepared in a large amount and kept in stock in the pharmacy to be divided for individual prescriptions

compounding the process of using raw ingredients and/or other prepared ingredients to prepare a drug product for a patient

concentrate a highly condensed drug product that is diluted prior to administration

conversion factor an equivalency equal to 1 that can be used when converting units of measure using the ratio-proportion method

D

days' supply a method of inventory management that tries to keep inventory value approximately equal to the cost to the pharmacy of the products sold in a certain number of days; calculated as the value of inventory divided by the average daily cost of products sold

DEA number a number issued by the Drug Enforcement Administration (DEA) to signify the authority of the holder to prescribe or handle controlled substances; made up of two letters followed by seven digits, the last of which is a checksum digit used to check the validity of the DEA number

decimal a fraction value in which the denominator is 10 or some power of 10

denominator the number in the bottom part of a fraction

depreciation an allowance made to account for the decreasing value of an asset

diluent an inactive substance that is added to a concentrate to make it less concentrated; can be a vehicle or a solvent

dilution the product obtained when an inactive ingredient, a diluent, is added to a concentrate

dimensional analysis method a conversion method in which the given number and unit are multiplied by the ratio of the desired unit to the given unit, which is equivalent to 1

discount a reduced selling price

dispensing fee amount charged over and above the pharmacy's purchase price of the medication; includes profit, cost of materials, cost of labor, and overhead

dose on a prescription, the indication of how much medication the patient will take at each administration

dosing schedule on a prescription, the indication of how often the drug is to be taken

dosing table a table providing dose recommendations based on the age and/or the weight of the patient; often used for determining the safe dose for a pediatric patient

drop set the number of drops an IV set takes to make 1 mL; also called drip set

E

electrolytes substances such as mineral salts that carry an electrical charge when dissolved in a solution

F

Fahrenheit a thermometric scale in which 212 degrees is the boiling point of water and 32 degrees is the freezing point of water

flow rate the rate, expressed in milliliters per hour or drops per minute, at which

formula a written document listing the ingredients and instructions needed to prepare a compound

fraction a portion of a whole that is represented as a ratio

G

generic name the name under which a drug is approved by the Food and Drug Administration; sometimes denotes a drug that is not protected by a trademark; also referred to as a USAN (United States Adopted Name)

grain the smallest unit of measure in the apothecary system that is used with any frequency in pharmacy

gram the basic unit for measuring weight in the metric system

gross profit the difference between the selling price and the pharmacy's purchase price; also called *markup*

H

household measure a system of measure used in homes, particularly in kitchens, in the United States; units of measure for volume include teaspoonful, tablespoonful, cup, pint, quart, and gallon; units for weight are pound and ounce

I

improper fraction a fraction with a value greater than 1 (the value of the numerator is larger than the value of the denominator)

infusion the administration of a large volume of liquid medication given parenterally over a long period

injection a method of administering medications in which a syringe with a needle or cannula is used to penetrate through the skin or membrane into the tissue below

intramuscular injection an injection given into the aqueous muscle tissue

intravenous infusion the injection of fluid into the veins

inventory a listing of all items that are available for sale in a business

inventory value the total value of the drugs and merchandise in stock in the pharmacy on a given day

IV piggyback (IVPB) a small volume of fluid and medication that is given intravenously in addition to a primary infusion over a short period of time

L

leading zero a zero that is placed to the left of the decimal point, in the ones place, in a number that is less than zero and is being represented by a decimal value

liter the basic unit for measuring volume in the metric system

lowest known place value the last digit on the right of a written numeral

M

markup rate expressed as a percentage, the markup divided by the pharmacy's purchase price and multiplied by 100

markup the difference between the selling price and the pharmacy's purchase price; also called *gross profit*

medication is flowing through an IV line; also called infusion rate and rate of infusion

meter the basic unit for measuring length in the metric system

metric system a measurement system based on subdivisions and multiples of 10, made up of three basic units: meter, gram, and liter

milliequivalent (mEq) the ratio of the weight of a molecule to its valence, used to measure the concentration of electrolytes in a volume of solution; also an amount of medication that will provide the patient with a specific amount (equivalent amount) of an electrolyte

millimole (mM) molecular weight expressed in milligrams

mini-drip set a drop set at a rate of 60 gtt/mL

mixed number a whole number and a fraction

molecular weight the sum of the atomic weights of all atoms in one molecule of a compound

N

net profit the difference between the selling price and the overall cost of an item

numerator the number in the upper part of a fraction

O

overall cost the sum of the cost to purchase the drug from the manufacturer and the cost to dispense the drug

overhead the pharmacy's overall cost of doing business; includes salaries, equipment, operating expenses, and rent

P

parenteral administered by injection and not by way of the gastrointestinal system

percent the number of parts per 100; can be written as a fraction, a decimal, or a ratio

percentage of error the percentage by which a measurement is inaccurate

pharmacy benefits management (PBM) a prescription processing service that manages insurance reimbursement for prescriptions to pharmacies

place value the location of a numeral in a string of numbers that describes the numeral's relationship to the decimal point

powder volume (pv) the space occupied by dry pharmaceuticals, calculated as the difference between the final volume and the volume of the diluting ingredient, or the diluent volume; the amount of space occupied by lyophilized (freeze-dried) medication in a sterile vial, used for reconstitution

prescription an order for medication for a patient that is written by a physician or a qualified licensed practitioner to be filled by a pharmacist

product the result of multiplying one number by another

profit income minus overhead

profit margin the difference between the cost of doing business (the pharmacy's purchase price, overhead, and preparation) and the selling price or receipts for a product

proper fraction a fraction with a value of less than 1 (the value of the numerator value is smaller than the value of the denominator)

proportion an expression of equality between two ratios

Q

quotient the result of dividing one number by another

R

ratio a numerical representation of the relationship between two parts of the whole or between one part and the whole

ratio strength a means of describing the concentration of a liquid medication based on a ratio such as *a* grams:*b* milliliters

ratio-proportion method a conversion method based on comparing a complete ratio to a ratio with a missing component

Roman numerals a numbering system that uses alphabetic symbols to indicate a quantity; uses the letters I, V, and X to represent 1, 5, and 10, respectively

route of administration on a prescription, the indication of how the medication is to be given

S

scientific notation a method used to write numbers that have a very large or very small numerical value; uses "× 10" with an exponent

signa **(sig)** from the Latin for write; the instructions for proper use of the medication included on each prescription, including the dose, route of administration, and dosing schedule

significant figures the figures in a numeral that are known values and have not been rounded or estimated in the process of mathematical calculation, plus the digit in the lowest place value, which is approximate

solute the substance dissolved in the liquid solvent in a solution

solution a mixture of two or more substances

solvent the liquid that dissolves the solute in a solution

subcutaneous injection an injection given into the vascular, fatty layer of tissue under the skin

sum the result of adding two or more numbers together

T

trailing zero a zero that appears at the end of a decimal string and is not needed except when considered significant

turnover rate the number of times the amount of goods in inventory is sold during a year; calculated by dividing total annual purchases of inventory by the average inventory value

U

unit the amount of activity associated with a medication that has biological impact on a patient

V

valence the ability of a molecule to bond, as indicated by its positive or negative charge, represented by a superscript plus or minus sign next to an element's chemical symbol

vehicle an inert medium, such as a syrup, in which a drug is administered

volume in volume (v/v) the number of milliliters of a drug (solute) in 100 mL of the final product (solution)

W

weight in volume (w/v) the number of grams of a drug (solute) in 100 mL of the final product (solution)

weight in weight (w/w) the number of grams of a drug (solute) in 100 g of the final product (solution)

Y

Young's Rule a formula used to determine an appropriate pediatric dose by using the child's age in years and the normal adult dose; [age in years/(age in years + 12 years)] × adult dose = pediatric dose

Index

ratio strength
    calculating, 149
    for solutions, 177–179
reimbursement for prescriptions, 237
Roman numerals, 10–11
    comparison with Arabic, 10*t*
    guidelines for interpreting, 11*t*
rounding
    decimals, 17–19
    numbers, 23
route of administration, 69

S

scientific notation, 13–14, 14*t*
scruples, 257
signa, 69
significant figures
    accuracy and, 27–28, 29*t*
    defined, 27
    rules for counting, 27*t*–28*t*
solute, 177
solutions
    alligations, 211–215
    defined, 177
    ratio strength, 177–179
    solute, 177
    solvent, 177
    volume in volume, 178–179
    weight in volume, 178–179
    weight in weight, 177–178
solvent, 177
sterile water, 179
stock solution, compounded,
    208–209
story problems, ratio-proportion
    method, 87
straight-line depreciation method,
    248
subcutaneous injection, 145
subtraction
    of decimals, 16
    of fractions, 3–7
sufficient quantity (QS), 202
sum, estimating, 21, 21*t*
syringes
    insulin, *158*
    oral, 125, *125*
    selection, 146

T

temperature chart, 137
    Celsius in, *137*
    Fahrenheit in, *137*
temperature measurement
    Celsius, 135
    converting Celsius and
        Fahrenheit temperature, 135
    Fahrenheit, 135
    temperature chart, 137, *137*
trailing zero, 18
turnover rate, 247

U

United States Pharmacopeia (USP),
    158
units
    calculating, 158–159
    defined, 158
    of insulin, 158
    of metric equivalents, 82*t*
    of temperature, 135

V

valence, 154
vehicle, defined, 87
volume
    calculating volume of injectable
        solution, 146
    powder volume, 167
    volume in volume, 178–179
volume in volume, 178–179

W

weight
    customized doses based on, 87
    weight in volume, 178–179
    weight in weight, 177–178
weight in volume, 178–179
weight in weight, 177–178

Y

Young's Rule, for pediatric doses, 100

Z

zero
    leading, 16
    trailing, 18